The East European
Political System

Westview Special Studies

The concept of Westview Special Studies is a response
to the continuing crisis in academic and informational publishing. Library budgets for books have been severely curtailed. Ever larger portions of general library budgets are
being diverted from the purchase of books and used for data
banks, computers, micromedia, and other methods of information
retrieval. Interlibrary loan structures further reduce the
edition sizes required to satisfy the needs of the scholarly
community. Economic pressures on university presses and the
few private scholarly publishing companies have greatly limited the capacity of the industry to properly serve the academic and research communities. As a result, many manuscripts
dealing with important subjects, often representing the highest level of scholarship, are no longer economically viable
publishing projects--or, if accepted for publication, are
typically subject to lead times ranging from one to three
years.

Westview Special Studies are our practical solution to
the problem. As always, the selection criteria include the
importance of the subject, the work's contribution to scholarship, and its insight, originality of thought, and excellence of exposition. We accept manuscripts in camera-ready
form, typed, set, or word processed according to specifica-
tions laid out in our comprehensive manual, which contains
straightforward instructions and sample pages. The responsibility for editing and proofreading lies with the author
or sponsoring institution, but our editorial staff is always
available to answer questions and provide guidance.

The result is a book printed on acid-free paper and
bound in sturdy, library-quality soft covers. We manufacture
these books ourselves using equipment that does not require
a lengthy make-ready process and that allows us to publish
first editions of 300 to 1000 copies and to reprint even
smaller quantities as needed. Thus, we can produce Special
Studies quickly and can keep even very specialized books in
print as long as there is a demand for them.

About the Book and Author

In this detailed survey of European communist systems, Dr. Hazan examines the formal structure of East European politics and the functions of party organizations as the true centers of power. Drawing on extensive primary sources and illustrations from the most recent period of Eastern Europe's history, he analyzes the role of the entire government infrastructure in consolidating the strength of the Communist party. He also focuses on party congresses, internal elections, organizational and personnel changes, and foreign visits against the background of the all-encompassing network of ritual that governs the political process.

Baruch A. Hazan teaches at the Institute of European Studies, Vienna. His publications include <u>Olympic Sports and Propaganda Games</u> (1982) and <u>Soviet Impregnational Propaganda</u>.

To my Spring 1983 class
at the Institute of European Studies, Vienna

The East European
Political System
Instruments of Power

Baruch A. Hazan

Westview Press / Boulder and London

Westview Special Studies on the Soviet Union and Eastern Europe

Copyright © 1985 by Westview Press, Inc.

Published in 1985 in the United States of America by Westview Press, Inc.;
Frederick A. Praeger, Publisher; 5500 Central Avenue, Boulder, Colorado 80301

Library of Congress Cataloging in Publication Data
Hazan, Baruch, 1942-
    The East European political system.
    (Westview special studies on the Soviet Union and
Eastern Europe)
    Includes index.
    1. Europe, Eastern--Politics and government--
1945-   . I. Title. II. Series.
JN96.A2H39 1985   320.947   85-15340
ISBN 0-8133-7064-7

Printed and bound in the United States of America

10 9 8 7 6 5 4 3 2 1

Contents

List of Tables and Figures ix
Foreword, *Lonnie R. Johnson* xi
Author's Note xv

1   Introduction   1

2   Elections   9

3   The National Assemblies   33

4   The Communist Party: Membership, Structure,
     Organization   61

5   Top of the Pyramid: Central Committee,
     Politburo, Secretariat, Control Commission . . . 109

6   The Congress 171

7   The Leaders 209

8   Church and State 235

9   The Judiciary 273

10   The Ritual 289

11   The Auxiliary Organizations 309

12   Conclusions 365

List of Acronyms 371
Index 373

Tables and Figures

TABLES

2.1   Composition of the Bulgarian National
Assembly, 1966-1981   12

2.2   Composition of the Polish Sejm, 1965-1976 . . .   13

2.3   Percentage of Votes Received by Principal
Hungarian Leaders, 1980 and 1975 General
Elections   28

3.1   Composition of the CSSR Federal Assembly,
1976-1986   41

4.1   Growth in Membership in the Communist Party
of Albania, 1941-1981   63

4.2   Composition of Membership in the Bulgarian
Communist Party, 1962-1976   64

4.3   Composition of Membership in the Communist
Party of Czechoslovakia, January 1966 and
January 1976   65

4.4   Composition of Membership in the Socialist
Unity Party of the German Democratic Republic,
1947-1980   66

4.5   Composition of Membership in the Hungarian
Socialist Workers' Party, November 1970 and
March 1975   67

4.6   Composition of Membership in the Polish United
Workers' Party, 1945-1975   68

4.7   Composition of Membership in the Romanian
Communist Party, 1960-1984   70

4.8   Growth in Membership in the League of
       Yugoslav Communists, 1945-1982   71

4.9   Enrollments and Losses in Membership in the
       League of Yugoslav Communists, 1970 and 1980 . .   73

4.10   Composition of Membership in the League of
       Yugoslav Communists, 1977   74

5.1   Change in Numbers of Central Committee
       Members, Romanian Communist Party, 1974-1979 . .   129

5.2   Composition of the Central Committee Elected
       by the 12th Romanian Communist Party Congress .   130

5.3   Ages of Central Committee Members of the
       Hungarian Socialist Workers' Party Before
       and After the 1980 Party Congress   131

5.4   Changes in Membership in the Central Committee
       of the Bulgarian Communist Party, 1976-1981 . .   134

5.5   Ages of the Central Committee of the Bulgarian
       Communist Party, 1976-1981   135

5.6   Professional Backgrounds of Members of the
       Central Committee of the Bulgarian Communist
       Party, 1981   135

5.7   Ages and Professional and Educational Backgrounds
       of Members of the Central Committee of the
       League of Yugoslav Communists, 1982   136

5.8   Professional Backgrounds of Members of the
       Central Committee of the Polish United
       Workers' Party, 1980   138

5.9   Changes in Membership in the Central Committee
       of the Polish United Workers' Party, 1976-1981 .   140

5.10   Professional Backgrounds of Members of the
       Central Committee of the Polish United
       Workers' Party, 1981   141

6.1   Key for Election of Delegates by Local Party
       Organizations to the 11th LCY Congress in
       Yugoslavia, 1978   183

7.1   Leadership Succession in Eastern Europe,
       Post-World War II Through 1984   211

FIGURES

2.1   Yugoslavia's Assembly: The System of Delegates .   16

Foreword

The centennial anniversary of Karl Marx's death provided an occasion for representatives of various political persuasions to evaluate the impact of his thought on the twentieth century. In the countries where "real socialism" exists, the accomplishments of Marxism-Leninism were once again proclaimed, and Marxism-Leninism was once again reconfirmed as the only encompassingly legitimate form of historical, societal, economic, and political analysis. Within this context Lenin is (incorrectly) regarded as the only legitimate heir to the Marxian heritage, and the next person in the lineage is usually a national representative of interpretation or revision in a particular country.

Liberal critics in Western Europe and the United States took advantage of the occasion to criticize the various self-proclaimed heirs of Marx. The less sophisticated critics belabored the obvious lack of success communist-inspired regimes have had, and the more sophisticated found ample opportunity (frequently reverting to theses from Sir Karl Popper's Open Society and Its Enemies) to argue that Marxism is an inadequate method for a scientific analysis of history, society, economics, politics, or anything else. Western Neomarxists, caught between the inacceptability of "real socialism" and the inadequacy of liberal criticism, have attempted to salvage and cultivate the philosophical dimensions of Marx, but, in doing so, they have been equally critical of the dogmatic, political forms of Marxism. Long before the centennial of Marx's death, Jürgen Habermas wrote: "The Russian Revolution and the establishment of the Soviet system are the historical facts by which the systematic discussion of Marxism, and with Marxism, has been paralyzed.

. . . The Soviet path to socialism only recommends itself
as a method for shortening the process of industrialization
in developing countries, one which is far removed from the
realization of a truly emancipated society, and indeed at
times has regressed again from the constitutional rights
attained under capitalism to the legal terror or Party
dictatorship."[1]

Marx by no means wrote for the political and economic
situation of Eastern Europe, and orthodox Marxists at the
turn of the century knew that the real proletarian revolution was to occur in an advanced capitalistic, Western
bourgeois democracy. Lenin was caught off guard in his
Swiss exile in 1917 by a revolution that, according to
Marxian principles, was going to occur in the wrong place
at the wrong time and that would not be carried out by
proletarian masses but rather by a small group of professional revolutionaries. With the exception of isolated
and short-lived communist uprisings and coups in Europe,
the workers of the world did not unite to throw off the
yoke of capitalism, and Lenin was left with the problem
of consolidating power in a country torn by the ravages
of war and hunger. The urgency of the immediate tasks of
political consolidation and economic recovery ran parallel
to a debate over principles--what ultimate course the
revolution was to take and how socialism was to be introduced. Lenin's theories of revolutionary party and state
organization were designed to compensate for the "gap"
Marx had left in his writings dealing with the political
and strategic problems of the transitional period after
class struggle and revolution but before the establishment
of a free, communist society. Lenin, and then Stalin,
had to provide the theoretical justification for political
and economic measures that were aimed at creating the type
of society upon which socialism could be built. In other
words, if Russian reality did not provide an adequate
basis for Marxian theory, then the most important task in
the long run was to reshape Russian reality so that it
could conform to Marxian theory (or at least a revision of
Marxian theory formulated by Stalin and executed under the
auspices of the program of "socialism in one country").
The collectivization of agriculture and the forced development of industry, i.e., the creation of a proletariat in
Russia, and in Eastern Europe after World War II, must be
interpreted in this light. Marxism was a philosophy
designed for industrialized societies that first had to
be created in Eastern Europe.

The introduction of communism in Eastern Europe after

World War II was not burdened by theoretical debates about
the nature of socialism or how it was to be attained.
With few exceptions, Moscow had control of the communist
national movements and demanded allegiance. The Red Army
liberated Eastern Europe from fascism and occupied it by
agreement among the Allies. It is counterproductive to
attempt to make the diplomatic agreements of Stalin,
Churchill, and Roosevelt appear controversial; Eastern
Europe was conceded to the Soviet Union's sphere of
influence. The "revolutions" in Eastern Europe were
fundamentally interrelated questions of strategy. From
the Soviet point of view, they involved the establishment
of the USSR's national security. On a subordinated,
country-to-country level, the immediate consideration dealt
with the acquisition and consolidation of political power,
and this involved a familiar pattern of circumventing
democratic institutions and parties. The domestic consolidation of the communist regimes in Eastern Europe along
the lines of the Soviet model (with the noticeable
exceptions of Yugoslavia and Albania), along with the
establishment of multilateral military and economic
assistance organizations in the East (and in the West),
has given Eastern Europe a monolithic appearance for the
Western observer.

The title of Dr. Hazan's book reinforces this
impression at first because the author has chosen the term
"system" instead of "systems." The methodological principle of a system analysis operates on two levels in this
context. The introductory and most apparent deals with a
structural and formal comparison between the general
Western understanding of democratic institutions and
practices and their nominal counterparts in the East. In
spite of the homonymity of terms, the ideological formulation of concepts hardly allows one to bridge this first
great gap in understanding, e.g., the meaning of democracy
in the West versus its definition in a Democratic People's
Republic. The second and more important level deals with
(1) an attempt to systematize the political and ideological
principles that, in the final analysis, justify the use of
the term "political system" in the geographical context
of Eastern Europe, and (2) the variations these political
principles undergo on a country-to-country basis. The
result is not only a theoretical description of the unity
of political theory in Eastern Europe but also a documen-
tation of the diversity of political practice in light of
the concessions made to adapt theoretical principles to
the idiosyncracies of individual countries, their

historical backgrounds and traditions, indigenous domestic problems, etc.

As Hugh Seton-Watson wrote in the introduction to his classic theory, Eastern Europe Between the Wars: "Eastern Europe cannot be separated arbitrarily from the rest of the continent, for the problems of the part are indissolubly connected with those of the whole. Yet the local factors must be understood if the position of Eastern Europe in the world is to be clear." These words may be even more true today than when they were written in 1945. Dr. Hazan's book is undoubtedly an important contribution to the literature of Eastern European studies, and although it is by no means conciliatory in tone, its wealth of information and frankness will contribute to a broader understanding of those essential "local factors" that are so important in the processes of opinion building and decision making. In this sense, Dr. Hazan's book will promote international understanding, one of the primary goals of the institution on whose faculty he serves.

Lonnie R. Johnson, Ph.D.
Institute of European Studies
Vienna Program

Notes

1. Theory and Practice, translated by John Viertel (London: Heinemann, 1974), p. 197.

Author's Note

An East European joke describes the visit of a general
to the building of the Ministry of Defense. After visiting
the departments of CPT (Combat and Political Training), AAFD
(Anti-Air Force Defense), IEPS (Ideological Education and
Political Studies), and MPAAF (Main Political Administration
of the Armed Forces), he finally reached the end of the
long corridor, where the letters "EXIT" marked the last door.
"Why was I not informed about the creation of the new
department?!" roared the general.

Like so many political jokes, this one includes more
than a grain of truth. Every political regime leaves its
imprint on the language spoken in the country. This includes
not only specific political concepts, but also the entire
phraseology dominating political, social, and cultural life.
This aspect of the East European political system has been
analyzed in the chapter dealing with the political ritual
of the East European political system. However, at this
point something must be said about the widespread use of
abbreviations in Eastern Europe. This practice (like virtually every political process or institution) has been borrowed from the Soviet Union where abbreviations are an integral part of everyday life. Although one can refrain from
analyzing the psychological motives behind this phenomenon
(simplifying complicated new political concepts, introducing
verbal discipline into everyday life communications, setting
an easily understandable code for uneducated citizens igno-
rant of the complex meaning of the full name of the organ
or department involved, etc.), one cannot avoid using them
when the East European political system is described.

Numerous abbreviations of East European organizations,
organs, and parties have been used in this book. They

appear in the abbreviations list at the end of the book;
in addition, each is spelled out on first use in the book.

Thus there is hope that the reader will be able to
decode sentences such as: "ADN reports that the GDR
government and the SED CC have greeted the LCY CC on the
SFRY national holiday."

Baruch A. Hazan

1
Introduction

"Eastern Europe" is primarily a political concept
rather than a geographical one; it is understood to mean
the socialist regimes of Albania, Bulgaria, Czechoslovakia,
the German Democratic Republic, Hungary, Poland, Romania,
and Yugoslavia. The two separate words "Eastern" and
"Europe" are purely geographical terms, but the concept
formed by their combination--"Eastern Europe"--is charged
with heavy political connotations and implies a socialist
political system that was originally modeled on the Soviet
system. It is one that differs fundamentally from the
political system of the countries of Western Europe (which
is also a political concept).

The political regimes of the East European countries
have certain common denominators. At the same time there
are a number of marked differences among them, some of
these differences being politically important. To take
the common denominators first: These regimes were all
established at the end of or soon after the end of World
War II, in most cases with the help of the Soviet army.
They are all governed by communist parties, although these
parties may sometimes be called "socialist" (the German
Democratic Republic, or GDR) and sometimes "workers"
parties (Albania, Hungary, Poland). They all consider
Marx, Engels, and Lenin to be their ideological sages (and
in Albania's case Stalin as well, though he has not yet
made a comeback in the other East European countries), and
they claim that their regimes are based on the "principles
of Marxism-Leninism." Finally, they all aspire to build
the "socialist society" (sometimes called "mature" or
"developed" socialism) as a stage in eventually building
communism.

On the other hand, these regimes do differ from one

1

another, quite apart from the differences in history and
geography that have molded their countries. All but two--
Albania and Yugoslavia--are members of the Soviet bloc's
military alliance, the Warsaw Pact, and this has important
political implications. All but the same two are members
of the Council for Economic Mutual Assistance--CEMA--the
East European version of the European Economic Community;
Yugoslavia, although a nonmember, maintains the status of
observer. Albania, since 1961, has been openly and
vociferously hostile to the Soviet Union, which it calls
"revisionist" (although Albania's political regime closely
reflects all the characteristics of the Soviet political
system--another common denominator of the East European
countries.) Yugoslavia, under Tito, also broke openly with
the Soviet Union in 1948, but over the years the two
countries have worked out a modus vivendi and now maintain
civil relations. In spite of the fact that Yugoslavia
is a founder member of the nonaligned movement, making
great efforts to cultivate relations with Third World
countries, and the fact that it calls its own system "self-
management," it is a communist state ruled by a communist
party just like all the other East European states.

Romania too is often regarded as something of a
maverick of the Eastern bloc, as it cannot always be
expected to echo the Moscow line precisely. It is the only
East European state to maintain diplomatic relations with
Israel, and its calls for disarmament embrace both super-
powers, not just the United States.

Hungary has in recent years introduced a number of
economic reforms that have encouraged private initiative
in an effort to improve its sluggish "socialist" economy;
indeed, these reforms have had their effect. Because the
concept of a "private economy" is anathema to orthodox
Marxist ideologists, these experiments have been
scrutinized with great suspicion by the Soviet Union and
the other East European countries, but they have gradually
been adopted by them and were even singled out for praise
by the Soviet party leader, Yuriy Andropov, at a meeting of
the Central Committee of the Communist Party of the Soviet
Union (CPSU) in February 1983.

Just as one might argue that the common denominators
are not enough in themselves to enable one to describe the
East European regimes as a uniform political system, one
could also argue that the differences are no bar to an
attempt to analyze them as a uniform system. I will argue
here that the differences mentioned (and those that will be
pointed out in later chapters) do not affect the general

nature of the East European regimes and that these regimes do in fact represent a uniform political system, the basic characteristics of which are the following.

TOTAL SUPREMACY OF THE COMMUNIST PARTY

The absolutely fundamental characteristic of the East European political system is the unlimited and uncontrolled--in a word, total--rule of the communist party. Despite the existence of some peripheral political parties in almost all East European countries (peasants' and Catholic parties), it is solely the communist party that decides whether such parties may exist and that sets the limits of their token political activities. Their existence is sanctioned and tolerated only insofar as these parties are useful and obedient to the communist party. There is certainly no sharing of political power and authority, which is reserved to the communist party leadership. Although the existing political parties may participate in the elections for the national assemblies (where, appearing together with the communist party in a uniform list sponsored by the Fatherland Front organizations, they have previously assigned seats), they in no way represent any opposition or alternative to communist party rule. Therefore, what Eastern Europe has is not merely a single-party political system, but a system in which the party and the state are totally identified with one another.

TOTAL IDENTIFICATION OF COMMUNIST PARTY AND STATE

All aspects of political life in Eastern Europe are dominated by the communist party. Although minor areas of political activity may occasionally be assigned to the peripheral parties--participation in propaganda campaigns sponsored by the communist party would be a common example--there is absolutely no doubt that these parties do not in any way affect the state system or political life. It is not only the peripheral parties that become auxiliary instruments of the communist party, but also the state itself. Party goals, such as the construction of socialism, identified and analyzed decades before the actual establishment of the socialist regimes, become state goals. Political opponents of the communist party are defined as enemies of the state and the people, and all state organs are subjugated to the goal of perpetuating

4

the supremacy of the communist party. Thus one of the
major tasks of the organs of law and order is not to dispense justice and safeguard law and human rights, but to
persecute and prosecute the political opponents of the
communist party, treat political opposition as a state
crime, eliminate all forms of social dissent, and enact
laws to legally justify all this. Subsequently, it is not
the fact that all the important state posts are occupied
by communist party leaders and officials that turns the
state into an instrument of the communist party, but rather
the fact that all state organs, including those constitutionally defined as nonpolitical or independent,
facilitate the implementation of party goals and perpetuate
the supremacy of the communist party. All this makes any
kind of legal opposition in Eastern Europe inconceivable.
Any form of dissent--political, social, or cultural--is
treated by the party as an acute manifestation of high
treason, punishable by the state organs. Any kind of non-
conformity is viewed with suspicion and quickly suppressed.

Consequently, it is not enough to describe the East
European political system as totalitarian or authoritarian.
It falls into a category of its own--one of absolute
party rule or, to coin a term, partiocracy, i.e., a system
in which the party and its political apparatus are superior
to the state organs, whose activity is directed by the party
toward facilitating the implementation of its goals and,
above all else, the perpetuation of its rule. Such a
political system requires claims of legitimacy.

STRANGE FORMS OF LEGITIMACY

Communist claims of legitimacy are based on un-
democratic, unorthodox, and often travestied practices
and processes. On the face of it the East European
political system displays the usual political processes
that exist in every democratic regime. Constitutions,
elections, national assemblies, and so forth are ostensibly
an integral part of the system. Aware of the questionable
legitimacy of their rule, the communist parties
meticulously maintain the pretense of democracy, calling
their regimes "people's democracies" and maintaining the
illusion of representative democracy based on carefully
orchestrated elections whose results are predetermined.
(Where else is it possible to have an election turnout of
99 percent, all voting in precisely the same way?) There
is, however, a very large gap between the democratic label

and the substance.

In a real democracy the legitimacy of the ruling party rests on the fact that it has won constitutionally organized free elections, in which the population has openly expressed its political preference for one of several parties by casting votes. A partiocracy goes beyond this. It bases its legitimacy not only on the ostensible democratic process of election, but on continuous and demonstrative support on the part of the population. This means that every important political step is to be demonstratively endorsed by the entire population. The result is a never-ending series of political rallies, meetings, demonstrations, letters of support, declarations, appeals and petitions, and similar "spontaneous campaigns" in support of the party policy and condemning the opponents or enemies of the party. In this way the party is able to boast a new kind of legitimacy, demonstrated not just at the ballot box, but every day in action. A precondition for organizing this kind of "legitimacy" is maintaining the population in a state of supportive mobilization.

CONSTANT SOCIAL MOBILIZATION

Life in a partiocracy is highly politicized. There is hardly an area of living that is free of some political significance. Sports, the arts, the use of leisure, private plans and aspirations, social habits and practices--in short, everything is politically important and consequently is controlled by the party. A submissive and conformist attitude on the part of the citizens is obligatory if unpleasant consequences are to be avoided. This is not enough, however. Passive compliance is necessary but insufficient. What is required is continuous, enthusiastic, and demonstrative support, which is carefully organized and controlled by the party. The result is the state of constant social mobilization in which the citizens of a partiocracy exist. They are subjected to a constant propaganda campaign, which seeps through to every area of life and involves every important step or measure initiated by the communist party. The people are daily required to enthusiastically endorse the party policy and condemn its enemies. This manipulated support is considered by the communist party as the ultimate proof of the legitimacy of its rule. Yet party personages count for little in such support; anyone who happens to be in party power can organize favorable demonstrations. When otherwise

democratic processes are made into pretenses devoid of
any real meaning, the method of succession to party leadership and other positions of importance is not established.

NO CLEAR RULES OF SUCCESSION

Because the state and its organs are in fact auxiliary
organs of the party, the normal democratic rules of
succession (elections, votes of no confidence, bona fide
resignations, etc.) do not apply to the partiocracy. The
supreme party organs or a selected group of party leaders
decide matters of succession and replacement and seldom if
ever disclose the reasons behind their moves. The lack of
a free press, public debates, and reliable open information
contributes to the uncertainty about why such changes take
place, what prompts them, and who decides them. Consequently, a premier can be killed at a cabinet meeting
(Mehmet Shehu, Albania), another can be demoted to chairman
of the national assembly (Stanko Todorov, Bulgaria), and
yet another simply ousted (numerous cases of state and
party leaders in all East European countries), without the
reasons for these developments ever actually being disclosed. Although explanations such as "expediency,"
"retirement," "deviations," or even "suicide" and "treason"
(Shehu) are often given, they invariably conceal the
specific reasons. Even when a formal decision is adopted
by one of the organs constitutionally entitled to do so
(parliament), this decision is in fact a post factum rubber-
stamp endorsement of a fait accompli brought about by the
party. One can assume that reasons like personal rivalry,
over-ambitious or too eagerly aspiring leaders, Soviet
preferences, and so on are plausible, but the real reasons
and actual procedures remain secret. The citizens have no
actual way of obtaining reliable information, because in
the partiocracy the party also has control over all
official information.

MONOPOLY ON INFORMATION AND ON THE TRUTH

Information in Eastern Europe is a party enterprise.
All the mass media belong to or are controlled by the
party. The sanctioned peasants' and religious parties and
the various public organizations and trade unions publish
newspapers and magazines, but their content is strictly
controlled by the party, and it does not vary from the

content of the communist party press. Alternative sources
of information are usually suppressed (although a very
limited quantity of some Western newspapers is sold in
Hungary and Yugoslavia) and their effects neutralized by
official propaganda campaigns.

Among its various monopolies the communist party holds
the monopoly on the truth. This means that the only
version of anything that is available is the one disseminated
by the party. Any differences would imply dissent and thus
is punishable. Although in real democracies the truth is
found out by debate, research, trial and error, experience,
exchange of information, analysis, and so forth, in
Eastern Europe the truth is simply announced by the
communist party. Doubts are dangerous and might lead to
independent thinking, which is not encouraged. Personal
analysis based on an individual's intellect and acumen is
not tolerated. The truth--the only and indisputable one--
is a matter of party pronouncement through the usual mass
media channels, which are controlled by the party organs.
Thus the mass media actually operate as party spokesmen,
presenting the picture as conceived by the party, suppress-
ing facts and dissenting opinions, inventing "facts"
when necessary, and in general, doing everything to
facilitate the implementation of party goals.

These are the main characteristics of the East
European political system. In addition, there are the
basic characteristics of every totalitarian regime--an
official and infallible ideology, terroristic police
control, and a monopoly of the means of military or other
armed control, which means turning the army into another
instrument of the party, and so forth. The differences in
political and economic structure among the East European
countries are peripheral and do not affect the general
nature of the system. They are principally differences of
degree and not of substance. All the characteristics
described in the following chapters are inherent in all
East European countries; that is why it is possible to
regard the East European regimes as one uniform political
system. It is the purpose of this book to describe and
analyze the basic structure and organs of the East European
political system and to point out the tremendous discrepancy
between the ostensible organs of authority and the real
center of power. Real and ostensible differences among
the various East European countries, as well as the overwhelming similarities, will be pointed out and explained and
the basic political processes and practices examined and
analyzed.

2
Elections

ELECTION CHARACTERISTICS AND SYSTEMS

One of the basic characteristics of the East
European political system is its meticulous adherence to
some of the structural and formal aspects of democracy.
Aware of their lack of legitimacy and intrinsic democratic
essence, the political regimes in Eastern Europe painstakingly go through the motions of demonstrating several
procedural and ritual institutions of real democracy,
such as constitutions, general elections, and parliament.
However, whereas in true democratic regimes these
institutions strengthen the democratic character of the
state, protect human rights, and guarantee some form of
popular participation in decision making, in Eastern
Europe they serve a double purpose: to "prove" the
democratic character of the regime and to strengthen the
dominance of the communist party by purporting to show that
this dominance is based not on power alone but also on
some ostensibly democratic practices.

In a real democracy the point of general elections is
to afford the population the opportunity to select and
elect representatives and to exercise a certain degree of
control over the performance of those representatives by
virtue of the right not to elect them again. The point of
elections in Eastern Europe is completely different. Like
almost all aspects of the East European political system
they are an instrument of the governing communist party for
achieving goals that have nothing to do with selecting
representatives or controlling their subsequent performance.
Instead the most important functions of general elections
in Eastern Europe are :

1. To serve as a visible demonstration of the democratic essence and nature of the system.

2. To provide the communist party with formal and legal proof of the endorsement of its programs and policies by the people, as well as to demonstrate the people's identification with the regime's goals and ideas.

3. To afford the regime the opportunity of developing an extensive propaganda campaign aimed at enhancing the people's loyalty, increasing their productivity, strengthening their political awareness, denouncing the regime's enemies, strengthening the regime's friendship with the USSR, and so forth. Almost all East European countries hold their general elections two or three months after their party congresses. This means that the election campaign begins shortly after the congress, thus making it possible to link the pre-congress and post-congress propaganda campaigns with the electoral one, with a view to maintaining the whole nation in a state of social mobilization and political alertness (combined with well-publicized working enthusiasm) for several months at a time. In the words of Pencho Kubadinski, Bulgarian Communist Party (BCP) Central Committee Politburo member and chairman of Bulgaria's Fatherland Front National Council: "Every electoral campaign increases the political and labor activity of the citizens in our country and is a political school for the people's masses. At the same time, elections are an impressive manifestation of the firm unity and cohesion of our people in supporting the policy of the BCP."[1]

4. To serve as nationwide exercises of the communist party's organizational and supervisory abilities. The preparation of a congress, the staging of a purge, or the exchanging of party membership cards are of a similar nature, but they all involve inner-party affairs, whereas elections have to do with the party-public relationship. Thus the general election campaign in each East European country is in fact a test of the party's ability and power to make all people do what the party tells them to do.

5. To provide the East European communist parties with the opportunity to increase the effectiveness of the organizational and mobilizational activity of their local organs and to improve their day-to-day work. The "accountability election" or "meet the voters" gatherings that are an integral part of the election campaign may not be an example of real democracy as understood in the Western world, but they have a certain effect on the daily running of affairs in villages or small towns, where it matters most to the common people.

6. To provide the communist party with the opportunity to publicly reward outstanding workers, party veterans, famous artists, and even athletes for their services. Since membership in the national assembly or parliament is not a demanding job--the various East European parliaments hold two to four regular sessions a year, each lasting a day or two, and their activity is devoid of any real political importance or effect--membership is considered to be first of all a matter of honor or a reward for a job well done (elsewhere). Thus among the Bulgarian National Assembly members elected in June 1981 were the writers Nikolay Khaytov, Pavel Vezhinov, Veselin Andreev, and others; the sculptor Sekul Markov; the composer Aleksandur Raychev; the painter Svetlin Vulchev; the actresses Nevena Kokanova and Margarita Duparinova; the first Bulgarian cosmonaut, Georgi Ivanov; the chairman of the Bulgarian Olympic Committee, General Vladimir Stoychev; and of course many outstanding workers, along with all the party and state leaders.[2] The situation in all other East European countries is identical.

In all East European countries the members of the state legislatures are elected in direct, general, and universal elections, citizens of voting age being eligible to vote without any discrimination based on race, religion, creed, or class. (The format of the general elections in Yugoslavia is somewhat different and will be explained later.) The pattern is identical: Local constituencies elect candidates by overwhelming majorities. These candidates have been proposed at meetings of the communist party-dominated Fatherland Front (also called National Front or People's Front depending on the country) and approved by the communist party. In almost all cases there is only one candidate per seat (thus rendering the function of selecting or choosing the candidates non-existent), and even in those very few cases in which two candidates compete for the same seat they are members of the same party and represent the same line and policy.

In fact, the constituencies do not elect their representatives at all but demonstratively endorse the selection already made by the communist party. In most East European countries there are no competing political parties that could at least theoretically provide the voters with alternatives. When other (noncommunist) parties exist (as in Poland), they are allocated a more or less constant quota of representatives by the communist party and precluded from any real possibility of presenting an alternative (let alone competing) political program.

Thus, in Bulgaria the Bulgarian Agrarian National Union
(BANU) is allowed to participate in the elections, and its
candidates run jointly with the communists on the Fatherland Front ticket without any opposition. (In Bulgaria the
principle is clear and firm: one unopposed candidate per
National Assembly seat.) The results of the general
elections since 1966 show that the number of communist
and agrarian representatives does not change much (see
Table 2.1).

Table 2.1
Composition of the Bulgarian National Assembly, 1966–1981

Party	1966	1971	1976	1981
Bulgarian Communist Party (BCP)	280	266	272	271
Bulgarian Agrarian National Union (BANU)	99	100	100	99
Nonparty*	37	34	28	30

*Nonparty candidates also run unopposed on the Fatherland
Front ticket and are mostly Komsomol members or famous
writers and artists.

Sources: Sofia Domestic Service in Bulgarian, 1830 GMT,
28 February 1981; Rabotnichesko Delo, 1 June 1981; and
Radio Free Europe (RFE) Situation Report, Bulgaria,
15 June 1981.

The election results in Poland (Table 2.2) are even
more illustrative. The greatest change between 1965 and
1976 was six seats, in the ruling communist party.
On 30 October 1956, Hungarian Premier Imre Nagy
announced the establishment of a multiparty system. The
experiment lasted exactly four days before being terminated
by Soviet troops. On the other hand, in 1967 Hungary
allowed multiple candidacies in both the National Assembly
and the local council elections. In 1967 there were double
candidacies for nine of the National Assembly's 352 seats.
In the next general elections in 1971 there were forty-
eight double and one triple candidacy. In 1975 the number
dropped to thirty-four, and in 1980 it decreased further
to fifteen.[3] There is no official explanation of the
phenomenon, but it seems that (aside from the fact that it
is difficult to transplant democratic practices to a nondemocratic environment) people were afraid or ashamed of
losing elections even though they all appeared on the same
ticket, represented the same political ideology, and

Table 2.2
Composition of the Polish Sejm, 1965-1976

Party	1965	1969	1972	1976
Polish United Workers' Party (PZPR)	255	255	255	261
United Peasants' Party	117	117	117	113
Democratic Party	39	39	39	37
Nonparty	36	35	36	36
Catholic Activists	13	14	13	13
Total	460	460	460	460

Sources: Trybuna Ludu, 3 June 1965, 5 June 1969, and
21 March 1972; Polytika, 3 April 1976.

promised to strive for the fulfillment of the same plans
and programs. Or perhaps just because of this, defeat was
seen as a reflection of their personal qualities--or at
least their image as perceived by the voters. The party
in Hungary tries repeatedly to stress that what matters is
the party policy and that the party always wins eventually;
thus there are no real losers or winners, and defeated
candidates remain respected citizens of excellent standing.[4]
Obviously, the opinion of the candidates is somewhat
different. Perhaps the idea of multiple candidacies would
have taken root if, instead of two communist candidates,
two candidates of different political creeds had competed.
Theoretically this is possible. The candidates are proposed or nominated at meetings of the Patriotic People's
Front, by an open ballot as a rule. Regardless of who
proposes the candidate, the name would have been approved
in advance by the communist party, and endorsement is
automatic. Still, one-third of the participants in the
meeting can put up another candidate. This, however,
requires not merely courage but also a certain measure of
self-destructiveness; as already noted, voting on the
proposal is open, and it is difficult to see how under the
watchful eyes of the party representatives one-third of
the participants would approve the candidacy of somebody
who would compete with the communist candidate. As a
matter of fact it is doubtful whether even the introduction
of secret voting would change anything in this respect.
    In 1981 it was announced in Hungary that the election
system (mainly the nomination of candidates) would be
reformed in order "to guarantee the representation of
other interest groups in the operation of the state system

and power structure, especially the organized representation of the larger and more significant social organizations,
larger work collectives, factories, agricultural cooperatives
and larger institutions." On 8 June 1985 the first general
elections according to the new and revised system took place
in Hungary. In a broadcast interview, Istvan Sarlos, member
of the MSZMP Central Committee Politburo and chairman of
the National Assembly, stated that 750 nominees were
competing in 352 constituencies. Answering questions of
listeners who telephoned to the studio, he admitted that
"some mistakes have been allowed," mainly in trying to
select competing nominees of the same background (two
professors, two workers, etc.), but he added that "the
1985 elections will serve as a school for perfecting
future elections."[5]

In Poland too the communist party permits a certain
number of double candidacies. There are 460 seats in the
Polish Sejm. Some 617 candidates competed in 1961, 625 in
1972, and 646 in 1980.[6] Notwithstanding the potentially
competitive element suggested by the larger number of
candidates, there never was any doubt about the results of
the elections. In fact the outcome was predetermined by
the order of appearance on the list, because candidates
at the end have no practical chance of being elected. And
of course, no alternative lists to those presented by the
Front of National Unity are allowed.

The elections in Yugoslavia are somewhat different
in structure, though not much in essence. Until 1969 the
Yugoslav elections were identical to those in the other
East European countries. Candidates were nominated at
public meetings and subsequently elected to the various
communal, provincial, republican, and federal assemblies.
Thus in 1969, when such elections were held for the last
time, 80,000 candidates were nominated for a total of
43,678 seats in all assemblies. The elections were semi-
open, with the nomination and possible election of nonparty people easier at the communal than at the provincial,
republican, and federal levels.[7] Because the theoretical
possibility of opposing the party candidates, however, was
a real one, the party leaders conceived a new system,
unique in its character, previously unknown anywhere in
the world, but easier to control and use to strengthen the
party dominance.

Thus in February 1974 the Yugoslav National Assembly,
consisting of a Federal Chamber with 220 members and a
Chamber of Republics and Autonomous Provinces with 88
members, adopted a new Constitution, whose Articles 132

through 152 provide for a new election system called the System of the Delegations.[8] The new system is rather complicated and time consuming (the 1978 elections lasted 5 months[9] and the 1982 elections 4 months[10]) and is based on electing about 70,000 to 75,000 delegations consisting of about 2,000,000 "delegates" to four kinds of assemblies (see Figure 2.1):

1. Communal Assemblies (in 501 communes) consisting of three chambers:
   (1) Chamber of Associated Labor,
   (2) Chamber of Communes, and
   (3) Sociopolitical Chamber.
2. Assembly of Intermunicipal Communities consisting also of three chambers:
   (1) Chamber of Associated Labor,
   (2) Chamber of Communes, and
   (3) Sociopolitical Chamber.
3. Assembly in a Republic or Autonomous Province consisting of three chambers:
   (1) Chamber of Associated Labor,
   (2) Chamber of Communes, and
   (3) Sociopolitical Chamber.
4. Assembly of the Socialist Federative Republic of Yugoslavia (SFRY) consisting of two chambers:
   (1) Federal Chamber with 220 delegates (30 delegates from each of the six republics and 20 delegates from each of the two autonomous provinces, all elected by the communal assemblies), and
   (2) Chamber of Republics and Autonomous Provinces with 88 delegates (12 delegates sent to Belgrade by each of the six republics and 8 delegates from each of the two autonomous provinces).

As had happened in the previous two elections (in 1974 and 1978), the 1982 elections were staged in four phases, each lasting about one month. Phase 1 was the registration of names of posible candidates (more names than seats), which took place in January and February. In Phase 2, which took place in March, workers in enterprises (members of the Basic Organizations of Associated Labor-- BOAL), peasants in cooperatives, individual farmers, white-collar workers, employees in various institutions, state officials, and members of the army elected "almost 3,000,000 members of delegations and delegates" throughout

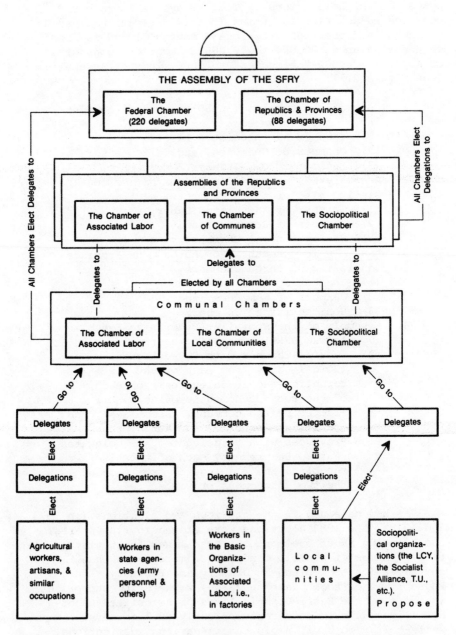

Figure 2.1   Yugoslavia's Assembly: The System of Delegates

Yugoslavia to represent them in higher bodies. During
Phase 3 in April more than 100,000 delegates were
selected from the previously mentioned millions of delegates
to serve in communal, provincial, and republican assemblies,
as well as in the National Assembly in Belgrade.[11] Finally,
in Phase 4 the May session (15-16 May 1982) of the National
Assembly elected the president of the SFRY National
Assembly,[12] chairmen of the National Assembly commissions,[13]
the president of the Federal Executive Council,[14] and other
officials.

According to the Yugoslav Constitution, the workers in
the enterprises and communities elect their delegations
directly and by secret ballot (Article 134), but only from
persons who were previously "registered." The basis for
the delegations' activity is the idea of "imperative
mandate," i.e., the rule that individual delegates or
complete delegations are obliged to follow the instructions
given to them by "their basic organizations," rather than
make their own decisions. By this procedure the authors of
the electoral law anticipated that the party would easily
increase its control, strictly directing the behavior of
the National Assembly members. Delegates trying to march
along their own road can easily be "recalled" by the party
and replaced. There must be no mistake about the aspect
of selection among different candidates: although in the
low-level assemblies the voters have the chance of selecting from among more candidates than there are seats, the
candidates for all high-level assemblies are in fact
appointed in advance by the party.[15]

Official Yugoslav sources presented the new system as
one launching "the idea of emissaries rather than of
representatives," a system that "overcomes the classical
bourgeoise and class representation and replaces it with
that of direct class rule of the majority through
emissaries or delegates."[16] Yet despite its novelty and
complexity the Yugoslav election system differs from the
system of the other East European countries only in its
format. The principles of total party control of nomination and outcome persist through the banning of real
competition.

In the East European countries general elections take
place every four or five years (Albania, 4; Bulgaria,
5; Czechoslovakia, 4; German Democratic Republic, 5;
Hungary, 5; Poland, 4; Romania, 4; Yugoslavia, 4). Despite
the fact that the length of the term is usually set by
the constitution, the exact date of the elections is not
determined until the last session of the outgoing national

assembly, which announces the date of the forthcoming
elections. This is an automatic rubber-stamp approval of
a previous decision adopted by the party Central Committee.

STAGES IN ELECTION CAMPAIGNS

There is usually only a very short period between the
"decision" of the National Assembly and election day. Thus
on 31 January 1980 the Polish Sejm adopted a decision to
hold general elections on 23 March 1980, stipulating that
the list of the candidates was to be completed and submitted for approval to the Front of National Unity by
27 February.[17] This left a little more than three weeks
for the election campaign. The Czechoslovak Constitution
allows at least sixty days between the National Assembly
decision and the election,[18] and the situation in Hungary[19]
and the other East European countries is similar.

The election campaign in Eastern Europe has two
stages: preparation and execution. Both stages are
organized by a formal coalition of political parties and
mass organizations, which exists in each East European
country (and whose activity will be analyzed in a separate
chapter). Although these coalitions go under different
names (Front of National Unity in Poland, National Front
in Czechoslovakia, Fatherland Front in Bulgaria, Democratic
Front in Albania, National Front in GDR, Patriotic People's
Front in Hungary, Socialist Alliance of the Working People
of Yugoslavia in SFRY, and Socialist Democracy and Unity
Front in Romania) they all are dominated and activated by
the respective communist parties.

Preparation

This stage consists of compiling the electoral
registers, defining the constituencies, forming election
committees, selecting and registering the candidates, and
publishing the list of the candidates.

The registration of the voters takes place at the
places of work--and nowhere else. The names of all
citizens entitled to vote are entered in the electoral
register. Citizens who are not registered cannot vote.
The electoral registers are compiled by the national
election committee with the help of the election committee
of each constituency. The registers are made accessible
to the general public approximately a month before the
election, so that errors can be corrected.

Voters who have a legitimate reason to expect to be unable to cast their votes in the constituency in which they are registered may obtain special (usually written) permission to vote in the constituency in which they find themselves on election day. Because the election results usually give percentage figures bordering on 100 percent, it is possible, at least theoretically, for a candidate to receive more than 100 percent of the votes if on election day enough "outside voters" are in his constituency.

At the same time the electoral register is being prepared, the national election organs are being set up. In some states, such as Hungary, the national election committee is appointed by the State or Presidential Council[20]; in others, such as the Czechoslovak Socialist Republic (CSSR), by the National Front.[21] Officially, the national election committee "must safeguard the legality of the elections, accept the list of candidates chosen by the nominating meetings, publish the electoral results, and if necessary, set the date for runoff elections."[22]

Another development that usually takes place at the same time is the publication of an "appeal" by the National Front to the people. The appeal explains the mechanism of the elections, encourages the people to participate in the imminent nominating meetings, and urges them to intensify their working enthusiasm and cast their votes for the candidates of the National Front.

These first organizational steps in the stage of preparing the elections are immediately followed by the relatively more important development of the election campaign--the nomination of the candidates and the submission of their names to the national election committee for examination and registration. This process takes place in nomination meetings organized by the National Front organizations at the places of work, residential areas, offices, army and police units, and so forth. The candidates may be recommended publicly and openly by any of the mass organizations grouped in the National Front. Incidentally, the East European press frequently praises the nomination of the candidates by an open vote as an "essential characteristic of socialist democracy."[23] The general criteria for nominating the candidates have been defined as "political maturity, class consciousness, good moral character, experience in organizing and conducting propaganda, devotion to socialist construction, readiness to fight for the interests of the working people, and so forth."[24]

As noted earlier, the communist party has a monopoly

over the nomination of the candidates. Its main leaders
are automatically nominated, as are other suitable candidates
chosen among front-ranking workers or people who have ex-
celled in various areas of life and whose candidacy is
considered a party reward for services rendered to the
socialist society. Because the name of each proposed
candidate has been previously made known by the party, all
meetings in the same constituency propose the same
candidate.

The higher the position of the candidate, the higher
the rank of the person who proposes him. Thus members of
the Politburo or prominent members of the Central Committee
are proposed by the highest party official of the constituency, usually the first secretary of the relevant
party committee. Failure of an outgoing member of
parliament to be renominated should not automatically be
considered a demotion or ousting. First of all, in some
East European countries, such as Yugoslavia, there is a
two-term limit.[25] Second, when the new candidate is proposed by the outgoing member of parliament himself, the
reason is obviously retirement or transfer to another post.
Such was the case with the Hungarian general elections in
1975, when the 75-year-old Professor I. Noszkay proposed
a new candidate to represent his constituency, saying that
"when one reaches the age of 75, one considers it natural
for one's constituency to seek a new candidate."[26]

It must be remembered that there is theoretically a
possibility of proposing candidates who oppose the official
National Front candidates (in most East European countries
this can be done by one-third of the participants in the
nominating meeting). The fact that the proposal has to be
approved by an open vote, however, renders the theoretical
right a meaningless act of suicidal courage, hardly likely
to be supported by one-third of the participants. On the
other hand, the so-called double candidacy (which does
not exist in Bulgaria and the CSSR) does not really add any
measure of true democracy, because both candidates belong
to the same party and represent the same political platform. Many East European politicians and journalists take
great pains to explain that a socialist election differs
fundamentally from its "bourgeois equivalent." CPCZ
(Communist Party of Czechoslovakia) Central Committee
Secretary Jan Fojtik, writing before the 1981 election in
the CSSR, said that the essence of the election was not to
offer a choice but rather to unite society for the purpose
of undisputed advancement toward the one and only aim--
strengthening and developing socialism.[27]

Even if the impossible really happened and an alternative candidate was proposed, there would be little likeli-
hood of his being accepted by the national election committee.
Thus, the nomination meetings are little more than a formal
act, purporting to lend an air of democracy to a fait
accompli of the communist party.

Before a nominee becomes an official candidate he must
be registered by the appropriate national election
committee and his candidacy must be made public. The
national election committee publishes the list of candidates
three to four weeks before election day. The list gives
the names of the candidates, their ages, and their occupa-
tions. The publication of the list is usually accompanied
by an appeal or an interim report of the national
election committee. Thus in the GDR the committee published on 18 May 1981 the list of candidates for the 14
June elections.[28] The committee, led by Paul Verner,
member of the Politburo, secretary of the Socialist Unity
Party (SED) Central Committee, and chairman of the GDR
National Front, stressed that the list was "an impressive
document of the common objectives and means of all parties
and mass media working together in the National Front . . .
it has led to new initiatives for successfully completing
the tasks of the 1980s as expounded by Erich Honecker at
the 10th party congress. So far the election movement has
clearly shown the identity of word and deed, the firm
alliance of workers and their socialist fatherland the
GDR." The examination of the candidates was defined by him
as "an example of true socialist democracy," and he concluded by saying that the objective of the election campaign
so far has been "to achieve further impetus for the
democratic movement throughout the country in order to
implement the resolutions of the 10th SED Congress to which
all parties and mass organizations, united in the National
Front, have given their consent."[29]

Despite the fact that the national election committee
is usually chaired by the National Front chairman, who is
a Politburo member, and that there is no chance that it
would do anything even vaguely opposing party policy, the
party Central Committee still keeps an eye on the election
committee's activity. It is not unusual for a special
Central Committee plenum to examine the progress of the
election preparations. Thus on 23 April 1981 the CPCZ
Central Committee met in Prague under the chairmanship of
Gustav Husak to discuss the progress of the preparations
for the June 1981 general elections.[30] The plenum adopted
a resolution praising the preparations and expressing the

conviction that "the elections will become a demonstration
of the unity of the party, the entire National Front and
all working people, and will contribute to the further
deepening of socialist democracy and the development of the
political and labor activity of the GDR citizens in the
realization of the program of the 16th CPCZ Congress."[31]
In addition the Central Committee pledged "to all party
bodies and organizations . . . to continue the demanding
and responsible task of preparing for the elections and to
continue effective political-organizational, mass-political
and agitation work so that the progress and results of
the elections bring about a decisive victory of the candidates of the National Front."[32]

The publication of the list of candidates completes
the preparation stage of the election campaign and marks
the beginning of the second stage, the execution stage or
actual campaign.

Execution

This stage consists of mass "election rallies" at
which the candidates are presented to their constituencies
and speak of their "programs." In fact the process is a
broad agitation campaign conducted by the communist party,
aimed at increasing the working enthusiasm of the population, as well as their political awareness and support for
party policy.

The election rallies at which the candidates are
presented to their constituencies are routine affairs at
which standard slogans are voiced and predictable pledges
made. Nevertheless, the election rallies serve several
interesting purposes. First of all, because all party
leaders (Politburo members, Central Committee secretaries,
and so forth) are also candidates, the rallies really serve
as a vehicle for presenting and explaining party policy.
The importance of the rally and the size of the audience
depend on the prominence of the candidate. Paradoxically,
"second-rate" candidates (manual workers, employees,
teachers, etc.) often play second fiddle at their own
election rallies, while the local party secretary or some
other party dignitary present at the rally basks in the
limelight. Such treatment demonstrates that it is not the
personalities but policy (and unanimous support for it) that
matters, and subsequently, that the main attention is
accorded to holders of political posts who are important in
day-to-day implementation of party policy, such as the first
secretary of the local party committee or the chairman of

the local people's council.

One knows in advance what will happen at an election rally; it is no different from any other agitation meeting. Subsequently, the participation in such rallies is not overwhelming, a fact frequently deplored in the East European press.[33] The most important rallies are, of course, those at which the party leader appears. The leader's speech on such occasions goes far beyond the borders of a regular election speech and represents an authoritative statement on the party's current policy. A typical rally of this type took place on 29 May 1980 at the ship and crane factory in Budapest's 13th district. The speaker was Janos Kadar, MSZMP (Hungarian Socialist Workers' Party) Central Committee first secretary.[34] In his speech he praised the democratic selection of candidates, maintaining that more than 2,200,000 people had taken part in the nomination process. He pointed out that there were 15 double candidacies (of the 352 parliament seats) as an example of democracy, and justified this low number by the "thoroughness of the selection process," which had provided in most cases one candidate per available position.

From this point on, Kadar's speech became a tight summary of his speech at the 12th MSZMP Congress. He acknowledged that the party and its leadership cannot provide foolproof answers but would try to provide the best possible living conditions; the achievements of socialism in Hungary were stressed against the background of the situation before the establishment of the socialist regime; he pointed to the steady increase in the standard of living, stressing the fact that 5,000,000 Hungarians travel abroad annually, that 510,000 people had bought new cars in the last 5 years, and that 1,500,000 people had moved into new accommodations during the same period. Kadar did not overlook certain difficulties in Hungary's economy, but restricted himself to the same facts (and even phrases) he had used at the MSZMP Congress. Thus, for instance, he warned the workers that "steadily increasing" does not mean "always increasing" and that the possibility of slower increase exists. He admitted that the quality of political leadership "and even the highest leadership" must be improved as a precondition of demanding better discipline from the workers. He attacked the "idle loafers" in society, branding them as criminals, and concluded this part of his speech with some statistics on the improvement of the domestic economy as a result of party policy.

The second part of Kadar's election speech dealt with

foreign affairs. He reiterated Hungary's firm support for
"progressive forces" throughout the world and confirmed the
party's and country's total support for Soviet foreign
policy. Speaking of Afghanistan, he expressed support for
the Babrak Karmal government, pledging solidarity with the
"revolutionary efforts of the Afghan people," and he
expressed agreement with the versatile aid that the USSR
had provided "the Afghan revolution."

After dwelling on some other international issues,
praising the part of Hungarian public organizations in
the international peace movement, he concluded his speech
by calling for a declaration of support for the policy of
the MSZMP in the form of votes cast on election day.[35]

The similarity between Kadar's speech and a speech by
Todor Zhivkov, BCP Central Committee secretary general and
State Council chairman, at a 6 June election rally in Sofia
is striking, but then it is yet another common feature
among so many others of the East European countries'
regimes. Zhivkov, like Kadar, praised the democratic
character of the election and admitted several minor
difficulties: "I admit that there have been cases in
which leaders at various levels were forced to listen to
severe criticism about themselves. No one can delude himself that everything proceeds smoothly in our country,
that we have no unsolved problems, that there are no just
demands which are still unfulfilled."[36] From this point
on, again like Kadar, Zhivkov surveyed Bulgaria's economic
successes "in the light of the 12th BCP Congress' decisions"
and pledged new successes in every area of life. Just as
Kadar's speech was a summary of an earlier one, this portion
of Zhivkov's speech was a summary of his speech at the
April 1981 BCP Congress. In international affairs Zhivkov
stressed that Bulgaria's peace-loving policy has been
universally recognized. He expressed the well known Soviet
position on every topical international issue and confirmed
Bulgaria's total support for the peace programs adopted by
the 24th, 25th, and 26th CPSU Congresses. He concluded
his speech by urging the voters to vote unanimously for
the Fatherland Front candidates.

Both Kadar's and Zhivkov's speeches are typical East
European election speeches. One notes immediately the
absence of any reference to local issues of interest to the
particular constituency involved, or of promises and
pledges relevant to the same constituency. In fact there
is nothing in these speeches the participants could not have
read daily in the newspapers.

The election rallies serve yet another purpose. The

entire election campaign is not only a useful opportunity
for increasing the people's consciousness by acquainting
them with party programs and policies, but also an occasion
for developing a broad agitation campaign aimed at increasing the workers' productivity and improving the quality
of production. A substantial part of the newspapers is
devoted to reporting working achievements in honor of the
forthcoming elections, as well as pledges for new successes.
When participants in the election rallies take the floor
they utilize the opportunity not only to voice their
support of party policy but to promise further development
and improvement in their quality of work. In fact, as
already pointed out, the election campaigns in Eastern
Europe are a direct continuation of the pre-congress and
post-congress propaganda campaigns and serve the same
functions. In all East European countries, as the following excerpt from Czechoslovakia points out for that
country, the election campaigns are openly viewed as
instruments for implementing the decisions of the most
recent party congress: "Election platforms of the
National Front should primarily become the key instruments
for creative implementation of the resolutions of the 16th
CPCZ Congress at the community, district, and regional
level."[37]

There are several other interesting aspects of East
European election campaigns, one of them touching upon
church-state relations. Strong atheistic propaganda is
officially the rule in all East European countries. However, during the election campaigns this propaganda
invariably ceases, and the churches are given breathing
space (with the possible exception of Albania, where the
church has been effectively eliminated as a factor of any
sociopolitical importance). In return, the regime expects
full cooperation and commitment, in an attempt to
demonstrate the total cohesion of the population and the
universal support the party policy enjoys.

A typical case involved the 1976 general elections
in the CSSR. The elections were set for 22 and 23 October.
On 15 September a meeting of the Christian Peace Conference
took place. It was attended by 200 representatives of the
fifteen churches authorized in the CSSR, included four
theological seminars, and dealt with the forthcoming
general elections. The main speaker was Karel Hruza,
director of the Church Secretariat at the office of
the Presidium of the government, who highly praised the
contribution of believers to building the socialist society
and their active participation in preparing for the

forthcoming elections.[38] Hruza explained that the main purpose of the campaign was to guarantee social security and material well-being and to create conditions that would make it possible for citizens to enjoy these benefits in peace and security.[39]

Jan Urban, chairman of the Brethren Church, replying on behalf of the representatives of all churches, spoke on the subject of "For Peace, Work and Bread," giving assurances of the committed support of church representatives in the elections.[40] In the discussion that followed, the other representatives of the churches also expressed full support for the election program of the National Front and pledged that "the believers will approach the elections with a sense of responsibility for bringing about a happy future for our nation within the framework of the socialist community."[41]

The church press also contributes its share to the election campaign by urging its readers to vote for the National Front candidates. This does not exhaust the ways in which the church in Eastern Europe participates in the election campaign. Usually, on the eve of the elections the church issues a declaration praising the party policy and pledging support for the election program of the National Front, "because this is a program which guarantees a peaceful development for the Motherland, a general prosperity for the republic, and growth in the people's standard of living."[42] In an earlier CSSR election the church pre-election declaration expressed support for the "decisive contribution of the socialist community led by the USSR, to the struggle for world peace."[43] Similar appeals and declarations are issued in Hungary[44] and other East European countries.

The reward is often in kind. Thus at the October 1976 plenum of the CPCZ Central Committee, Gustav Husak thanked the CSSR churches for having supported the National Front program and candidates in the election campaign. Apparently as a token of this appreciation, a seat was given in the Slovak National Council to Gejza Navratil, chairman of the Slovak branch of Pacem in Terris, an organization of Catholic clergy supporting the regime. Previously only the Protestant church had been represented by Pastor Jan Konvit, who was then confirmed as a member of the Slovak contingent of the Federal Assembly's Chamber of Nations.[45] However, much more important (for the church) are the tacit concessions, which are never publicized in the communist press, such as an easing of antireligious propaganda, allowing the churches to fill vacant places of various priests and bishops, slightly increasing the <u>numerus</u> <u>clausus</u> of the theological seminars, and so forth. All this, however, does not change the official status of the church in Eastern Europe, which is dealt with in a separate chapter.

THE ELECTION

Election Day

Election day is an official holiday, during which "spontaneous" celebrations, dancing, and singing are organized outside the polling stations. The voters begin to arrive at the earliest possible time. Failure to show up can be costly, because it usually is interpreted as a way of expressing protest. After several hours of voting, long before the end of election day, the overwhelming majority of the voters have already exercised their voting right. In the afternoon special messengers or even committees visit the houses of those who have failed to show up, to find out why.

The voters cast their votes personally; proxies are not permitted. The ballot papers are placed on the table at which the election committee is sitting, next to the ballot box. After a voter has been checked against the electoral register, he is issued a ballot paper. There is a polling booth, but the voter may enter it only if he wants to modify the ballot paper. Thus, use of the booth indicates that a change has been made, and very few voters, if any, dare to enter it. The overwhelming majority simply cast their ballots as soon as they receive them from the election committee, and thus fulfill their duty. Small wonder that the National Front candidates are elected by majorities of 99.75 percent, 99.87 percent, or even 100 percent.

Election Results

Elections in Eastern Europe never produce any surprises. Not only is it known in advance that the National Front candidates will be elected, but even the name of the future national assembly chairman is known. Thus, several weeks before the 1978 general elections in Yugoslavia, it was known that the Serb Dragoslav Markovic would be elected president of the new National Assembly to replace the Macedonian Kiro Gligorov.[46] It was all arranged.

When one reads the election results of various East
European countries, one has the impression that they are all
the same result, reprinted again and again. Several
examples from recent East European elections will suffice
to illustrate this point: In Bulgaria's 1981 general
elections there were 6,526,782 registered voters. Some
6,519,674, or 99.93 percent, cast their ballots for the
Fatherland Front nominees. There were only 577 ballots
cast against the nominees.[47] In the GDR in 1981 there were
12,352,362 registered voters. Some 12,254,613 votes were
cast. This represented a 99.21 percent turnout. A total
of 12,235,071 valid votes, or 99.86 percent of the votes,
were cast for the joint National Front lists. A total of
16,645 votes were cast against the list.[48] In the CSSR
general elections in 1981, some 10,725,609 voters, or
99.96 percent, voted for the National Front candidates.
The election turnout was 99.98 percent.[49] In Hungary,
some 99.30 percent of those who took part in the 1980
general elections voted for the candidates of the
Patriotic People's Front.[50] The percentage of the votes
received by some of the leaders in this Hungarian
election and the one preceding it can be seen in Table 2.3.

Table 2.3
Percentage of Votes Received by Principal Hungarian
Leaders, 1980 and 1975 General Elections

Name and Position	1980	1975
Janos Kadar, MSZMP Central Committee first secretary	99.8	99.8
Karoly Nemeth, MSZMP Central Committee Secretary and Politburo member	99.2	99.7
Gyorgy Lazar, Politburo member, premier	100	99.8
Gyorgy Aczel, Politburo member, deputy premier	99.7	99.8
Pal Losonczi, Politburo member, Presidential Council chairman	99.9	99.9
Frigyer Poja, minister of foreign affairs	100	99.9
Sandor Gaspar, Politburo member and trade union secretary general	99.2	99.6
Istvan Sarlos, Politburo member and Patriotic People's Front secretary general	99.9	99.5

Source: Radio Free Europe Situation Report, Hungary,
16 June 1980.

The election results are invariably interpreted in the same way. For the CSSR in 1981: "In the election the Czechoslovak people again expressed their agreement with the policy of the Czechoslovak Communist Party and the National Front, and support for the program of the 16th party congress, for the friendship and alliance with the USSR, and for Czechoslovakia's adherence to the socialist community."[51] For the GDR in 1981: "With this result our country's citizens have with great unanimity expressed their confidence in their candidates and support for the aims set out in the National Front election manifesto, which is dedicated to the people's well-being and to the preservation of peace. . . . By our joint work we will guarantee to all our citizens prosperity and full employment, growth and stability, social security and a sense of belonging, as well as a peaceful life. This path was indicated by the 10th SED Congress."[52]

It must be stressed that votes in Eastern Europe are usually counted manually--an excessively painstaking and time-consuming process--which leaves the door open to suspicions about manipulation and "doctoring" the results. But by any realistic criterion the East European elections are in fact a plebiscite by which the public is required to endorse--partly of its own will and possibly partly otherwise--people selected by the party to form parliamentary bodies. The leading role of the party in all stages of the election campaign is more than evident, and it has been described with impressive simplicity: First the party selects the candidates; then it trains and rehearses the electoral commissions, also handpicked; then it sends agitators in pairs to visit all voters. The party assures that "a favorable atmosphere" is created in general and in the polls in particular.[53] In localities where party influence is small, factory organizations of the party are entrusted to look after the elections; party district committees dispatch instructors to supervise the entire process in towns and villages, and on the two election days (in the CSSR the general elections last two days), party committees are in full session to intervene where necessary and to purvey regular reports to higher bodies. Finally, party activists insure the "undisturbed counting of votes," having first excluded from the polling stations all those who had no business there. Vote counting is not declared closed until the subordinate commission receives instructions to this effect from the superior commissions, all under the close watch of party officials.[54]

Obviously, what is described here is a basically
nondemocratic process involving the automatic approval of
candidates selected by the party, with no possibility of
alternatives. The entire process is considered a demonstrative act of approval of party policy and of the nature
of the regime; therefore, nonparticipation is considered
a counterdemonstration, which often involves unpleasant
consequences (hence the tremendously high participation
percentage). In addition to electing deputies to the
national assemblies, the general elections in Eastern
Europe are supposed to be an expression of the will of the
people to follow the party policy along the road toward
socialism, to demonstrate national unity and cohesion,
and to increase the people's political consciousness and
working enthusiasm.

NOTES

1. Pencho Kubadinski, BCP Central Committee Politburo
member, in Rabotnichesko Delo (Bulgaria), 25 March 1981.
2. East European Report no. 1906, Foreign Broadcast
Information Service (FBIS), 5 August 1981, p. 1037.
3. Radio Free Europe (RFE) Situation Report, Hungary,
18 June 1980.
4. Magyar Hirlap (Hungary), 18 June 1980.
5. Radio Budapest, 22 June 1981, in RFE Situation
Report, Hungary, 27 August 1981; Budapest Domestic Service
in Hungarian; 1715 GMT, 20 May 1985, in Daily Report
(FBIS), 21 May 1985.
6. RFE Situation Report, Poland, 24 March 1977
and 20 March 1980.
7. RFE Situation Report, Yugoslavia, 21 March 1978.
8. Ibid.
9. Ibid., 5 June 1978.
10. RFE Research and Analysis Department (RAD)
Background Report, Yugoslavia, no. 114, 14 May 1982.
11. Ibid.
12. TANJUG Domestic Service in Serbo-Croatian, 1249
GMT, 15 May 1982; Daily Report (FBIS), 17 May 1982.
13. TANJUG Domestic Service in Serbo-Croatian, 1225
GMT, 15 May 1982; Daily Report (FBIS), 17 May 1982.
14. TANJUG Domestic Service in Serbo-Croatian, 0944
GMT, 16 May 1982; Daily Report (FBIS), 17 May 1982.
15. RFE Situation Report, Yugoslavia, 5 June 1978.
16. J. Djordjevic, Demokratija i Izbori (Zagreb, 1977),
pp. 47-48.

17. RFE Situation Report, Poland, 6 February 1980.
18. RFE Situation Report, CSSR, 13 October 1976.
19. RFE Situation Report, Hungary, 13 June 1975.
20. Ibid.
21. RFE Situation Report, CSSR, 13 October 1976.
22. Nepszabadsag (Hungary), 3 May 1975.
23. Komarom Megyei Dolgozok Lapja (Hungary), 14 May 1975.
24. The Representative System of the CSSR (Prague, 1974), p. 112.
25. Borba (Yugoslavia), 21 February 1978.
26. Magyar Nemetz (Hungary), 24 May 1975.
27. Rude Pravo (CSSR), 19 May 1981.
28. ADN (German General News Service) International Service in German, 1239 GMT, 18 May 1981; Daily Report (FBIS), 20 May 1981.
29. Ibid.
30. Prague Domestic Service in Czech, 1330 GMT, 23 April 1981; Daily Report (FBIS), 24 April 1981.
31. Ibid.
32. Ibid.
33. Szolnok Megyei Neplap (Hungary), 30 May 1975.
34. Nepszabadsag, 30 May 1980.
35. Ibid.
36. Rabotnichesko Delo, 6 June 1981.
37. Pravda (CSSR), 13 February 1981.
38. Svobodno Slovo (CSSR), 16 September 1976.
39. Ibid.
40. Radio Hvezda (CSSR), 1630 GMT, 15 September 1976.
41. Ibid.
42. Declaration of the CSSR Christian Peace Conference, Radio Prague, 1830 GMT, 21 September 1981.
43. Declaration of the CSSR Churches and Religious Societies, RFE Situation Report, CSSR, 6 October 1976.
44. Uj Ember (Hungary), 1 June 1975; Magyar Nemetz, 18 May 1975.
45. RFE Situation Report, CSSR, 10 November 1976.
46. RFE Situation Report, Yugoslavia, 5 June 1978.
47. Bulgarian Telegraph Agency (BTA) in English, 1325 GMT, 9 June 1981; Daily Report (FBIS), 9 June 1981.
48. ADN International Service in German, 2043 GMT, 14 June 1981; Daily Report (FBIS), 16 June 1981.
49. Czechoslovak News Agency (CTK) from Prague in English, 1613 GMT, 7 June 1981; Daily Report (FBIS), 8 June 1981.
50. Nepszabadsag, 10 June 1980.

32

51. CTK from Prague in English, 1613 GMT, 7 June 1981; Daily Report (FBIS), 8 June 1981.

52. ADN International Service in German, 2043 GMT, 14 June 1981; Daily Report (FBIS), 16 June 1981.

53. "Party Organizations Preparing For Elections," Zivot Strany (CSSR) no. 10, 1981, pp. 8-10, in RFE Situation Report, CSSR, 16 June 1981.

54. Ibid.

3
The National Assemblies

The East European parliaments are the best illustration of the tremendous discrepancy that exists in Eastern Europe between the formal existence of democratic organs and institutions and the nondemocratic reality, marked by the total inability of these organs and institutions to influence the decision-making process or even take a meaningful part in it. All East European constitutions explicitly provide that all legislative authority rests exclusively with elected parliaments or assemblies, that the parliaments have a crucial role in defining the basic rights and duties of the citizens and the state organs, and that all other state organs that may issue laws, regulations, decrees, ordinances, and directives (such as the presidium of the national assembly, the state council, the council of ministers, the individual ministries, and so forth) in fact derive their authority from the parliament. Yet the East European legislatures seldom do more than give rubber-stamp ex post facto endorsements and legal attestation of the executive (and other legislative) acts of other state organs. They play no active or at least meaningful part in formulating public policy, controlling the executive or influencing the country's political life in any way. As in all other areas of life in Eastern Europe, parliamentary activity is completely dominated and controlled by the communist parties and is utilized for purposes that have little if anything to do with normal democratic practices. Although in recent years there have been several examples in Poland and Yugoslavia (to be discussed later) that suggest a certain deviation from the accepted practice in the activity of those parliaments, these examples were the exception to the rule and hardly changed the overall picture of parliaments controlled by the communist parties.

33

FORMAL STRUCTURE

There is nothing in the formal structure of the East European parliaments that suggests their actual political emasculation. In fact their structure resembles that of most West European legislatures:

1. <u>Albania</u>. Article 66 of the Albanian Constitution defines the 250-member unicameral People's Assembly as the "highest and most important organ of the governmental structure." It holds two regular annual sessions.

2. <u>Bulgaria</u>. Articles 66-89 of the Bulgarian Constitution, which deal with the 400-member unicameral National Assembly, describe it as the "supreme organ of state power" and stipulate that it shall hold three regular annual sessions. In fact, without amending the constitution, the Bulgarian National Assembly has held in recent years four annual sessions,[1] something that did not affect its basic characteristics and functions.

3. <u>The CSSR</u>. The Federal Assembly consists of 350 members and two chambers: a 200-member Chamber of the People and a 150-member Chamber of Nations, 75 of whose members are Czechs and 75 Slovaks. The Federal Assembly holds two regular annual sessions.

4. <u>The GDR</u>. Here the legislature is called the People's Chamber (Volkskammer). It consists of 500 members, has one chamber, and holds two regular annual sessions.

5. <u>Hungary</u>. The 352-member unicameral National Assembly holds four regular annual sessions.

6. <u>Poland</u>. The 460-member unicameral Sejm holds two regular annual sessions. However, since August 1980, when the activity of the Solidarity trade union began, the Sejm has stepped up its activity to hold numerous sessions.

7. <u>Romania</u>. The 360-member unicameral Grand National Assembly holds two regular annual sessions.

8. <u>The SFRY</u>. Yugoslavia has a 308-member bi-cameral Federal Assembly. One chamber, the Federal Chamber, consists of 220 delegates "from self-managing organizations and committees

and sociopolitical organizations in the
republics and the autonomous republics."
The smaller Chamber of Deputies and Autonomous
Provinces has 88 members, who comprise
delegations from "assemblies of the republics
and assemblies of the autonomous republics."[2]

In addition, the East European parliaments have
parliamentary committees similar to those of Western
parliaments, although their sessions are closed and little
if any information on their debates is ever released.
Their official rights and prerogatives are again similar
to those of West European parliaments and include
legislating laws, proclaiming elections, adopting the
budget and the national plan, amending the constitution,
electing and approving the council of ministers, electing
or approving judges, controlling the performance of
ministers and ministries, ratifying state documents, and
declaring war. The Romanian Constitution even goes so
far as to list twenty-three specific prerogatives of the
Grand National Assembly, ranging from adopting and
amending the Constitution to appointing and recalling the
supreme commanders of the armed forces.[3]
Various East European sources often stress specific
functions of the parliaments, related to facilitating the
implementation of party tasks. Thus Stanko Todorov, chairman of the Bulgarian National Assembly, listed "improving
the political system and developing socialist democracy"
and "implementing the instructions of the 12th BCP
Congress" among the most important functions of the
Bulgarian National Assembly.[4]
The resemblance in the structural characteristics is
as far as the resemblance between the East European and the
West European parliamentary system goes. In everything
connected with their real functions there is no comparison,
and one thing must be clearly understood about East
European parliaments from the beginning. As noted in the
list above, these parliaments meet two to four times a
year. Their sessions last only for two or three days,
sometimes even less. This means that for the rest of the
year the country's supreme legislating body is not sitting.
Having described the structural resemblance to West
European parliaments, one should add that this great gap
between parliamentary sessions accounts for a significant
structural difference between the East European and Western
parliamentary systems. Obviously, the East European
parliaments cannot be expected to exercise the full range

of their constitutional prerogatives during their brief
sessions. Furthermore, the agenda of these routine
sessions is more or less standard: adopting the plan and
budget, listening to the reports of the prime minister and
the minister of finance, approving by-elections, and so
forth. A special organ was therefore created in all East
European countries, which in fact implements the duties of
the national assemblies. Its structure and functions are
similar in all East European countries, although its
official name varies from one country to another.

1. Albania. The special state organ is called the
   Presidium of the People's Assembly and consists
   of a president, two vice-presidents, a secretary,
   and ten members. The president is the titular
   head of state.
2. Bulgaria. The State Council, as it is called,
   has twenty-nine members including a chairman
   (the titular head of state), a first deputy
   chairman, three other deputy chairmen, and a
   secretary.
3. The CSSR. The Presidium of the Federal Assembly
   has forty members, half of whom are Czechs and
   half Slovaks. The head of the Presidium is
   the country's head of state.
4. Hungary. The Presidential Council has a
   chairman, two deputy chairmen, a secretary,
   and seventeen members. At present, Hungary
   is one of the three East European states (the
   other two being Poland and the SFRY) in which
   the titular head of state, i.e., the chairman
   of the State Council, is not also the leader
   of the communist party. In Albania, Bulgaria,
   the GDR, the CSSR, and Romania the two positions are held by the same person.
5. Poland. The Council of State has a chairman
   (head of state), four deputy chairmen, a
   secretary, and eleven members.
6. Romania. The Council of State has a president
   (the head of state), five vice-presidents, a
   secretary, and nineteen other members.
7. The SFRY. The nine-member State Presidency
   consists of one member from each of the six
   republics and the two autonomous provinces
   plus the current president of the LCY (League
   of Yugoslav Communists) Central Committee
   Presidium. The presidential post rotates

annually among the eight members other than
the Central Committee Presidium President.[5]

The East European state councils are elected by the
parliaments of the respective countries from among their
members. Thus a new form of democracy is created, namely
government by the representatives of the representatives.
Actually, the East European state councils are something
between mini-parliaments and collective "presidents."
They exercise the real legislative functions between
parliamentary sessions, issuing decrees, representing the
state in the international arena, interpreting laws, calling elections, convening the parliaments, holding
plebiscites, concluding treaties, appointing and recalling
diplomatic representatives, appointing civil servants--
in short, acting as a parliament. Although theoretically
responsible to the national assembly, the state council
in fact directs and regulates the work of the parliament,
serving as a useful party vehicle for issuing official
decrees. At their regular sessions the East European
parliaments automatically vote their approval of the
decrees issued by the state councils.

When other political parties exist, along with the
ruling communist party, they are also represented in the
state councils, their leaders usually serving as first
deputy chairmen. Thus in 1982 Petur Tanchev, the leader
of the Bulgarian Agrarian National Union, was the first
deputy chairman of the Bulgarian State Council.[6] In the
GDR Gerald Goetting, leader of the Christian Democratic
Union; Heinrich Homann, chairman of the National Democratic
Party; and Manfred Germach, leader of the Liberal Democratic
Party of Germany, were deputy chairmen of the State
Council. In Poland, Tadeus Mlynczak (Democratic Party),
and Zdizislaw Tomal (United Peasants' Party), were deputy
chairmen of the Polish Council of State. Sometimes
illustrious figures or even noted actors or writers can
become state council members. Thus in Bulgaria in 1982
the poet Georgi Dzhagarov was deputy chairman of the
State Council.[7]

Although the sessions of the East European parliaments
are usually open to the general public, little is known
about the way in which the state council conducts its
business. One only learns about its output--in the form
of laws and decrees--but never anything about the discussions and debates, voting procedures, and so forth.
However, the fact that the overwhelming majority of the
state council members are party leaders leaves no doubt

about who really directs the state council activity. As
are all other state organs in Eastern Europe, the state
councils are party-dominated bodies whose main function is
to lend a measure of legality to the unrestricted party
rule.

The relationship between the state councils and the
parliaments of the respective East European countries is
interesting. Officially, the parliament elects and thus
controls the activity of the state council. In fact, however, the entire activity of the parliaments consists of
either approving acts and decrees of the state council,
or routinely adopting the national plan and budget. The
following example illustrates the degree to which the East
European parliaments are dominated by the state council.

Hungary's new National Assembly, elected on 8 June
1980, held its constituent session on 27 June. Following
established practice, it first elected its own leadership,
determined the composition of its eleven standing
committees, and voted into office a new Presidential
Council. Then, despite the fact that the National
Assembly was still in session, the Presidential Council
immediately convened in order to issue a decree on the
merger of the ministries of education and culture, and it
submitted to the National Assembly its recommendations
regarding nominees for the new Council of Ministers, the
president of the Supreme Court, and the Chief Prosecutor,
all of whom were unanimously accepted by the 352 members
of the National Assembly.[8] What made the whole show
absurd was the fact that even the Presidential Council
did not decide independently on those matters, but simply
approved a decision of the MSZMP Central Committee. All
personal appointments and changes, which ostensibly were
enacted by the Presidential Council and approved by the
National Assembly, were in fact made by the party Central
Committee at its 24 June plenum, i.e., three days before
the National Assembly session.[9] On 26 June the National
Council of the Patriotic People's Front (the broad
coalition of mass movements and political parties
ostensibly organizing and conducting the elections in
Eastern Europe) heard a report by Janos Kadar, MSZMP
Central Committee first secretary, on the Central Committee
plenum's decisions, unanimously adopted the Central
Committee's personnel proposals, and decided to submit
them jointly with the MSZMP to the "proper authorities."[10]
Thus three separate bodies--the People's Patriotic Front,
the Presidential Council, and the National Assembly simply
rubber-stamped decisions previously adopted by the MSZMP

Central Committee.

One final word on the subject of the state councils. Although all East European constitutions clearly state that the national assembly is the supreme state organ, at least one constitution--that of Yugoslavia--in fact confirms the superiority of the Federal Presidency (Yugoslavia's state council). Whereas Article 282 of the Yugoslav Constitution states that the Federal Assembly is "the highest agency of authority" in Yugoslavia,[11] Article 319 presents a different picture. This article deals with the procedure to be followed in the (unlikely) event of the Federal Assembly refusing to accept a proposal of the Federal Presidency. After describing the steps involved in resolving the conflicting situation, Article 319 states that "in the event that agreement is not reached . . . the competent Chamber of the Assembly of the SFRY shall be dissolved and the mandate of the Presidency of the SFRY shall cease."[12] This sounds fair enough, until one reaches the next paragraph of the article: "Until the new Presidency of the SFRY is elected, the old Presidency of the SRFY whose term has expired, shall carry out its duties."[13] This last paragraph actually establishes the Supremacy of the Presidency over the Federal Assembly, because in the time between a "competent chamber" being dissolved and a new one elected, the Federal Presidency, with all its power, would be free to make any changes it pleases without any control.

NATIONAL ASSEMBLY MEMBERS

One must realize that the East European parliaments' members are not the choice of the people, but the choice of the party, and that subsequently they represent party interests and not the interests of specific districts, groups, or social sectors. One must further realize that hardly anybody expects an East European parliament--a faceless collection of party and state apparatus members, outstanding workers, agrarians, teachers, writers, and actors--to act as a real parliament during the infrequent and short sessions in which they approve decisions that have already been made in their name by other state and party organs. Consequently, since the important business is done elsewhere, membership in the national assembly is nothing more than a reward for achievements in various areas or loyal services rendered to the party. There is no real effort to promote the emergence of real parliamentarism and parliamentarians on the part of the party,

and with minor exceptions, no real parliamentary debate
exists. Thus, one can safely conclude that normal parliamentary activity does not exist in Eastern Europe. Subsequently, there are no parliamentarians.

The members of the East European parliaments are people
who follow a career somewhere else (see Table 3.1). They
include the main party and state leaders, the leaders of the
mass public organizations and the trade unions, members of
the party and state apparatus, and representatives of various
professions and vocations (elected on the basis of personal
achievement and not as representatives of their respective
groups), who continue their own jobs regardless of their
membership in the national assemblies. The varied occupational breakdown of national assembly membership does not
prove helpful in influencing government. Regardless how
many workers, teachers, or cultural figures, how many male
and female members, or what ages the members are, the
performance of the East European national assemblies is
always the same: uniformly and loyally serving the
interests of the communist party. This activity has three
main features: paucity of parliamentary outcome, the total
lack of surprises, and the strict control over the parliamentary activity by the communist party.

PAUCITY OF PARLIAMENTARY OUTCOME

The East European state councils are the real
legislative bodies of these countries. Issuing the main
legislative documents and decrees (by which they usually
give legal authencity to party decisions), they strip the
parliaments not only of any real authority but also of
their functions. The result is that the East European
parliaments have very little to do. It has already been
noted that they hold two to four regular sessions a year.
The amazing fact is that even these infrequent sessions
often produce no new laws.

One such typical session was the Bulgarian National
Assembly 21 March 1981 session. It opened on the afternoon
of that day and ended with a brief meeting on the following
morning. No new law was enacted and no old law amended.
Apart from the routine approval of decrees issued since the
previous session (20-22 December 1977) and of by-elections
to replace deceased deputies, its only business was a
report by (then) Prime Minister Stanko Todorov. This
report was also a routine element in Bulgaria's parliamentary
practice; the obligation for the prime minister to make such

Table 3.1
Composition of the CSSR Federal Assembly, 1976–1986

Composition Characteristic and Breakdown by Group	Number and Percentage of Members	
	1976-1981	1981-1986
Social-occupational composition		
Workers	102 (29.1%)	92 (26.3%)
Agriculturalists (i.e., all working in farming sector)	47 (13.4%)	51 (14.6%)
Technical and economic employees	52 (14.8%)	63 (18.0%)
Party and other political functionaries	110 (31.4%)	113 (32.3%)
Intellectuals	18 (5.1%)	
Armed forces	12 (3.4%)	31 (8.9%)
Others	9 (2.6%)	
Ethnic composition[1]		
Czechs	199 (56.9%)	202 (57.7%)
Slovaks	123 (35.1%)	122 (34.9%)
Hungarians	19 (5.4%)	18 (5.1%)
Ukrainians[2]	4 (1.1%)	4 (1.1%)
Poles	3 (0.9%)	2 (0.6%)
Germans	2 (0.6%)	2 (0.6%)
Age at time of election		
Under 35	62 (17.7%)	60 (17.1%)
35-50	157 (44.9%)	127 (36.3%)
51-60	114 (32.6%)	133 (38.0%)
Over 60	17 (4.9%)	30 (8.6%)

1. In the total population of the CSSR, the ethnic composition according to the 1979 census was Czechs, 63.8 percent; Slovaks, 30.5 percent; Hungarians, 4.0 percent; Ukrainians, 0.4 percent; Poles, 0.5 percent, and Germans, 0.5 percent.
2. Czech citizens of Russian and Ukrainian origin.

Sources: Pravda, 14 May 1981, p. 2; Rude Pravo, 25 June 1981, p. 1; Ceteka (in English), 1 July 1981; and Radio Free Europe Situation Report, CSSR, 13 July 1981 (for percentages and age composition).

a report at the beginning of every year is incorporated in the 1971 Constitution. Todorov's report was, as always, unanimously approved.[14] Incidentally, despite the constitutional requirement, in 1974, 1976, 1980, 1981, and 1982 the Bulgarian prime minister failed to submit his annual report on the activity of the government.[15] No explanation was given and nobody asked any questions.

Even when laws are enacted by the East European parliaments, their quantity is minimal. Thus on 31 January 1980 the Polish Sejm convened for the last time in its seventh term. On that occasion its total output for the entire four-year term was summarized. In the seventh term the Sejm passed only forty-two laws and four decrees, compared with 103 laws and eleven decrees in the 1972-1976 period. Some twenty-eight sessions were held.[16]

The Hungarian Parliament elected for the period of 1971-1975 had an even poorer record. During that parliamentary period it enacted only twenty-three laws.[17] For the sake of comparison, the Hungarian Presidential Council elected in 1975 enacted in less than eighteen months thirty laws and decrees having to do with both Hungary's international relations and domestic or internal problems in regard to social relations, the economy, and cultural life.[18] Thus the reason for the low parliamentary outcome is obvious: in Eastern Europe the state councils are the real legislatures.

Even when a session of an East European parliament produces a substantial output (as the exception to the rule), the procedure involves no heated debate or unusual discussions. Thus the 30-31 March 1982 regular (and short) session of the Bulgarian National Assembly succeeded in dealing with several important matters, including the amendment of no fewer than 130 of the 424 articles of the Bulgarian Penal Code. The amendments dealt with the decriminalization of minor offenses and sharpening the penalties for major, especially economic, crimes. The amendments were presented to the National Assembly members, who promptly moved to adopt them without any debates.[19] Once again, the National Assembly was used to authorize legislature produced elsewhere.

PREDICTABILITY

There hardly is any need to stress again that the activity of the East European parliaments has nothing to do with the established practices of the Western

parliamentary democracies. Nonconfidence votes, heated
debates, spirited confrontations--in short, the basic
characteristics of the democratic parliaments--are not a
part of the East European parliamentary system. Instead,
there are short and routine sessions that deal with routine
matters, approval (usually unanimous) of what is to be
approved, and boring predictability. In each East
European parliament there are two standard annual sessions:
one dealing with the annual report of the prime minister
(usually the first annual session), and the other--the last
annual session--dealing with the national plan and budget
for the following year.

The prime minister's report reviews the country's
economic achievements during the previous year, stresses the
importance of implementing the decisions of the most recent
communist party's congress, and outlines the tasks for the
current year. Some minor weaknesses are usually admitted,
against the background of impressive successes in almost
every area of life.

The 15th session of the CSSR Federal Assembly, which
took place on 9-10 April 1980, was devoted to the annual
report of the premier. Lubomir Strougal, chairman of the
CSSR Council of Ministers, presented the government's
record over the past year, ostensibly seeking the assembly's
approval. The (unanimous) approval was granted after brief
speeches made by seventeen members, who actually repeated
various parts of Strougal's report. Two undramatic questions were asked: on the preparations for the Seventh
Five-Year Plan (1981-1985) and on domestic food supplies.
Both questions were equally undramatically answered: the
plan preparations are progressing normally, and appropriate
directives would be dispatched to the enterprises; the
1979 meat shortage was caused by crop failure. The
unanimous approval of the premier's report testified to
the members' satisfaction with both the report and the
answers to their questions.[20]

The 12-13 April session of the Bulgarian National
Assembly followed exactly the same lines,[21] as do all
East European parliaments annually. Later parliamentary
sessions dealing with the annual plan and budget belong
to the same category of predictability, devoid of any real
surprises. These sessions take place almost simultaneously
in all East European countries, usually at the end of
November and beginning of December. The main speakers
are the ministers of finance (or the chairmen of the state
planning committee) and the premiers, who present the
national budget and plan respectively for the following

44

year. The sessions seldom continue more than the usual day or two, and the budget and plan are unanimously approved following several routine interpellations and speeches that repeat sections of the two major speeches. (Exceptions, seldom as they are, will be discussed later.) The budget itself is never published in detail; the published law on the state budget adopted by the national assemblies out-lines only in broad terms the state income, expenditures and surplus (always!), and the general sums allocated to various economic, social, and cultural enterprises.

The reports on the national assemblies' sessions never fail to stress the unanimity of opinion of the national assembly members. A typical example is the announcement about the 27 November 1981 session of the Romanian Grand National Assembly:

> The proceedings of the Fourth Session of the Eighth Legislature of the Grand National Assembly, which started this morning in Bucharest, resumed in the afternoon with further discussions on the agenda points. Various deputies addressed the plenum, express-ing their complete endorsement of the documents under discussion, praising President Nicolae Ceausescu's vital contribution to drafting them, and pledging to do their utmost to contribute to Romania's socioeconomic development.
>
> The deputies then proceeded to vote on the first three points of the agenda. The Grand National Assembly unanimously passed the bill on the adoption of the Uniform National Plan of the Socioeconomic Development of the Socialist Republic of Romania for 1982; the bill on the adoption of the development plan of agriculture and the food industry for 1982; and the bill on the adoption of the 1982 budget.[22]

Very similar announcements were published after the comparable sessions of the National Assemblies of the GDR,[23] Bulgaria,[24] the CSSR,[25] and Hungary.[26]

The reason for the routine discussion of such important matters as the national plan and budget and their quick and automatic approval is simple: the real discussion and the real approval take place at a special Central Committee plenum, which precedes the National Assembly session and which deals with precisely the same matters--i.e., the national plan and budget. Thus a 25 November 1981 plenum of the Romanian Communist Party Central Committee dealt with the 1982 plan and budget[27] (among other matters) and "debated and endorsed them."[28] This Central Committee plenum preceded the National Assembly session dealing with the same matters by two days. The Bulgarian Communist Party Central Committee met on 9 December 1981 and approved the 1982 national plan and budget[29] one day before the National Assembly did the same thing.[30] Once again, as in the case of the National Assembly, the approval of the Central Committee was "unanimous."[31] The same procedure took place in the CSSR,[32] Hungary,[33] and so forth. Thus the Central Committee approval of the plan and the budget is the precondition for submitting them for approval to the national assembly. The speakers at the Central Committee plenum are the same speakers who present the plan and the budget to the national assembly[34] and the real debates (if any, because seldom is anything published on the discussions that might or might not take place at this forum) take place at the Central Committee plenum.

If there are some exceptions, they nevertheless do not affect the general character of the East European parliamentary procedure. Thus, until 1980 the Polish Sejm acted in the same way as the parliaments of all other East European countries, i.e., as a rubber-stamp, approving organ of party decisions. The annual plan and budget were automatically adopted without any meaningful discussion, despite the deteriorating economic situation in the country, something that prompted Piotr Stefanski, then the deputy speaker of the Sejm, to define that body as a "factory producing laws."[35] Even as the Polish economic situation was sinking into crisis, the national plans and budgets in 1979 and 1980 were automatically approved by the Sejm.[36] During 1980, however, following the workers' unrest, the establishment of the Solidarity trade union, and the ousting of the party boss Edward Gierek and many other top party and state officials, the Sejm departed from the familiar practice of unanimously endorsing all party proposals. The 1981 plan and budget, for instance, were not "unanimously adopted," but were "referred to Sejm commissions for analysis."[37] Radio Warsaw could not hide its astonishment: "A new departure of the Sejm was the many questions put to Henryk Kisiel, deputy chairman of the Council of Ministers, and Marian Krzak, minister of Finance, immediately after they presented the plan and budget."[38] The approval given the budget and plan was conditional, pending recommendations of the Sejm commissions:

"The Sejm passed a motion provisionally approving the budget, which in case of the central budget, will give it validity for the first quarter of the year. The Sejm preferred to give provisional approval rather than to hastily approve the full plan and budget, to the detriment of their analysis and possible correction."[39]

The Polish television was no less surprised, its report illustrating the intensity of the shock caused by the newly discovered quasi-democratic parliamentary procedures: "The Sejm of the Polish People's Republic met in Warsaw today. One item on the agenda was deputies' question time, during which government members replied to interpellations. The so-called question hour in fact took two and one-half hours. Questions asked of ministers dealt, among other things, with measures to improve the supplies of medicines, the allocation of larger stocks of fertilizers and foodstuffs to the private farming sector, forms of utilization of the Agricultural Development Fund, Penal Code, amendments, the situation in the power and heating industries, the future of the system of education for children and young people and of history teaching in the schools."[40]

In Yugoslovia, the mixed national and ethnic characteristics of the population have also caused certain departure from the standard East European parliamentary pattern. Local or ethnic interests, on several occasions, have proved stronger than uniform party discipline, causing the rejection of a law or a resolution proposed by the government. The most famous case was the resignation of the Slovene government in December 1966, following the rejection of a new social security law by the Social Council of the Slovene Assembly. In this case, as in similar ones when the assembly rejects a proposal of the executive branch, the latter was obliged to rewrite the draft, taking into consideration the remarks and suggestions made by the Assembly and its committees.[41]

In October 1978 the second chamber of the SFRY Federal Assembly—the Chamber of Republics and Provinces—rejected the government's draft resolution on economic development for the following year as "too general, unclear and undefined, and therefore inadequate for effective implementation of the economic development policy."[42] Eventually, after some corrections, the plan was adopted. There were no surprises in the following year; the plan and budget were adopted without any difficulties.[43] Nevertheless, it seems that following Tito's death, Yugoslavia more than any other East European country showed a somewhat liberal attitude toward at least some basic parliamentary rules. Although still far away from the accepted practices of the Western democracies, the SFRY Federal Assembly and especially the Chamber of Republics and Autonomous Provinces, where the local and ethnic interests are more sharply evident, had in 1981 reached the stage of having relatively long discussions, interpellations, and criticism of the federal government.[44] Nevertheless, there was no real change in the basic character of the SFRY Federal Assembly, which despite its occasional democratic "transgressions" is still a solid example of the East European parliamentary pattern.

On occasions, even the East European press has to admit the emasculated character of the socialist countries' parliaments. Thus, in June 1977, after the first six regular sessions of the Hungarian National Assembly elected on 15 June 1975 had produced only one question time--during the winter 1976 session--when one member had made use of his right of (harmless) interpellation, Magyar Hirlap noted: "Never have so few interpellations been recorded in the annals of the parliament . . . one might well ask why question time has virtually vanished from the National Assembly."[45]

Another occasion for standard sessions, devoid of any parliamentary surprises, is the first session of a newly elected national assembly, which approves the composition of the new government. The approval (with the recent exception of Poland, discussed below) is automatic. Thus, on 25 June 1981, the newly elected GDR People's Chamber "unanimously elected the members of the State Council."[46] On 26 June, the People's Chamber elected in the same manner the members of the Council of Ministers.[47] The first session of Bulgaria's Eighth National Assembly, which took place on 16-17 June 1981, elected in the same fashion the Bulgarian State Council and Council of Ministers, despite the major structural (merging of various ministries) and personnel (new premier, Grisha Filipov) changes.[48] The transfer of former Premier Stanko Todorov to the post of chairman of the National Assembly did not evoke any interpellations, questions, or remarks. On precisely one of these same two days, 17 June 1981, the newly elected CSSR Federal Assembly unanimously elected or approved their Assembly Presidium,[49] the chairman and the deputy chairman of the Federal Assembly,[50] and their new government.[51] There were no reports of any debates in the GDR, Bulgaria, the CSSR, or even Yugoslavia after the 1982 elections. Apparently, the usual procedure (the names of the "candidates" read by the proposed premier, followed by the parliament automatically and unanimously approving by open vote) was clearly strictly observed.

Once again Poland, at least before the announcement of martial law (and subsequently, the suspension of all hitherto achieved democratic characteristics of political life) showed some traces of real democratic practices. In December 1981 the Sejm members, and especially the representatives of the various Catholic groups in the Sejm, repeatedly subjected the government to severe criticism and even demanded that the Sejm consider initial drafts of each year's economic plan and budget, instead of simply rubber-stamping the final versions as had been the practice hitherto. Another proposed change would have given the Sejm the right to be consulted on matters of changes at ministerial level. (The accepted practice in Eastern Europe is for the parliament to be "informed" on the ministerial changes, whenever they take place.) Moreover, it was demanded that ministers be obliged to appear before the relevant Sejm committees at these committees' request in order to answer questions and provide information.[52] Although these demands were not met, the election of a new State Council and Council of Ministers on 12 February 1981 departed from the accepted pattern. Thirty-three Sejm members voted against the recall of Krzysztof Kruszewski from his post as minister of education and training, and thirty-five abstained; seven members voted against the recall of Tadeusz Skwirzynski from his post as minister of forestry and timber industry, and fifteen abstained.[53] There were more objections to and abstentions in the election of new persons to these and other posts.[54] The entire procedure was carried live by Radio Warsaw. Nevertheless, the Polish example was not followed by any of the other East European parliaments, which continued to approve automatically the composition of their governments, and in Poland itself the relative democratization was short-lived.

In conclusion, the legislative activity of the East European parliament is predictable and restricted. The majority of the sessions are routine (budget and plan; premier's report and election of state organs), and the rest deal predominantly with the ex post facto endorsement of laws and decrees enacted by the state council. The common denominator of all parliamentary sessions is the lack of any decision-making power on the part of the parliaments. Long before the convocation of the sessions the matters that ostensibly are going to be debated by the parliaments have already been decided by the Central Committee of the communist parties.

OVERT PARTY INTERFERENCE IN LEGISLATING

The fact that the East European communist parties actually control the activities of their respective countries' parliaments has already been stressed. It has also been explained that usually there is little if any parliamentary debate, simply because such debate is meaningless, matters having already been decided elsewhere. Nevertheless, when circumstances require it, the communist leaders do not hesitate to influence directly the activity of their legislatures. Two examples will illustrate this point, one from Bulgaria, the other from Yugoslavia.

The 11th session of the 7th Bulgarian National Assembly (30-31 October 1979) dealt with an amendment of the 1972 law on scientific degrees and titles.[55] It seems that the new law was intended to implement a previously unknown 1977 Politburo decision on scientific cadres. The main point of the "considerable amendments and supplements" was to raise the requirements of candidates for scientific and teaching posts, to set additional criteria for evaluating the scientific dissertations, and to give detailed new tasks to the Higher Assessing Commission in selecting and assessing scientific cadres.[56]

The bill was presented in the National Assembly by Nacho Papazov, chairman of the Committee on Science and Technological Progress, on behalf of the Council of Ministers, which acted formally as its sponsor.[57] Only two deputies were reported to have taken the floor to comment on the bill: Professor Angel Balevski, chairman of the Bulgarian Academy of Sciences, and Professor Blagovest Sendov, former rector of Sofia University. According to the press reports of their statements, however, they seem to have fully approved the bill, except for "some concrete suggestions" made by Balevski, and "some remarks" made by Sendov.[58] Obviously, these remarks contained nothing revolutionary, because the bill was "unanimously approved" at the first reading.[59]

The next day, Vladimir Bonev, then the chairman of the National Assembly, read a letter that, according to him, had been received from Todor Zhivkov, BCP Central Committee secretary general (then still first secretary) and chairman of the State Council. The letter stated that at the previous day's plenary session "interesting discussions" had taken place and "questions which deserve serious attention" had been raised during "the debates." It would be useful, Zhivkov said, for the Legislative Commission, together with other appropriate agencies and organizations, to carefully and thoroughly consider the suggestions made, as well as other suggestions that might be made during a broader study of the bill. He added that the main issue was to achieve full agreement between the suggested amendments and the situation that had made them necessary, an implication that the bill did not quite correspond to the requirements of the 1977 Politburo decision.

Finally, Zhivkov suggested that rather than amending the law on scientific decrees and titles it might be more expedient to adopt a new law on scientific organizations that would cover the above-mentioned matters. He proposed, therefore, that further discussions of the bill be postponed. It was reported that the Council of Ministers then withdrew the bill and the deputies voted, again unanimously, for postponing the approval of the bill.[60]

What could possibly have prompted the letter of Zhivkov, which in effect overruled a "unanimous" decision of the National Assembly and replaced it by another-- completely opposite--"unanimous" decision? One possible explanation of Zhivkov's letter would be that indeed, as Zhivkov claimed, genuine debates on the bill did not take place during the first day of the session, and that both Balevski and Sendov, and possibly some other deputies, made valid critical remarks. In that case the press reports obviously did not report correctly what happened at the National Assembly session. But then more questions immediately arise: if at least some National Assembly members criticized the bill, which was introduced by the government, then why was the bill unanimously adopted? Why did the chairman submit the bill to the vote without taking into consideration the remarks (if any)?

Another plausible explanation could be that the "interesting discussion" Zhivkov mentioned in his letter did not take place in the National Assembly, but elsewhere. It is possible that in the course of these discussions Zhivkov was contacted and asked to intervene. This explanation, of course, presents the Bulgarian National Assembly in its usual role--a voting machine--unanimously voting for and against the same bill in the course of less than twenty-four hours, obediently following party instructions. Whatever the explanation, the conclusion is obvious: Zhivkov had the authority and power to interfere with the National Assembly's legislative activities by killing a bill after it had been unanimously approved.

One can assume that Zhivkov is hardly the only East European leader who enjoys the prerogative of influencing the parliamentary activity of his country. On the contrary, there are other examples. Thus, in October 1978, Tito, who at that time was preoccupied with the issue of his succession, was intensely promoting the notion of the "collective leadership." One of his ideas was to amend Article 151 of the Yugoslav Constitution by making the one-year term a rule for most elected and appointed bodies.[61] In order to promote his idea Tito sent a letter to the Federal Assembly on behalf of the State Presidency, justifying the proposed constitutional change as being a "more consistent implementation of the principle of collective work, decision making and responsibility in (various) assemblies and other collective organs."[62]

In the case of the Yugoslav Federal Assembly Tito was acting "on behalf of the State Presidency," and the effect of his letter was not immediate (although eventually positive); however, Zhivkov's letter had an urgent character, aggressive style, and immediate effect, reversing a unanimous decision of the National Assembly. Both letters are examples of the authority and power of the East European communist leaders vis-à-vis their parliaments.

Another interesting characteristic of East European parliamentary life is the so-called "nationwide discussion." These discussions on the subjects of legislation, notably the pain, supposedly take place all over the respective countries, in local party meetings, and at factories and other workplaces; their purpose is to influence the legislature. Thus, in 1977 in Bulgaria, a bill on the activity of the National Assembly deputies and people's counselors was put forward for nationwide discussion. The aim of the discussion was to manifest the "ever-growing socialist democracy in Bulgaria"--a phrase used by all Bulgarian dailies.[63]

At the 12-13 April 1977 session of the Bulgarian National Assembly, Vladimir Bonev then the chairman of the National Assembly, reported that 1,338 proposals had been made at these public discussion meetings, and that 459 written proposals relating to the bill had been sent directly to the National Assembly.[64] The bill, which regulated the relations of the deputies and the people's counselors with their constituencies as well as their relations with the mass organizations such as the Father-land Front, was criticized as "formalistic."[65] Other weaknesses of the proposed law were pointed out by the daily press.[66] Yet the National Assembly simply ignored the nationwide discussion and the subsequent suggestions. At the relevant session only four National Assembly members took the floor and made statements, which simply rephrased the main principles of the draft law, reported to be "personally introduced by Todor Zhivkov";[67] the statements added nothing of importance in the way of suggestions or content. After allegedly making some corrections (with which Todor Zhivkov had reportedly agreed[68]) the National Assembly voted the bill into law.

Hungary, like all other East European countries, follows the same pattern "in order to enhance the democratic nature of legislation." Thus the resolution of the 11th MSZMP Congress of March 1975 directed the party members "to further improve the social publicity given to legislation by discussing the drafts in a broad circle before they are adopted, as well as to make a systematic and good use of the remarks and proposals of citizens and social organs."[69]

It was understood that preparation of legislation by social debate should be applied to drafts of bills that affect the public at large. Such was the case with the draft law on internal trade, also in Hungary. As a result of the "social debate" of this draft law, introduced by the Patriotic People's Front (PPF), 500 changes were proposed, thirty-nine of which were forwarded to the Ministerial Preparatory Committee by the PPF National Council. Some twenty-four of the proposed changes were eventually written into the draft, which was submitted to a joint session of the National Assembly's commercial and legal administrative and judicial standing committees. The two committees had one day—17 March—to study the draft. Some eleven changes were introduced by them,[70] notably fewer than the participants in the "social debate" made. At the National Assembly session of 23 March 1978 the bill was passed by the customary unanimous vote, the one-day debate producing no amendments.[71]

The entire procedure was turned into a farce by a published interview with Janos Inokai, one of the National Assembly's deputy speakers.[72] Although he stressed the importance of the social debates, Inokai was critical of the fact that not all members of the National Assembly were informed about the proposals put forward in the course of social debates, nor did they know to what extent the ministry in charge of the bill had taken into account suggestions from the public in drawing up the bill to be placed before the standing committee of the house.

"Therefore," Inokai concluded, "it would be useful to provide information on such questions to the members of the
National Assembly."[73]

Two things are immediately apparent: first of all
Inokai was not very happy with the social debates; inevitably these debates or social discussions curtailed the
legislative prerogatives (already few) of the National
Assembly. Second, during and following most social debates
the members of the National Assembly did not know what was
going on, i.e., who amended what, and so forth, and therefore just voted in their automatic and obedient manner.

It seems that the "social debates" and the "nationwide discussions" have no real effect on the activity of the
East European parliaments. They serve mostly as a propaganda instrument for "public participation" in legislation,
and, when needed, as yet another device for exercising
party influence (through the "people's proposals") on the
work of the national assemblies.

One sentence from an interview with Professor
Sylwester Zawadzki, member of the Polish Sejm and
professor of constitutional law at Warsaw University,
epitomizes the relations between the party and the
parliament in the East European countries: "The Marxist-
Leninist party gives political direction to the work of
both the Parliament and the Government. Parliament and
Government both work to carry out a common program for
building socialism. It does not mean, however, that under
these conditions the importance of the Sejm's constitutional functions is reduced."[74]

PROPAGANDA FUNCTIONS

Propaganda--both domestic and international--is an
integral part of East European politics. So closely do
East European propaganda and policy intertwine that sometimes it is impossible to distinguish between them, or to
decide where one ends and the other begins. On special
occasions, the national assemblies too are mobilized for
participating in various communist domestic and international propaganda campaigns.

When in 1977 in the CSSR, the civil rights of the
citizens became a major issue following the publication of
Charter-77, the CSSR Federal Assembly was called upon to
take part in the party campaign against the demands for
more civil rights and liberties in the CSSR. On 5 April
1977, at the climax of the Charter-77 issue, both chambers

of the Federal Assembly convened in Prague to discuss as
the main issue the problem of human rights.[75]   The speakers
at this session were Jan Fejes, the CSSR prosecutor general,
Josef Ondrej, chairman of the Supreme Court, and Bohuslav
Chnoupek, minister of foreign affairs.   Some fourteen
Federal Assembly members took part in the discussion,
after which the session adopted a resolution.[76]   The
various speakers stressed that human rights in the CSSR
enjoy a tremendous scope, and that they are solidly pro-
tected by broad political, economic, social and legal
guarantees, and pointed out that the citizens enjoy in
fact "unlimited rights and freedoms."[77]

Foreign Minister Chnoupek deplored what he called the
"international campaign against the CSSR and the other
socialist countries,"[78] stressing that such action on the
part of the capitalist countries can harm détente.   The
subsequent resolution adopted by the Federal Assembly
repeated the various statements made during the session and
enumerated the "broad rights and freedoms" of the CSSR
citizens.   It pointed out that the Czechoslovak social
system is to be defended against those who violate the law,
and recommended that the prosecutor general and the Supreme
Court center their attention on an effective defense of the
CSSR social system and act in such a way as to ensure
"just and timely punishment of all who by their actions
have come into conflict with the laws of the land."[79]
Thus the CSSR Federal Assembly both joined the propaganda
campaign aimed against Charter-77 supporters and gave
parliamentary approval to past and future police and
judicial action against the civil rights campaign.

Often the propaganda activity of the East European
parliaments is coordinated and aimed at giving effective
support to various international propaganda campaigns
organized by the Soviet Union.   Thus when in June 1981 the
USSR Supreme Soviet issued an appeal "To The World
Parliaments and Peoples" urging them to support the basic
trends of Soviet foreign policy and oppose the principles
of U.S. foreign policy, all East European parliaments with
the exception of the Albanian People's Assembly issued
declarations endorsing the USSR Supreme Soviet appeal and
supporting USSR foreign policy.   The numerous identical
phrases in these declarations[80] and the uniformity of the
manner in which support of the USSR Supreme Soviet appeal
was expressed leave no doubt as to the well planned and
coordinated nature of the entire campaign.

Apropos of the planned nature of parliamentary
activity, it is like everything else in Eastern Europe--

all aspects of life and government are subjected to central planning. Ridiculous as it might sound, in 1976 Romania published an ambitious Five-Year Legislative Plan (1976-1980) that was to include the drafting of the Civil Code, the Code of Civil Procedure, the Family Code, the Code on Minor Violations of the Law, and so forth. [81] By mid-1979, i.e., almost four years after the publication of the plan, none of the heralded significant legislative texts had been published. [82] This was not the first time that Bucharest had announced new laws without producing them. At the 10th Romanian Communist Party (RCP) Congress (1969) Ceausescu announced the forthcoming preparation of new Civil and Family Codes. Like many other sweeping reforms and grandiose schemes that Ceausescu likes to announce, and that encourage hope but eventually prove largely illusory, the Civil and Family Codes were not enacted.

SUMMARY

This survey of the characteristics and activity of the East European parliaments suggests several general conclusions about the parliamentary system in Eastern Europe:

1. Parliaments in a democratic society serve as a counterbalance to the executive branch of government and exercise a substantial amount of control and supervision over the activity of the latter. They serve as a forum for criticism, advice, opinion, deliberation, and decision making in enacting the country's legislation.

The East European political system maintains the structural separation of power inherent in the Western democracies. However, the three branches of the East European system are flesh and blood of the same body—the communist party. They are connected, interrelated, and in the final account subjected to the interests, goals, and needs of the communist party. Therefore, the East European separation of power does not exist in fact, something that completely neutralizes the normal functioning of the parliaments. Thus, instead of being a forum for criticism, supervision, and support for the government, the East European parliaments are organs of deliberate and manipulative support and endorsement of the party policy, as well as instruments of automatic legalization of the lawmaking activity of the state councils.

2. Despite all this, or perhaps because of it, the East European parliaments meticilously preserve all the

basic and external principles of normal parliamentary
activity--regular sessions (rare as they are), voting,
interpellations, commissions, and by-elections. The routine
and standard way they dispose of their "duties" makes it
easier to preserve the external characteristics of democratic
procedure. However, special but not infrequent events such
as a letter or demand on the part of the party leader can
direct parliamentary activity in a way that has nothing to
do with normal parliamentary practice, and sometimes even
contradicts the previous day's activity of the parliament
(as we have seen from the case of Todor Zhivkov's letter
to the Bulgarian National Assembly). Such activity, as
well as various appeals and declarations of a purely propaganda nature, the (normally) automatic endorsement of
everything submitted for approval, and the unusually brief
and infrequent sessions expose the real character of the
East European parliaments and the emptiness of their routine
activity.

3. Although minor or trivial matters can sometimes
serve as reasons for mild and limited criticism of some
aspects of economic or social life, the party general policy
and, above all, its foreign policy are never subjected to
any serious discussion, let alone criticism on the part of
the parliaments. The short sessions are usually reserved
for endorsing the state council's acts and decrees and other
routine activity. The East European parliaments never serve
as a forum for debating state policy vis-à-vis topical
international affairs (unless a declaration supporting
Soviet foreign policy and condemning the West is to be
issued). Actually, it is impossible to visualize the
East European parliaments as instruments for criticizing
the party. After all it is the party that most of the East
European members of parliament represent, and everything
related to debating or discussing party policy is done
exclusively in party forums.

4. Despite the fact that from time to time some East
European parliaments do demonstrate sparks of real debate
or discussion (Poland, the SFRY), it is difficult to
envisage their developing into forums of real and meaningful parliamentary activity. After all, the basic
characteristics of the East European political system is
the party monopoly in every sphere of life. Violating
this principle in any particular area (parliaments) would
inevitably change the essence of the entire political
system, something the communist parties would hardly
agree to.

NOTES

1. Radio Free Europe (RFE) Situation Report, Bulgaria, 10 May 1982.
2. Ustav Socijalisticke Federativne Republike Jugoslavije, the SFRY Constitution (Belgrade, 1974), Article 236.
3. Romanian Constitution, Article 43.
4. Otechestven Front (Bulgaria), 22 January 1982.
5. Borba (Yugoslavia), 4 July 1981.
6. Otechestven Front, 18 June 1981.
7. Ibid.
8. RFE Situation Report, Hungary, 3 July 1980.
9. Nepszabadsag (Hungary), 27 June 1980.
10. Ibid.
11. SFRY Constitution, p. 16.
12. Ibid., p. 153.
13. Ibid.
14. RFE Situation Report, Bulgaria, 28 March 1978.
15. Ibid., 10 May 1982.
16. RFE Situation Report, Poland, 6 February 1980.
17. RFE Situation Report, Hungary, 16 April 1975.
18. Ibid., 22 March 1977.
19. Rude Pravo (Czechoslovakia), 10 and 11 April 1977.
20. Rabotnichesko Delo (Bulgaria), 14 April 1977.
21. Bucharest Domestic Service in Romanian, 2000 GMT, 27 November 1981; Daily Report (FBIS), 30 November 1981.
22. East Berlin ADN International Service in German, 1501 GMT, 17 December 1980; Daily Report (FBIS), 19 December 1980.
23. Sofia BTA in English, 1335 GMT, 18 December 1980; Daily Report (FBIS), 19 December 1980.
24. Rude Pravo, 17 December 1980; Daily Report (FBIS), 19 December 1980.
25. Nepszabadsag, 20 December 1980.
26. Bucharest Domestic Service in Romanian, 1600 GMT, 25 November 1981; Daily Report (FBIS), 27 November 1981.
27. Bucharest AGERPRESS in English, 2000 GMT, 26 November 1981; Daily Report (FBIS), 27 November 1981.
28. Sofia Domestic Service in Bulgarian, 1400 GMT, 9 December 1981; Daily Report (FBIS), 10 December 1981.
29. Rabotnichesko Delo, 11 and 12 December 1981.
30. Sofia Domestic Service in Bulgarian, 1400 GMT, 9 December 1981; Daily Report (FBIS), 10 December 1981.
31. Prague Domestic Service in Czech, 1000 GMT, 9 December 1981; Daily Report (FBIS), 9 December 1981.
32. Nepszabadsag, 5 December 1981; Daily Report (FBIS),

8 December 1981.

33. Sofia Domestic Service in Bulgarian, 1830 GMT, 15 December 1980; Daily Report (FBIS), 16 December 1980.

34. Polityka (Poland), 21 October 1978.

35. RFE Situation Report, Poland, 12 January 1979; 11 December 1979.

36. Warsaw Domestic Service in Polish, 2200 GMT, 19 December 1980; Daily Report (FBIS), 22 December 1980.

37. Ibid.

38. Ibid.

39. Warsaw Domestic TV Service in Polish, 2030 GMT, 19 December 1980; Daily Report (FBIS), 22 December 1980.

40. RFE Research and Analysis Department (RAD) Background Report, SFRY, no. 240, 8 November 1978.

41. TANJUG in English, 19 October 1978, in RFE B.R./SFRY/8 Nov. 1978.

42. Borba, 27 November 1980.

43. RFE Research and Analysis Department (RAD) Background Report, SFRY, no. 342, 14 December 1981.

44. Magyar Hirlap (Hungary), 4 June 1977.

45. East Berlin ADN International Service in German, 0956 GMT, 25 June 1981; Daily Report (FBIS), 26 June 1981.

46. East Berlin ADN International Service in German, 1528 GMT, 26 June 1981; Daily Report (FBIS), 29 June 1981.

47. Sofia Domestic Service in Bulgarian, 1300 GMT, 17 June 1981; Daily Report (FBIS), 18 June 1981. Also Sofia BTA in English, 1442 GMT, 17 June 1981; Daily Report (FBIS), 18 June 1981.

48. Prague Domestic Service in Czech and Slovak, 1200 GMT, 17 June 1981; Daily Report (FBIS), 18 June 1981.

49. Prague Domestic Service in Czech and Slovak, 1400 GMT, 17 June 1981; Daily Report (FBIS), 18 June 1981.

50. Prague CTK in English, 1540 GMT, 17 June 1981; Daily Report (FBIS), 18 June 1981.

51. RFE Situation Report, Poland, 4 December 1980.

52. Warsaw Domestic Service in Polish, 2108 GMT, 12 February 1981; Daily Report (FBIS), 13 February 1981.

53. Ibid.

54. Durzhaven Vestnik no. 36, 9 May 1972.

55. Rabotnichesko Delo and Otechestven Front, 31 October 1981.

56. RFE Situation Report, Bulgaria, 12 December 1979.

57. Rabotnichesko Delo, 31 October 1979.

58. Ibid.

59. RFE Situation Report, Bulgaria, 12 December 1979.

60. Ibid.

61. Nin (SFRY), 28 October 1979; RFE Situation Report,

SFRY, 6 November 1979.
    62. <u>Nin</u>, 28 October 1979.
    63. <u>Otechestven Front</u>, 23 February 1977; Trud
(Bulgaria), 24 February 1977; <u>Zemedelsko Zname</u> (Bulgaria),
19 March 1977, etc.
    64. <u>Rabotnichesko Delo</u>, 13 April 1977.
    65. <u>Otechestven Front</u>, 27 February and 11 March 1977.
    66. Ibid., 23 March 1977.
    67. Ibid.
    68. <u>Rabotnichesko Delo</u>, 14 April 1977.
    69. MSZMP 11th Kongresszusa, 1976, Budapest, Ch. II
("To Further the Development of Relations"), p. 162;
RFE Situation Report, Hungary, 4 April 1978.
    70. <u>Magyar Hirlap</u>, 24 March 1978.
    71. Ibid.
    72. <u>Magyar Hirlap</u>, 12 March 1978.
    73. Ibid.
    74. <u>Student</u> (Poland) no. 6, 13-26 March 1980, p. 4.
    75. <u>Rude Pravo</u>, 6 April 1977.
    76. Ibid.
    77. Ibid.
    78. Ibid.
    79. Ibid.
    80. Prague <u>Prace</u> in Czech, 1 July 1981; <u>Rabotnichesko
Delo</u>, 8 July 1981, etc.
    81. <u>Scinteia</u> (Romania), 21 December 1977; RFE Situation
Report, Romania, 27 January 1978.
    82. RFE Situation Report, Romania, 12 June 1979.

4
The Communist Party: Membership, Structure, Organization

This chapter deals with the East European communist parties, mainly, who the communist party members are, how they are admitted to the party and how they lose their membership, and the structure and functions of the basic and intermediate party organs.

MEMBERSHIP

The East European political system is a single-party system. Other parties do exist in some East European countries (for example, the Peasants' Party and Democratic Party in Poland and the Bulgarian National Agrarian Union in Bulgaria), but this does not alter the character of the system. These parties exist because the ruling communist parties allow them to exist as "proof" of the democratic character of the system. They are in no way political opposition or rivals of the communist parties. On the contrary, they fully cooperate with the communist parties in the parliaments or national assemblies and other organs, and in a way they belong to the category of auxiliary organizations, a subject discussed in a separate chapter. These other parties do not contribute anything to the country's decision-making process or to making or executing policy.

The East European communist parties are relatively small. They are elitist, highly disciplined, and strictly controlled organizations, structured in a tight hierarchical manner and totally subjected to the authority and power of their top organs.

Only a fraction of the population may join the party. Restricted membership, complicated admission procedures,

and frequent purges (in whatever form), have kept the East
European communist parties to a compact proportion of about
7-8 percent of the population. The membership and social-
occupational composition of some of the East European
communist parties will show the similarities from one country
to another.

Albania

Table 4.1 shows the number of members in the Albanian
Workers' Party (AWP) from 1941 to 1981. In November 1981,
at the 8th AWP Congress, it was reported that of the total
of 122,600 party members, nearly 38 percent were workers,
29.4 percent peasants (members of the cooperative agricultural farms), and 32.6 percent office workers. Women
constituted 30 percent of the total, 2.5 percent more than
at the time of the previous congress.[1]

Bulgaria

Table 4.2 shows the number of members in the BCP by
social-occupational group, from 1962 to 1976. Somewhat
later, by the end of 1977, the BCP had 812,000 members,
41.8 percent of whom were workers, 22.4 percent peasants,
and 30.3 percent white collar workers. Women accounted
for 28.2 percent of the total membership.[2]
On 31 March 1981, at the 12th BCP Congress, the party
leader, Todor Zhivkov, reported that there were 825,876 BCP
members, 352,649 of whom were "members of the workers'
class."[3] He also pointed out that 29.7 percent of the party
members were women.[4]

The CSSR

Table 4.3 shows the number of members in the CPCZ by
social-occupational group in January 1966 and again in
January 1973. By 1976 the CPCZ had 1,382,860 members,
167,885 of whom had "candidate" status.[5] (In some East
European countries, such as the CSSR, complete admission
to the party is preceded by a period of one to two years
during which the member has "candidate" status. During
this period the candidate is to prove himself worthy of
being a full member of the communist party.) Somewhat
later, in 1978, there were 1,473,112 members,[6] and in March
1980 there were 1,538,179 members.[7]
In April 1981 at the 16th CPCZ Congress, Gustav
Husak reported that there were 1,538,179 CPCZ members.

Table 4.1
Growth in Membership in the Communist
Party of Albania, 1941-1981

Year	Membership
1941	200
1943	700
1944	2,800
1948	29,137
1952	44,418
1955	48,644
1961	ca 53,000
1966	66,326
1969	ca 50,000
1971	86,985
1976	101,500
1981	122,600

Sources: Zeri I Popullit (Albania), 24 March 1954, 4
November 1971, 3 November 1976; Tirana Radie, 1 November
1966; Pruga E Patrise (Albania), March 1969, p. 65; AWP
Central Committee report to 8th party congress, Tirana ATA
(Albanian Telegraph Agency) in English, 1323 GMT, 1
November 1981; Daily Report (FBIS), 2 November 1981.

Some 321,000 new members had been admitted since the
previous congress, 61 percent of whom were workers, 7.8
percent peasants (members of the cooperative farms), and
22.1 percent white collar workers. Women accounted for
27.3 percent of the party membership.[8]

The GDR

In 1976 the SED had 2,043,697 members.[9] In October
1980 there were 2,130,671 members and candidate-members,[10]
and in April 1981 at the 10th SED Congress, a total of
2,172,110 members was reported. Of this number, 57.6
percent were workers--"the highest level since the creation
of the SED." A total of 42.5 percent of the SED members
were younger than 40 years of age, and "one-third of the
party members were women."[11]
The social-occupational composition of the SED is no
different from that of the other East European communist
parties, as shown in Table 4.4. Some 30.6 percent of the
party members were reported to have university and higher
technical education, and 33.7 percent had party

Table 4.2
Composition of Membership in the Bulgarian Communist Party, 1962–1976

Social-Occupational Group	Number and Percentage of Members			
	Nov. 1962 (8th BCP Congress)	Nov. 1966 (9th BCP Congress)	Apr. 1971 (10th BCP Congress)	March 1976 (11th BCP Congress)
Workers	196,449 (37.2%)	234,693 (38.4%)	280,480 (40.1%)	326,974 (41.1%)
Peasants	169,601 (32.1%)	178,464 (29.2%)	182,563 (26.1%)	181,655 (23.0%)
White collar and others	162,624 (30.7%)	198,022 (32.4%)	236,433 (33.8%)	281,167 (35.6%)
Total	528,674 (100%)	611,179 (100%)	699,476 (100%)	789,796 (100%)

Sources: Rabotnichesko Delo (Bulgaria), 6 November 1962 and 30 March 1976; Radio Free Europe (RFE) Situation Reports, Bulgaria, 25 November 1966 and 30 March 1976.

Table 4.3
Composition of Membership in the Communist Party
of Czechoslovakia, January 1966 and January 1976

January 1966			January 1973		
Industrial workers	511,917	(30.2%)	Industrial workers	544,194	(44.1%)
Agrarian workers	46,062	(2.7%)			
Collective farmers	91,109	(5.4%)	Collective farmers	57,998	(4.7%)
Government officials	113,350	(6.7%)			
Public workers	27,246	(1.6%)			
Scientific workers	3,796	(0.2%)	White collar workers	389,944	(31.6%)
Engineering and technical workers	293,277	(17.3%)			
Workers in arts and culture	9,218	(0.5%)	Housewives pensioners, others	241,846	(19.6%)
Students	6,372	(0.4%)			
Housewives	68,659	(4.0%)			
Pensioners	293,577	(17.4%)			
Others	168,641	(9.8%)			
Totals	1,698,011			1,234,000	

Sources: Zivot Strany (CSSR), September 1966 (in CSSR
press review, 13 October 1966); Otazky Miru A Socialismu
(CSSR), July 1973, pp. 91-92.

education.[12] The age distribution of the SED's members was
as follows:[13]

age	percentage of party membership
under 31	23.1
31 to 40	19.1
41 to 50	22.9
51 to 60	17.8
61 to 65	3.9
above 65	13.2

Table 4.4
Composition of Membership in the Socialist Unity
Party of the German Democratic Republic, 1947-1980

Social-Occupational Group	Percentage of Membership					
	1947	1957	1961	1970	1976	1980
Industrial workers	48.1	33.8	33.8	47.1	56.1	56.9
Officials and intelligentsia	22.0	42.3	41.3	28.1	20.0	21.7
Peasants	9.4	5.0	6.2	5.8	5.2	4.7
Others	20.5	18.9	18.7	19.0	18.7	16.7

Sources: Edward Langer, "Zum Bildungsstand der SED
Funktionare," Die Orientirung (GDR), no. 2, 1968, p. 7;
World Marxist Review, August 1970, supplement, p. 6;
East Berlin Radio, 18 May 1976; Einheit (GDR) vol. 35,
no. 10, October 1980, p. 1021.

Hungary

In 1966 it was reported that 40 percent of the party
members were workers and "former workers" (presumably now
doing desk jobs), and that 37.3 percent were intelligentsia.[14] More comprehensive information was published at
the 10th and 11th MSZMP Congresses (see Table 4.5). By
July 1978 it was reported that there were 770,000 party
members, and by March 1985, 831,000 members.[15]

Poland

The profound political and social crisis that shook
Poland in 1980-1982 had a great impact on the party membership and its social composition. Extensive purges as
well as voluntary resignations from party membership were
reported. Until this period the PZPR membership had
increased more or less steadily, occasional purges only
checking the growth for a time. In January 1945 there
were 30,000 party members. Data for succeeding years are:
July 1946--364,000; July 1947--848,000; December 1948--
1,500,000 (after fusion with the socialists); December
1950--1,360,000; June 1952--1,129,000; March 1954--
1,297,000; January 1956--1,344,000; March 1959--1,067,000;
July 1961--1,270,000; January 1963--1,397,000; January
1965--1,640,000; June 1966--1,848,000; March 1967--

Table 4.5
Composition of Membership in the Hungarian Socialist
Workers' Party, November 1970 and March 1975

Social-Occupational Group	10th MSZMP Congress (November 1970)		11th MSZMP Congress (March 1975)	
Industrial and farm workers	282,674	(42.7%)	343,070	(45.5%)
Intelligentsia (white collar)	252,222	(38.1%)	347,594	(46.1%)
Others (armed forces, students, pensioners)	127,104	(19.2%)	63,336	(8.4%)
Totals	662,000	(100.0%)	754,000	(100.0%)

Sources: Nepszabadsag (Hungary), 29 November 1970; A. Magyar,
(Szocialista Munkaspart XI Kongresszusa (Budapest, 1975),
p. 18.

2,296,000; December 1971--2,270,000; November 1975--2,453,000;
and December 1976--2,500,000.[16] The social-occupational
composition of the PZPR during most of this period is given
in Table 4.6.

During 1980 no precise and reliable information on party
membership was published. Then on 29 June 1981 the Polish
Press Agency (PAP) in Warsaw reported that party membership
was 2,870,000. The drop vis-à-vis 1980 was explained at the
9th Extraordinary PZPR Congress in July 1981, when the
PZPR Central Auditing Commission reported: "Between 1 July
1980 and 31 May 1981, 311,100 people were removed from the
party register or excluded from the ranks of the PZPR.
Some 190,000 of them handed in their party cards. . . .
Unfortunately, the proportion of workers in the party went
down from 46.4 percent to 44.7 percent."[17]

On 12 June 1982 the Polish authorities staged a twelve-
hour "phone-in" radio program with top party and government
officials, to mark the first six months of martial law.
Wlodzimierz Mokrzyszczak, PZPR Central Committee Politburo
candidate-member and Central Committee secretary for
internal organizational matters, who appeared on the
program, disclosed some official data on PZPR membership.
According to him, in June 1982 there were 2,488,000 PZPR
members and candidate-members--"a loss of some 660,000 since
July 1980."[18] However, he added that the rate of decline
was decreasing and that workers still accounted for 41
percent of the party membership.[19]

Table 4.6
Composition of Membership in the Polish United Workers' Party, 1945-1975

Social-Occupational Group	Number and Percentage of Members			
	December 1945	September 1957	October 1970	November 1975
Industrial workers	130,620 (62.2%)	511,917 (39.9%)	939,064 (40.9%)	995,918 (40.6%)
Peasants	59,220 (28.6%)	164,224 (12.8%)	266,236 (11.6%)	242,847 (9.9%)
Intellectuals	20,160 (9.6%)	497,804 (38.8%)	975,890 (42.5%)	1,052,337 (42.9%)
Others (artisans, pensioners, housewives, etc.)	-- --	109,055 (8.5%)	114,810 (5.0%)	161,898 (6.6%)
Totals	210,000 (100.0%)	1,283,000 (100.0%)	2,296,000 (100.0%)	2,453,000 (100.0%)

Sources: Nowe Drogi (Poland), January-February 1947, p. 29, and May-June 1948, p. 30; Zicie Warszawi (Poland), 25 October 1953; Trybuna Ludu (Poland), 18 November 1957; Warsaw Radio, 3 November 1970; Polish Perspectives, November 1975, p. 5.

Romania

Romanian sources publish data on party membership and
composition fairly regularly. This practice allows a more
comprehensive profile of the Romanian Communist Party to
be drawn (see Table 4.7).

During 1976 some 106,000 new party members were
admitted, of whom 83.5 percent were workers and peasants,
and 16.5 percent functionaries and intellectuals. About
33.7 percent were women, bringing their strength in overall
party membership to 25.8 percent.[20] In October 1977 party
membership reached a total of 2,700,000, 51 percent of whom
were workers, 19 percent peasants, and 22 percent white
collar workers and intelligentsia.[21] Some 112,305 new
members were admitted in 1977, 71.71 percent of whom were
workers, 12.96 percent peasants, and 15.29 percent white
collar workers and intelligentsia. Women represented
37 percent of the new members.[22] By the end of 1980 there
were 3,044,336 party members, "74.80 percent of this total
number of party members carrying on activities in the sphere
of material production."[23] Some 45.69 percent worked in
industry, construction, and transportation, and 23.3 percent worked in agriculture.[24] Some 132,000 new party
members were admitted in 1980, 84.33 percent of whom were
workers and peasants.[25]

A plenary session of the RCP Central Committee took
place on 31 March 1982. A document adopted by the session
pointed out that "on December 1981 the RCP counted
3,150,812 members. The share of party members within the
total population working in the area of the material production went up from 74.80 percent by the end of 1980, to
76.03 percent at present. Over the last year as many as
19,361 intellectuals became members of the RCP. As many
as 56,000 women rounded off the party membership, this
figure representing 46 percent of the total number of
members admitted over the last year. The share of women
within the party went up from 28.71 percent in 1981 to
29.62 percent in 1982."[26]

The same document also revealed the principles of
admission during 1982:

The admission to the party will be further oriented
toward primarily admitting the highly qualified
workers of all the branches of the national economy,
that are to represent 57 to 65 percent of the total
number of working people to become party members
this year. The fact will be ensured that peasants

Table 4.7
Composition of Membership in the Romanian Communist Party, 1960-1984

Social-Occupational Group	Number and Percentage of Members			
	June 1960	March 1970	December 1975	November 1984
Workers	426,000 (51.0%)	867,290 (43.4%)	1,288,717 (ca 50.0%)	1,920,000 (ca 56%)
Peasants	186,000 (22.0%)	531,447 (26.6%)	515,487 (ca 20.0%)	540,000 (ca 16%)
Intelligentsia	83,000 (11.0%)	481,083 (24.0%)	511,642 (ca 22.0%)	710,000 (ca 21%)
Others	131,000 (16.0%)	119,900 (6.0%)	103,088 (ca 8.0%)	230,000 (ca 7%)
Totals	826,000 (100%)	1,999,720 (100%)	2,418,934 (100%)	3,400,000 (100%)

Source: Scinteia (Romania), 21 July 1960, 20 March 1970, 24 April 1976, and 20 November 1984.

further stand for at least 15 percent of these
people admitted to the party, and in the counties
where the population working in agriculture is
more numerous they represent at least 25 percent
of the new members of the party.

In order to ensure the growth of the share
represented by women within the ranks of the party
and to preserve a stable balance as concerns the
distribution of members according to their age, in
1982 women shall stand for at least 50 percent of
the total number of people admitted to the party,
and at least 70 percent will come from the Union
of the Socialist Youth.[27]

Continued emphasis on these guidelines has continued
to affect party membership; at least through 1984 when a
report at the 13th RCP Congress in November announced that
the proportion of women in the party had increased to more
than 32 percent, and that 23 percent of all members were
under 30 years of age.

Yugoslavia

As in all other East European countries, party membership in Yugoslavia is growing in the long run, as Table 4.8
shows. On 18 October 1979, the LCY Central Committee held

Table 4.8
Growth in Membership in the League of Yugoslav
Communists, 1945-1982

Year	Membership
1945	140,000
1948	448,175
1952	779,382
1956	635,984
1960	898,300
1964	1,030,041
1970	1,111,682
1974	ca 1,100,000
1978	1,774,624
1982	2,117,083

Sources: Komunist (SFRY), 15 October 1964 and 6 April
1967; Borba (SFRY), 24 October 1970, 27 February 1975,
and 19 October 1979; Belgrade TANJUG in English, 0900 GMT,
16 June 1982; Daily Report (FBIS) 17 June 1982.

a plenum at which the following data on party membership
was revealed: On 30 June 1979 the LCY had 1,855,638 members,
of whom 630,904 (34 percent) were "highly qualified, semi-
qualified, and unqualified workers and peasants." Between
1972 (when the LCY had 1,009,947 members) and the end of
1978 (1,774,624 members), 1,021,411 new members had joined
the party. This means that in the same period 256,734 had
lost their party membership.[28]

Incidentally, Yugoslavia is the only East European
country that publishes regular data on the expulsion of
party members: "The largest falloff in membership was in
1970, when 91,851 members were expelled, dropped from the
rolls, or resigned. There was a large drop in membership
between 1953 and 1958, when the LCY lost 148,114 members,
and the largest number of expulsions in the recent past
was in 1972, when it was 12,941 members."[29] Often as well,
when Yugoslav sources cite data on the social composition
of the LCY, they also reveal information on the specific
share of each social group among those expelled from the
party (see Table 4.9).

The age of breakdown of LCY members in the two years
covered by Table 4.9 was:[30]

Age	1970	1980
Under 27	218,184	673,800
28-40	433,956	723,410
41-55	331,080	485,910
56 or older	65,181	143,390

According to other official statistics, in 1978 alone--
a Congress year--181,320 new members were admitted.[31] It
was further revealed that in 1979, 35.5 percent of the
party members were young people up to 27 years of age.
There were 451,000 female members--24 percent of the
total party membership.[32] The social-occupational composition of the members (two years earlier) was as shown in
Table 4.10.

At the beginning of 1980 there were "more than
1,950,000 party members."[33] Among those who enrolled in
the first three months of 1980 (total of 48,334), 34,874
or 72.2 percent were young people below the age of 27,
and 13,922 or 28.8 percent were women.[34]

At the beginning of 1981 there were 2,041,272 LCY
members, "only 602,184 of whom were workers, which means
that we have not yet carried out the recommendation of the
June 1978 11th LCY Congress to create a workers' majority
in the party."[35] Some 199,446 new members were admitted

Table 4.9
Enrollments and Losses in Membership in the League of Yugoslav Communists, 1970 and 1980

Year/Social-Occupational or Other Group	Total	Enrolled	Expelled	Removed from Rolls	Resigned from LCY
1970					
Total	1,049,184[1]	31,885	10,178	20,680	15,224
Workers	310,555	9,210	5,502	8,584	7,410
Other employed persons	411,663	6,304	2,282	5,867	3,917
Private farmers	68,425	2,800	1,207	1,636	1,292
Secondary and university students	54,428	10,563	185	1,838	173
Yugoslav People's Army and others	204,113	3,008	1,002	3,755	2,432
Women	201,946	7,540	1,123	4,172	3,066
1980					
Total	2,026,521	199,185	3,686	8,995	2,574
Workers	600,722	58,918	1,752	3,262	1,111
Other employed persons	840,582	48,827	1,145	1,651	654
Private farmers	87,109	8,319	310	575	102
Secondary and university students	201,034	62,084	73	1,924	138
Yugoslav People's Army and others	297,074	21,037	406	1,583	569
Women	521,823	65,928	401	2,518	712

1. The discrepancy between this figure and the corresponding one in Table 4.8 is unresolved, owing to different sources and, possibly, data obtained at different times in the same year.

Source: Komunist (SFRY), 5 February 1982, p. 13.

Table 4.10
Composition of Membership in the League of
Yugoslav Communists, 1977

Social-Occupational Group	Number of Party Members	Percentage
Blue collar workers	470,883	29
White collar workers	113,661	7
Peasants	81,187	5
Humanist intelligentsia	227,323	14
Administrative officials	194,849	12
Managers and functionaries	113,661	7
Army and police forces	97,424	6
Unemployed	48,712	3
Pensioners, students, etc.	276,035	17
Total	1,623,735	100%

Source: Borba (SFRY), 7 January 1979.

in 1980, most of them workers.[36] Finally, in June 1982
the LCY had a total membership of 2,117,083 members. At
the end of 1981 some 649,378 party members were workers.[37]
    The above data on party membership in the East
European countries allow the following general conclusions
on the membership of the communist parties in Eastern
Europe:
    1. The party membership in Eastern Europe is
constantly growing. Despite frequent purges or other
methods of reducing membership and getting rid of "unwanted" elements, such as an exchange of party cards
(discussed later in this chapter), in the long run the
number of party members is increasing steadily.
    2. All East European communist parties are eager to
demonstrate the high percentage of workers among their
members. However, the data on the percentage of workers
in these parties are not reliable. It is understandable
that the East European communist parties strive to
demonstrate their proletarian character. After all, the
communist party was supposed to lead the proletariat.
Some communist parties (SED, CPCZ) report that the absolute
majority of party membership consists of workers; the usual
percentage reported by the other East European communist
parties is between 45 and 50 percent. Unfortunately there
are absolutely no data to show what percentage of the
workers are party members by comparison to the percentage
of white collar workers and intelligentsia who are party
members. Thus, official sources usually indicate that
white collar workers and intelligentsia account for 15-25

percent of party members. The percentage of white collar
workers and intelligentsia in the population, however, is
much lower, which means that in any country a much greater
percentage of the white collar workers and intelligentsia
than of workers are party members. Most East European
countries fudge the percentages and speak only of the
percentage of workers among those who have been admitted
to membership. Yugoslavia is the only country that
occasionally provides more substantial data.

3. Some social segments are clearly underrepresented
in communist party membership. The percentage of women
among party members is much lower than their percentage
in the population. In fact this is a situation that has
been admitted by several East European countries, and steps
to improve the situation have frequently been announced.
Thus a 1973 plenum of the RCP Central Committee analyzed
the condition of women in Romania and noted an increase in
the percentage of women admitted to the RCP.[38] However,
another RCP Central Committee plenum on 22-23 March 1978
expressed "dissatisfaction with the representation of
women in the party."[39] The problem is evidently a continuing one, because subsequent Central Committee plenums
have continued to promote membership by women in the
party.[40]

The issue of admitting more women to the communist
party has also focused the attention of the Albanian
Workers' Party authorities. The official party organ
Zeri I Popullit criticized local party organizations and
pointed out that "when it is time to accept the most
outstanding women into the party, [these organizations]
show lack of confidence in their abilities as political
militants of the party line and as social activists."[41]
The result has been that in many places "only 20 to 30
percent of the young people admitted to the party were
women."[42]

STRUCTURE

The communist parties of Eastern Europe maintain a
dictatorship in the name of the workers' class, which itself has only minority representation in the party. How
is it possible that a small political party, which has only
a fraction of the population as members, maintains such
strict control, in fact a monopoly, over all areas of human
life? The answer lies in the structure of the party and
the principal of "democratic centralism," which serves as

the foundation of this structure.

The structure of the communist party represents a rigid pyramid, consisting of several layers. Thus in April 1982 the Romanian Communist Party consisted, from the top down, of its Politburo and Central Committee, 40 county organizations, the Bucharest municipal organization and 242 other municipal and town organizations, 2,705 commune organizations, 7,218 organizations led by party committees at the level of enterprises, institutions, agricultural units, production sections and sectors, and 65,219 basic organizations in units, workshops, farms, etc.[43] The party in its structure is basically a hierarchical apparatus subjected to strict party discipline (total obedience to the higher party level, and ultimately to the supreme party organs), which is necessary in order to maintain effective control over the implementation of policies and programs, and in fact, over all sociopolitical, scientific, cultural, and personal activities.

Centralism and democracy, these two basic conceptual cornerstones of the communist party's structure and operation, were defined in the following way by Professor Habilitatus Adolf Dobieszewski, director of party studies at the PZPR Central Committee Higher School of Social Science.:[44] "The essence of a centralist party construction, in the Leninist meaning of that word, is homogeneous, efficient management for implementation of the goals of socialism. The homogeneous management requires: (1) subordination of the entire party to the will of the party majority; (2) subordination of the lower elements of the party's structure and their leadership to the higher elements and their leadership; and (3) voluntarily accepted discipline, equally binding on all party members."

"Democracy," according to Prof. Dobieszewski, means "the equal opportunity for all members of the party to formulate the party's program and its general line: i.e., the equal opportunity for all members of the party to participate in the formation and recall of their own party organizational authorities (from the basic party organization to the authorities of the entire party), and to control, participate in, and influence the direction of party activity; [and] the opportunity for party members and organizations, from basic organizations to voivodeship organizations, to undertake independent actions to influence the pursuance of the general line of the party."

The PZPR statutes define democratic centralism along the same lines:

The supreme organizational principle of internal
party life is democratic centralism. It constitutes a condition of ideological and political
uniformity as well as unity of party activity.
The principles of democratic centralism are the
following:
1. all managerial party authorities, from the
lowest to the highest, are elected in a democratic
manner;
2. all party resolutions are passed by a majority
of the votes;
3. all party authorities are responsible to the
organization that elected them and, also, are
obliged to file reports of their activity;
4. all members and organizations must observe
the same party discipline and the minority must
submit to the resolutions of the majority;
5. resolutions and directives of the higher party
authorities must be carried out by the lower ones.[45]

It is hardly necessary to add that the entire structure
of the East European communist parties and the conceptual
principles to which they are subjected are identical to
those of the Communist Party of the Soviet Union. The
bottom layer of the pyramid of the East European communist
parties is formed by tens of thousands of "basic" or
"primary" party organizations (formerly "cells"), or units,
set up in the places in which the members work--in factories, workshops, business enterprises, state farms,
governmental and other offices, the army, educational
establishments, institutions, cultural enterprises--in
short, wherever at least three communists work.
    Lenin defined the primary party organizations as
"the cells of the revolutionary working class party,
performing agitational and propaganda work, as well as
organizational activity, and acting with determination in
all domains of public life."[46] At the beginning of the
communist rule in Eastern Europe the primary party
organizations were formed according to the territorial
principle (i.e., wherever at least three communists lived);
today, however, it is preferred to establish them at the
places of work, as mentioned above. It should be pointed
out that the party organizations in the army are something
of an exception in the regular party hierarchy, since they
are not controlled by a higher layer (there is none as such),
but directly by the main political administration of the
armed forces, which in turn, is directly controlled by the

party's Central Committee.

There is no difference between the various East European communist parties as regards the tasks of the primary party organizations, as enumerated in their party statutes. The tasks can be summarized as follows:

1. Organizational work among the masses to facilitate the implementation of party tasks, decisions, resolutions, plans, and programs.

2. Agitational-propaganda activity springing from party ideology (or rather slogans, aimed at explaining the need to implement the aforementioned tasks, decisions and so forth, inspiring the masses by evoking what the communist press defines as their "working enthusiasm," and, in short, connecting the need for harder and better work with party ideology and principles. This task includes the control of the mass media, and first of all the local press, through several channels including primary party units on the staffs of the newspapers and other mass media.

3. Recruitment of new party members, which will be analyzed later in this chapter. At this point it need only be pointed out that the actual process of admitting new party members takes place at the level of the primary party organizations, subject to the approval of the party organs of the next layer up.

4. Political indoctrination of party members through courses on Marxism-Leninism, party history, discussion of current events, and so forth.

5. Social mobilization of the population, which includes not merely mobilizing the masses for implementing party tasks (which is a separate task), but maintaining the population in a state of permanent mobilization for various propaganda and economic campaigns, such as implementing national plans, maintaining better labor discipline, organizing "socialist competition" for fulfilling the Five-Year Plan, reprimanding citizens for "unsocialist" behavior, and, in short, maintaining a high degree of social tension as a means of preventing unwanted activity and an instrument for inducing loyalty and cooperation.

6. Control of the activity of the management of
   production and trade enterprises, as well as
   agrarian farms, organizations, etc. The primary
   party organizations thus bear a large share of
   responsibility for implementing industrial and
   agrarian plans.
7. Maintaining "vigilance" -- a very common word in
   the Eastern bloc, which translates simply into
   reporting any activity that might be considered
   harmful, disloyal, or detrimental to the
   implementation of party tasks.
8. Control of the activity of the local municipal
   organs.
9. Struggle against "antiparty" or "antisocialist"
   tendencies in cultural life, the arts, and so
   forth.

In addition to all this, the primary party organizations in the armies of the East European communist countries are charged with responsibility for strengthening
the political training of the soldiers, selecting candidates for officer careers, etc. [47]
If one could sum up all these functions in one
sentence, it would be that the primary party organizations
control every area of public activity through active
participation in economic, political, and cultural life.
Although, as already noted, party statutes in all East
European countries devote much space to defining and explaining the functions of the primary party organizations,
one still finds frequent party resolutions and decisions,
and articles in the party press, explaining the functions
of the primary party organizations and dealing with their
activity, apparently in an ongoing effort to improve it.
In one such article Dr. Heinz Puder, SED Central Committee
department deputy head, pointed out:

The basic organizations link the party with all
working people. They bear a great responsibility
for having the working people rally closely around
the party and for organizing the masses in the
implementation of our party policy, which is oriented
to man, to the prosperity and happiness of the
people.
It is necessary to increase the responsibility
of all party organizations and every communist for
further developing the socialist national consciousness and for having the working people take part

> still more comprehensively in the various forms
> of management and planning.
>
> The primary party organizations must . . .
> ever more effectively shape a truly socialist
> attitude toward labor . . . they must be ahead
> of all citizens in terms of labor discipline
> and energy. . . . They must foster collective
> consultation and creative debate on how best to
> implement the party resolutions . . . and they
> must improve political training.[48]

The primary party organization consists of a minimum
of three members, but it may include as many as 300
members. Its highest organ is the annual plenary session
(or general assembly) of all members. The party statutes
charge this meeting with supervising the implementation of
the primary party organization's main tasks. Unless
otherwise instructed, the primary party organization
holds a regular monthly meeting. Attendance is obligatory,
and the topics discussed are standard--implementation of
economic plans, current party policy, and so forth. The
real burden of daily work rests on the shoulders of the
primary party unit's committee (3-11 members), elected by
the larger units at their annual session, and these
committees' bureaus (an even narrower circle of leadership,
consisting of the secretary of the primary party organization, a deputy or deputies if the unit is a large one,
and 2-4 members of the bureau). A Romanian party source
describes the responsibility of the bureau as follows:

> As the executive organ of the general assembly
> elected to lead all current activities of the
> base organization, the bureau has to carry out
> special tasks. It is called upon to organize and
> ensure the application of the decisions of the
> general assembly and the carrying out of the tasks
> stemming from party and state decisions, to
> judiciously distribute the resources of the base
> organizations in order to cover all sectors,
> regions, and problems, to constantly oversee
> adherence to internal party democracy and
> communist discipline, and to create all the
> conditions so that each party member will actively
> take part in all the activities of the organiza-
> tion. Similarly, it is also asked to organize
> all propaganda work and political-ideological
> training for the communists and to instruct

and coordinate the collective's activities for
agitators and editorial staffs or gazettes,
satirical gazettes, and radio stations. In
addition, it prepares on-time general assemblies
and exercises a systematic review in all fields
of activity, promptly informing its superior
organ about special problems."[49]

The work of the secretaries and their associates is
closely watched and evaluated by higher party authorities
(usually, but not always, the leadership of the next layer
up) and is subjected to frequent resolutions and decisions
of the party central organs. Such was the March 1977
resolution of the BCP Central Committee Secretariat, "On
Further Strengthening the Role of the Secretaries of the
Primary Party Organizations."[50] The resolution stressed
that the performance of the 28,000 secretaries of the BCP
primary organizations did not always correspond to the
standards of party requirements. The list of their shortcomings is long. They "did not understand the essentials
of their tasks and did not exercise enough control over
the administrative and economic managers," which was "the
secretaries' basic obligation as political leaders of labor
collectives." They did not work "systematically and
persistently for the organizational consolidation of the
primary party organization"; many secretaries "resort to
forms, means, and methods that are alien to the party
style . . . others duplicate the functions of economic and
state officials or underestimate the importance of
ideological and political activities among party members
and nonmembers." An intermediate conclusion of the resolution is that "all this belittles the vanguard role of the
BCP." The resolution goes on to enumerate certain
"considerable and objective" weaknesses in selecting and
training the party secretaries ("apathetic persons have
been elected; some of them do not know enough and often
use an incorrect style of work," and so forth). The rest
of the resolution deals with measures for improving the
quality of the party secretaries: Only people who are
"selflessly devoted to the working class and socialism,
. . . ready to fight under any circumstances for the
implementation of the party line," may be elected as
secretaries of the primary party organizations. They will
have to undergo a special Marxist-Leninist training (the
resolution specifies what courses this training is to
include), and ultimately, they will be subjected to
stricter control, and systematic and periodic evaluation by

the party's higher organs. Special attention must be paid
to "reserve cadres," i.e., potential secretaries.

In order that the secretaries may work more effectively,
the resolution recommends that they be relieved of all
obligations that interfere with their party functions.
Duplication should be avoided. Their state of health must
be periodically checked and recorded and their wages as
party functionaries should not be lower than the wages
they received in their professional capacity prior to their
election as secretaries of primary party organizations.
Finally, the resolution recommends various material incentives, and that the secretaries be awarded orders, medals,
and titles in an attempt to improve the quality of their
work. The mass media and the Unions of Bulgarian Writers
and Cinematographers were instructed to "depict the
secretaries of the primary party organizations as modest,
selfless, and respected leaders."[51]

On 13 July 1981 at the 9th Extraordinary PZPR Congress,
the PZPR Central Auditing Commission reported that the
wages of all party workers had been substantially increased. The salaries of the secretaries of the basic
party units were increased from 5,711 to 11,300 Zloties
a month.

ADMISSION--RULES AND POLICY

In general the rules governing admission to the East
European communist parties follow the pattern established
by the CPSU. The minimum age of the applicants in most
of the East European party statutes is 18 years,[52] but
practice shows that one is not considered a candidate
before the period of his membership in the youth communist
organization ends, usually at the age of 24 to 26. An
applicant must fill in an application form consisting of
searching questions, and submit his detailed personal
curriculum vitae. The application must be endorsed by two
sponsors (in some countries, three) with at least two years
of good standing as party members (in Poland, three years).[53]

It must be immediately pointed out that it is no easy
matter for a candidate to find the necessary sponsors to
endorse his application. After all, according to party
statutes, the sponsors "bear responsibility for the
trustworthiness of their recommendations," and in times of
a purge this can be a liability. The application is considered by the committee or the bureau of the primary party
organization at the applicant's place of work. This is the

same primary party organization that he will join if he is admitted to the party ranks. After reviewing the application, the committee makes a "recommendation," which, if positive, means that the applicant will be invited to a meeting of the entire primary organization and will be asked to relate his life story and answer the party members' questions. Usually, he is asked first of all to explain why is he seeking admission to the party, why at this particular moment and not earlier (or later), and what makes him worthy of being a party member. After the grilling, the primary party organization votes on the application. If the decision is positive, it must then be affirmed by the higher tier of party authority, i.e., the district or city committee of the party.

Having successfully negotiated all these hurdles, the applicant becomes first a candidate-member for a period of one to two years, during which time he may not vote or be elected to party posts but may attend the meetings of the primary party organization. This probationary period is used to make sure that the candidate would make a worthy party member. If he passes this prolonged test, then the candidate once again goes through the same complete process of admission--including sponsors and checks--and if everything is in order he becomes a party member.

This basic procedure is used for admitting new party members to the communist party in all East European countries, with slight differences from one country to another. Thus, in Yugoslavia until 1952, the criteria for membership in the LCY were the same as in the USSR, i.e., a prospective member was required to be at least 18 years of age, to have the written recommendation of two party members who had themselves been members for at least two years, and to submit a written biography. Applications were then reviewed by the relevant primary party organization and forwarded to the higher authority; if everything was approved, the candidate was admitted for a probation period of eighteen months. At the 8th LCY Congress the requirements were modified to eliminate written recommendations and probationary status.[54]

Admission of new members to the party can be simultaneously a simple and a very complicated matter. It becomes simpler when the party is interested in somebody, for instance an outstanding worker or a famous athlete, and the entire process becomes proforma, everything being done smoothly and automatically in a minimum of time. On the other hand, admission can be a very important and complicated matter, because (along with the

exchange of party cards and purges) it is one of the basic
ways of tailoring party membership and balancing the party's
social composition. The party therefore regulates the
admission policy very carefully and thoroughly, striving
to limit the admission of those from certain social sectors
and to encourage the admission of others, all according to
the specific party needs at a given moment. When despite
all this the quality of party membership ceases to satisfy
the leadership (or Moscow), there are other, swifter means
of regulating the party membership, which will be examined
later on in this chapter.

There are some social groups whose members are readily
admitted and sometimes even urged to join. Such is the
case with the army. When official data on the social
composition of the East European communist party is published, the military personnel are usually hidden in the
"others" category. However, when data on party membership
among the military is published, it is clear that officers
are one of the most overrepresented groups in the party.
Thus, in 1978, it was revealed that "the Yugoslav Army
comprises 250,000 officers, noncommissioned officers,
soldiers, and civilian employees"[55] and that among them,
by the end of August 1978, there were 100,000 party
members.[56] Another example: in a speech at an army
conference to mark the 1,300th anniversary of the Bulgarian
state, Army General Dobri Dzhurov, BCP Central Committee
Politburo member and minister of national defense, revealed
that "over 85 percent of the officers and generals of the
Bulgarian People's Army are party members."[57] Finally,
official Yugoslav sources claimed in 1977 that "over 98
percent of all commanding officers are LCY members."[58]

A constant concern of the East European communist
parties is to maintain or at least to claim a high percentage of industrial workers as party members. Frequently,
recruitment procedures for this particular group are
relaxed. A drop in the percentage of industrial workers is
usually kept secret, and when revealed is accompanied by
special concern expressed on the part of the party. Thus
in July 1981, the PZPR Central Committee, in referring to
the exodus from the party in the wake of the rise of the
Solidarity trade union movement, admitted that "between
1 July 1980 and 31 May 1981, 311,100 people were removed
from the party register or excluded from the ranks of the
PZPR. Some 190,000 of them handed in their party
cards. . . . Unfortunately, the proportion of workers in
the party went down from 46.4 percent to 44.7 percent."[59]

One should treat all official data on party membership

published by the East European communist parties with
proper reservation. First of all there is the problem of
lack of verification, i.e., there is no way of checking
personally the party register. Second, the uncertain
definition of a "worker" in Eastern Europe makes all East
European statistics questionable.

The admissions policy of the communist parties is
subjected to frequent decisions by the party's highest
organs. Several examples will illustrate the nature of
these: A plenum of the RCP Central Committee on 29 March
1977 heard reports on the strength, composition, and organizational structure of the RCP as of 31 December 1976, and
on the implementation of the party's cadres policy.[60] It
was reported that in 1976, 106,000 new members were
admitted to the party, 83.5 percent of whom were workers
and peasants and 15.6 percent intellectuals and functionaries. About 33.7 percent of the new members were women,
bringing their strength in the party membership to 25.8
percent.[61] In order "to further strengthen the leading
role of the party," the 29 March 1977 RCP Central Committee
plenum decided that the basic criteria for admission to
the party ranks should continue to be "moral-political"
and "professional" qualifications. Priority was to be
given, as until then, to workers and peasants, who should
represent "at least 80 percent of new party members."
The ratio of women admitted to the party was to be increased to at least 35-40 percent. Members of the Union
of Communist Youth (the Romanian Komsomol) were to be
encouraged to join and efforts were supposed to be made to
enlist engineers, technicians, and "basic cadres" of
research and drafting institutes.[62]

There were two more RCP Central Committee plenums
in 1977 that also dealt with the issue of improving
party membership. At both of these plenums, the one on
21-22 September 1977[63] and the other on 26-27 October
1977,[64] it was urged that the admission of members of
"working class origin" be intensified.

Another RCP Central Committee plenum dealing with
improving the RCP social composition took place on 22-23
March 1978.[65] After reviewing the party membership and
social-occupational composition (2,747,110 members, some
73.26 percent of whom were engaged in "material production"[66]), and the social-occupational composition of
members admitted in 1976 (some 106,000 new members were
admitted, 71.71 percent of whom were workers, 12.96
percent peasants, and 15.29 percent intellectuals[67]),
as well as the increased percentage of the women (33.7

percent among the newly admitted members in 1976),[68] the
plenum concentrated on the party's admissions policy. It
was pointed out that efforts were being made "to implement
the instructions of Comrade Nicolae Ceausescu" (the party
leader) to raise party membership and increase the percentage of the party's working class contingent. (The
secretary general of the RCP had criticized the efforts
made in this respect in a speech at the 21-23 September
1977 RCP Central Committee plenum.) As far as women were
concerned, the RCP Central Committee expressed dissatisfaction with the degree to which they were represented in
the party: "Although 26.4 percent of all party members are
women, this is not an adequate reflection of the fact that
they make up 46.33 percent of the country's nonfarming
labor force and 62.27 percent of the personnel employed by
agricultural production cooperatives."[69] In view of the
situation the plenum concluded that women must in the future
amount to 35 to 40 percent of all new members, with special
emphasis laid on recruiting women working in the agro-
industrial complexes.[70]

The problem continued to focus the attention of the
RCP Central Committee, and the issue of admissions policy
and the social composition of the RCP were repeatedly discussed by later Central Committee plenums. Thus on 31
December 1980 a Central Committee plenum adopted a document
dealing with the effectiveness, composition, and organizational structure of the RCP.[71] This document stated that
132,000 new members had joined the party in 1980, 84.33
percent of whom were workers and peasants. Following
Ceausescu's exhortation to "strengthen the revolutionary
class character of the party and develop a strong workers'
nucleus," 94,780 workers joined the party in 1980, raising
the percentage of workers to 54.62 percent, compared with
54.00 percent in 1979.[72]

A further Central Committee plenum took place on 25
March 1981, and again the same issue was discussed.[73]
Ceausescu's recommendations have evidently sitll not been
implemented, because the percentage of women in the party
was reported as 28.75 percent (27.97 percent in 1977),[74]
a far cry from the ambitious 35-40 percent recommended
by Ceausescu.

Finally, at the already cited 31 March 1982 RCP
Central Committee plenum, it was reported that "the share
of women within the party went up from 28.71 percent in
1981 to 29.62 percent in 1982."[75]

In the CSSR the problem of admission to the party and
social-occupational composition also occupies the attention

of the party organs. In the words of a <u>Rude Pravo</u>
editorial: "the whole history of the CPCZ is proof
that the success of its policies has always depended
on the quality of the party's rank and file."[76]   In order
to insure further successes the editorial recommended overcoming several faults in party admission, such as admitting
too many candidates "working in auxiliary, less important
sectors," and "admitting too many employees of the
management."[77]

  The Central Committees of all other East European
communist parties hold plenums devoted to the issue of
party membership and social-occupational composition,
and issue similar instructions related to increasing the
percentage of workers and women in the party. Still, the
more or less equal proportion of workers, peasants, and
intellectuals, as well as women, in all East European
communist parties (see Tables 4.2-4.7, 4.9, and 4.10)
gives the impression that the existing (more or less)
uniform social-occupational composition of the parties is
a consequence of tacit party policy. It seems fair to
suppose that despite all Central Committee decisions and
recommendations, the composition of the parties reflects
policy or preferences set at forums other than the parties'
Central Committee.

EXPULSION, EXCHANGE OF PARTY CARDS

  Selective recruitment based on detailed instructions
and recommendations is only one way of controlling party
membership. Another, much swifter way is simply to "oust"
unwanted members or elements. In the past it was done by
terminating the membership (and sometimes the life) of the
party members. In recent years, however, it has been done
in a more sophisticated and nonviolent way, namely, by a
procedure known as the exchange of party membership cards.
This procedure takes place every few years, the idea being
to review the behavior of the party members (thus keeping
them under the pressure of the "ever-watchful eye") and to
issue new membership cards only to those members who have
been found worthy of remaining party members. The entire
process is carried out by means of personal interviews
with all party members by special commissions.

  Although all East European communist parties use the
instrument of the exchange of party cards to regulate party
membership, they naturally deny that the procedure is a
purge of unwanted party members. There are two additional

common denominators: in all East European countries the
exchange of party cards is a nonviolent campaign, and there
usually are no repercussions for those who have been denied
new party cards. The percentage of those denied new
membership cards is usually around 1 percent of the total
party membership.

Almost all East European communist parties exchanged
their members' cards in the late 1970s and early 1980s.
It was common for the party to explain in the party
press its reasons for doing so and deny that it was in
fact a "mild purge" of the party membership.

In the GDR the SED conducted its party cards exchange
campaign in 1980. The key article explaining the campaign
was written by Horst Dolhus, SED Politburo candidate-member
and Central Committee secretary.[78] The article recalled
the decision of the 11th SED Central Committee plenum "to
check the party documents and regular SED membership and
candidacy registrations between 1 March and 30 April 1980,"
and then explained the entire campaign:

> The checking of party membership cards and of the
> regular registrations of all comrades and the
> personal talks are neither a reexamination of party
> statutes nor a purge. . . . The check implies two
> important organizational-political tasks. First we
> must make a careful check of the party membership
> card, and its validity must be confirmed through a
> check mark. And then there will be a check of the
> proper registration of each member's and candidate's
> personal data. For that purpose each comrade
> will have to fill out a questionnaire. The most
> important thing in the political requirement of
> document checks is talking personally with all
> members and candidates. The whole idea in preparing,
> conducting, and analyzing the check is to boost
> the activities of the primary organizations and
> all comrades in the continued implementation of
> the resolutiovs of the 9th SED Congress and in
> preparation of the 10th SED Congress."[79]

Further, the article recommended that the conversations with the members be really personal, meaning that
"they should not be held in groups, but individually, in
a frank and comradely atmosphere." An evaluation would be
required of the personal contribution of each member to
implementing party decisions and resolutions. A meticulous
record would be kept of everything said at the individual

interviews, and stored for future reference. Each of
these conversations should be conducted by "a member of
the executive"; however, "no more than two comrades should
conduct the conversation." The article stressed further
"that the personal conversations improve the political
effectiveness of all the basic organizations' party work
in terms of our comrades' great ideological steadfastness,
their class point of view, and their fully assuming
responsibility for implementing the instructions of the
11th SED Central Committee plenum." Finally, the article
pointed out that "it is particularly important to reinforce
all members' and candidates' understanding of and unanimous position on the requirements worked out at the 11th
SED Central Committee plenum in order to make our economy
more efficient, on participating in the party's ideological
struggle, and on personally contributing to preserving
peace and further strengthening the party ranks."[80]
    These lengthy quotations from Horst Dolhus' article
clearly illustrate the main goals behind the exchange of
party cards: "shaking the party up" by improving its
social composition, facilitating the implementation of
party decisions, strengthening the members' ideological
background, and improving the quality of their economic
and political activity. In fact those are the reasons
given by all East European countries for conducting the
exchange of party membership cards. In addition, it is
sometimes pointed out that the exchange of party cards
strengthens the unity of the party. Here is one of the
reasons given in the CSSR for the 1980 exchange of party
cards: "The exchange of party membership cards was a
meaningful political action, which continued the process
of upgrading the membership bases. The unity of the party
ranks was once again demonstrated on this occasion, and
it confirmed that its members fully agreed with the policies
of the Central Committee concerning the fulfillment of the
decisions of the 15th Congress, and that they are determined to fulfill their assigned tasks with honor."[81]
    When the resolution of the CPCZ Central Committee
plenum of 4 and 5 December 1978, which announced the
exchange of party cards in the CSSR, was published, it
stressed that the "work of all party members will be
assessed in a demanding and complex manner," and that the
implementation of various economic tasks was the main
reason behind the campaign.[82] The resolution also
stressed the more pleasant aspects of the exchange: it was
supposed to serve as "an occasion to honor the devoted work
of communists who have been consistently implementing party

policy and serving the interests of society, and have been
models in carrying out their tasks."[83]
  It seemed that the 1979 exchange was probably different from the 1970 CPCZ exchange of party cards, which
followed the events of August 1968 and served the purpose
of purging "ideologically unstable" elements. In the course
of the 1970 exchange, 326,817 party members (21.67 percent
of the total party membership at that time) lost their
party cards.[84] In the course of the exchange, which continued throughout the second half of 1979, it became
apparent that the campaign was not a purge (as at least
seven Rude Pravo editorials during this period stressed).[85]
It had a distinctly exhortive character, and really sought
"to activate the ranks of the party."[86] The thrust was
unmistakably toward rousing the membership to work harder
and produce more against the background of economic
difficulties.[87] While the process of exchanging the party
cards was going on, new members continued to be admitted to
the party and thus it is not possible to assess precisely
how many party members were denied new membership cards.
A Bratislava Pravda editorial of 4 January 1980 came nearest
to citing a figure: "the party has parted ways with less
than 1 percent of its membership." The same editorial
called the 1979 exchange of party cards a success, stressing that "never before has the exchange of party cards been
such a profoundly invigorating process which leaves a mark
on every communist."[88]
  Unusually (for Eastern Europe), another CSSR magazine
had a different opinion: "Even after the exchange of party
cards and despite the party's ridding itself of many inactive members, there still remained in our ranks comrades
who do not always behave as true communists should behave."[89]
  Relatively much more and more precise information is
available concerning the 1980 exchange of party cards in
Romania. At the 22-23 March 1978 plenum of the RCP Central
Committee, Ceausescu pointed out that "careless selection
of candidates for party membership had led to the need to
expel a comparatively large number of members each year,
either because they proved to be poor party workers, or
because of violations."[90] There were several indications
during the same year hinting that an exchange of party
cards was imminent. Finally, on 29 March 1979 another
Central Committee plenum adopted a resolution on exchanging
the party cards.[91] Although in other East European countries the exchange of party cards is a more or less periodic
affair (thus in the CSSR there were exchanges in 1963, 1970,
and 1979), in Romania the last exchange had been in 1948.

At that time 192,000 party members were expelled.[92]

A Scinteia editorial of 2 February 1980 marked the beginning of the campaign. This article stressed that the exchange of party cards should not be "considered as merely a purely technical operation, but rather as an action with a profoundly political content," designed the "ensure the analysis of the communists' activities and strengthen their party responsibility and revolutionary spirit."[93] The article noted the usual instructions for the campaign: holding individual conversations with each party member, activating each member, eliminating mistakes and shortcomings, and so forth. The bureaus of the municipal, county, and city party committees were charged with responsibility for conducting the campaign.

Near the end of the year the party press was already publishing some conclusions drawn from the exchange of party cards. Thus, for instance, it was revealed that "individual discussions have been held by the bureaus of the primary organizations with nearly all communists, and general meetings have been held in more than 99.5 percent of the organizations to discuss the conclusions resulting from the campaign."[94] It was reported that the personal meetings had taken place in a constructive atmosphere and that "the action to exchange the party documents has placed its mark for a long time throughout political-organizational activity."[95] "Closer relations" were established between the party organs and the members and "strict order in recordkeeping" was introduced.[96] A variety of shortcomings were eliminated and "solemn commitments" signed by party members. In addition it was reported that "the positive impact of the exchange of party cards is also making itself felt in production . . . in the struggle to exemplarily fulfill the plan."[97] Despite the "good results" that had been achieved, it was also reported that "in some party units in enterprises, institutions, and agricultural plants the individual decisions . . . had a formal and shallow character, the shortcomings and violations of some party members and the infringement of the obligations involved in the quality of party members were treated with indulgence, and the cases concerned were not treated as political and educational matters."[98]

Finally, a plenum of the RCP Central Committee held on 25 March 1981 reviewed the entire campaign and reported the final results. Ceausescu, who spoke at the plenum, referred once again to the need to improve the party's social composition. He reported that "30,000 former party members have not received new cards, which is a relatively small

number when we think of the over 3,000,000 membership."[99]
More precise numbers were cited several days later: "Some
2,900,091 communists from the total number of 2,936,093
party members . . . received the new party member cards,
that is, 99.72 percent of all party members; 30,210 party
members were not handed over the new party membership cards,
in accordance with decisions adopted in this respect by the
party organization they belonged to, and therefore they
were excluded from among the party members. At the same
time, several party members in whose activity shortcomings
were manifest were sanctioned and were seriously warned to
eliminate their shortcomings immediately and to adopt
progressive attitudes in production, in family life, and in
the entire social life."[100]

The exchange of party cards in Bulgaria in 1979-1980
was not much different. The decision to exchange the party
cards was adopted by an RCP Central Committee plenum on
19 December 1977.[101] More than a year before the BCP Central
Committee plenum decision, Todor Zhivkov, speaking from the
rostrum of the 11th BCP Congress (July 1976), mentioned the
necessity of exchanging the party cards, defining it as "an
important political, ideological, and organizational undertaking of the party . . . aimed at increasing the energy and
responsibility of the communists," and he added "we are not
undertaking a purge."[102]

An editorial in Rabotnichesko Delo of 9 January 1978,
which dealt with the matter, reported that since 1944 party
cards had been exchanged twice. The first time was in
1953-1955, and the reason given--changing the name of the
Bulgarian Workers' Party (communists) to Bulgarian
Communist Party. The second exchange took place in
1967-1969, "because of expiration of membership cards."[103]
(Incidentally, this was the first time that the second
exchange had been officially mentioned. Nothing is known
to have been published on the step at that time, nor was
there any indication that party membership cards were
valid only for a specific period of time. No special
explanation was given for the new exchange, other than the
standard "uniting and strengthening party ranks."[104]

By the end of 1980 the first official data on the
scope of the campaign were published. Dunavska Pravda
of 18 December 1980 reported that the exchange of party
cards had been completed and that "it resulted in the
expulsion of 3.7 percent of all party members."

One interesting aftermath of the exchange of party
cards in Bulgaria was an article by Milko Balev, BCP
Central Committee secretary (and later Politburo member),

entitled "Review of Combat Ranks," published in <u>Pravda</u>
(Moscow) on 3 February 1981. Quoting the party decisions
and Zhivkov's statements on the importance of the campaign,
Balev stated that "this exchange of party cards was
radically different from previous ones." Then he explained
why, and in fact revealed that this was a most regular
affair, identical to the campaigns conducted in Romania,
the CSSR, and the GDR:

> The operation which just ended was one of the
> measures taken by the BCP in recent years to
> increase its creative and constructive role . . .
> a part of our work to further strengthen and
> develop the primary party organizations. . . .
>   It was not prompted by any crisis phenomenon
> and does not have the nature of a purge. . . .
>   It was just a specific, frank and principled
> talk with every communist about the current problems
> of party activity and about his personal contri-
> bution to the implementation of the course out-
> lined by the BCP. It was aimed at further
> strengthening the party ranks' ideological and
> political unity. [105]

Those are exactly the phrases and justifications used
in all other East European countries, and they deny the
Bulgarian exchange any special or extraordinary character.
Furthermore, Balev's report of the mechanics of the
exchange leave again no doubt as to its routine character.
Finally, the results of the exchange, as reported by Balev,
are also identical with the results reported by all other
East European countries: "the quality of the BCP membership improved," there was an "improvement in the work of
the primary party organizations," "the exchange was a
convincing manifestation of the communists' determination
to continue to steadily follow the BCP's Leninist course,"
and so forth. [106]
Reporting the numerical results of the exchange
Balev stated:

> The BCP jettisoned those workers, including
> certain leading workers, who had lost the
> qualities of a communist and were failing to
> conform with the dictates of the program and
> the party rules, who were flouting the law of the
> land and the norms of social morality, who were
> harboring petit bourgeois and philistine

inclinations, and undermining the party's
prestige and influence among the masses. The
party organizations were qualitatively improved
by refusing to issue new cards to 3.8 percent
of their previous members, penalizing 2 percent
of the BCP members for specific transgressions,
and deferring the issue of new cards to 2 percent
of the members."[107]

It seems that if there was anything unusual in the
exchange of party cards in Bulgaria, then it was only the
unusually high percentage (almost 8 percent) of those who
were denied new cards (both permanently and temporarily).
    Hungary is a country in which the exchange of party
cards really is a periodic and routine affair. Between
1945 and 1977 party cards were exchanged six times.[108]
The most recent exchange was announced by a 23 October 1975
plenum of the MSZMP Central Committee.[109] The intention
to conduct such a campaign was announced several months
earlier, in March 1975 at the 11th MSZMP Congress.[110]
Central Committee Secretary Arpad Pullai, who spoke on the
fourth day of the congress, spoke about the intended exchange and repeated the familiar phrases: "The exchange of
party cards will be an important political event in party
life and will strengthen the party's ideological, political,
and operational unity. . . . What we have in mind is not
a purge."[111]
    Those key phrases were repeated in every article and
statement dealing with the exchange. Finally, after the
exchange was completed, an MSZMP Central Committee plenum
was convened on 22 June 1977. At the plenum it was reported that as a result of the exchange of party cards,
2.7 percent of the members left the party either of their
own accord or at the behest of the primary organizations.[112]
    All in all, it seems that the exchange of party cards
really is what the East European communist parties claim,
namely, an instrument for "improving the party membership"
and "strengthening the party's organizational, economic,
and political activity." It is an instrument for
periodically regulating the party membership and a nonviolent way of sanctioning some party members or intensifying the enthusiasm and devotion of others. It is not,
however, the only way of achieving these goals. The
expulsion of party members for "abuse of authority"[113]
or other reasons happens regularly. Purges (although
rare) still exist, as the examples of the CSSR in 1969-1970
and Poland in 1981 proved. Still, there is one basic

difference between the exchange of party membership cards
and other means of regulating the social composition of
party membership, namely, the extensive involvement of the
primary organizations in the process of exchanging party
cards, and the fact that the entire campaign is presented
as an instrument for activating not only the party members
but the primary organizations themselves.

PARTY STRUCTURE--UPPER LAYERS

Between the apex of the party pyramid and the broad
base of the primary party organizations there are two or
three layers of party organizations corresponding to the
respective levels of government administration, i.e.,
region, city, district, and so on. In Bulgaria, for
instance, the order is: primary party organizations,
community, district, city, and okrug (region) party
organizations. In Albania it is primary party organizations, city, district, region; in Romania, primary party
organizations, commune, town, country; in Poland, primary
party organizations, commune, county, province, and so
forth. In all East European countries, the top level of
the party structure comprises the party's leading organs
(Central Committee, Secretariat, Politburo, and the party
congress, which are discussed in separate chapters).

The supreme organ of each intermediate party layer
is the conference (which corresponds to the party congress
on the national level). Each conference is attended by
delegates of the lower level organizations. The conference,
which meets every two years, reviews and approves reports,
debates party activity and elects the party committee
(which manages the corresponding party organization), and
elects delegates to the conference of the appropriate
higher party level, or to the party congress. The
conferences of the intermediate party layers are in fact
sounding boards. One cannot expect an organ that meets
only every other year to manage the affairs of the
respective party organizations. It is the committee
elected by the conference that is responsible for implementing the instructions and directives of the higher
party organs and supervising the activities of the lower
party organs.

The committee of the county (or okrug), the highest
intermediate layer, meets every three months. It is in
constant contact with the party center through its secretary (or first secretary), who usually is a Central

Committee member. The committee of the town or commune
meets every two months. It is the immediate superior of
the primary party organization. Clearly, even an organ
that meets once every two or three months cannot manage
the day-to-day activities of the party organizations.
Routine party affairs at the level of the county, town,
and commune are handled by the bureaus of the party
committees. The bureau itself is managed by an even
smaller organ--the Secretariat, composed of the first
secretary and the other secretaries of the party organization.

To summarize, theoretically the supreme organ of each
intermediate layer is the party conference to which the
lower layers send delegates. The conference elects the
party committee of the respective town, district, or
county, which in turn elects its bureau and the Secretariat,
which manage the activity of the respective party organization.

The committees and their secretaries are responsible
to their particular conference to which they report the
implementation of their tasks. Simultaneously, they
receive their orders and instructions from the level above
and report to its leading organs. There is thus a dual
responsibility or dual subordination: one horizontal, to
the conference of the same level, and the second vertical,
to the higher party organs. This feature is an integral
part of the principle of democratic centralism. The
division of authority at each level (conference, committee,
bureau) serves a single aim: to create the feeling among
the rank-and-file party members that they are involved in
decision making. In fact at each level the real authority
rests with the first secretary and secretaries, who head
the executive organs of the party organization.

In Poland, the relationship among the different
party layers is governed by a statute issued by the 3rd
PZPR Congress in 1959 and amended by subsequent congresses.
This document defines the principle of democratic centralism. The following rules apply to the relationship among
the various levels of the party hierarchy:

- o All party resolutions are passed by a majority
     vote;
- o All directing authorities, from the lowest to
     the highest, are elected in a democratic manner;
- o All party authorities are required to report to
     the party organizations that elected them;
- o Maintenance of party discipline is required and

the minority is subordinate to the resolutions of the majority;
o   Resolutions and directives from higher party
    authorities must be carried out by lower
    ones.[114]

The amendments did not affect these principles.

Although one could summarize the tasks of the various
layers' committees in one sentence--implementing the
instructions and resolutions of the level above--party
statutes in all East European countries assign them a wide
range of tasks. Thus the committees of the regional
(okrug) layer are required to ensure the implementation of
party directives; to facilitate the development of
criticism and self-criticism and the education of communists
in the spirit of an uncompromising attitude toward dis-
orders; to direct the study of Marxism-Leninism by party
members; to organize the communist education of the
workers; to direct and control the work of the district
and city party organizations and approve the secretaries
of the district and city committees; to establish regional
party schools; to appoint the editor-in-chief of the
regional party newspaper, subject to the approval of the
Central Committee; to propose candidates to regional
people's committees and councils (organs of the state
administration); to propose candidates for membership in
the national assembly; to direct the work of the communists
in the regional people's committees and in the regional
organs of the mass organizations; to manage the party's
economic affairs on a regional level (budget, personnel,
funds, etc.); to provide regular information for the
Central Committee by submitting a periodic report on its
activities; and to elect a bureau consisting of nine to
eleven persons, as well as a first secretary and two or
three other secretaries, who must be approved by the
Central Committee.

The district, city, and commune party organizations,
on the other hand, have the primary duty of directing
and controlling the primary organizations and keeping the
members' personal records. They also have the specific
authority to approve or disapprove the primary units'
decisions on admitting new members to the party or expelling members.

During the time they serve as party functionaries,
secretaries and bureau members of the regional, district,
and city committees are released from their regular
employment and work full time as party officials. The

bureau members usually act as heads of the various departments to which the apparat and the work of the intermediate organizations are subdivided, such as agitation and propaganda, industry, agriculture, culture, and so forth. The common denominator of all party committees on all levels below the Central Committee, Politburo, and Secretariat level is that no independent action is permitted. Everything must be approved by the level above. Every activity must be reported and accounted for. Every act must be based on relevant party decisions and instructions, and strict party discipline must govern all aspects of party life.

The activity of the functionaries of the intermediate party layers is constantly scrutinized by the top party organs. After all, the proper functioning of the country's administrative and economic systems depends to a large degree on the performance of the local party organs. The scrutiny and control is sometimes executed by special control organs of the party (discussed separately), and sometimes by the Central Committee or even the Politburo. Thus in July 1978 Janos Brutyo, chairman of the MSZMP Central Control Committee, subjected to critical analysis the conduct of some 700,000 party members.[115] He lashed out with particular vehemence against some leaders' "abuse of authority," which was defined by him as "one of the gravest disciplinary offenses." "It takes different forms," Brutyo pointed out, "but each is rooted in the fact that such leaders forget in whose name they wield power." Then he listed many examples of "abuse of authority":

o Leaders who overrate their authority and jurisdiction, and make their decisions without listening to the advice of others, or without consulting the particular collective entitled to express an opinion;
o Leaders who pay little or no heed to party resolutions and government decrees, and even act contrary to them, in hope that past merits or personal connections will enable them to get away with it;
o Leaders who stifle or punish criticism--the most serious type of "abuse of authority."

It is a measure of the party's concern over the "abuse of authority" that, in the words of Brutyo, "during the two-and-a-half years since the 11th party congress, 102 people have been expelled from the party owing to this grave

violation of communist conduct. This is nearly twice the
number expelled on these grounds in the five years between
the 10th and 11th party congresses."[116]

In Czechoslovakia in 1980, the CPCZ Central Committee
decided to conduct a "comprehensive evaluation of the
nomenclatura cadres of party organs." To quote the
decision:

> Experience of party agencies and organizations
> from all the previously conducted comprehensive
> evaluations in past years confirms the need for
> constantly and comprehensively evaluating the
> preparedness, commitment to work, political
> participation, and especially, the achieved
> results of the cadres' activities. . . .
>   The difficulty and complexity of the manage-
> ment of political and social processes, as well
> as the economic processes related to building
> the developed socialist society, necessarily raises
> the demands for the sophistication and quality of
> cadres in all areas of life.[117]

As a result of this "evaluation," the performance of party
leaders at the intermediate levels was closely scrutinized
and numerous cases of "abuse of authority" were subsequently revealed by the daily press.

The party press of the East European countries constantly and repeatedly stresses that the career of party
functionaries depends on their performance. In the words
of Sandor Jakab, MSZMP Central Committee party and mass
organizations department head: "If a leader is unable to
satisfy the requirements, if he hinders the enforcement of
policy, then he must be removed. We do not believe in
compulsory and systematic rotation because that creates
uncertainty and a feeling of impermanence. There are other
ways of controlling the activity of our leaders in such a
way as to avoid professional blindness and political
errors."[118]

The RCP Central Committee also is permanently preoccupied with the performance of local party cadres. Many
Central Committee plenums (29 March 1977,[119] 26-27 October
1977,[120] 22-23 March 1978,[121] to mention just three) have
dealt with this issue. Criticism is often voiced against
"persisting subjectivism, formalism, and poor political
and ideological training."[122] The 26-27 October 1977
Central Committee plenum decided "to put selection and
promotion of cadres in party, state, and mass organizations

under the direct control of the RCP Central Committee and local party organs,"[123] thus apparently depriving the state apparatus of jurisdiction over them.

The results of the RCP's efforts to closely evaluate the activity of the personnel of the intermediate layers were soon disclosed. On 31 March 1978 Scinteia reported that over 8,000 cadres who met political, professional, and moral prerequisites had been promoted to positions on the "classified list" of party bodies during the previous years.[124] This means, of course, that the people who had held those positions must have been kicked out to make way for others.

In addition to the special decisions, resolutions, inspections, and other acts of control on the part of the communist parties' leading organs, the activity of the intermediate levels' committees is periodically reviewed by the party congresses. The draft theses on the country's socioeconomic and political development, published shortly before each party congress, and the Central Committee report at the congress (which is in fact almost identical to the theses), devote much space to reviewing the activity of the intermediate party organs.

It is not only performance or party resolutions and other documents that determine the career of the party leaders at the intermediate level. The communist system vaguely resembles the political structure of the feudal society. Each member of the Politburo has his "vassals" among the party's lesser leaders at the regional and city levels. These are officials who have been appointed or promoted under his patronage. Consequently, the ups and downs in the career of the patron affect the fate of the "vassal." A typical case was the 1977 ousting of Boris Velchev, until then BCP Central Committee secretary and Politburo member.

Boris Velchev had been a Central Committee secretary since 1959 and Politburo member since 1962. On 12 May 1977 the Bulgarian newspapers reported that he was ousted by a Central Committee plenum "for reasons of expediency," a formula indicating that the reasons for the move were political. The fact that he was also deprived of his Central Committee membership indicated that these political reasons were indeed serious. (The real reasons for the ousting of high party officials are seldom if ever published in Eastern Europe.)

Almost exactly one month after the removal of Valchev, the Yambol Okrug (region) BCP committee held a plenum (10 June 1977), which was attended by Todor Zhivkov

himself. (The attendance of the first party leader
usually indicates that the plenum of the regional committee
is to adopt important personnel decisions, for instance,
the appointment of a new first secretary of the committee
or the ousting of the previous leader.) The Yambol plenum
released Khristo Georgiev, first secretary of the BCP
Yambol Okrug committee, from his post and also removed him
from membership in the okrug's party committee for "gross
violations of party methods and style of work, for
political shortsightedness, for hamstringing the okrug
party organization, and for attempts to introduce a
spirit of dispute within the cadres."[125]

Georgiev was one of the only two okrug party first
secretaries in Bulgaria's twenty-seven okrugs who were
elected at the pre-congress accountability-election meetings in February-March 1976, prior to the 11th BCP
Congress (these meetings are explained in the chapter on
the party congresses), and it was precisely those two
meetings (the other was in Vratsa) that were attended by
Boris Velchev. Various observers linked the ousting of
the Yambol Okrug party organization first secretary with
the ousting of his patron.

Extensive changes in Bulgaria's diplomatic corps
in June-July 1977 were also viewed as an aftermath of
Velchev's ouster.[126] It seemed probable that some of those
who had been released from their ambassadorial posts were
people of his personal choice, who enjoyed his trust. Many
of them were replaced in an unusual hurry--before even the
State Council conferred its formal approval.[127]

When the removal of a regional party committee
secretary is not the result of political mistakes or a
political play in the leadership, the standard formula
explaining the removal is "transfer to another post."
This formula usually indicates failure in fulfilling the
plan. Thus on 25 and 26 February 1980, Todor Zhivkov,
BCP Central Committee first secretary, visited Vidin city.
He was accompanied by Aleksandur Lilov, BCP Central
Committee secretary. Both took part in a plenum of the
okrug party committee, which released the first secretary
of the okrug committee, Lyudmil Pendelashki, because of
"transfer to other work."[128] Krustyu Nikolov, chairman of
the Vidin city People's Council, (the Bulgarian equivalent
of mayor), was also released,[129] something that added to
the impression that the okrug's leaders were being
penalized.

In Poland, where many voivodeship first secretaries
were released during 1980-1981, the formulas used were

"illness,"[130] "resignation" (without any further explanation),[131] "resignation" (accompanied by expression of
gratitude for the past activity),[132] and so forth. And
apropos of Poland, by the end of 1980 intense pressure from
angry and resentful members of the PZPR had forced the
leadership to make far-reaching concessions toward
"democratization" of the party. A December 1980 plenum
of the PZPR Central Committee approved new party election
rules.[133] Some of them were clearly aimed at loosening
control and promoting democratization:

1. Delegates at party meetings could nominate up
   to 50 percent more candidates than the number
   of positions to be filled, instead of only 15
   percent under the previous rules, something
   intended to give the voters greater opportunity
   for choice;
2. Secret balloting was extended to election of
   first secretaries and executive committees;
3. Limits were placed on simultaneously holding
   party and state posts, a measure aimed at
   ending the concentration of power in the hands
   of local or national party bosses.

These rules differed considerably from the Soviet party
election rules on which the original Polish rules were
based.
     Simultaneously, the Polish party published numerous
articles dealing with the issue of democratization in
internal party life. One of them, "Electoral System
as a Mechanism for Turning Over Authority in the Party,"
by Professor Edward Erazmus,[134] examined additional means
of lending an air of democracy to internal party elections,
such as rotation, limiting to two terms the period during
which one could hold a party post, and so forth. Martial
law, which was introduced in December 1981, put an end to
these attempts to refresh the procedures governing internal
party life in Poland.
     One must not forget that the post of first secretary
of a regional party committee can also serve as jumping
board to more responsible posts. After all, many of
the top party leaders in East Europe were themselves at one
time regional first secretaries. As we have seen, plenums
that deal with personnel changes are attended by high
party officials as a rule, and this applies to promotions
as well. Thus in Bulgaria in December 1981, at a plenum of
the okrug party committee, the first secretary of the

Kurdzhali Okrug party committee, Georgi Petrov, was released from his post and "transferred to a responsible
post in the BCP Central Committee."[135] The new post was
not specified, but the indications ("responsible" post and
BCP Central Committee), as well as the presence of Todor
Zhivkov at the plenum, left no doubt that Petrov had been
promoted. Incidentally, the post was given to the hitherto
first secretary of the Komsomol Central Committee, Georgi
Tanev,[136] who at that time was being groomed for even more
responsible posts in the party apparatus.

To sum up, the organizational structure of the East
European communist parties is a strict hierarchy, resembling
a broad-based pyramid, and consisting of primary party
organizations and three layers of local and regional level
party organizations, all of which are subordinate to the
top level of the party hierarchy, namely, the Politburo,
Central Committee, and Secretariat. If this structure is
partially a remnant of the parties' clandestine past
(cells), today the elaborate organization is necessary,
as the party leaders frequently say, so that the implementation of party decisions, policies, and campaigns can be
properly supervised. The entire party organization at all
levels is subjected to strict party control, meaning that
the organs at each level are responsible to the organs of
the level above (and to the conference of its own level,
which convenes every two years). Instructions and
directives pass down the chain from top to bottom;
responsibility flows in the opposite direction. Party
officials at the regional level are often members of
higher party organs (thus regional first secretaries are
usually members of the Central Committees), and their
regional posts can serve both as a jumping board to even
more responsible positions or as a scapegoat position for
weaknesses of the entire party organization.

NOTES

1. AWP Central Committee report to the 8th party
congress, Tirana ATA (Albanian Telegraph Agency) in
English, 1323 GMT, 1 November 1981; Daily Report (FBIS),
2 November 1981.
    2. Rabotnichesko Delo, 20 December 1973.
    3. Ibid., 1 April 1981.
    4. Ibid.
    5. G. Husak, "Confidently and Creatively Along the
Leninist Road," World Marxist Review, June 1976, p. 12.

6.   Nova Mysl (CSSR) nos. 7 and 8, 1978.

7.   Rude Pravo (CSSR), 21 May 1979.

8.   Prague Domestic Service in Czech, 0822 GMT, 6 April 1981; Daily Report (FBIS), 8 April 1981.

9.   Neues Deutschland (GDR), 21 May 1976.

10. Einheit (GDR), vol. 35, no. 10, October 1980, p. 1021.

11. SED Central Committee report to the 10th SED Congress, Neues Deutschland, 12 April 1981; Daily Report (FBIS), 30 April 1981.

12. Einheit, vol. 35, no. 10, October 1980, p. 1021.

13. Ibid.

14. Nepszabadsag (Hungary), 29 November 1966.

15. Nepszabadsag, 23 July 1978 and 25 March 1985.

16. R. Staar, Communist Regimes in Eastern Europe (Stanford, California, 1977), p. 133.

17. Polish Press Agency (PAP) in Russian, 0300 GMT, 14 July 1981; Daily Report (FBIS), 14 July 1981.

18. Radio Warsaw, 12 June 1982, in RFE Situation Report, Poland, 1 July 1982.

19. Ibid.

20. Scinteia (Romania), 7 April 1977.

21. RFE Situation Report, Romania, 11 October 1977.

22. Scinteia, 31 March 1978.

23. Bucharest AGREPRES in English, 1916 GMT, 25 March 1981; Daily Report (FBIS), 26 March 1981.

24. Scinteia, 26 March 1981.

25. Ibid.

26. Bucharest AGERPRES in English, 0910 GMT, 3 April 1982; Daily Report (FBIS), 5 April 1982.

27. Ibid.

28. Borba (SFRY), 19 October 1979.

29. Komunist (SFRY), 5 February 1982, p. 12.

30. Ibid., p. 12.

31. Borba, 24 July 1979.

32. Ibid., 19 October 1979.

33. Ibid., 14 June 1980.

34. Komunist, 30 May 1980.

35. Borba, 29 June 1981.

36. Politika (SFRY), 16 June 1981.

37. Belgrade TANJUG in English, 0900 GMT, 16 June 1982; Daily Report (FBIS), 17 June 1982.

38. Romania Libera (Romania), 7 January 1981, pp. 1, 3.

39. Scinteia, 24 March 1978.

40. Bucharest AGERPRES in English, 1916 GMT, 25 March 1981; Daily Report (FBIS), 26 March 1981.

41. Zeri I Popullit, 18 September 1980; FBIS East

Europe Report, no. 1830, 28 November 1980.

42. Ibid.

43. Bucharest AGERPRES in English, 0910 GMT, 3 April 1982; Daily Report (FBIS), 5 April 1982.

44. Zycie Partii (Poland), no. 2, 1981, pp. 2-3.

45. Statute of the Polish United Workers Party, FBIS East Europe Report, no. 1899, 17 July 1981, p. 22.

46. V. Lenin, "Theses on the Tasks of the Second Comintern Congress," Werke, vol. 31 (Berlin, 1956), p. 235.

47. A. Schoenberg, "Party Experience," Neuer Weg (GDR), vol. 37, no. 5, 1982, pp. 181-183.

48. Heinz Puder, "Basic Organizations--Foundations of the Party," Einheit, vol. 35, no. 9, September 1980, pp. 963-967.

49. I. Moga, "The Bureau of the Base Organization--A Collective Organ," Munca de Partid (Romania), August 1981, p. 79.

50. Partien Zhivot (Bulgaria), no. 8, 1977.

51. Ibid.

52. For example, PZPR Statutes, Chapter III, Article 3, Lodz 1973, p. 7.

53. Ibid.

54. Komunist, 15 July 1965, paragraph I of the party statute, in Osmi Kongress SKJ, Belgrade, 1964.

55. Military Balance 1978, Institute of Strategic Studies, London.

56. Narodna Armija (SFRY), 31 August 1978.

57. Narodna Armiya (Bulgaria), 28 May 1981.

58. Review of International Affairs (SFRY), nos. 656 and 657, 5 August and 20 August 1977.

59. PAP in Russian, 0300 GMT, 14 July 1981; Daily Report (FBIS), 14 July 1981.

60. Scinteia, 7 April 1977.

61. Ibid.

62. Ibid.

63. Ibid., 23 September 1977; RFE Situation Report, Romania, 11 October 1977.

64. Scinteia, 27 and 28 October 1977.

65. Ibid., 24 March 1978.

66. Ibid.

67. Ibid.

68. Ibid.

69. Ibid.

70. Ibid.

71. Scinteia, 28 March 1981.

72. Ibid.

73. AGERPRES in English, 1916 GMT, 25 March 1981;

Daily Report (FBIS), 26 March 1981.
74. Ibid.
75. Bucharest AGERPRES in English, 0910 GMT,
3 April 1982; Daily Report (FBIS), 5 April 1982.
76. Rude Pravo, 8 January 1981.
77. Ibid.
78. Horst Dolhus: "An Important Phase in the Development of Our Fighting Alliance--On the 11th Central Committee
Plenum Resolution on the Control of Party Documents,"
Neuer Weg, vol. 35, no. 3, pp. 93-97.
79. Ibid.
80. Ibid.
81. Rude Pravo, 8 January 1981.
82. Ibid., 6 December 1978.
83. Ibid.
84. Radio Prague, 14 December 1970, RFE Situation
Report, CSSR, 14 December 1978.
85. Rude Pravo, 19 July, 14 August, 10 September,
20 September, 11 October, 5 November, and 28 November 1979.
86. Ibid., 19 July 1981.
87. Ibid., 10 September 1979.
88. Pravda (CSSR), 4 January 1980.
89. Zivot Strany (CSSR), no. 3, 1980, p. 7.
90. Scinteia, 24 March 1978.
91. Ibid., 30 March 1979.
92. Ibid., 24 December 1955.
93. Ibid., 2 February 1980.
94. Munca de Partid, November 1980, p. 10.
95. Ibid., p. 19.
96. Ibid., p. 29.
97. Ibid., January 1981, p. 19.
98. Ibid.
99. Bucharest AGERPRES in English, 1954 GMT, 25 March
1981; Daily Report (FBIS), 26 March 1981.
100. Bucharest AGERPRES in English, 1845 GMT, 31 March
1981; Daily Report (FBIS), 2 April 1981.
101. Rabotnichesko Delo, 20 December 1977.
102. RFE Situation Report, Bulgaria, 27 January 1978.
103. Rabotnichesko Delo, 9 January 1978.
104. Ibid.
105. Pravda (Moscow), 3 February 1981.
106. Ibid.
107. Ibid.
108. Partelet (Hungary), November 1975, in RFE
Situation Report, Hungary, 28 June 1977.
109. Nepszabadsag, 24 October 1975.
110. Ibid., 18 March 1975.

111. Ibid., 24 March 1975.

112. Ibid., 24 June 1977.

113. Ibid., 23 July 1978.

114. PZPR III Zjazd, Warsaw, 1959, pp. 1213-1237.

115. Nepszabadsag, 23 July 1978.

116. Ibid.

117. Rovnost (CSSR), 19 August 1980.

118. Sandor Jakab, MSZMP Central Committees party and mass organization department head, in Beke es Szocialismus, July 1978; RFE Situation Report, Hungary, 12 August 1975.

119. Scinteia, 7 April 1977.

120. Ibid., 27-28 October 1978.

121. Ibid., 24 March 1978.

122. Ibid., 7 April 1977.

123. Ibid., 28 October 1977.

124. Ibid., 31 March 1978.

125. RFE Situation Report, Bulgaria, 15 June 1977.

126. RFE Situation Report, Bulgaria, 9 September 1977.

127. Ibid.

128. Cherveno Zname (Vidin, Bulgaria), 28 February 1980.

129. Ibid., 4 March 1980.

130. Warsaw Domestic Service in Polish, 0400 GMT, 14 October 1980; Daily Report (FBIS), 14 October 1980.

131. Bydgoszcz Domestic Service in Polish, 1600 GMT, 13 October 1980; Daily Report (FBIS), 14 October 1980.

132. Warsaw Domestic Service in Polish, 2000 GMT, 11 October 1980; Daily Report (FBIS), 14 October 1980.

133. Zicie Partii, no. 2, 1981, pp. 1-3.

134. Ibid., no. 3, 1981, pp. 5-7.

135. Rabotnichesko Delo, 15 December 1981.

136. Ibid.

5
Top of the Pyramid:
Central Committee, Politburo,
Secretariat, Control Commission

According to the statutes of all East European
communist parties, the party congress is the supreme organ
of the party. In reality, of course, nobody expects this
huge, pompous, and mostly demonstrative meeting, which
usually takes place every four or five years, to direct
daily party life. Nevertheless, the congress has one
important function, namely, to elect the party's top
organs--the Central Committee (which in turn elects the
Politburo and the Secretariat) and the Central Control
Commission. In addition, the congress delegates to the
Central Committee the authority to act as the supreme
party organ during the period between congresses. The
Central Control Commission (which appears under slightly
different names in the various East European communist
parties and will be discussed later in this chapter) also
has an important role, albeit in a circumscribed field,
mostly watching over the unity of the party and the
political and moral conduct of the party members.

THE CENTRAL COMMITTEE

The party statutes of the East European communist
parties describe the functions of their Central Committees
in identical terms: the Central Committee represents the
party externally, i.e., vis-à-vis other communist parties,
establishes party institutions and directs their activity,
nominates the editorial boards of central party newspapers,
controls the performance of the party cadres, administers
funds, controls the performance of the state organs,
approves the state plan and budget prior to the debates of
the national assemblies, and approves the appointments of

persons to top party and state positions. Even this list
is incomplete, as an example document on Central Committee
functions will show. On 13 November 1980 the MSZMP Central
Committee adopted a resolution setting out the role and
functions of the Central Committee.[1] This resolution in
fact completely summarized the tasks and functions of all
the East European Central Committees. The document is
reprinted here in its entirety.

"It is an important lesson of our party's more than
six decade-long struggle that its elected bodies--first of
all the Central Committee--are indispensable for fulfilling
its historic mission and maintaining its leading role.
For this reason, the Central Committee periodically examines
its own activity and coordinates it with the requirements
of current tasks facing the party. Most recently, it made
an extensive resolution in 1968 to improve its working
methods. In connection with goals defined at the party's
12th Congress, the Central Committee found it necessary to
evaluate the working methods of its own executive organs:
the Political Committee [Politburo] and the Secretariat.
"The Central Committee establishes:
"The MSZMP sets its policies according to the
principles of Marxism-Leninism, and the Leninist norms are
consistently implemented in the party's life and activity.
Elected bodies make decisions at all levels; the Central
Committee determines the tasks through longer-term and
principled resolutions; the mid-level and lower-level party
organs and the party's branch organizations carry out their
tasks with a great degree of independence and authority.
"Through ideological and political leadership, the
party makes certain that the principles and goals of
socialism are implemented in our society. Respecting the
independence of state and social organizations, it
implements its policies and resolutions through Communists
who work there.
"Following the directives of the party congress, the
Central Committee continuously defines the tasks matured by
social progress, eliminates the contradictions and
coordinates the interests of the working classes and
strata; it mobilizes and organizes society's creative
forces for the most important tasks in building socialism.
"I.
"The Central Committee endorses the present practice
of the party's high-level executive bodies, which distills
and expresses the party's many decades of experience in
principles and politics.

111

"1.   According to the organizational by-laws, the
Central Committee is, between two congresses, the party's
primary body of political control, and its rights, duties
and responsibilities are established accordingly. Its
fundamental task is to implement, through ideological and
political means, the line adopted at the party congress.
It manages and controls all party organs and organizations,
and represents the party in various state and social
organizations, and in international relations. In its
leadership and control, it deals with the tasks in the
various areas of social life according to their importance.
It decides on all fundamental questions of party policy,
and on personal matters within its jurisdiction.
"2.   The Central Committee is the party's collective
guiding organ, and the main guardian of party unity and
discipline. In its activities, it implements the principle
of democratic centralism. It makes decisions collectively,
and makes personal responsibility a part of the execution.
In decision making, it considers the interests of the
people, weighs the expected social and political effects
of its decisions, and determines the political and organizational tasks of the party organizations accordingly.
It considers in its decisions the various interests that
exist in society. There is opportunity at the meetings of
the Central Committee for democratic and creative discussion and for airing various views. Free discussions,
criticism, and self-criticism guard the party against
mistakes; they are indispensible requisites for correct
decisions, exact implementation, and party unity. The
democracy within the party has a decisive effect on the
essential features of our system, i.e., socialist democracy.
"3.   The Central Committee adopts a five-year plan in
which the resolutions of the congress are to be implemented
and which determines the main aspects of the activity of
the central party organs. It works on the basis of annual
work plans recommended by the Political Committee. The
tasks included in these plans determine the main direction
and more important areas in the work of the Politburo,
the Secretariat, and the mid- and lower-level party organs,
during the relevant year.
"4.   The Politburo and the Secretariat are the
executive organs of the Central Committee. Their activity
is managed and controlled by the Central Committee.
"The Politburo controls the party's political activity
between two Central Committee meetings. It decides
questions within its jurisdiction and directs the party's
international activity. It is responsible to the Central

Committee for its decisions and work. It prepares the
Central Committee meetings and recommends the agenda.

"The Secretariat decides personnel and organizational
questions under its jurisdiction; matters requiring
political decisions are submitted to the Politburo. It
organizes, coordinates, and supervises the implementation
of resolutions made by the elected central bodies. It
directs the apparatus of the Central Committee so that it
can fulfill its basic tasks in preparing decisions and in
organizing and supervising their implementation. It
coordinates the activity of the Central Committee and
the regional party organs.

"The Politburo reports to the Central Committee about
its own activity, including its international activity,
in the form of agenda items, reports, and proposals.
The Politburo and the Secretariat regularly inform the
Central Committee members in writing about their activity.

"5. The Agitation and Propaganda Committee and the
Committee on Economic Policy, elected by the Central
Committee, help the party's leading organs by discussing,
and taking a stand on, ideological and practical questions
under their jurisdiction. They do preparatory work for the
Politburo and evaluate individual proposals and performance.

"6. The Central Committee also sends out special
committees, made up of its own members, to examine individual questions, to work out proposals, and to supervise
the implementation of resolutions. Depending on the kind
of questions, the committees may also submit their proposals
directly to the Central Committee. According to necessity,
they also involve in their work a large circle of special-
ists in a given area, including nonparty members.

"7. The Central Committee is responsible for implementing the principles of cadre policies. It decides on
cadre questions that come under its jurisdiction. The
Politburo has preliminary consultations with members of
the Central Committee, who work in the relevant area.

"8. The two leading organs, i.e., the Central
Committee and the Central Control Committee, are
coordinated. The Central Committee, when necessary,
initiates meetings with the Central Control Committee.
The chairman and secretary of the Central Control
Committee participate as permanent observers in all
Central Committee meetings.

"The Central Committee invites to its expanded meetings leading officers of party, state, and social bodies,
including nonparty members, all of whom have the right to
participate in the discussion.

"9. The Central Committee informs the party membership, the directing bodies of state and social groups, and
the public about its meetings. It issues communiques
about its meetings, summarizing speeches, discussions,
and the essence of the resolutions. These communiques
must be considered official party documents. To inform
the public, the Central Committee issues, as necessary, its
resolutions and speeches in a suitable form.
"II.
"The term of the Central Committee members is the
period between two congresses. They have equal rights and
responsibilities.
"1. Central Committee members are not and cannot be
personally dependent on the party's executive organs. For
this reason, the Central Committee reserves the right to
decide on personnel changes and make other decisions, which
might affect the posts of the members. In especially
urgent cases--if the member involved accepts the proposal--
the Politburo may also decide, but the decision must be
submitted to the Central Committee for subsequent approval.
"2. Central Committee members participate in the
resolutions, in meetings, in decision making, in the party's
everyday activity, and in the work of their own local
organizations. They have the right to voice their opinion
in Central Committee meetings also on matters that are not
included in the agenda; they may also request that important
issues be put on the agenda. Central Committee members are
personally responsible for their work in the committee and
for the decisions made there. Even outside meetings, they
are required to represent the views of the Central
Committee and are responsible for party unity and discipline.
"3. Central Committee members may submit comments
and proposals directly to the Politburo and the Secretariat.
They may turn with their questions and comments to any
party, state, and social organ, which in turn is required
to respond and, if necessary, to act.
"4. It is the right of the Central Committee members
to look into the activity of the Central Committee's
departments, to gain direct experience in the activity of
regional party organs and organizations, and to participate
in their meetings. They have the opportunity, by special
authority as temporary or permanent associates, to
participate in the work of a Central Committee department.
"5. Central Committee members are informed about the
more important items discussed in the meetings of the
Politburo and the Secretariat. They may look into proposals, resolutions, and documents dealt with by executive

organs and committees and that assist them in their work. They regularly receive the documents and informative material concerning domestic and foreign affairs and party events, and a list of the main topics that are put in the given time period on the agenda of the party committees of Budapest, the counties and so forth.
"III.
"The Central Committee's working method, in accordance with the respective 1968 resolution, has progressed in the right direction. Further strengthening the party's leading role, more coordinated cooperation between party, state, and social organs, and the tasks we face that pose higher requirements, demand, first of all, that the Central Committee continue with its proven methods and improve its guiding and controlling activity.
"1. In accordance with the needs of socialist progress, and in addition to economic development and foreign policy, the Central Committee must pay more attention in the future to domestic affairs and ideological questions.
"2. To better prepare decisions, the Central Committee should discuss important questions more often during preparation. Proposals should include, when possible, alternate solutions. When differences of opinion arise in the evaluation of the essence of a given problem, they also must be made known.
"3. The Communist leaders of state, social, and mass organizations should report on their work to the Central Committee and should present individual matters of the agenda, depending on the topic under discussion.
"4. Central Committee members should be more involved in the preparation of personnel decisions.
"5. The participation of the Central Committee members in public life, i.e., in domestic and international affairs, in party programs, in party meetings, and in membership meetings must be better organized.
"6. Central Committee members should receive, as information, the work plan of committees that work alongside the Central Committee. They should be invited, according to need, or at their request, to the meetings of these committees and panels.
"7. By 1 November, the members of the Central Committee submit for the annual work plan of the party organs their proposals on questions they consider important. The Politburo should evaluate these proposals and make a report to the Central Committee about their adoption.
"8. At the middle of the period between two congresses, the Central Committee should regularly examine the

implementation of congress resolutions."

The conclusion is obvious: there is absolutely
nothing that does not fall within the Central Committee's
capacity and authority. Officially it acts as the country's supreme decision maker, legislator, and even court.
In reality, however, the Central Committee is not that
active. There are two basic reasons: its size and the
infrequency of its plenums.

The East European communist parties' Central Committees
are large and cumbersome organs. The AWP Central Committee
has 81 full members and 40 candidate-members[2]; the MSZMP
Central Committee, 127 members[3]; the RCP Central Committee,
245 full members and 163 candidate-members[4]; the PZPR
Central Committee, 200 full members and 70 candidate-
members[5]; the BCP Central Committee, 192 full members and
139 candidate-members[6]; the LCY Central Committee, 165
members.[7] On 16 March 1982 the LCY Central Committee
adopted a decision reducing future Central Committee membership from 165 to 157 members, although in practice the
membership remained 165 because according to the decision,
the presidents of the eight republican and provincial
Central Committees became ex officio members of the LCY
Central Committee.[8] The CPCZ Central Committee has 123
full members and 55 candidate-members,[9] and the SED Central
Committee 156 full members and 57 candidate-members.[10]

One does not expect organs of this size to act
quickly and make routine decisions related to standard
everyday matters. Furthermore, one does not expect such
an organ, which holds three or four regular plenums (or
sessions) a year, each lasting for a day or two, actually
to manage and direct the country's political life. For all
practical purposes, therefore, the East European Central
Committees vaguely resemble these countries' national
assemblies although they are much more authoritative and
involved in important decisions; they serve as their own
kind of "parliament," while the Politburo (or Presidium)
and the Secretariat (both described later in this chapter)
are the real decision makers and executives.

The East European Central Committees resemble the
parliaments in yet another way. Each has twenty to thirty
departments, which cover (roughly) the areas of concern
covered by the committees of every normal parliament:
foreign relations, foreign trade, social services, transportation, industry, culture, sports, education, science,
mass media, and so forth. However, some of the Central
Committee departments are secret, and their real functions,

and sometimes even their names, have not been revealed.
Other departments demonstrate the special nature of the
East European political system: agitation and propaganda
(all East European Central Committees), party political
education (all), political organization department (CPCZ),
Western Affairs (SED), Cadres Abroad (BCP), etc.

Security engulfs the work of the Central Committee
to a large extent, and even organizational changes are not
regularly reported by the newspapers. Thus in 1980
occasional references in the Bulgarian press revealed (or
rather implied) that several BCP Central Committee departments had been reorganized in late 1979 or early 1980.
Rabotnichesko Delo on 5 February 1980 mentioned en passant
for the first time a Military-Administrative Department of
the Central Committee, which had been formed by merging the
former Military Department and the Administrative Department, which had existed since 1965. Col. Gen. Velko Palin
was mentioned as head of the new department.[11] A Mass-
Information Media Department, which had been set up in 1974
and which quietly disappeared at the beginning of 1977,
was again established.[12] Lalyu Dimitrov, former editor-in-
chief of the daily Otechestven Front, was named head of
this department.[13]

The same source also mentioned a new Transportation
and Communication Department, headed by Atanas Popov.[14]
Later references in the press[15] revealed that the former
Organizational Department had been divided into the Organi-
zational Department and the People's Councils and Mass
Organizations Department, and that the former Cadres, Party
Organizations, and Business Trips Department, had changed
its name (and probably functions) to Cadres Abroad
Department.[16]

It must be stressed once again that these changes were
not officially reported anywhere. It was not said when
the changes took place, what prompted them, how the
decision was adopted, or what the entire procedure was.
The fact that the changes did take place was gleaned from
occasional references in the newspapers.

Since secrecy is a sine qua non, the activity of the
East European Central Committees (let alone their minutes,
protocols, debates, etc.) is largely obscure. Nevertheless,
from time to time references in the East European media (in
addition to standard and laconic communiques) throw some
light on the activity of the Central Committees.

There are two kinds of Central Committee plenums:
regular and extraordinary. There are also two kinds of
regular plenums: some are attended only by Central

Committee members, while others are also attended by other
figures (state officials, economic figures, leaders of
mass organizations, media representatives, local party
leaders, and so on), according to the topic of the plenum.
Such meetings are called "expanded" or "enlarged" plenums
and seem to be held when matters of general importance,
not directly related to party affairs, are being discussed.
Many of the Central Committee routine plenums are "expanded." They usually deal with economic matters and
follow the same pattern: a report on the relevant economic
matter by the Central Committee secretary responsible for
the economy, a briefing on topical international developments, usually given by the Central Committee secretary
responsible for foreign policy or for relations with
"fraternal" and other parties, discussion of the matter
(seldom if ever published), and a resolution. Occasionally,
the number of "guests" at expanded plenums surpasses the
number of regular Central Committee members. Thus on
1 June 1982 the RCP Central Committee held an "expanded"
plenum dealing with the "current stage of building socialism
in Romania" and various ideological and educational matters.
It was attended by 360 guests--"cadres which are carrying
out their activity in party organizations and bodies, in
mass and civic bodies and the economy, and, in the field of
educational-political and cultural work, in scientific
research, education, press and radio-television."[17]

When party affairs are concerned, or "organizational
matters" discussed (usually meaning personnel changes in
the top party and state organs, including the Central
Committee itself), there are no outsiders, and the announcements published after such plenums are brief and laconic.
This is not unusual. Even after more or less routine
plenums the communiques (if any) are short and dry, as the
following, typical example of a communique on a regular SED
Central Committee plenum illustrates:

> The SED Central Committee met for its 13th session
> in Berlin on 11 and 12 December 1980.
> The Politburo report was presented by Guenter
> Mittag, member of the Politburo and secretary of
> the Central Committee. Gerhard Schuerer, candidate-
> member of the Politburo and chairman of the State
> Planning Commission, moved the draft of the 1981
> economic plan.
> Fifteen comrades spoke during the discussion.
> The Central Committee endorsed the Politburo
> report and the speeches on moving the 1981 economic

plan. It gave its consent to the bills on the
1981 economic plan and the 1981 budget.[18]

Sometimes an extraordinary plenum may also be an
"expanded" one. This does not mean that more information
is available. On the contrary, sometimes even the fact that
such a plenum took place is not published, or at least is
published only much later.

An "important Central Committee plenum"[19] was reported
to have taken place in Bulgaria on 1 and 2 July 1976. The
plenum was reported only after it had ended, and even then
the report said only that it dealt with "measures to ensure
the consistent and all-round implementation of the decisions
of the 11th BCP Congress."[20] An indication of the importance of the plenum was given by the fact that Todor
Zhivkov "read a detailed report" and had a concluding
speech. (Their contents were never published.) Some
twenty persons were listed as having taken the floor, and
the brief announcement ended by saying that "the plenum
unanimously adopted an appropriate resolution."

The unusual format of the announcement (bearing in
mind that this was an expanded plenum), indicated that
harsh criticism of serious shortcomings may possibly have
been made at the plenum, or that some unpopular measures
had been adopted. However, despite frequent references in
the Bulgarian press to the importance of the BCP Central
Committee July 1976 plenum, its actual topic, let alone
speeches and debates, has never been published.

After certain other Central Committee plenums long
and detailed communiques are issued. As a rule, this is
only the case after a routine plenum, when nothing unusual
has happened. The adoption of the national plan and budget
by the Central Committee usually is an appropriate occasion
for a detailed communique. Such was the communique published after the 3 December 1981 MSZMP Central Committee
plenum.[21] It listed the participants: "In addition to the
members of the Central Committee the plenum was also
attended by the heads of the departments of the Central
Committee, the first secretaries of the county party
committees, the secretaries of the Budapest party committee,
the chairman of the Central Control Committee, the members
of the Council of Ministers, the chairman of the National
Material and Price Control Board, the chairman of the
Central Statistics Office, the chairman of the State Office
on Wages and Labor, and the heads of the central press."
The communique then announced the topics dealt with: "The
Central Committee discussed and approved: a report submitted

by Comrade Andreas Gyenes, secretary of the Central
Committee, on topical international issues; and a proposal
submitted by Comrade Ferenc Havasi, member of the Politburo
and secretary of the Central Committee, on guiding principles for the 1982 plan and state budget."[22] The
communique then went on to express the well known stand
of the MSZMP on all topical international issues, as well
as the principle points of the plan and the budget. A
similar communique of the LCY Central Committee on its
4 December 1980 plenum,[23] which also dealt with the state
plan and budget, reads like a copy of the corresponding
MSZMP Central Committee communique.

Sometimes, when the occasion requires, even if an
extraordinary plenum is involved, its decisions are published in their entire length. Such was the case with the
RCP Central Committee plenum of 9 February 1982, which
adopted a resolution of "Resetting of Prices and Augmentation of Remuneration of Working Personnel."[24] The plenum
drastically increased the price of basic foodstuffs in
Romania, and the subsequent resolution was needed not only
to announce the "resetting" of prices but also to justify
the new measure.

It is interesting to note that in some cases the
population is called upon to implement decisions taken by
the Central Committee that have never been published in
full. Such was the case with the already described BCP
Central Committee July 1976 plenum. Several weeks after
the initial (post-plenum) announcement, references started
appearing in Rabotnichesko Delo (the party daily) of the
"extreme importance" of the plenum. An editorial published
about three weeks after the plenum read: "The July plenum
is one of those party forums which, because of the con-
fluence of certain circumstances, transcend the normal
functions of party congresses and plenums--analyzing and
elaborating on party's tasks for a given period. . . .
These forums enrich and develop the very general line of
the party."[25] Although the newspaper stressed that only
party members were to be "acquainted" with Zhivkov's report
at the plenum and the subsequent decisions, it also indicated that "the entire population is called upon to fulfill
the 'program' contained in the report."[26]

The case of the BCP Central Committee April 1956
plenum is even more extreme. This was the plenum that
"unmasked" the personality cult of Vulko Chervenkov. It
launched the "BCP April line," which is constantly referred
to and praised by all important party documents, decisions,
and speeches as marking the beginning of a new era. Yet

the "historic plenum's" decisions and minutes have never
been reported. After the 12th BCP Congress, in April 1981,
it was announced that Zhivkov's speech at the April 1956
Central Committee plenum would be published. So far, its
contents—more than twenty-six years after the plenum and
more than two years after the death of Vulko Chervenkov,
and many years after the death or removal of most of the
participants in this plenum—are still too sensitive to be
published. This omission does not prevent the party from
constantly referring to the plenum as the "beginning of a
new era."

On some occasions, the Central Committee serves as an
authoritative and appropriate body for expressing the party
stand on a sensitive issue. Such was the 25 March 1981
plenum of the RCP Central Committee, which dealt with international issues and reviewed the party's and state's international policy. A rather long resolution published
after the plenum[27] surveyed the various topical international issues and elaborated the RCP stand. It also
stressed two points on which Romania differs from the other
East European countries—the position on Poland and Romania's
postulates on independence: "The highly-principled stand of
the RCP was approved in respect to the situation in Poland,
and solid support was expressed for surmounting the difficulties encountered by the communists, the working class,
and the Polish people itself, without any outside interference. . . . Romania firmly declares for the observance
of people's freedom and independence, of each nation's
sacred right to develop self-reliantly on the road of progress
and civilization, without any outside interference."[28] The
repeated reference to refraining from outside interference,
coming from the highest party forum between congresses,
acquired a special resonance.

Occasionally, a Central Committee plenum has apparent
propaganda purposes. Such are the plenums dealing
primarily with foreign affairs, whose main (if not sole)
purpose is to express adherence to the principles (or
recent proposals and initiatives) of Soviet foreign policy.
The 21 April 1982 plenum of the CPCZ Central Committee had
such character. The main speaker was Vasil Bilak, Presidium
(Politburo) member and Central Committee secretary. He surveyed the international situation and reinterated the well
known Soviet position on each issue, accusing the United
States of imperialism and "anti-Sovietism," "striving to
eliminate the policy of détente," "refusing to reconcile
itself to the fact that it (United States) has lost its
dominating position in world policy and economy," "striving

to change the postwar arrangement of the world," "intensifying the arms race," "trying to weaken the socialist
community," "striving to disrupt the Polish leadership's
endeavor to consolidate the situation in the country," and
so forth.[29] At the same time, total support was expressed
for all Soviet "peace initiatives," stressing that "The
Soviet peace initiatives aim at averting the danger of a
world nuclear war . . . and also correspond to the vital
interests and peace wishes of the Czechoslovak people."[30]
Needless to say, on such occasions all speeches and
resolutions are immediately and frequently referred to by
the media.

During 1980-1982 the plenums of the PZPR and LCY
Central Committees were an exception to the pattern in the
rest of the East European political system. In Poland it
was a result of the activity of the Solidarity trade union
and the subsequent "renewal" of party life, while in
Yugoslavia, the Central Committee tried to cope in various
ways with the situation that emerged after the death of Tito.

In Poland, the Central Committee plenums were stripped
of all secrecy. Not only were the agenda of these plenums
(often very sensitive) published in full and all speeches
and debates reported, but on several occasions, the plenums
were carried live by Warsaw Radio, and some portions even
by state television. Such was the case with the 11th PZPR
Central Committee plenum, which took place on 9-10 June
1981, and which dealt with the preparations for the Extraordinary 9th PZPR Congress. Party leader Kania's opening
remarks were televised,[31] his speech on the preparations
for the Extraordinary 9th Congress carried live by Radio
Warsaw,[32] and the subsequent debates, some of which included rather critical remarks and observations, as well as
overt opposition to the entire party leadership, were also
reported. For example, "Jerzy Putrament [speaker]: In
the Political Bureau there is no connection between
decisions and their being transformed into concrete
political action. At least a partial change of the
Political Bureau is necessary."[33] Or, "Janusz Prokopiak
[speaker]: . . . a secret ballot should express the attitude
toward the entire leadership."[34]

On other occasions the Central Committee plenum was
utilized to admit mistakes committed by the leadership.
Thus at the 5 September 1980 plenum of the PZPR Central
Committee, Kania (whose speech was read by an announcer on
radio and television), pledged himself unequivocally to a
faithful implementation of the agreements with the strikers.
He also went out of his way to endorse the legitimacy of

the strikers' grievances, bluntly accepting the regime's
responsibility for "distortions and mistakes" in social and
economic policy. On the trade union issue, he promised
both a "renewal" of the existing trade union system and an
acceptance of the "new trade unions," specifying that he
would hold the workers to their promise that the new
organization would be loyal to socialism and the party.[35]

Many Central Committee plenums in Poland--which held
many more than the usual three or four plenums per year--
dealt with personnel matters (expelling former party leader
Gierek and former Premier Jaroszewicz at the 2 October 1980
plenum and adding a large number of new members to the
Central Committee; rejecting the proffered resignation of
Politburo members Olszowski, Grabski, and Ney at the 29-30
March 1981 plenum, and so forth), sensitive organizational
matters (accepting the major democratic reforms demanded by
the party rank and file at the 29-30 April 1981 Central
Committee plenum), the ouster of Kania himself at the 17-18
October 1981 plenum, and so forth. There was no secrecy.
Speeches, debates, decisions, and results were closely
followed and discussed by the entire nation. The intro-
duction of martial law in Poland on 13 December 1981 put
an end to this situation, which was not normal for the East
European political system and was regarded by the other
East European countries as an aberration.

The death of Tito on 4 May 1980 created a serious
vacuum at the top of the LCY. Because there obviously
was nobody capable of stepping into Tito's shoes, the LCY
Central Committee had to deal with many organizational
matters: i.e., deciding at the June 1980 Central Committee
plenum that there would not be an LCY president for "the
next two years," but that the former chairman of the Central
Committee Presidium, who acted as deputy party president in
Tito's lifetime, would be president of the Central
Committee Presidium for a one-year period[36]; establishing
an elaborate rotation system[37] that covered all leading
posts in the party and state hierarchy; proposing and
adopting various changes in the LCY statute[38]; reducing
the Central Committee membership[39]; and preparing the
documents (resolution, etc.) of the 12th LCY Congress.[40]
All in all, the LCY Central Committee had twenty-eight
plenums between the 11th and 12th LCY Congresses, an
average of six or seven a year, more than the usual average
of other East European countries. In addition, most of the
speeches and discussions were also extensively reported by
the Yugoslav press. However, it has to be stressed that
this situation was a result of Tito's death and the delicate

federative balance of Yugoslavia, which necessitated both profound organizational changes in the LCY structure and the introduction of the rotation principle for all top positions in the party and the country. Consequently, this situation created in Yugoslavia too the need for more Central Committee plenums and more extensive reports on their debates and results.

Two final observations about the nature of the Central Committee plenums in Eastern Europe may be made. First of all, one immediately notices that "topical international issues" are discussed at almost every Central Committee plenum. The main reason is the need to constantly and officially adhere to Soviet foreign policy and express authoritative support for the various Soviet initiatives in the international arena.

The second observation concerns the nature of the Central Committee activity. It has been pointed out that the Central Committees of the East European communist parties hold about four plenums a year. This does not mean that the Central Committee--as an organ--does not function all the time. The members and the candidate-members of the Central Committee are only a part of the apparatus of this organ. Even when there is no plenum, the various departments and sessions of the Central Committee function continuously. Foreign delegations are hosted; local delegations are sent to foreign countries; regulations, instructions, and orders are issued; and continuous control is exercised. In short, the party apparatus functions constantly, without dependence on the Central Committee plenums.

Who are the Central Committee members and how are they elected? Let us begin with the second question. The Central Committee members and candidate-members are elected --in toto--by the party congress at a closed session on its last day. There is no information available as to the procedure followed during the closed session. (The special case of the Extraordinary 9th PZPR Congress will be described in this chapter.) The chairman of the final session of the congress (which usually follows the closed session at which the Central Committee is elected) simply reads out the names of the Central Committee members, adding the inevitable phrase "unanimously elected." Because the "closed" session is usually a short one (it lasted for only one hour at the 1981 BCP, SED, CPCZ, and AWP congresses), it can be safely assumed that debates and real discussion hardly form a part of selection to the Central Committee. Some of the criteria involved in selecting the Central

Committee members were revealed by Albanian party leader
Enver Hoxha at the 6 November 1981 session of the 8th AWP
Congress. Presenting the list of the new Central Committee
members and candidate members and asking the Congress'
delegates to approve the list, Enver Hoxha said:

> It is now up to the congress to discuss and approve
> this list. Some of the criteria used in preparing
> the list are well known by the party. We have
> tried to implement these norms and criteria to the
> best of our ability in order to select the most
> distinguished party members, primarily for their
> loyalty to the party, Marxism-Leninism, the people,
> and the construction of socialism in Albania,
> qualities which have characterized the party
> leadership elected by the 7th AWP Congress. This
> is the main criterion that has guided the repre-
> sentation in carrying out this duty.
>
> Another criterion that we have borne in mind
> was the selection of capable candidates, that our
> Marxist-Leninist party may always remain mature
> in its thinking, clear and fully capable of leading
> the struggle and our socialist revolution. As
> always we have tried to carry out a sound Marxist-
> Leninist combination between experienced communists
> and young comrades of both sexes. The party
> interests require that new blood should be brought
> into the leadership. The new candidates are not of
> the same age as the older cadres, but we have kept
> in mind that bright men and women should be brought
> into the leadership, young men and women who are
> not only politically and ideologically sound, but
> also capable in the work and struggle to implement
> the party's line; young men and women who have
> shown their maturity in carrying out the important
> functions entrusted to them.
>
> Among a large number of communists, we have
> tried to select the best among those who have
> distinguished themselves and whom we know through
> letters and documents, as well as through the
> contacts we have had with the majority of them.
> I can say without exaggeration that the party has
> educated and trained a large number of able
> communist cadres. This is also proven by the
> fact that the party put at our disposal about
> 2,000 candidates, but we have selected the best
> party members. And, as we shall all see, we

believe that those we are putting forward are
such members . . . [words indistinct] every
congress delegate has the full right to remark
on who should remain on the list, among those
that have been proposed, and who should be
dropped, as well as proposing someone else in
his place."[41]

First of all, it should be pointed out that no delegate at the congress made use of his "full right to remark
on who should remain on the list." As usual at all party
congresses, the new Central Committee was unanimously
approved by the congress' delegates. There are two
interesting elements in Hoxha's speech. Throughout the
paragraphs just quoted he constantly referred to some
unspecified and mysterious "we": "We have tried to implement
the norms . . ." "We have borne in mind . . ." "We have
tried to carry out . . ." and so forth. An intelligent
guess could be that the "we" involved in preparing the
Central Committee list were simply the Politburo and the
Secretariat, but one must remember that Hoxha did not
say this.

The second element involved real information. Hoxha
revealed that "the party put at our disposal about 2,000
candidates." Since the AWP Central Committee elected by
the 9th AWP Congress consisted of 81 full members and 40
candidate-members,[42] the inevitable conclusion is that 6
percent of those candidates proposed were selected. However, who it was that proposed the candidates, when, how,
and to whom remains secret. Still, even this information
is much more than the other East European communist parties
reveal.

Yugoslavia is the only East European country that uses
a formula in forming the party Central Committee. The LCY
Central Committee plenum of 20 March 1978 decided that the
Central Committee (then 165 members plus Tito) would
consist of twenty representatives from each of the six
republican parties (nineteen plus the president of the
Republican Central Committee, who is an ex-officio member
of the LCY Central Committee); fifteen representatives from
each of the two provincial parties (fourteen plus the
president of the Provincial Committee); and fifteen representatives of the army--altogether 165 members, in addition
to Tito, who held a position of such preeminence in
Yugoslavia, being head-of-state and party leader for life,
and not a part of the formula.[43]

As a matter of fact, the Yugoslav republics and

provinces nominate their representatives to the LCY Central
Committee at their own congresses, which precede the LCY
Congress. Thus they elect (altogether) their own top
organs (republican or provincial Central Committee and
Presidium), delegates to the Congress of the LCY, and
representatives to the LCY Central Committee.[44] Consequently, the show of "electing" a new Central Committee is
avoided. In fact, the members of the new Central Committee
come already elected (or "nominated") to the LCY Congress.

Romania too has revealed some of the procedure involved in the election of the RCP Central Committee. At
the 11th RCP Congress in 1974 the 408 Central Committee
members were elected from among 570 candidates proposed at
conferences of the thirty-nine county party committees and
the Bucharest Municipal Party Committee. This meant that
more than 162 more candidates were proposed than there were
seats available. In reality, however, these candidates
had been put up not only for the 408 seats of full and
candidate-members, but also for the seventy-three seats on
the Central Auditing Commission. As a result, the number of
candidates exceeding vacancies was only eighty-nine. In
fact, a special congress commission, of which the Ceausescus
were members, made proposals for appointments to the Central
Committee, thus restricting the little freedom of election
left to the congress. When delivering his closing speech
at the 11th RCP Congress, Ceausescu mentioned that the new
Central Committee had been elected "quasi-unanimously,"
but he later refrained from any reference to the Central
Committee election in his speech at the 12th RCP Congress.[45]

The election of the PZPR Central Committee at the
Extraordinary 9th PZPR Congress was a special case. This
was, in fact, the only time that the election of an East
European Central Committee was subjected to democratic
procedures. The list of candidates for the Central
Committee was compiled by the Congress' Electoral Commission
and initially consisted of 200 names--the exact number of
seats to be filled. According to commission chairman
Bednarski, provincial delegations added some nominations
after examining the list, and a 279-member list was presented
to the congress on the third day. There was a separate list
of 105 candidates to fill seventy Central Committee
candidate-member positions.

Under the rules, the delegates were given ballots
listing the 279 candidates and voted in secret for the 200
candidates of their choice by crossing off seventy-nine
names. The room for choice was sufficient for the delegates
to withhold Central Committee membership from eleven of the

then-incumbent fifteen Politburo and Secretariat members
who were on the list. An absolute majority of delegates
struck off the names of Politburo members Grabski,
Jablonski, Jagielski, Moczar, and Zabinski, as well as
Politburo candidate-members Fiszbach, Kruk, and Ney,
secretaries Kurowski and Cypryniak, Secretariat member
Gabrielski, and the first secretaries of almost all the
big provinces: Katowice's Zabinski, Warsaw's Kociolek,
Poznan's Skrzypczak, Bydgoszcz's Bednarski, Gdansk's
Fiszbach, and Krakow's Dabrowa.[46]

Only the list of elected Central Committee members was
published--not the list of the candidates who ran. Nor did
the regime publish the number of votes received by the
elected members. But numerous Polish press reports have
referred to people who ran and lost, and the number of
votes garnered by each of the victors and losers was
apparently broadcast by mistake in an early report on
Polish television and became known to Polish and Western
reporters. The figures for Jaruzelski, Kania, Olszowski,
Rakowski, and Barcikowski were cited by a reporter in the
18-19 July Olsztyn paper Gazeta Olsztynska. According to
this report, Jaruzelski received 1,615 votes; Kania,
1,335; Barcikowski, 1,262; Olszowski, 1,090; and Rakowski,
1,085. According to the Polish commentator Jerzy Sadecki,[47]
1,070 was the minimum number of necessary votes.

As a rule, the exercise of electing a new Central
Committee is designed to remove those elements that had,
for various reasons, become undesirable, while promoting
people faithful to the party leader and his closest associates. In fact, election to the Central Committee is one
way of paying for services rendered. To put it even more
bluntly, election to the Central Committee is one way in
which the communist feudal lords reward the loyalty of their
most important vassals. It is also an effective way of
injecting new blood into the party leadership, including
guaranteeing representation of particular sectors of
society, state, and public organizations, youth, and the
party apparatus.

Let us review some of the changes in the Central
Committee membership that took place at the 1980-1981 party
congresses in some East European countries.

Albania

Presenting the new Central Committee to the 8th AWP
Congress in November 1981, Enver Hoxha first clarified the
reasons for dropping about 20 percent of the old Central

Committee members. Stressing that "there were no political problems," and that the Central Committee members who had been dropped "are Comrades with good past, good and resolute party leaders who are prepared to lay down their lives for the party, and who have worked and struggled with determination,"[48] Hoxha divided those who had been dropped from Central Committee membership into three groups: "Those who are unable to carry out their duties as members of the leadership owing to their old age"; "those who have not been put forward for health reasons"; and finally, "members who, despite their efforts and the assistance given to them by the party in their work and struggle, have not justified themselves as members of the leadership, have failed to act energetically and maturely in carrying out the tasks entrusted to them. In other words, some have not shown brilliance in their work."[49] Hoxha then described the composition of the new Central Committee:

> I will now give you some concise data about the composition of the new AWP Central Committee. The average age of the Central Committee members elected by the 7th AWP Congress was 50.7 years. The new proposals bring the average age down to 49. This average age, in our opinion, is normal for a high forum like the Central Committee. . . . If we compare the educational standards of the Central Committee elected by the 7th AWP Congress with the candidates proposed, we have 18 percent more people with higher education in party or state schools; 32 percent more with higher state education in various specialities, 11 percent of whom hold scientific titles or awards; 22 percent more comrades who have completed their studies at the party school or its higher courses. . . . The [new] list includes candidates from some sectors that had not been represented, such as science, literature, and art, journalism and culture . . . as well as a better balance between male and female members.[50]

One has to assume that by "better balance between male and female members" Hoxha meant fewer women in the Central Committee, for the Central Committee elected by the 7th AWP Congress included sixteen female members and seven female candidate-members, whereas the Central Committee elected by the 8th AWP Congress included only twelve female members and seven female candidate-members.[51]

Romania

The Central Committee elected by the 12th RCP Congress
in November 1979 (see Tables 5.1 and 5.2) was a larger body
than the previous Central Committee (408 versus 361 members),
and some fresh blood was added in the form of 96 new full
and 133 new candidate-members.[52]

Table 5.1
Change in Numbers of Central Committee Members,
Romanian Communist Party, 1974-1979

Committee and Date	Full Members	Candidate-Members	Total
Central Committee elected by the 11th RCP Congress, November 1974	205	156	361
Central Committee on the eve of the 12th RCP Congress, November 1979	205	147	352
Central Committee elected at the 12th RCP Congress, November 1979	245	163	408

Source: Radio Free Europe Research and Analysis Department
(RAD) Background Report, Romania, no. 24, 5 February 1980.

The majority of the new Central Committee full members
was made up of first secretaries of county party organizations; all forty county first secretaries became Central
Committee members.[53] Those who were removed from Central
Committee membership were mostly older party members
associated with the late party leader Gheorghe Gheorghiu-
Dej, others tainted by corruption, and any considered to
have doubtful loyalty to the party secretary-general. As
in Albania, the new Central Committee included more representatives of the intelligentsia: engineers, seven university professors, and writers such as Dimitru Radu
Popescu.[54] However, unlike in Albania, the number of female
Central Committee members increased. The old Central
Committee included thirty-seven women; the new one has
100. Taking into consideration the increase in total
Central Committee membership, this means that the proportion of women members grew from 10.25 to 24.51 percent.
In addition, one could clearly distinguish representatives
of various social or professional groups among the Central

Table 5.2
Composition of the Central Committee Elected
by the 12th Romanian Communist Party Congress

	Number and Percentage of Members					
Membership Category	Full Members		Candidate-Members		Total	
Members of the old Central Committee reelected	127	30.6%	30	7.3%	155	38%
Candidate-members of the old Central Committee elected to full member-ship on the new Central Committee	32	13%	–	–	32	7.8%
Members of the new Central Committee who had not been members of the old Central Committee	88	35.9%	133	82%	221	54%

Source: Radio Free Europe RAD Background Report, Romania,
no. 24, 5 February 1980.

Committee members: representatives of the agricultural
production cooperatives, jurists, representatives of the
Central Consumers' Union, the military, etc., as well as
representatives of Romania's Hungarian and German
minorities. [55]
    The Central Committee elected by the 13th RCP Congress
in November 1984 is still larger than the 1979 committee--
265 full members and 181 candidate-members (total, 446)
of whom 70 are women. [56]

Hungary

    In March 1975 the 11th MSZMP Congress elected 125
members to the Central Committee. Seven of them died between April 1975 and November 1978, leaving the Central
Committee with 120 actual members at the time of the 12th
MSZMP Congress in March 1980. [57]
    The 12th MSZMP Congress increased the size of the
Central Committee from 125 to 127 members. It reelected
94 and dropped 26 incumbent members, which means that there
were 33 new members. By comparison, the 11th Congress
reelected 82 and dismissed 19 incumbent members, making the

number of new members 43--the single largest influx of "new
blood" into the Central Committee since party leader Janos
Kadar came to power. It is interesting to note that the
12th MSZMP Congress not only failed to continue along the
same line, but also dropped 14 of the 43 new members chosen
in 1975.[58]

The 120 members of the Central Committee on the eve
of the 12th MSZMP Congress fell into the age groups shown
on the left in Table 5.3. For the 127 members of the
new MSZMP Central Committee, details are available for the
ages of only 106, as shown on the right in Table 5.3.

Table 5.3
Ages (by Age Groups) of Central Committee Members of the
Hungarian Socialist Workers' Party Before and After
the 1980 Party Congress

Age Group	Number of Members on the Eve of the Congress	Number of Members after the 12th Congress Election*
Below 30	0	0
30-40	1	4
40-50	11	11
50-60	82	69
60-70	18	16
70-80	7	5
80 and over	1	1

*Ages of 21 members are not shown because data are
not available.
Source: Radio Free Europe RAD Background Report,
Hungary, no. 192, 1 August 1980.

One notices immediately the absence of any Central
Committee members younger than 30 years of age, as well as
the only slightly increased number in the 30-40 age group.
On the other hand, there was only a slight decrease in the
numbers in the 60-70 and 70-80 age groups.

The 12th MSZMP Congress increased the number of women
in the Central Committee from 16 to 18; they now constitute
14.1 percent of the total Central Committee membership,
still considerably below the share of women in the total
party membership and far lower than their share in the
population as a whole.[59]

As in all other East European countries, the Hungarian
Central Committee is in fact a representative body, providing representation for professional and social-occupational groups. Some 81 of its seats in 1980 were reserved

for officialdom; i.e., 37 seats went to the party apparatus, 30 to the state apparatus, and 14 to the leadership of various mass organizations. As in other East European Central Committees, it was obvious that many of the Central Committee members hold their membership ex officio, as a result of the fact that they were holding another official state or party post. Thus, among the 37 party-apparatus seats in the Central Committee, 19 seats were alloted to the MSZMP Central Committee first secretary and five other secretaries, the heads of the eight Central Committee departments, the editors of the two most important party publications (Nepszabadsag and Tarsadalmi Szemle), and the directors of the three most important central institutes of the Central Committee (the Party Academy, the Institute of Social Sciences, and the Institute of Party History).[60] The first secretaries of ten of the country's nineteen counties were also elected Central Committee members.

The same picture emerged in the state officials group. The prime minister, his four deputies, and all important ministers were elected Central Committee members, in addition to the presidents of the National Bank, the People's Central Control Commission, the National Committee on Technological Development, and so forth.[61] In addition, there were also the usual representatives of the army, industry, agriculture, mass media, and the spheres of arts, culture, science, and education, as well as the Hungarian Ambassador to Moscow (which is also the case in almost all other East European countries).

Most of the twenty-six Central Committee members who were not reelected by the 12th MSZMP Congress were obvious cases of retirement, turnover, or transfer to another post. Seven cases were clear cases of demotion, although not all of the seven were sent out into the wilderness completely but instead were transferred to other, though lower, state and party posts.

Bulgaria

The Central Committee elected by the 12th BCP Congress in April 1981 had 197 full members, compared with 154 elected by the 11th BCP Congress, and 139 candidate-members, compared with the 121 elected five years earlier.[62] Party membership between the congresses increased from 789,797 to 825,876 members,[63] or 4.5 percent, while Central Committee membership increased by 27.9 percent (full members) and 14.9 percent (candidate-members); thus, the size of the

Central Committee does not necessarily follow the development of the party membership. At the 11th BCP Congress in 1976, the trend was the opposite: party membership had risen by roughly 13 percent, but only 5 percent more full Central Committee members and 10 percent more candidate-members were elected.[64]

In the five years between the 11th and 12th BCP Congresses, the number of full Central Committee members was increased on two occasions by no less than twenty-one,[65] whereas only one Central Committee member--Boris Velchev (also Politburo member and Central Committee secretary)-- was ousted.[66] Some eight Central Committee members and two candidate-members died between the two congresses. Thus on the eve of the 12th BCP Congress the Central Committee consisted of 166 full and 105 candidate-members (see Table 5.4).

The average age of all 197 full members was 57.5 years of age.[67] The composition of the Central Committee by the age groups of its full members is illustrated by Table 5.5.

The chart shows that the largest increase was in the 61-70 age group, not because of the newly elected Central Committee members (only eight in this group), but mainly because many of those reelected had passed into this age group. Eight of the Central Committee members were older than 80 years of age and one of the three Central Committee members younger than 40--Lyudmila Zhivkova--died three months after the 12th Congress. As usual, women were strongly underrepresented. Despite the increased number of full Central Committee members, the number of women among them decreased from 14 to 11. (Five of the former 14 women members were not reelected and only 2 were added). Among the candidate-members, the number of women increased somewhat, from 14 to 19, but so did the total number of candidate members, so that the proportion has not improved.[68]

Some 28 of the reelected 147 Central Committee members have been members of the committee since 1966, 27 since 1971, and 32 since 1976. The membership of 20 of them is even more recent--since the 1977 and 1978 Central Committee plenums. The number of those elected at the 7th BCP Congress (1958) and the 8th BCP Congress (1962) was seven and ten respectively. Nine of the Central Committee members have survived since the 6th BCP Congress (1954). Three of them, however, with occasional interruptions.[69] Todor Zhivkov has been a Central Committee member since 1948, Ruben Avramov since 1945, and Tsola Dragoycheva since 1937.[70]

Table 5.4
Changes in Membership in the Central Committee of
the Bulgarian Communist Party, 1976-1981

Category	Full Members	Candidate-Members
Elected at the 11th BCP Congress, 1976	154	121
Ousted between congresses	-1	-
Died between congresses	-8	-2
Promoted from candidates to full members between congresses	+14	-14
Newly elected between congresses	+7	-
Situation on the eve of the 12th BCP Congress, 1981	166	105
Not reelected at the 12th BCP Congress	-19	-33
Promoted from candidates to full members	+30	-30
Moved from Central Control Commission to Central Committee	+6	+4
Newly elected	+14	+93
Total after the 12th BCP Congress	197	139
Subtotal reelected to the same positions	147	42

Source: Radio Free Europe RAD Background Report, Bulgaria,
no. 134, 12 May 1981.

The educational level of the Central Committee members
was rather high. At least nineteen of them had higher party
education, and 122 formal higher education in the following
areas: law, 21; philosophy, philogy, 25; economics, 16;
engineering, 24; architecture, 1; arts, 1; medicine, 6;
agronomy, 8; natural sciences, 1; military, 15; and
international relations, 4.[71]
As for the professional backgrounds of the Central
Committee members, the predominance of party and state
officials is obvious, as elsewhere in Eastern Europe (see
Table 5.6).[72]

Table 5.5
Ages (by Age Groups) of the Central Committee
of the Bulgarian Communist Party, 1976-1981

| | 12th BCP Congress (1981) | | | 11th BCP Congress (1976) |
Age Group	Reelected	Newly Elected	Total	Total
Under 40	1	2	3	2
41-50	28	14	42	35
51-60	57	17	74	69
61-70	43	8	51	28
Over 70	17	1	18	17
Unknown	1	8	9	3

Source: Radio Free Europe RAD Background Report, Bulgaria,
no. 134, 12 May 1981.

Table 5.6
Professional Backgrounds of Members of the Central
Committee of the Bulgarian Communist Party, 1981

Professional or Occupational Area	New	Reelected	Total
Government and administration	13	66	79
Party	23	47	70
Mass organizations	1	12	13
Scientists	-	7	7
Writers	1	5	6
Journalists	2	3	5
Workers	4	5	9
Diplomats	4	-	4
Industrial managers	1	-	1
Agricultural managers	1	-	1
Pensioners	-	2	-
Subtotals and total	50	147	197

Source: Radio Free Europe RAD Background Report, Bulgaria,
no. 134, 12 May 1981.

Most of the nineteen Central Committee full members
who were not reelected were people whose careers had been
on the decline for several years. Some of them (two Heroes
of Socialist Labor) were obviously due for replacement by
new workers, and some apparently retired.[73] There is no
evidence of any purge.

Yugoslavia

Some 95 of the 163 members of the Central Committee[74] elected by the June 1982, 12th LCY Congress were newly elected. This turnover (58.3 percent) is larger than the usual 33-40 percent. Only fifteen (9.2 percent) of the Central Committee members elected by the 12th LCY Congress were women.[75] The ages and the professional and educational structure of the new Central Committee are given in Table 5.7.

Table 5.7
Ages (by Age Groups) and Professional and Educational Backgrounds of Members of the Central Committee of the League of Yugoslav Communists, 1982

Characteristic	Number and Percentage of Members	
Age Group		
Below 30	13	(7.9%)
31-50	47	(28.9%)
51-55	16	(9.8%)
56 and over	87	(53.4%)
Professional background		
Party functionaries	90	(55.2%)
Managers	25	(15.3%)
Scientists and white collar	18	(11.1%)
Workers	13	(8.0%)
Farmers	1	(0.6%)
Army	15	(9.2%)
Artists	1	(0.6%)
Education		
Professional education (highly skilled and skilled)	17	(10.5%)
Higher education and high school education	131	(80.4%)
Secondary and elementary education	15	(9.1%)

Source: Borba (Belgrade), 30 June 1982.

Poland
The new Central Committee that emerged from the 8th PZPR Congress in February 1980 was numerically unchanged, slightly older, and included more women.[76] Unlike the Central Committee that was to be elected by the Extra-ordinary 9th PZPR Congress in June 1981, the 1980 Central

Committee did not undergo any spectacular change. The
newly elected organ consisted of 143 full members and 108
deputy members, which meant a numerical increase of three
in the first category and decrease of three in the
second.[77] By comparison, the Extraordinary 9th PZPR
Congress elected a new Central Committee consisting of 200
full members and 70 candidate-members.[78]

Five of the 140 full members and seven of the 111
candidate-members elected by the 1975 PZPR Congress had
died, so only 135 full members and 104 candidate-members
lived to see the 8th PZPR Congress. Of the 135 living
members, 97 were reelected, 34 dropped, and four transferred
to the Central Auditing Commission. Of the 104 candidate-
members, 23 were promoted to full membership, 49 retained
their candidate status, three were transferred to the
Central Auditing Commission, and 29 were dropped.[79]

The overall turnover in 1980, especially of full
Central Committee members, was considered lower than it was
in 1975, when as many as 63 of the 140 full members were
either total newcomers (48) or advanced from candidate-
membership (15). Among the 108 candidate-members, 72 were
new additions to the Central Committee (nearly 60 percent).[80]
The usual professional groups found their regular representation in the new Central Committee (see Table 5.8).
Women were underrepresented on the Central Committee and
also in the PZPR, although their number in the Central
Committee increased slightly (15 full members as compared
with 11 in 1975, and 14 deputy members as compared with 9
in 1975).[81] The average age of the Central Committee
members elected by the 8th PZPR Congress was 52.5--nearly
three years older than in 1975--and the average age of the
deputy members was 48.5, also three years older than at the
previous congress. The 51-55 age group was the strongest--
31 percent (20 percent in 1975); those aged 56 and over
numbered 48 (29 in 1975). Members of the 40-50 age group,
who were numerically the strongest in 1975 (64), dropped
to only 48.[82]

The Central Committee elected by the 8th PZPR Congress
did not survive unchanged until the 9th PZPR Congress.
Between February 1980 and July 1981, 17 of the Central
Committee full members were removed (including five cabinet
members, three Central Committee secretaries, and five
voivodeship first secretaries); 16 were added (three were
elected and 13 promoted from deputy membership). Of the
deputy members, six were ousted (three voivodeship first
secretaries, two ministers, and one television official)
and eight added (one party journal editor-in-chief, one

Table 5.8
Professional Backgrounds of Members of the Central
Committee of the Polish United Workers' Party, 1980

Professional or Occupational Area	Full Members	Deputy Members
Party apparat officials		
CC secretaries	10	0
CC department heads	13	6
Voivodeship secretaries	25	33
Subtotal:	48	39
Government and state officials		
Council of ministers members	20	7
Deputy ministers	5	2
Generals	6	9
Heads of central offices	3	0
Ambassadors	3	0
Subtotal:	37	18
Cultural workers		
University professors	5	4
Journalists incl. RTV	5	8
Writers	1	0
Subtotal:	11	12
Industry		
Managers	0	5
Technical personnel	7	5
Foremen	11	4
Miners	3	0
Other skilled workers	14	11
Subtotal:	35	25
Agriculture		
State and collective farm managers	4	2
Individual peasants	1	3
Subtotal:	5	5
Others		
Mass organization heads	6	4
Profession unknown	1	5
Subtotal:	7	9
Grand total:	143	108

Source: Radio Free Europe Situation Report, Poland,
29 February 1980.

television official, two voivodeship first secretaries, and four workers).[83]

The secret ballot by which the new Central Committee at the Extraordinary 9th PZPR Congress was elected was tantamount to a vote of nonconfidence in the old professional party apparatus by the congress' delegates. Only 16 full Central Committee members elected by the 9th PZPR Congress were reelected, and two former deputy members and one member of the Central Control Commission were promoted to full membership; the overwhelming majority, 181 members, were total newcomers. The situation with the candidate-members was similar: only five former deputy members were reelected as candidate-members (all five were army generals), two were transferred from the Central Control and Audit Commissions,[84] and 63 were new arrivals (see Table 5.9).

Sweeping changes were made with regard to the social and professional composition of the PZPR Central Committee (see Table 5.10). People involved in industrial production made up the largest single group, about 40 percent of the Central Committee members. At the same time, the party and state "establishment" was radically reduced. Only three former Central Committee secretaries, five cabinet members, two deputy ministers, and eight voivodeship first secretaries were on the new committee, while none of the seventeen Central Committee department heads were included in it. In other words, the group that formerly accounted for well over half the Central Committee membership was reduced to a mere 8.5 percent.[85] Among the full Central Committee members elected by the Extraordinary 9th PZPR Congress there were only fifteen women or 7.5 percent, compared with nearly 10.5 percent in 1980.[86]

The changes that took place at the Extraordinary 9th PZPR Congress were indeed extraordinary. They reflected the turmoil of Polish society in the summer of 1981 and the pressure of rank-and-file party members to renew the leadership and general party life. Such changes had never taken place in any other East European party congress, and therefore they are not a part of the general conclusions about the social composition and professional background of the Central Committees elected by the party congresses in Eastern Europe. However, the following conclusions can be reached from the other East European congresses surveyed in this chapter.

Table 5.9
Changes in Membership in the Central Committee of the Polish United Workers' Party, 1976-1981

Category	Full Central Committee Members		Central Committee candidates	
	After 8th PZPR Congress	After 9th PZPR Congress	After 8th PZPR Congress	After 9th PZPR Congress
Reelected	97	16	49	5
Promoted from deputy membership	23	2	--	--
Promoted from Central Control Commission	--	1	--	1
Promoted from Central Audit Commission	--	--	3	1
Newcomers	23 (16.8%)	181 (90.5%)	56 (51%)	63 (90%)
Total	143	200	108	70

Source: Radio Free Europe RAD Background Report, Poland, no. 221, 3 August 1981.

Table 5.10
Professional Backgrounds of Members of the Central
Committee of the Polish United Workers' Party, 1981

Professional or Occupational Area	Full Members		Deputy Members	
Party apparat officials				
CC secretaries	3	(10)	0	(0)
CC department heads	0	(13)	0	(6)
Regional and local secretaries	8	(25)	14	(33)
Secretaries of factory				
party cells	14	(0)	7	(0)
	25	(48)	21	(39)
Government and state officials				
Council of Ministers members	5	(20)	1	(7)
Deputy ministers	2	(5)	4	(2)
Generals*	6	(6)	3	(9)
Heads of central offices	0	(3)	0	(0)
Ambassadors	0	(3)	0	(0)
	13	(37)	8	(18)
Industry				
Managers	3	(0)	3	(5)
Technical and supervisory				
personnel	16	(7)	4	(5)
Foremen	15	(11)	2	(4)
Miners	14	(3)	2	(0)
Other skilled workers	34	(14)	9	(11)
	82	(35)	20	(25)
Intellectual Professions				
University professors	9	(5)	6	(4)
Journalists	1	(5)	0	(8)
Writers	0	(1)	0	(0)
Teachers	6	(0)	1	(0)
Doctors	9	(0)	1	(0)
Others	1	(0)	1	(0)
	26	(11)	9	(12)
Agriculture				
State and collective farm				
managers	7	(4)	0	(2)
Agricultural workers	1	(0)	1	(0)
Individual farmers	29	(1)	2	(3)
	37	(5)	3	(5)
Other occupational groups				
Mass organization officials	2	(6)	1	(4)
Party veterans	4	(0)	1	(0)
Local administration officials	1	(0)	1	(0)
Transport and services	9	(0)	5	(0)
Others	1	(1)	1	(5)
	17	(7)	9	(9)
Total	200	(143)	70	(108)

*In addition to those in government positions.
Source: Radio Free Europe RAD Background Report, Poland,
no. 221, 3 August 1981.

Conclusions About Central Committees

About one-third of the Central Committee membership is usually renewed at the party congresses. This seems to be the accepted quota of renewal. Most of those who fail to be reelected are not victims of a purge, but casualties of the turnover or of their already declining political careers. The Central Committee itself is both an authoritative and representative body. Officially responsible for conducting the party affairs between congresses, it is the supreme party organ when no congress is sitting, and, among other things, it affords representation to the most important professional and social groups in the country. It has to be stressed that it is not people who are being represented in the Central Committee, but various levels of party hierarchy, industrial branches, sections of the state apparatus, the army, and so forth. In fact, most of the Central Committee members (the PZPR Central Committee elected by the Extraordinary 9th PZPR Congress being an exception) hold their seats because of some party or state function they fulfill (district party secretaries, ministers, leaders of various political organizations, and so forth). At least one social sector—women—is strongly underrepresented on all East European Central Committees. The percentage of women in the Central Committees is not only much lower than their proportion in the population, but even lower than their percentage in party membership.

The members of the Central Committee are not subjected to any public criticism. The rank-and-file party members have absolutely no control over the composition of the Central Committee, let alone any opportunity to demand that certain members be ousted or others elected. In only one East European country—Poland—has there ever been open criticism of the Central Committee composition. On 23 September 1980, Zycie Warszawy, a mass circulation Warsaw daily, published an article by Sejm deputy Jerzy Buc, entitled "Driving Forces and Brakes." The article, which was immediately summarized, translated, and disseminated abroad by the official Polish press agency PAP,[87] attacked the composition of the PZPR Central Committee. Quoting the statistical data on the Central Committee membership published by the weekly Polityka on 23 February 1980, Buc stressed that the representatives of the government and the central authorities accounted for over 63 percent of the entire Central Committee, whereas workers accounted for only slightly over 10 percent, and farmers for 2 percent: "In my view workers and farmers and representatives of the

intelligentsia and other professions, in the broad sense
of the term, should account for the essential majority in
the PZPR Central Committee and the Sejm. The percentage
of representatives of chief organs of state administration
in the Central Committee and the Sejm should be limited to
a necessary minimum, which is substantiated by reasons of
the country's security."[88]

How secure are the Central Committee members in their
seats? It has already been pointed out that roughly one-
third of them are dropped at each congress. Although this
proportion is nothing to be ashamed of, it is not a great
honor either. Still, for the Central Committee members
there at least is the comforting thought that "a trouble
shared is half a trouble," and that in most cases being
dropped from the committee really is part of the routine
turnover. Nevertheless, it must be remembered that the
turnover is neither automatic nor obligatory. Furthermore,
being subjected to the turnover means that one is expendable,
simply because there are Central Committee members who are
above this "hazard." The group of the "elders" in the
Bulgarian Central Committee has already been mentioned.
The situation in all other Central Committees is similar.
Each one has its own "dinosaurs" who display amazing
longevity in their positions. Thus the Central Committee
elected by the 12th MSZMP Congress in 1980 included five
members who had figured in all Central Committees since
1948 when the "merger" congress of the communist and
socialist parties took place (Antal Apro, Sandor Gaspar,
Karoly Kiss, Istvan Szabo, and Rezso Nyers). One could
add Janos Kadar and Gyula Kallai, who were also elected to
the Central Committee in 1948 and again in 1951, but were
soon afterwards arrested, victims of Rakosi's personality
cult, and thus were unable to run for reelection at the
3rd MSZMP Congress in May 1954. After Rakosi's fall in
July 1956, however, both were immediately readmitted to the
Central Committee.[89] Similar cases exist in Albania,
the CSSR, and the GDR.

Changes in the Central Committee between congresses
are rare and extraordinary events. It was a rule of Janos
Kadar, MSZMP leader, since 1962 to make no changes in the
Central Committee membership between congresses; therefore,
whenever a Central Committee member died, he was not replaced. Thus, although the 10th MSZMP Congress in 1970
elected a 105-member Central Committee, only 97 were still
at hand at the 11th party Congress in 1975.[90] The tradition
was broken at the 2 July 1975 Central Committee plenum,
when new members (Istvan Huszar and Pal Losonszi) were added

both to the Politburo and the Central Committee.[91] Another
plenum on 29 March 1979 relieved Sandor Jakob of his post
as head of the Central Committee Party and Mass Organization Department, which he had chaired since 1970, "with
recognition of his good services and pending his appointment
to another important office." He was replaced by his
deputy Tibor Baranyai.[92] On 25 June 1982 a special MSZMP
Central Committee plenum approved a number of personnel
changes in the Central Committee membership. The official
announcement read:

> For requirements of practical work, the MSZMP
> Central Committee resolved certain changes in
> leading posts:
> o It relieved Andras Gyenes from his post of
>   Central Committee secretary and from member-
>   ship of the Central Committee.
> o It elected Gyorgy Aczel as Central Committee
>   secretary,
> o It relieved Peter Varkonyi from his post of
>   editor-in-chief of the central party organ
>   Nepszabadsag and elected him Central Committee
>   secretary,
> o It elected Janos Brutyo as Central Committee
>   member,
> o It elected Sandor Rajnai as Central Committee
>   member.
> o It relieved Janos Berecz from his post as head
>   of the Central Committee Foreign Affairs
>   Committee and appointed him editor-in-chief
>   of Nepszabadsag,
> o It appointed Matyas Szuros as head of the
>   Central Committee Foreign Affairs Department,
> o It relieved Imre Gyorgy of his post as head of
>   the Central Committee Agitation and Propaganda
>   Department,
> o It appointed Erno Lakatos as head of the Central
>   Committee Agitation and Propaganda Department.[93]

The scope of the changes was unprecedented for
Hungary. Furthermore, the election of Janos Brutyo to the
Central Committee seemed somewhat puzzling against the
background of the following announcement, disseminated less
than one hour after the afore-quoted announcement of the
MSZMP Central Committee: "The Central Control Commission
of the Hungarian Socialist Workers' Party (MSZMP) held a
session on June 24. The posts of personnel were discussed.

Janos Brutyo's request to no longer be president and member
of the Central Control Commission because of retirement was
accepted, and his service acknowledged."[94] There was no
explanation either for the extensive changes or the question
of why Brutyo "retired" from the Central Control Commission
on 24 June but became a member of the Central Committee
the next day.

In the other East European communist parties the
dismissal of Central Committee members has always been a
more or less ordinary (albeit rare) event. Although on
occasions the face-saving formula of "retirement" or
"transfer to another post" is used, sometimes the dismissal
is accompanied by harsh words. Thus a plenum of the RCP
Central Committee on 26 November 1981, which dealt with
"organizational matters" (meaning personnel changes), used
two formulas. Leonte Rautu was "released from the RCP
Central Committee and the Political Executive Committee and
from his post as rector of 'Stefan Gheorghiu' Academy,"
without any reason being given; Dimitru Popescu was released from his position as RCP Central Committee secretary
"because of appointment as rector of the 'Stefan Gheorghiu'
Academy"; Ilie Radulescu was released from his post as RCP
Central Committee secretary "in connection with his appointment as general manager of Romanian Radio and Television."
On the other hand, Virgil Trofin was "excluded from the
Central Committee and punished by a vote of censure and
warning", and Vasilie Ogherlaci also was "excluded from
the Central Committee . . . and punished by a vote of
censure and warning."[95] As often in such cases it was
stressed that the RCP Central Committee was actually
approving a decision that had already been taken by the RCP
Political Executive Committee (the RCP Politburo). As
usual, the reason for the dismissal, sanction, or warning
was not disclosed.

Although changes in the Central Committee between
congresses are rare, as already noted, sometimes new
members are added. This event can follow the death of a
Central Committee member or result from the promotion of
people who have been appointed to responsible posts that
carry semi-mandatory Central Committee membership. A CPCZ
Central Committee plenum on 1 December 1977, following the
death of Central Committee secretary Jan Baryl, elected
Milos Jakes, until then chairman of the party Control and
Auditing Commission, Central Committee member, candidate-
member of the Presidium (the CPCZ Politburo), and Central
Committee secretary. Two more persons, Antonin Brabec and
Frantisek Pitra, were elected Central Committee members.[96]

Similar plenums took place in Bulgaria in 1957, 1961, 1972, and 1977, involving a few persons only and believed to have had the purpose of replacing deceased members and promoting persons who had been raised to prominence. Thus the 19 December 1977 plenum elected Andrey Lukanov, deputy chairman of the Council of Ministers; Belcho Belchev, minister of finance; Ivan Sakarev, minister of construction and construction materials; and sixteen more persons (mostly ministers or state committees' officials) as Central Committee members. It also elected three new Politburo members (Ognyan Doynov; Minister of National Defense Dobri Dzhurov; and Foreign Affairs Minister Petur Mladenov) and three new Central Committee secretaries.[97] This change added nineteen new members to the Central Committee, to increase its membership to 173. A similar plenum took place on 20-21 July 1978, when Yordan Yotov, editor-in-chief of Rabotnichesko Delo, and Veselin Nikiforov, president of the National Bank, were elected Central Committee members; Todor Bozhinov and Stoyan Mikhaylov were elected Central Committee secretaries; and former Central Committee secretary Ivan Prumov was ousted.[98]

It is an amazing fact that the Central Committee, which is a strictly party organ, ostensibly not a part of the state apparatus, actually dismisses members of the state apparatus and appoints others. Sometimes the nature of the changes is not published, the communiques laconically stating that "the Central Committee adopted recommendations for filling of jobs in the state apparatus,"[99] as the communique published after the 29 March 1979 plenum of the MSZMP Central Committee read. On other occasions the exact nature of the changes in the state apparatus made by the Central Committee is disclosed. Thus the 13-14 September CPCZ Central Committee plenum removed two deputy prime ministers--Jan Gregor and Frantisek Hamouz--as well as the minister of agriculture and nutrition, Bohuslav Vecera.[100] The 22 April 1978 plenum of the MSZMP Central Committee made changes both in the Central Committee membership and in state bodies, replacing ministers in the Council of Ministers and even making a change in the Presidential Council (Imre Katona elected secretary of the Presidential Council).[101]

A special plenum of the PZPR Central Committee on 9 February 1981 received the resignation of Jozef Pinkowski, then the premier, and appointed General Wojciech Jaruzelski as premier.[102] There are many more such examples of the Central Committee acting as an organ superior to the council of ministers and even the state council, ousting and electing officials to these state organs, and in general, demonstrating party superiority to any state bodies.

It is interesting to point out that when Central Committee members are relieved of their posts in the state administration (and obviously demoted), it does not necessarily mean that they automatically lose their Central Committee membership. When in 1978 in Bulgaria, Sava Dulbokov and Mako Dakov lost their posts as deputy chairmen of the Council of Ministers[103] and were transferred to less lucrative positions (Sava Dulbokov as deputy chairman of the Fatherland Front), both retained their Central Committee membership and were reelected Central Committee members at the 12th BCP Congress.[104]

It must be stressed that despite the fact that similar changes do take place occasionally between congresses in all East European countries, they all are exceptions to the rule that the most substantial changes in Central Committee membership take place only during the party congresses.

Poland in the period of 1980-1981 was a true exception. The efforts to cope with a situation rapidly getting out of control as a result of the rise of the Solidarity trade union movement, Moscow's evident dissatisfaction with the situation, and the frantic scramble of the political leadership to maintain its dominance in the face of Solidarity's burgeoning popularity all combined to cause frequent and substantial changes in all leading party and state organs. These frequent changes were also an attempt to clear the party of all responsibility for the (admitted) mistakes and shortcomings, and turn individual leaders into scapegoats. (The party is always right; it is some officials who make mistakes.)

Both the PZPR Central Committee plenum on 24 August 1980 (with Gierek still the party leader, although the main report was already being read by his successor Stanislaw Kania)[105] and the session of the State Council the same day[106] made extensive personnel changes in the Politburo, the Secretariat, and the Central Committee, as well as in the Council of Ministers. Less than a fortnight later, another Central Committee plenum ousted Gierek himself and other Central Committee and Politburo members.[107] Another month later--another plenum, and this time the reasons for dismissing former leaders from the Central Committee were painfully articulated: "The Central Committee . . . resolves to recall from the Central Committee: Comrades Edward Babiuch and Zdzislaw Zandarowski for allowing distortions in interparty life, for shaping an incorrect style of party work, and for inadequate concern for the quality of party ranks; Jerzy Lukaszewicz for errors in directing the ideological activities of the party and institutions of the ideological front and for shaping a propaganda line divorced from reality; Jan Szydlak for errors in economic policy and support for arbitrary action in this field; Tadeusz Wraszyczyk for errors in planning and managing the economy; Tadeusz Pyka for incorrect style of management and work with economic personnel, and for irresponsible bearing in the first phase of talks with the strike committee in Gdansk."[108]   In addition, the "resignation" of three Central Committee members was accepted, one of them "because of poor state of health," the other two without any explanation.[109]   The same plenum elected fifteen new Central Committee full members (mostly workers) and eight new candidate-members.[110]

Less than two months later, another Central Committee plenum was held, with more changes. This time it was Gierek himself and his premier, Piotr Jaroszewicz, whose "party responsibility was terminated,"[111] meaning simply that both were kicked out of the party. The official announcement on the plenum included several phrases that should dispel any doubts as to the supremacy of the Central Committee over all state organs:

> In connection with the decision adopted by the 6th plenum of the party Central Committee concerning excluding former members of the party leadership from the Central Committee, the 7th PZPR Central Committee plenum instructs Comrades Edward Babiuch, Jerzy Lukaszewicz, Tadeusz Pyka, Jan Szydlak, Tadeusz Wraszczyk, and Zdzislaw Zandarowski to resign their parliamentary seats which they have received during the elections to the Sejm on the recommendation of the Central Committee.
> The Central Committee instructs Comrade Edward Gierek to resign the parliamentary seat and the post of member of the State Council, which he received in the elections to the Sejm on the recommendation of the Central Committee.
> The 7th plenum also instructs Comrade Piotr Jaroszewicz to resign his seat which he obtained in the elections to the Sejm on the recommendation of the Central Committee.[112]

This communique is an admission of the fact that members of the Sejm owe their seats to the party Central Committee. When the Central Committee requires their

resignation from the Sejm, the fact that they had been
elected by the people (and not by the Central Committee)
does not change anything. In addition, the announcement
on the plenum illustrates the fact that the party Central
Committee controls the composition (and of course the
performance) of the Sejm and the State Council.

More PZPR Central Committee plenums in 1981 approved
additional changes in the membership of the main state and
party organs. General Jaruzelski replaced Premier Jozef
Pinkowski at the 9 February 1981 plenum,[113] and finally,
on 18 October 1981, he replaced Kania as PZPR first
secretary.[114] The Polish mass media even reported the
number of votes cast for Jaruzelski (something extraordinary) as 180 of the 184 votes cast. Kania's resignation, on the other hand, was accepted by a vote of 104 to
79.[115] All these were only some of the changes in the
membership of the PZPR leading organs that took place during the 1980-1981 period.

Important and authoritative as the East European
Central Committees are, one should keep in mind that they
meet infrequently, and even then they serve mostly as a seal
of approval for decisions already taken by the Politburo,
or as an instrument for issuing orders and instructions
initiated by the Politburo or the Secretariat. Despite the
fact that its departments and apparatus function continuously, the Central Committee's entire activity is
subjected to the needs and goals of the most powerful
party organ--the Politburo.

THE POLITBURO

The Politburo (called Presidium in the CSSR and
Yugoslavia and Political Executive Committee in Romania)
is the most important organ in the East European political
system. In fact, it is the single most powerful political
body in the world.

Formally, the Politburo is elected by the Central
Committee from among its members at its first plenum,
following immediately its own election on the last day
of the party congress. The Central Committee secretaries,
the Secretariat, and the Control and Auditing Commission
are also elected in the same way at the same time. The
plenum is a very short one (one to two hours), after which
the names of the Politburo members are read out to the
congress' delegates by the first secretary of the Central
Committee.

The fiction of the Central Committee supremacy over
the Politburo is preserved by the occasional reports the
Politburo submits to the Central Committee,[116] which are
little more than post factum briefing on measures and
steps already taken by the Politburo.

The Politburo is a relatively small organ. In August
1981 the Politburo of the Albanian Workers' Party consisted of 11 full members and 5 candidate-members; the
BCP Politburo, 11 full members and 3 candidate-members;
the CPCZ Presidium, 12 members and one candidate-member;
the SED Politburo, 17 members and 8 candidate-members;
the MSZMP Politburo, 13 members and no candidate-members;
the PZPR Politburo, 15 members and 2 candidate-members;
the RCP Political Executive Committee, 27 members and 22
candidate-members (the RCP Political Executive Committee
also has a Permanent Bureau, composed of 15 members and
no candidate-members, which in fact is the real Politburo);
and finally, the LCY Presidium, which has a set membership
of 24.[117]

Officially (as all East European communist parties'
statutes claim), the Politburo "directs the work of the
Central Committee between plenums." In fact, however, the
Politburo controls every single area of life. It directs
the Central Committee; issues and executes policy (utilizing the Central Committee to a large degree in the same way
the National Assembly is utilized--as a rubber stamp);
issues directives and regulations to practically all
authoritative organs and agencies, institutions and
administrations; supervises the implementation of policy;
punishes and promotes--in short--governs the country. The
Politburo is the living example of the concentration of
power and lack of any division of authority in the East
European political system.

The Politburos of all East European communist countries consist of each country's real elite, i.e., the
holders of the most important positions in the party and
state hierarchy, and the leaders of the mass organizations.
It is a political body that blends together all political,
executive, legislative, and even judicial power and
authority, and thus holds the reins of the country in its
hands.

There is a very fine equilibrium in the composition
of the Politburo. Its size is governed by set regulations
in Yugoslavia only, but some basic characteristics of its
membership are evident throughout Eastern Europe. First of
all, the party's first (or general) secretary is obviously
a member of the Politburo. So are at least some (but not

all) of the Central Committee secretaries, the leader of
the party organization in the capital city, a representative
of the army (usually the minister of defense), the prime
minister, sometimes the minister of foreign affairs, and
occasionally the chairman of the national assembly and the
leader of the Fatherland Front. As already mentioned,
Yugoslavia is the only East European that has set regulations for Politburo membership. A special plenum of the
LCY Central Committee on 27 February 1978[118] set the Politburo membership at twenty-four according to the following
key:

> twelve members from the six republican parties
>   (two from each);
> two members from the two provincial parties
>   (one from each);
> six presidents of the six Republican Central
>   Committees;
> two presidents of the two Provincial Committees;
> one representative of the army;
> one President of the LCY--at that time, Tito.
>   (After the death of Tito the title President
>   of the Party was abolished, because "it was
>   impossible for a single person to replace Tito."[119]

This key gives more meaning to the announcement on the
election of the Politburo by the Central Committee elected
by the 12th LCY Congress, which read as follows:

> The following persons have been elected members of
> the LCY Central Committee Presidium--Bosnia-
> Herzegovina: Nikola Stojanovic, Franjo Herljevic;
> Croatia: Dusan Dragosavac, Vladimir Bakaric;
> Montenegro: Veljko Milatovic, Miljan Radovic;
> Macedonia: Dimce Belovski, Kiro Hadzhivasilev;
> Slovenia: Mitja Ribicic, Milan Kucan; Serbia:
> Dragoslav Markovic, Dobrivoje Vidic; Voivodina:
> Petar Matic; Kosovo: Ali Sukrija.
>   Ex-officio members of the LCY Central
> Committee Presidium are: Hamdija Pozderac, Jure
> Bilic, Dobroslav Culafic, Andrej Marinc, Dusan
> Ckrebic, Krste Markovski, Marko Djuricin, Sinan
> Hasani, Dane Cuic.[120] [The ex-officio members
> are the six presidents of the six Republican
> Central Committees, the two presidents of the
> two Provincial Committees, and the representa-
> tive of the army.]

Thus, throughout Eastern Europe the Politburo is to a large extent a representative organ, which affords representation to the most important centers of power in each country. The representative function of the Politburo was confirmed in fact in Yugoslavia. When Edvard Kardelj, a member of the LCY Presidium, died on 10 February 1979, his seat was taken by Hamadija Pozderac, a Muslim, who was elected to the Presidium obviously in order to give the 1,800,000 Yugoslav Muslims representation at the highest level.[121] The membership of a "representative of the army" in the LCY Presidium[122] is further confirmation of the Politburo's representative functions.

It has already been pointed out that the Politburo members are supposedly elected by the newly elected Central Committee at its first plenum on the last day of the party congress. (Again Yugoslavia is an exception. For example, in 1978 the list of the "proposed" Presidium members was published several months before the 11th LCY Congress.[123] Actually, the exception is not in the procedure used, but only in the fact that the list was actually published in advance.) It can safely be assumed that Politburo membership is hardly a matter of debate by the Central Committee. The first plenum of the newly elected Central Committee apparently only approves a list of the party Politburo, Secretariat, and Control Commission that has been prepared in advance by the previous Politburo itself.

The work of the Politburo is veiled in total secrecy. Very little apart from official brief communiques or announcements (in addition to major decisions in the areas of economics and policy, various messages of greetings and condolences, and so on) is ever published. One does not know how often the Politburo meets (one can assume at least once a week), what procedures are followed during the meetings, and whether there is any voting. In fact, on some occasions one even does not know whether a particular person is still a member of the Politburo. This was the case with BCP Politburo member Tano Tsolov, who was a candidate-member of the BCP Politburo from 1962 to 1966 and became a full member in 1966. His last public appearance was on 22 March 1979,[124] and he was generally believed to have been seriously ill after that date (most probably a stroke from which he did not recover). On 26 February 1980 he was formally released from his post as deputy chairman of the Council of Ministers, which he had held since 1971, but the move was not reported until several months later.[125] Actually the appointment of Todor

Bozhinov to the same post in September 1979, and his promotion to the Politburo two months earlier, were a clear indication that Bozhinov was taking over the functions of Tsolov, who was not expected to return to active political life.[126] Still, for about two years (until the 12th BCP Congress, when he was not reelected as a Politburo member) it was not officially known whether Tsolov was still formally a member of the Politburo or whether he had been relieved by a secret Politburo decision.

Each member of the Politburo has his own area of responsibility. Although sometimes it is an area that has nothing to do with the state leadership (ideology, for instance), in most cases it is an area that theoretically is managed by a specific ministry. When the relevant minister himself is a member of the Politburo (as ministers of foreign affairs and defense usually are), it is safe to assume that they are in charge of their specific field of responsibility. Often, however, especially in the various economic areas, the Politburo member dealing with the subject is far more important than the relevant minister. This fact demonstrates again the superiority of the Politburo over the state organs and confirms the Politburo's position as the East European countries' real cabinet.

The East European press usually never deals with the Politburo procedures, or how it actually operates. Again, the exception is Yugoslavia, where the LCY Central Committee adopted a "procedure concerning the organization and manner of work of the Presidium."[127] According to the official announcement "the rules of procedure represent a continuation of the democratic practice which over the years has become customary in the LCY, or rather in the work of its highest organs." The most important parts of the rules are:

> The Presidium of the LCY Central Committee is a democratic organ. It is not a formal, but a truly collective body in which all its members by collective work participate in the making of decisions and in the creation of policy about all questions of the LCY and our society. This means that all its members, regardless of their functions and permanent or temporary duties, are responsible for the work of the Presidium.
>
> Individual duties of the Presidium members do not give them the right to adopt, without the agreement of the Presidium, decisions that bind anyone unless the Presidium empowers a member of

the Presidium to do so.[128]

The rules also stress that the Presidium members are
in charge of individual spheres of work and permanent or
ad hoc tasks. The Presidium chairman is responsible for
the "over-all division of work," as well as the "preparation of the sessions and the decisions."[129]

Some of the routine functions of the Politburo,
usually noted in the press, are reviewed briefly in the
topics that follow.

Appointment of Certain Officials

Every important appointment—regardless of whether
the party or the state apparatus is involved—is initiated
by the Politburo. Although the national assembly (or the
state council) stamp of approval is needed for state
appointments, and Central Committee agreement for party
appointments (or "election"), the decision in each case is
taken by the Politburo. In fact, the East European
communist parties do not hide this situation, and official
documents often point out that the Central Committee (or
other organ) "confirms" decisions previously taken by the
Politburo. Thus, the already cited 26 November 1981 plenum
of the RCP Central Committee, which made significant changes
in the membership of the Central Committee and the Political
Executive Committee, only "confirmed the decision on the
personnel changes, previously adopted by the Political
Executive Committee."[130] Sometimes appointments are made
even without the formal approval of the Central Committee.
Thus the PZPR Politburo on 19 September 1980 appointed Josef
Klassa head of the Central Committee Press, Radio, and TV
Department, and Kazimierz Rokoszewski head of the Central
Committee Personnel Department.[131] There was no indication
that the Central Committee was involved in this decision,
which is strange, since according to party statutes the
Central Committee is superior to the Politburo.

The same is true in regard to removing members from
the Politburo. Again, although the Central Committee
approves post factum, the decision taken by the Politburo
is final. The ousting of major leaders is discussed in a
separate chapter. Let us then only state at this point
that in everything related to appointing or ousting members
of the party and state leading organs (including itself),
the Politburo is the only decision maker.

Approval of Contacts with Foreign Leaders and of Visits Abroad

The leaders of the East European socialist countries like "personal contacts." Each of them travels abroad frequently and is very much involved in receiving foreign guests, negotiating with them, signing agreements, etc. As a rule, a visit abroad or a meeting with a counterpart is followed by a Politburo meeting, which "approves the results" of the meeting or the visit, in almost all cases without ever specifying what these results were, or at most describing them in very general and noncommittal terms. Thus on 18 February 1981 the PZPR Politburo "approved the results of Kania's talks in the CSSR and the GDR,"[132] stating that "these talks were important regarding the development of friendly relations with our neighbors and for the cooperation of the PZPR with the CPCZ and the SED, as well as for the cooperation of our states in all fields."[133] Nothing was said as to what made the talks important.

In similar terms the BCP Politburo on 2 February 1981 "expressed satisfaction with the meeting between Mr. Todor Zhivkov and Mr. Nicolae Ceausescu, which proceeded in the spirit of cordiality and mutual respect characteristic of the relations between the two neighboring countries and peoples. The Politburo of the Central Committee of the BCP assessed highly the concrete results achieved during the talks."[134] Almost the same sentence had been used several months earlier when the BCP Politburo approved the results of another Zhivkov-Ceausescu meeting.[135] In both cases there was no clue to what these "concrete results" actually were. This standard phrase "the Politburo approves the results of the visit of . . ." seems to be a part of the semantic ritual of the East European political system. There is no precedent of any East European Politburo refusing to approve the results of any official visit of the party leader. Still, sometimes, this phrase acquires certain political significance. This was the case with the visits of Poland's state and party leader Jaruzelski to all East European countries in April-June 1982. The short (usually one-day) visits were obviously aimed at obtaining the support of the Warsaw Pact member-countries for the various measures taken by the Polish government during the martial law period. The announcements of the various Politburo after the visit (all of which "approved the results of the visit") were in fact a vote of confidence for Jaruzelski's policy.

On other occasions, the Politburo not only "approves the results" of the talks, but also expresses its admiration for the performance of the party leader during the talks. Thus, after the visit of the FRG chancellor Helmut Schmidt to the GDR in December 1981, the SED Politburo resolved: "The Politburo of the SED Central Committee, the State Council, and the Council of Ministers of the German Democratic Republic discussed the results of the meeting between Erich Honecker, general secretary of the SED Central Committee and chairman of the GDR State Council, and Helmut Schmidt, federal chancellor of the Federal Republic of Germany, at Lake Werbellin from 11 to 13 December 1981. They highly assessed the course and results of the meeting and thanked the general secretary of the SED Central Committee and chairman of the GDR State Council for the work performed by them."[136]

There again was no explanation of the concrete results of the talks or even the specific topics discussed, apart from the standard and obligatory issues of détente, peace, security, and so forth.

Decisions on Important Industrial and Agrarian Matters

Sometimes Politburo decisions and resolutions on important industrial and agrarian matters are published at least as summaries by the mass media. Thus on 30 August 1978 all Bulgarian dailies carried a full-page summary of a decision the Politburo was said to have adopted "recently." It was aimed at solving the acute labor shortage in agriculture due to migration, unwillingness of young people to work on the land, low professional qualities required, and slow progress of mechanization. Although the decision indicates the direction in which the solution was to be sought, neither the full decision nor any of the procedures involved in its adoption were published.

Sometimes, instead of a decision or a resolution on the economic situation, the Politburo word is spoken in the form of a report to the Central Committee. Such was the report of the CPCZ Politburo to the Central Committee "On Results of Fulfilling the Conclusions of the 15th CPCZ Congress and on Further Action on Their Implementation," which was read by party leader Gustav Husak at the 11th plenum of the CPCZ Central Committee.[137] The report surveyed various areas of economic development, reported successes and shortcomings, and pledged new successes. As usual, it was published in the form of a summary.

On certain occasions similar reports or decisions are

published jointly by the Politburo and other organs.
Such was the April 1981 decision of the SED Politburo and
the GDR Council of Ministers "On the Broad Public Discussion of the Directives of the 10th SED Congress to the
Five-Year Plan for the Development of the SED Economy in
the Years 1981-1985."[138]   The decision had an apparent
propaganda character and did not include any important
political elements.

Decisions Related to Particular Party and State Organs, Industries, Organizations, and Institutes

Sometimes the Politburo issues instructions or
decisions that affect only a single institution or area.
Such was the BCP Politburo decision "On Increasing
Rabotnichesko Delo's Role in the Building of the Developed
Socialist Society,"[139] which listed the newspaper's weaknesses and achievements and set measures for improving its
effectiveness. The decision covered every conceivable area
subjected to newspaper reporting (policy, culture and arts,
relations with the USSR, economy, social issues, etc.) and
stressed that everything printed must truly reflect the
party's directives in great detail. Precise instructions
and directions in all areas of journalistic activity were
included in the decision.
On 18 March 1980 the SED Politburo issued a similar
resolution entitled "Tasks of the Universities and Colleges
in the Developed Socialist Socity."[140]   Surveying the tasks
and responsibilities of the universities ("The principal
task of the universities and colleges is to train and
educate the students and junior scientists at a high
professional level and in the spirit of Marxism-Leninism,
the scientific world view of the working class"[141]), the
SED Politburo resolution articulated detailed instruction
regarding the study of Marxism-Leninism and the specific
areas of study, research, and so forth. Simultaneously,
instructions were issued to the local municipal, party, and
Komsomol organs in everything dealing with their relations
with the local establishments of higher education.[142]
On some occasions the Politburo overtly interferes
with the work of specific ministries and issues decisions
and resolutions related to the professional work of the
ministry. It is not unusual for a ministry to report
directly to the Politburo, and then receive specific
instructions. Such was the case with the 26 June 1982
meeting of the Albanian Politburo, which discussed
educational matters:

The AWP Central Committee Politburo has approved
the conclusions of the popular discussion on
raising the quality of work in schools. Under the
chairmanship of Comrade Enver Hoxha, first secretary
of the AWP Central Committee, a meeting of the
Politburo was held at the premises of the AWP
Central Committee to examine a report presented
by the Ministry of Education and Culture on the
conclusions emerging from the popular discussion
held on the question of raising the standard and
quality of work in schools in accordance with
the tasks set out by the Eighth AWP Congress. . . .
        The Politburo approved the conclusions
approved by the Ministry of Education and Culture
and adopted relevant decisions that will serve to
further raise the development and quality of the
entire educational work of our schools that they
may better meet the present and future demands
for the education of the younger generation and
the training of higher cadres. [143]

        Sometimes, the Politburo treats the government itself
as if it was a subordinate ministry, demands specific
actions, and requires strict obedience. Thus on 22 June
1982 the Executive Political Committee of the RCP Central
Committee discussed the issue of reducing the consumption
of oil products. "Considering that the consumption of
thermal energy is exaggerated, the Executive Political
Committee asked the ministries, centrals, enterprises,
the research and design institutes to take adequate measures
in view of diminishing the consumption of hot water . . .
eliminating the loss in the transport of thermal energy . . .
improving the technological processes and diminishing the
consumption of energy and thermal and fuel resources."
Accordingly, the Romanian government was instructed in a
matter-of-fact way as follows: "The government is to make
monthly analyses of the way in which the measures stipulated
are implemented, and to take action for their adequate
application." [144]
        During the same meeting, the Executive Political
Committee "approved the results" of Jaruzelski's visit to
Romania on 4 June, and Ceausescu's visit to Iraq (16-17
June) and Jordan (17-18 June), and it adopted a noncommittal
statement on the need for peacefully solving the conflict
between Iran and Iraq. In addition, the leading party
organ adopted a decision on holding municipal elections:
"The Executive Political Committee debated the proposals

concerning the preparation and unfolding of the all-country
elections for deputies of the people's councils at the
level of municipalities and of the districts of Bucharest
town, of towns and communes. The elections will take place
on Sunday, November 21, 1982."[145]

Elections obviously are a matter to be discussed and
decided upon by the national assembly. However, the fact
that the RCP Executive Political Committee dealt with it
(and even set the date for the elections) is not unusual
in Eastern Europe. There is absolutely no area in which
the Politburo cannot issue instructions and resolutions
or demand responsibility. Even such areas as sports,
cinematography, music, and even fashion have been subjected
in the past to Politburo decisions and recommendations.

In conclusion the East European Politburo is a self-
perpetuating organ that includes the most important leaders
of the country. Regardless the fact that officially it
is a party organ and not a state organ, it exercises full
authority and power in every single area of life, including
those areas that ostensibly are under the control of
particular state organs, and thus manifests the principle
of uniformity of party command over all areas of life in
Eastern Europe. It combines the power and authority of
the three branches of government (whose members are subject
to party discipline anyway, and thus to the authority of
the Politburo), and it serves as a living monument of party
supremacy in the East European political system.

THE SECRETARIAT

The Central Committee Secretariat is an important
organ consisting of full-time party functionaries who
assist the Politburo and serve as an instrument of continuity
within the party. It is one of the few party top organs that
is in constant operation. Its position is further enhanced
by the fact that the Central Committee secretaries are major
participants in the Central Committee plenums, usually
reporting on behalf of the party leadership, this despite
the fact that not all Central Committee secretaries are
also Politburo members.

Although theoretically the administrative arm of the
Politburo, in fact the Secretariat is an organ of real
authority. Officially its activity is restricted to implementing policy set by the Politburo. In reality, it trans-
mits party orders from top to bottom, supervises the
selection and activity of the secretaries at the lower

levels of the party pyramid, and controls the activity of
the entire party organization.

Occasionally the Secretariat also deals with matters
that have nothing to do with party life. Thus in Bulgaria
on 7 June 1982, the BCP Central Committee Secretariat discussed the employment of sociologists and psychologists
in Bulgaria's industrial plants. A decision was issued
"outlining the basic tasks of the sociologists and
psychologists in the enterprises," and various organs and
public bodies, such as the trade unions, the Komsomol, and
so on, were instructed "to facilitate the employment of
sociologists and psychologists in material production."[146]

Sometimes the Secretariat deals with matters of public
importance, such as the treatment of citizens' letters and
complaints by various party and state organs.[147] However,
most of its work is related to the party organizations and
apparatus. Together with the secretaries of the region,
district, and city committees and other full time functionaries, its staff comprises the backbone of the party
apparatus. Despite the existence of special party control
organs, it is mainly the Secretariat that controls,
evaluates, and guides the activity of the lower-level
secretaries. Thus in Bulgaria in March 1977 the Secretariat
subjected the performance of the 28,000 secretaries to the
basic party organizations to close inspection and issued a
resolution entitled "On Further Strengthening the Role of
the Secretaries of the Basic Party Organizations."[148] The
resolution, which has already been examined in the chapter
dealing with the party structure, enumerated various shortcomings in the work of the secretaries of the primary party
organizations and suggested many moral and material
incentives aimed at improving their work.

The Secretariat is nominally elected by the Central
Committee, together with the Politburo, at its first plenum
following its own "elections" by the congress. Its
membership varies from country to country, and in August
1981, following the party congresses in several East
European countries, the composition was as follows:

In Albania, the AWP Central Committee Secretariat
consists of the party first secretary, Enver Hoxha, and
three secretaries; in Bulgaria, the BCP Central Committee
Secretariat consists of the party secretary general, Todor
Zhivkov, and ten secretaries; in Czechoslovakia, the CPCZ
Central Committee Secretariat consists of the party's
secretary general, Gustav Husak, eight secretaries, and two
members of the Secretariat. The status of Secretariat
member, as opposed to party secretary, used to exist in

several East European countries, but in 1981 Czechoslovakia
was the only country to preserve it. In East Germany,
the SED Central Committee Secretariat consists of the
party's secretary general, Erich Honecker, and nine secretaries. The SED is the only East European Communist Party
that openly publishes the areas of responsibility of each
party secretary. Thus Joachim Herrmann is in charge of
Agitation and Propaganda; Paul Verner, security; Herman
Axen, international affairs; and so forth.[149] In Hungary,
the MSZMP Central Committee Secretariat consists of the
party first secretary, Janos Kadar, and five secretaries;
in Poland in August 1981, the PZPR Central Committee
Secretariat consisted of the then party first secretary
Stanislaw Kania and six secretaries; in Romania, the RCP
Central Committee Secretariat consists of the party secre-
tary general, Nicolae Ceausescu, and nine secretaries.
Finally, in Yugoslavia, the LCY has a system that is slightly
different (in name only) from the other East European communist parties. Instead of a Secretariat, the LCY Central
Committee has a secretary of the Central Committee Presidium
and nine Executive Secretaries of the Central Committee
Presidium.[150]

The composition of the Secretariat in East European
countries changes frequently. Thus the BCP Secretariat
changed several times after the 11th BCP Congress. Boris
Velchev was ousted, Todor Bozhinov and Stoyan Mikhaylov were
elected BCP Central Committee secretaries, and Ivan Prumov
was transferred to another post.[151] Later on Milko Balev
and Misho Mishev were elected Central Committee secretaries,
and finally, at the 12th BCP Congress, Vasil Tsanov and
Chudomir Aleksandrov were added, to bring the number of
party secretaries to ten.[152]

While theoretically equal, some of the Central Committee
secretaries are "more equal" than others. The more important ones are easy to identify; they are the Central
Committee secretaries who are also members of the Politburo.
(In Albania two out of eight secretaries, in the GDR seven
out of nine, in Hungary four out of five, in Poland four
out of six, and in Romania six out of the nine Secretariat
members are members of the Central Committee Executive
Political Committee Permanent Bureau. Finally, in
Yugoslavia, where the balance of power after Tito's death
is a serious matter, no executive secretary is a member of
the LCY Presidium.)[153]

The transfer of a party secretary does not necessarily
mean disgrace, as the case of dismissal from the Politburo
does. Often they are just shifted to other duties. Thus

on 26 October 1976 an MSZMP Central Committee plenum released secretary Arpad Pullai, who had been Central Committee
secretary for nearly ten years, "with full recognition of
his merits," to take up "another important assignment,"
which turned out to be the ministry of transportation and
telecommunication.[154] No official explanation was given.
Similarly, in Romania, an RCP Central Committee plenum on
23 March 1980 elected National Defense Minister Ion Coman
party secretary and released Dumitru Popa from that position. On 29 March Popa was appointed minister of industrial
construction.[155]

Frequent shifts such as these, from party to state
posts and back, is a typical characteristic of the Ceausescu
regime in Romania. It seems one way of preventing accumu-
lation of too much power by a person who does not belong
to the leader's family. This characteristic of nepotism
in Romania will be described in the chapters dealing with
the East European leaders.

Sometimes secretaries are dismissed under less
pleasant circumstances. It is enough to mention the case
of Bulgaria's Boris Velchev (already discussed), and Poland
during the 1980-1981 period when sometimes it was very
difficult to keep abreast of the frequent personnel changes
in the top party organs.

In conclusion, the Central Committee Secretariat is
a very important organ composed of Politburo members and
top party functionaries. It does not hold plenums or
sessions, but simply acts continuously and serves as a
link between the Politburo and the other levels of the
party pyramid, supervising both the performance of the
lower party organs in the implementation of party instructions and the activity of various components of the
state system.

THE CENTRAL CONTROL COMMISSION

The Central Control Commission is the third top party
organ "elected" by the party Central Committee at its first
plenum on the last day of the party congress. This is the
organ responsible for making disciplinary investigations,
screening party members, hearing appeals against decisions
of lower party organs, and auditing the records of party
organizations in economic and financial matters. The name
of the commission is different in the various East
European countries. In Albania, Bulgaria, and the CSSR
it is called the Central Control and Auditing Commission;

in the GDR, the SFRY, and Poland it is called the Central Control Commission; and in Hungary, the Central Control Committee. In Romania the organ is called the Central Collegium. (In the GDR, Poland, and Romania there is a separate Auditing Commission, which deals mostly with the party's financial affairs.)

The size of the Central Control Commission also varies. Thus the BCP Central Control and Auditing Commission comprises 121 members,[156] but the SFRY Central Control Commission consists of only fifteen members.[157]

The activity of the Control and Auditing Commission is frequently the subject of party resolutions and theoretical articles. One such article, "Pressing Issues in the Evolution of the Control Activities of the Party," written by Miroslav Capka, chairman of the CPCZ Central Control and Auditing Commission, describes the Commission's activity in the following way: "The CPCZ Control and Auditing Commission has its important mission in strengthening the ideological and organizational unity of the party . . . consistently monitoring the upholding of the party statutes and norms . . . controlling the fulfillment of resolutions of the congress and the Central Committee . . . bringing to accountability those who disrupt statutes, party and state discipline, communist morals and ethics . . . assisting in overcoming shortcomings . . . controlling the effectiveness of the ideological and organizational work and monitoring the work and results in this area . . . developing political work . . . controlling the ideological influence of communists, etc."[158] In short, the Control Commissions are in charge of verifying the matching of word and deed, and comparing intentions and results.

The Central Control Commission presents one of the most important reports at the party congress. In this report the chairman of the commission surveys its activity since the previous congress. Important data related to the number of party members who have been punished or ousted during the period are revealed, as well as data on complaints of party members and how the complaints have been dealt with.[159]

Frequently the commission submits special or intermediate reports of its activity. Thus, the 23 July 1978 issue of the Hungarian party daily Nepszabadsag carried an article by Janos Brutyo, then chairman of the MSZMP Central Control Committee. Brutyo reported on the Committee's activity in controlling the conduct of the party members. Subjects such as party unity, party members' support for party policy, party members' political and moral

responsibility for mistakes, level of leadership, and so
forth were inspected. Despite the overall positive results,
Brutyo pointed out serious weaknesses that had been discovered (as noted earlier), such as "leaders who overrate
their authority and jurisdiction . . . leaders who pay
little or no heed to party resolutions and government
decrees . . . leaders who abuse authority by punishing
those who criticize, and so forth."[160] According to
Brutyo, "during the last two-and-a-half years 102 people
have been expelled from the party for serious violations
of communist conduct."[161]

In conclusion, the Central Control Commission is one
of the main watchdogs of the party. Although not
responsible for decision making or policy formulation,
the Central Control Commission is instrumental in supervising the implementation of policy decisions adopted by
other top party organs and controlling the moral,
ideological, and professional standards of the party
members.

NOTES

1. "The Central Committee's Ways and Means--the
Central Committee's Resolution of 13 November 1980,"
Partelet (Budapest), no. 12, December 1980, pp. 18-21.
2. Zeri I Popullit (Tirana), 8 November 1981.
3. Nepszabadsag (Budapest), 28 March 1980.
4. Scinteia (Bucharest), 24 November 1980.
5. RFE Research and Analysis Department (RAD)
Background Report, Poland, no. 221, 3 August 1981.
6. Rabotnichesko Delo (Sofia), 5 April 1981.
7. Borba (Belgrade), 21 March 1978.
8. Vecernje Novosti (Belgrade), 17 March 1982.
9. Rude Pravo (Prague), 11 April 1981.
10. Neues Deutschland (East Berlin), 17 April 1981.
11. Rabotnichesko Delo (Sofia), 5 February 1980.
12. Ibid., 1 February 1980.
13. Ibid.
14. Ibid.
15. Ibid., 19 March 1980 and 15 April 1980.
16. Ibid., 6 November 1980.
17. Bucharest Domestic Service in Romanian, 1300 GMT,
1 June 1982; Daily Report (FBIS), 2 June 1982.
18. East Berlin ADN International Service in German,
1415 GMT, 12 December 1980; Daily Report (FBIS), 16
December 1980.

19. Rabotnichesko Delo (Sofia), 3 July 1976.

20. Ibid.

21. Nepszabadsag (Budapest), 5 December 1981;
Daily Report (FBIS), 8 December 1981.

22. Ibid.

23. Belgrade TANJUG Domestic Service in Serbo-
Croatian, 1127 GMT, 5 December 1980; Daily Report (FBIS),
11 December 1980.

24. Bucharest AGERPRES in English, 1833 GMT, 10
February 1982.

25. Rabotnichesko Delo (Sofia), 26 July 1976.

26. Ibid.

27. Bucharest AGERPRES in English, 1930 GMT, 26 March
1981; Daily Report (FBIS), 27 March 1981.

28. Ibid.

29. Rude Pravo (Prague), 22 April 1982; Daily Report
(FBIS), 26 April 1982.

30. Ibid.

31. Warsaw Domestic Television Service in Polish,
1730 GMT, 9 June 1981; Daily Report (FBIS), 10 June 1981.

32. Warsaw Domestic Service in Polish, 1405 GMT,
9 June 1981; Daily Report (FBIS), 10 June 1981.

33. Warsaw PAP in English, 0800 GMT, 10 June 1981;
Daily Report (FBIS), 10 June 1981.

34. Ibid.

35. Trybuna Ludu (Warsaw), 6 September 1980.

36. Borba (Belgrade), 13 and 14 June 1980.

37. Belgrade Domestic Service in Serbo-Croatian,
1325 GMT, 17 February 1982; Daily Report (FBIS), 18
February 1982.

38. Politika (Belgrade), 17 March 1982; Daily Report
(FBIS), 19 March 1982; Borba, 18 May 1982.

39. Vecernje Novosti (Belgrade), 17 March 1982.

40. Belgrade TANJUG Domestic Service in Serbo-
Croatian, 1055 GMT, 7 June 1982; Daily Report (FBIS),
9 June 1982.

41. Tirana Domestic Service in Albanian, 1700 GMT,
7 November 1981.

42. Zeri I Popullit (Tirana), 8 November 1981.

43. Borba (Belgrade), 21 March 1978.

44. Vecernje Novosti (Belgrade), 20 May 1982.

45. RFE RAD Background Report, Romania, no. 24,
5 February 1980.

46. Trybuna Ludu (Warsaw), 18-19 July 1981.

47. Gazeta Krakovska (Krakow), 18-19 July 1981.

48. Tirana Domestic Service in Albanian, 1700 GMT,
7 November 1981.

49. Ibid.

50. Ibid.

51. Directory of Officials of the People's Socialist Republic of Albania (Washington, D.C.: 1980), pp. 27-29, and Zeri I Popullit (Tirana), 8 November 1981.

52. RFE RAD Background Report, Romania, no. 24, 5 February 1980.

53. Ibid.

54. Ibid.

55. Ibid.

56. Scinteia, 23 November 1984.

57. RFE RAD Background Report, Hungary, no. 192, 1 August 1980.

58. Ibid.

59. Ibid.

60. Ibid.

61. Ibid.

62. RFE RAD Background Report, Bulgaria, no. 134, 12 May 1981.

63. Zhivkov's report at the 12th BCP Congress, Rabotnichesko Delo, 1 April 1981.

64. RFE RAD Background Report, Bulgaria, 16 June 1976.

65. RFE RAD Background Report, Bulgaria, 1 February 1978.

66. RFE Situation Report, Bulgaria, 16 May 1977.

67. RFE RAD Background Report, Bulgaria, no. 134, 12 May 1981.

68. Ibid.

69. Ibid.

70. Ibid.

71. Ibid.

72. Ibid.

73. Ibid.

74. Normally the LCY Central Committee consists of 165 members. However, at the 12th LCY Congress, the president of the Croatian League of Communists Central Committee and the president of the Vojvodina League of Communists Provincial Committee were elected to the LCY Central Committee, despite the fact that they could have been ex-officio members. Consequently, the LCY Central Committee elected by the 12th LCY Congress has 163 members. (Belgrade Domestic Service in Serbo-Croatian, 1041 GMT, 29 June 1982; Daily Report [FBIS], 7 July 1982.)

75. All data related to the 12th LCY Congress are taken from Borba (Belgrade), 30 June 1982.

76. Trybuna Ludu (Warsaw), 16-17 February 1981.

77. Ibid.

78. Ibid., 18-19 July 1981.
79. RFE Situation Report, Poland, 29 February 1980.
80. Ibid.
81. Ibid.
82. Ibid.
83. RFE RAD Background Report, Poland, no. 221, 3 August 1981.
84. Ibid.
85. Ibid.
86. Ibid.
87. Warsaw PAP in English, 1416 GMT, 23 September 1980; Daily Report (FBIS), 24 September 1980.
88. Ibid.
89. RFE RAD Background Report, Hungary, no. 192, 1 August 1980.
90. RFE Situation Report, Hungary, 11 March 1975.
91. RFE Situation Report, Hungary, 8 July 1975.
92. RFE Situation Report, Hungary, 12 April 1979.
93. Budapest MTI in English, 1715 GMT, 25 June 1982; Daily Report (FBIS), 28 June 1982.
94. Budapest MTI in English, 1812 GMT, 25 June 1982; Daily Report (FBIS), 28 June 1982.
95. Bucharest Domestic Service in Romanian, 1700 GMT, 26 November 1981; Daily Report (FBIS), 27 November 1981.
96. RFE Situation Report, CSSR, 8 December 1977.
97. Sofia BTA in English, 1655 GMT, 19 December 1977.
98. Sofia Domestic Service in Bulgarian, 1900 GMT, 21 July 1977.
99. Nepszabadsag (Budapest), 30 March 1979.
100. RFE Situation Report, CSSR, 22 September 1976.
101. Budapest MTI in English, 1821 GMT, 22 April 1978; Daily Report (FBIS), 24 April 1978.
102. Trybuna Ludu (Warsaw), 10 February 1981.
103. Sofia Domestic Service in Bulgarian, 1830 GMT, 28 April 1978.
104. Rabotnichesko Delo (Sofia), 5 April 1981.
105. Warsaw Domestic Television Service in Polish, 1807 GMT, 24 August 1980; Daily Report (FBIS), 25 August 1980.
106. Warsaw Domestic Television Service in Polish, 1812 GMT, 24 August 1980; Daily Report (FBIS), 25 August 1980.
107. RFE Situation Report, Poland, 19 September 1980.
108. Warsaw Domestic Service in Polish, 0700 GMT, 6 October 1980; Daily Report (FBIS), 6 October 1980.
109. Ibid.
110. Ibid.

111.   Warsaw Domestic Service in Polish, 0001 GMT,
3 December 1980; Daily Report (FBIS), 3 December 1980.
   112.   Ibid.
   113.   Trybuna Ludu (Warsaw), 10 February 1981.
   114.   Ibid., 19 October 1981.
   115.   Ibid.
   116.   Bratislava Domestic Service in Slovak, 1630 GMT,
26 April 1982; Daily Report (FBIS), 27 April 1982.
   117.   RFE East European Leadership List, 12 August 1981.
   118.   Borba (Belgrade), 28 February 1978.
   119.   Vjesnik (Zagreb), 4 June 1980.
   120.   Belgrade TANJUG Domestic Service in Serbo-Croatian,
1604 GMT, 29 June 1982; Daily Report (FBIS), 30 June 1982.
   121.   Vecernje Novosti (Belgrade), 1 March 1979.
   122.   Ibid.
   123.   RFE RAD Background Report, Yugoslavia, no. 96,
23 May 1978.
   124.   RFE RAD Background Report, Bulgaria, no. 134,
12 May 1981.
   125.   RFE Situation Report, Bulgaria, 10 July 1980.
   126.   RFE RAD Background Report, Bulgaria, no. 134,
12 May 1981.
   127.   Belgrade TANJUG Domestic Service in Serbo-
Croatian, 1308 GMT, 9 November 1978.
   128.   Ibid.
   129.   Ibid.
   130.   Bucharest Domestic Service in Romanian, 1700 GMT,
26 November 1981; Daily Report (FBIS), 27 November 1981.
   131.   Warsaw PAP in English, 2014 GMT, 19 September
1980; Daily Report (FBIS), 22 September 1980.
   132.   Warsaw Domestic Television Service in Polish,
1830 GMT, 18 February 1981; Daily Report (FBIS), 19
February 1981.
   133.   Ibid.
   134.   Sofia BTA in English, 1848 GMT, 2 February 1981;
Daily Report (FBIS), 3 February 1981.
   135.   Sofia BTA in English, 1830 GMT, 25 October 1980;
Daily Report (FBIS), 27 October 1980.
   136.   East Berlin Domestic Television Service in
German, 1830 GMT, 15 December 1981; Daily Report (FBIS),
16 December 1981.
   137.   Prague Domestic Service in Czech, 1730 GMT,
17 March 1978; Daily Report (FBIS), 20 March 1978.
   138.   Neues Deutschland (East Berlin), 29 April 1981;
Daily Report (FBIS), 4 May 1981.
   139.   Rabotnichesko Delo (Sofia), 28 January 1977.
   140.   Neues Deutschland (East Berlin), 20 March 1980;

(FBIS), East European Report, no. 1786, 16 May 1980.

141. Ibid.

142. Ibid.

143. Tirana Domestic Service in Albanian, 1800 GMT, 26 June 1982; Daily Report (FBIS), 29 June 1982.

144. Bucharest AGERPRES in English, 1740 GMT, 22 June 1982; Daily Report (FBIS), 23 June 1982.

145. Ibid.

146. Sofia BTA in English, 1847 GMT, 7 June 1982.

147. Rabotnichesko Delo (Sofia), 21 April 1982; Daily Report (FBIS), 27 April 1982.

148. Partien Zhivot (Sofia), no. 8, 1977, in RFE Situation Report, Bulgaria, 5 August 1977.

149. RFE East European Leadership List, 12 August 1981.

150. Ibid.

151. Sofia Domestic Service in Bulgarian, 1900 GMT, 21 July 1978.

152. Sofia Domestic Service in Bulgarian, 1600 GMT, 4 April 1981.

153. RFE East European Leadership List, 12 August 1981.

154. Budapest Domestic Service in Hungarian, 29 October 1976, in RFE Situation Report, Hungary, 3 November 1976.

155. RFE Situation Report, Romania, 18 April 1980.

156. Rabotnichesko Delo (Sofia), 7 April 1981.

157. Borba (Belgrade), 30 June 1982.

158. Nova Mysl (Prague), in Czech, no. 12, 7 November 1980, pp. 87-98.

159. Trud (Sofia), 2 April 1981.

160. Nepszabadsag (Budapest), 23 July 1978.

161. Ibid.

6
The Congress

According to the party statutes of all East European communist parties, the party congress is the supreme party organ. Originally conceived as an annual event by the Bolshevik party, over the years the party congress of the East European communist parties (and indeed of the CPSU itself) has evolved into being an every-fifth-year event, following in each case a routine pattern based on Soviet practice. Theoretically, and also officially, the agenda of all East European party congresses is identical: a report of the Central Committee read by the party leader, followed by debates on that report (which in fact repeat various parts of the report), speeches of the leaders of the foreign delegations (also known as the greeting messages of their parties' Central Committees), adoption of the Central Committee report, report of the Central Control-Auditing Commission and other party organs, adoption of the party program, and election of the top party organs (the Central Committee, Politburo, Secretariat, and Central Control-Auditing Commission).

Although the party congress is undoubtedly an important and solemn gathering, which serves well to show the party's unity and provides a good opportunity for meetings between local leaders and the communist party delegations from all over the world that attend the congress, one can hardly expect this cumbersome and theatrical affair to serve de facto as the party's supreme organ. Furthermore, the congress meets every five years only. (Extraordinary congresses such as the Extraordinary 9th PZPR Congress in July 1981 are rare exceptions.)

In the final analysis, one cannot imagine the party leadership waiting for the congress to make personnel changes in the Central Committee or formulate the party's line at a given moment. The inevitable conclusion is that the congress is yet another fiction aimed at creating the impression of a democratic rule and procedure within the party and providing an opportunity for rewarding outstanding workers and worthy activists by electing them delegates to the congress.

The congresses of the East European communist parties have two very important tacit functions characteristic of the entire East European system: keeping the population in a state of constant mobilization, and keeping the party in a state of constant control and purges. In fact, the congress is yet another of the many instruments and events aimed at preserving and increasing the social pressure over the population by keeping the citizens in a constant state of having to perform additional tasks and demonstrate their loyalty to the party, by adhering to its line and implementing its programs. The second function (permanent control and purge) relates to the character of the communist parties. The pre-congress campaign, with its "accountability-election meetings" (to be discussed later), provides the party leadership with an excellent opportunity for weeding out unloyal, incapable, or undesirable cadres, shifting officials from one post to another, purging party ranks, and rewarding loyal supporters. In short, the pre-congress campaign is a useful instrument for shaking up the party, or rather dusting it off, in an attempt to enhance its performance and structure.

This chapter will deal with the entire congress campaign, starting with the decision to hold a congress, then the pre-congress campaign, the congress itself, and its decisions.

DETERMINING THE DATE OF THE CONGRESS

The congress does not convene at the end of a pre-set time or on particular dates. It has already been pointed out that the congress was originally conceived as an annual event, but that today as a rule it convenes every five years unless the Central Committee, which determines the date of the party congress, decides otherwise. A special congress may be convened at any time, or the date of an already announced congress can be postponed or changed. Sometimes the actual date of the congress is announced only shortly before the congress itself. In any event, the common denominator is the fact that it is the Central

Committee that sets the date (although one can safely
assume that the "operative" decision had been adopted by
the Politburo).

Thus a plenum of the PZPR Central Committee on 19
October 1979 decided to hold the 8th PZPR Congress on 11
February 1980.[1] On 9 February 1978 the fifth plenum of
the LCY Central Committee decided that the 11th LCY
Congress would take place in June of the same year.[2] The
precise date was determined later. The BCP Central
Committee plenum on 29 July 1980 set 31 March 1981 as the
opening date of the 12th BCP Congress.[3] The date of the
12th LCY Congress, June 1982, was set as early as
September 1980 by the LCY Central Committee.[4]

On the other hand, although it had been known for
months that the 11th MSZMP Congress would take place in
March 1975, the precise date was officially announced only
shortly before the congress actually opened. A Yugoslav
newspaper[5] announced on 15 January 1975 that an LCY
delegation had been invited to take part in the 11th
MSZMP Congress from 17 March to 22 March 1975, but official
Hungarian sources revealed the date only on 26 February,
maintaining that a Central Committee plenum, which had
taken place on the same day (26 February), had decided to
hold the 11th MSZMP Congress from 17 to 22 March 1975.[6]

Sometimes the date shifts. For example, a PZPR
Central Committee plenum on 2 December 1980 decided that an
Extraordinary PZPR Congress would take place in April 1981:
"In conformity with Article 29 of the PZPR statute, the
Central Committee has decided to convene the Extraordinary
9th Party Congress toward the end of the first and the
beginning of the second quarter of next year. The Central
Committee has set up a Congress commission composed of more
than 200 members."[7] Yet on 7 April 1981 Radio Warsaw
reported that the Politburo had decided that the 10th PZPR
Central Committee plenum, due to convene "in the last days
of April," would decide on the precise date of the
Extraordinary 9th PZPR Congress.[8] This Extraordinary
Congress was eventually held in July 1981.

Usually, the Central Committee plenum that sets the
dates of the party congress also decides its agenda and
some procedural matters related to the congress. Thus, on
26 July 1981 the AWP Central Committee decided to hold
the 8th AWP Congress in November 1981 (it began on 1
November 1981) and set the following agenda:

1. Report on the activity of the AWP Central
    Committee, to be delivered by Enver Hoxha,

AWP Central Committee first secretary;

2. Report of the Central Control and Auditing
    Commission, to be delivered by Comrade Pilo
    Peristeri, chairman of the Central Control
    and Auditing Commission;

3. Report on the directives of the 8th AWP
    Congress on the seventh Five-Year plan for
    the development of the economy and culture
    of the People's Socialist Republic of
    Albania for the years 1981-1985, to be
    delivered by Comrade Mehmet Shehu, AWP
    Central Committee and Politburo member and
    chairman of the Council of Ministers of the
    People's Republic of Albania;

4. Election of the AWP's central organs.[9]

The same plenum also decided the manner of electing
the congress' delegates: one delegate with voting rights
for every 150 party members, and one delegate without voting
rights for every 150 candidate-members.[10]

This agenda, which is the standard agenda of all East
European communist party congresses, follows the practice
established by the CPSU. The agendas of the 12th RCP
Congress[11] and the 12th BCP Congress[12] are identical.

Although the dates of the congress and its agenda are
usually fixed by the same Central Committee plenum, there
are exceptions from time to time. Thus the BCP Central
Committee decision on the 11th BCP Congress was taken well
in advance--on 4 July 1975--setting the dates for the
congress from 29 March to 2 April 1976, but the committee
said that the agenda, the form of representation, and the
way of electing delegates to the congress would be
determined later. This was done on 29 January 1976.[13]

On the other hand, the decision of the BCP Central
Committee 29 July 1980 plenum, which set the date for the
12th BCP Congress, was much more elaborate. It decided the
agenda, the form of electing delegates (one for every 500
members--the same as for the previous congress), and the
beginning and end of the accountability-election conferences
(pre-congress meetings of the party organizations at all
levels, examined later in this chapter), which were to
elect the congress' delegates.[14] Zhivkov, who reported to
the BCP Central Committee plenum, announced an interesting
innovation in the congress proceedings: in addition to the
plenary sessions, the congress was also to work in various
sections, devoted to the basic aspects of the country's
development--namely, party, political, organizational and

ideological work; economic policy; science, education, and
culture; foreign policy and international relations; and
state bodies and public organizations.[15] These procedural
changes were evidently expected to give the congress a
more businesslike character than before, when the congresses
were increasingly dominated by the speeches of the foreign
guests and irrelevant statements by rank-and-file members.

A last example is the decisions concerning the 12th
LCY Congress. The first--the decision adopted by the 30
September 1981 LCY Central Committee plenum--announced
that the Congress would be held in June 1982 and described
the manner of nominating the candidates and electing the
delegates to the congress,[16] and the second--the decision
of the 9 April 1982 LCY Central Committee plenum--set the
exact dates of the congress (26-29 June 1982) and announced
the agenda.[17]

Setting the date of the congress and publishing its
agenda precede the pre-congress campaign, which begins
with the publication of the congress' theses.

THE THESES

Several months before the congress itself, the party's
Central Committee publishes the "theses" or "guidelines"
for the congress. The "guidelines" for the 12th MSZMP
Congress, which began on 24 March 1980, were published
on 9 December 1979.[18] The "draft theses" for the 12th BCP
Congress, which began on 31 March 1981, were published on
16 February 1981.[19] The purpose of the early publication
is to start the nationwide pre-congress mobilization
campaign as soon as possible by launching a nationwide
discussion of the theses, usually in the form of public
meetings organized by the countries' mass organizations.
It must be pointed out that although in the past the
theses or guidelines were available to party members only
and the discussion on them was an inner-party affair,[20]
today the theses are openly published and subjected to
discussion by the "politically interested public."[21]

The guidelines or theses are usually written in
matter-of-fact terms. They cover every area of national
life and party policy, and outline both the future party
line and the country's international and domestic policy.
The "Guidelines for the 11th MSZMP Congress" (1975)
consisted of a preamble and seven parts:

1. The International Situation: Main Trends

and Tasks in Foreign Policy;
2. The Further Improvement of Social Conditions;
3. Tasks of Economic Construction;
4. Tasks With Regard to the Living Standard and Social Policy;
5. Ideological and Educational Tasks;
6. Tasks of the Party and Mass Organizations;
7. On the Development of the Party's International Activity and Relations.[22]

"The Theses" of the 12th BCP Congress, which were published (as "draft theses") on 16 February 1981,[23] about six weeks before the opening of the congress, consisted of only five chapters (and the obligatory preamble of ideological-propaganda character), but they covered exactly the same subjects:

1. On the World Situation and the International Activity of the Party and State;
2. On the Socioeconomic Development of the People's Republic of Bulgaria;
3. On the Development of Science, Artistic Culture, Education, and the Mass Information Media;
4. On Improving the State Construction and Social Management, and On Further Developing the Social Democracy;
5. On Enhancing the Party's Leading Role.

As already noted, there is no area of political, economic, cultural, or scientific life that is not dealt with by the congress' theses. Although there is seldom anything sensational in the theses, they always include up-dated information about party membership, social-occupational composition, and even the ousting of party members. Thus the theses of the 12th BCP Congress revealed that "more than 30,000 individuals" had been ousted from the party in the process of exchanging party membership cards.[24] This exchange of party cards was mentioned by Zhivkov in his report to the 11th BCP Congress and presented as an "important political, ideological, and organizational undertaking of the party that must be transformed into a review of our fighting ranks."[25]

The tone of the theses is usually optimistic with a leaning toward complacency. Although marginal difficulties, shortcomings, weaknesses, and mistakes are admitted and criticized, the general mood is absolutely positive, and success in every conceivable area is reported or pledged.

The theses, or the congress guidelines, serve as the basis of the party Central Committee report at the congress (an additional reason for the optimistic tone and the abundance of success reported). In fact, very long parts are incorporated in their entirety in the Central Committee report. During the period between publication of the "draft theses" and the congress, the theses are subject to nationwide discussion, and resulting amendments and additions (never too many) are incorporated in the final draft, which is then adopted by the congress.

The theses or guidelines are not the only document related to the congress and published by the party that is discussed during the pre-congress period. Thus when the CPCZ was preparing its 15th Congress, it published on 15 November 1975, five months before the Congress opened (12 April 1976), a "Central Committee Letter to Party Bodies and Organizations."[26] The letter, which occupied two newspaper pages, explained the party policy at that time and its future plans. The letter was discussed at all pre-congress meetings.

Five years later, when the 16th CPCZ Congress was been prepared, a set of thirty "slogans" for the congress was published.[27] They reflected the party policy and its main goals in all areas. They related not only to the forth-coming 16th CPCZ Congress (April 1981)--a party affair--but also the June 1981 general elections--a matter of the national assembly and the government. The first four slogans concerned the party, its unity and its leading role, and recognized its sixty meritorious years of existence. The next six slogans related to general and local government elections, mostly stressing the party's links with the people and its commitment to socialist democracy. Two general slogans dealt with the cohesion of the CSSR's two national elements (Czechs and Slovaks), including the various minorities, and the unity between workers, cooperative peasants, and the intelligentsia. The following four slogans simultaneously praised and exhorted the trade unions, the younger generation, women, and the armed forces respectively. Six slogans were devoted to economic matters, such as implementing the plan and increasing the effectiveness of economic management. Two slogans dealt with the two general ideological imperatives--Marxism-Leninism, and proletarian and socialist internationalism. Then three slogans followed dealing with the USSR, including the notorious catchwords coined by Klement Gottwald after the 1948 takeover: "Forever With the Soviet Union!" The final three slogans

concerned "the international unity of the communist movement," "the firm unity of the socialist community," and the
all-inclusive "May unity and militant solidarity be cemented
between the countries of the socialist community, the international working class, and the national liberation movement."[28]

Similar sets of slogans published in the CSSR and all
other East European countries on the eve of their national
holidays, or 1 May, include radical condemnations of
imperialists, Maoists, Zionists, revanchists, militarists,
hegemonists, and other renegades of the communist vocabulary,
but the CPCZ Congress slogans did not single out any
inimical targets. They were clearly not intended to start
a new propaganda campaign on the eve of the party congress,
but only to pinpoint certain points to be discussed at the
pre-congress meetings.

Occasionally it is not only the theses and a party
letter or slogans that are published before the congress,
but various documents that are part of the congress'
agenda, such as the Central Committee report or even the
final resolution of the congress, as was the case with the
12th LCY Congress.[29] These documents are then turned into
subjects of discussion by the party organizations.

The pre-congress campaign takes place on two parallel
levels: one for the entire population, and the other for
party members only. The campaign involving the entire
population does not differ much from other mobilization
campaigns, such as the election campaign. In public meetings, organized through the sociopolitical and mass
organizations such as the National Front or the Komsomol,
the participants discuss the various pre-congress documents,
make proposals and suggest amendments, hear information
on party policy and plans, and--perhaps most important--
report their working successes, demonstrate their loyalty
to the party and the regime, and pledge new economic
successes. Often these meetings adopt or approve a document voicing their pledges. A typical such document was
the one adopted by the GDR FDJ (the GDR Komsomol), entitled
"FDJ Central Council Resolution on Tasks for the 10th
SED Congress."[30] This document, which was subsequently
approved by all FDJ pre-congress meetings, stated:

> The 12th plenum of the SED Central Committee
> has determined that the 10th SED Congress will
> be held in the period 11-16 April 1981. The
> youth of our country has greeted this resolution
> with enormous approbation. They are filled with

pride and joy that under the leadership of the
SED and its Central Committee and the Committee's
secretary general, Comrade Erich Honecker, the
policies of the 8th and the 9th SED Congresses
are being so successfully implemented.

For the members of the FDJ and the Ernst
Thaelmann Organization of Young Pioneers, the
preparation of SED Congresses always involves
special accomplishments. Thus, the Central
Council calls upon the members of the FDJ, young
workers, cooperative farmers, members of the
intelligentsia, school children, apprentices,
students, and the members of the armed forces to
take part in the "FDJ Party Congress Initiative"
under the slogan "The Best for the 10th Party
Congress! Everything For the Good of the
People!"[31]

The document included the following concrete pledges:

o To strengthen loyalty to the party and friendship with the USSR, and uphold the revolutionary
   traditions;
o To save M 1,366,300,000 through good management
   in the "material economy" action;
o To save 67,723,000 work hours;
o To collect 334,950 tons of scrap metal and
   56,400 tons of used paper;
o to Produce a profit of M23,000,000 in the "food
   economy" action;
o To rebuild or extend 9,554 dwellings;
o To study the party resolutions, create brigades
   for rendering economic assistance wherever needed,
   develop various cultural programs, and so forth.[32]

Important as it is, the pre-congress campaign that
involves the entire population is no different from other
similar mobilization campaigns. The pre-congress campaign
of the party itself, however, is a completely different
matter. It encompasses the entire party structure, climb-
ing step after step through the different layers of the
party pyramid, and affects the leadership at all levels.

THE ACCOUNTABILITY-ELECTION CAMPAIGN

The 12th MSZMP Congress was scheduled to open on

24 March 1980. The pre-congress campaign had already started
in November 1979. Between 15 November and 15 December 1979
the 803,778 MSZMP members attended special pre-congress
accountability meetings at their 24,000 to 25,000 primary
party organizations.[33] At these meetings they heard reports
from their secretaries and evaluated their performance since
the last congress. They also elected a special nominating
committee (a chairman and three to seven members), which was
in charge of recommending the new leaders of the primary
organizations, which were to be elected at the second round
of the election-accountability meetings.[34] The second round
was held in January 1980. These meetings were the more
important ones. The congressional guidelines (which were
published on 9 December 1979 in Nepszabadsag) were discussed
and any changes were forwarded to the next party layer.
Then the primary units elected their leadership for the
following five years and their delegates to the party
conferences of their immediately supervisory party
organization. The importance of these meetings was shown
by the fact that they were attended by an average of 85-90
percent of their members, often the attendance being even
100 percent. It was estimated that every third member
present addressed such a meeting at one point or another.[35]
The leadership turnover was about 30 percent.[36]

These accountability-election meetings in Hungary and
throughout Eastern Europe serve an additional and very
important role, namely, to provide an opportunity for an
exercise in democracy. After all, how many opportunities
does the rank-and-file member of the communist party get to
voice his opinion and affect the election of his leadership? Thus, the meetings clearly avail an opportunity for
members to let off some steam and demonstrate the equal
rights of all party members. Nevertheless, one must
remember that the election of the new leadership is always
open. The communist parties do not trust secret elections.
Furthermore, proposals for new leaders may be made only to
the nominating committee, which afterwards selects the
"prescribed" candidate.

Each party organization at the higher level (city,
district, etc.) holds similar meetings. At this level,
they are called "conferences" and are usually attended by
higher party officials, the conferences of the districts
being usually attended by members of the Politburo. Their
agenda is a full one. They hear the secretary's report,
hold a discussion on the theses or the guidelines, elect
their own executives, their delegates to the conference
of the higher level, and/or their delegates to the party

congress itself.

The last conferences to precede the congress usually are the conferences of the party organizations of the capital, and the ministries of defense, foreign affairs, and internal affairs. They are attended by the party's first secretary, who delivers a major report which deals not only with internal party affairs, but in fact encapsulates his forthcoming report to the party congress. Such was the speech of Todor Zhivkov at the 17 March 1981 meeting of the BCP Sofia city organization, which preceded the 12th BCP Congress,[37] and the speech of Gustav Husak at the 8 March 1981 meeting of the Prague city party organization, preceding the 16th CPCZ Congress.[38] While dwelling primarily on the progress of the pre-congress campaign and party life, both also touched upon relations with the USSR and various international and economic issues.

Incidentally, in the CSSR and Yugoslavia (both being federations), the party congress is preceded by mini-congresses of the party organizations of the federation's basic units. These congresses closely follow the procedure and agenda of the party congress, namely, approve the report of the first secretary of the republican or provincial party secretary, elect the top organs of the republican or provincial party organization, and so forth. Occasionally, however, there is a local twist or a topical issue, which add some interesting nuances to these gatherings.

Thus, the 12th LCY Congress (June 1982) was preceded by the congresses of the party organizations of the six Yugoslav republics and two provinces, which took place in April-May 1982. They all elected their new top organs and delegates to the party congress. Still, at almost each of them there was something different, characteristic of that republic or its involvement in certain sensitive international issues. The congress of the Kosovo party organization (Kosovo being then engulfed by social unrest, various parts of its population demanding to join "Greater Albania," to obtain a status of federative republic within Yugoslavia, or simply to acquire more rights and achieve equality with the other federative republics and provinces), adopted a resolution stating: "The Kosovo communists will also in the future decisively oppose the nationalistic slogan 'Kosovo--A Republic' as a reactionary slogan aimed at wrecking togetherness. . . . They will fight against all migration trends."[39]

The congress of the Macedonian party organization (Macedonia being the subject of the perennial Yugoslav-

Bulgarian controversy) condemned "Bulgarian chauvinism" and accused the Bulgarian leaders of not being ready to recognize a separate Macedonian nation or give rights to the Macedonian national minority in Bulgaria.[40] The congress of the communist organization of Bosnia-Herzegovina (a republic populated by many nationalities, of whom the Moslems, Serbs, and Croats are the largest) strongly condemned "all sorts of nationalism" and pledged to protect the country's and party's unity.[41]

The mainstream in pre-congress party conferences is the more conventional ones in the other East European countries. One of the main differences between the conferences and the meetings of the primary party organizations (in addition to the seniority of the party leader attending) is the fact that primary party organizations elect only their own leaders and delegates to the conference of the higher level, while these conferences also elect delegates to the party congress itself. Thus in Hungary in 1980, only party organizations having more than 1,200 members were entitled to elect delegates directly to the party congress.[42] Although this is the rule followed by almost all East European parties (the numbers, of course, vary from country to country in accordance with the size of party membership), exceptions are possible. The LCY used a rather complicated key for electing delegates to its 11th Congress in June 1978. It was decided that there would be 2,303 participants with delegate status: 1,629 delegates (see Table 6.1) elected by local party organizations following the ratio of one delegate to 1,000 party members; 470 delegates elected by the republican and provincial party congresses (60 delegates for each republican party, 40 delegates for the two provincial parties, 30 delegates representing the army's party organization); the 165 members of the LCY Central Committee; 24 members of the Statutory Commission; and 15 members of the Control Commission.[43]

So much for broad numbers--but how these numbers themselves were constituted was further regulated by an even more precise key to ensure that the delicate balance of nationalities living in Yugoslavia was observed,[44] as shown by Table 6.1. Precisely the same key was used for electing the delegates to the 12th LCY Congress, the LCY Central Committee also explaining the specific criteria that were to be observed in selecting the delegates.[45]

The primary party organizations usually exchange (replace) one-third of their leaders, but the ratio in the

Table 6.1
Key for Election of Delegates by Local Party Organizations
to the 11th LCY Congress in Yugoslavia, 1978

Party Organization	Number of Party Members	Number of Delegates (1:1000 ratio)	Additional Delegates	Total
Bosnia-Herzegovina	256,144	256	60	316
Montenegro	58,354	58	60	118
Croatia	288,048	288	60	448
Macedonia	105,770	106	60	166
Slovenia	101,965	102	60	162
Serbia proper	462,731	463	60	523
Kosovo	72,313	72	40	112
Vojvodina	178,842	179	40	219
Army	92,900	93	30	123
Federal agencies	12,015	12	--	12
Totals	1,629,082	1,629	470	2,099

Source: Komunist (Belgrade); 27 March 1978.

higher party levels is much lower. Very seldom is a meaningful number of regional party first secretaries replaced
during the pre-election accountability-election meetings.
Thus in the 1980 pre-congress campaign in Hungary only one
of the nineteen first secretaries of the party regional
(county) organizations failed to gain reelection.[46]
    As already noted, the main party leaders attend the
conferences of the higher party organizations. Often they
attend more than one meeting. Thus in March 1981 Todor
Zhivkov, BCP Central Committee first secretary (and after
April 1981, secretary general), attended the conferences
of the BCP Plovdiv city organization,[47] the Sofia city
party organization,[48] and the army party organization.[49]
    Until the Extraordinary 9th PZPR Congress, the regular
PZPR Congresses followed the same pattern. The campaign
preceding the 8th PZPR Congress was launched on 19 October
1979, at the 16th PZPR Central Committee plenum.[50] Party
leader Gierek immediately commenced intensive pre-congress
activity. On 9 November he spoke at a party conference in
a mine in the Silesian town of Sosnowiec.[51] On 16 November
he spoke at a gathering of political and organizational
activists in the coastal city of Szczecin.[52] The speeches
set the tone of the entire pre-congress campaign, namely,
one of accusing local leaders and minor-rank officials of

fault for the country's economic difficulties and creating
a false impression of the regime's achievements and
accomplishments, mostly attributing them to the higher party
leadership. Thus the usual mood of self-satisfaction that
prevails in every pre-congress campaign was established
even where there was absolutely no ground for it. Reading
the optimistic and cheerful speeches of Gierek and his
deputies one could not imagine the events that were going
to shake Poland in the next few months. Gierek's speech
in Sosnowiec was characteristic of the prevailing
optimistic tone: "We are undergoing further expansion and
are becoming an even more civilized and affluent nation.
The might of our state is growing. The point now is that
having achieved our aim for the near future we must not
think that we have already achieved everything. . . .
We will now search for new goals in order to further
improve and perfect our life and working conditions."[53]

The same tone prevailed also at the forty-nine PZPR
regional (voivodeship) conferences. Low turnover of
leaders, reports on successes, and achievements and pledges
for new successes were the main trends, amidst some mild
and well controlled criticism of local leaders.

The campaign preceding the Extraordinary 9th PZPR
Congress in July 1981 was a completely different story.
The situation in Poland had changed radically. The
Solidarity trade union had established itself as a power
factor in the country's political life. Gierek and most of
his closest associates were ousted in disgrace, and the
political and economic crisis reached new peaks, or rather
depths. Obviously, because the congress was an extraordinary one called to deal with an extraordinary situation,
the pre-congress campaign could not follow the routine
pattern. Soon after the beginning of the campaign it
became apparent that it had turned into a very controversial political exercise. Much of the excitement was
a result of the introduction of a new provision stipulating
that both the delegates to the congress and the leaders of
the local party organizations were to be elected by secret
ballot, which of course, produced surprises in the election
of the congress delegates and in the unusually high turnover of leadership at the local level. The turnover
included replacement of 50 percent of the first secretaries
and 40 percent of the members of the primary party
organizations' executive committees, as well as 75 percent
of the leadership of village, town, and urban district
committees.[54]

A second factor strongly influencing the pre-congress

campaign was a letter from the Soviet leadership, signed by Brezhnev himself, to the PZPR Central Committee, and containing both an evaluation of the situation and suggestions to the Polish leaders about how to resolve the country's economic and political difficulties. The letter expressed criticism of the Polish leaders for failing to implement a program that would have reasserted the party as a central factor in Poland's life. But most significant in the context of the pre-congress accountability-election campaign was the implication contained in the letter that both Stanislaw Kania and Wojciech Jaruzelski, "as well as other Polish comrades," had failed to heed the earlier warnings from Moscow about the danger that might result for Poland from the continuing crisis. Nevertheless, the letter stopped short of demanding the resignation of the PZPR top leaders.[55] The letter placed the PZPR on the defensive, and during the pre-congress campaign the leaders repeatedly had to defend and justify themselves. Thus in his speech at the Plock voivodeship accountability-election conference, which took place on 15 June 1981, Stanislaw Kania said that reading the USSR leader's letter, the PZPR leadership "realized with all clarity that our country's credibility within the Warsaw Pact alliance had fallen and this is something that must be treated seriously."[56] What complicated the picture even more and made the pre-congress campaign unique was the fact that for the first time in Eastern Europe the struggle of different factions within the PZPR leadership had become a part of the campaign itself. The "Poznan forum," and the "Katowice forum," which called uncompromisingly for a return to faithful (and Moscow-true) Marxism-Leninism, and other similar conservative factions extensively reported and acclaimed by Moscow[57] demonstrated the schism in the PZPR top leadership and thus added another unusual aspect to the already extraordinary atmosphere of the 1981 pre-congress campaign.

The letter of the Soviet leadership, which was followed by similar letters from several republican branches of the CPSU to various Polish voivodeships, as well as from groups of workers in the Soviet Union's plants to their brother workers in Poland, was read at almost all pre-congress meetings and conferences, gave rise to genuine and often heated discussion, and thus inserted, in fact, an international aspect to the campaign.

At a later stage of the campaign, when delegates to the congress started to be elected, the participants in the conferences showed a marked reluctance to elect the

candidates put forward by the Politburo. Quoting the
election instruction published in April by the Politburo,
the local activists demanded the election of local representatives to the congress, and not the officials sent to
attend the conference. Occasionally, Kania himself had to
intervene and settle heated disputes between Politburo
members attending the local accountability-election
conferences and the local activists.[58] The final outcome
of the pre-congress campaign was a spirit of uncertainty.
Some 80 percent of the delegates elected during the
campaign were newcomers, i.e., persons elected for the
first time in their life.[59] Consequently, in sharp
contrast to the established practice in all other East
European countries, nobody could predict what direction
the Extraordinary 9th PZPR Congress would follow.

Back once again to more conventional pre-congress
campaigns, the participation of Politburo members in high
level accountability-election conferences has already been
pointed out but does not exhaust their roles in the
campaigns. As a rule, toward the end of a campaign most
of the Politburo members publish lengthy articles, which
comprise a report on the activity of their ministries (or
spheres of responsibility) for the period since the last
previous congress. In this way the leaders' contributions
blend into the "accountability atmosphere" that characterizes the pre-congress campaign. Three such articles that
preceded the 12th BCP Congress in 1981 were the following:
an article by Army General Dobri Dzhurov, Politburo member
and minister of National Defense, entitled "Party Leadership
is the Foundation of the Army's Cohesion and Power,"[60] in
which he described the BCP as the source and inspirer of
all achievements and successes of the Bulgarian People's
Army; an article by (then) Premier and Politburo member
Stanko Todorov, entitled "Real Democracy--the Foundation
of Socialism's Political System,"[61] which presented the
Bulgarian political system as a shining example of
democracy; and an article by Petur Mladenov, Politburo
member and minister of foreign affairs, entitled, "Policy
of Peace, Understanding, and Cooperation,"[62] which
analyzed Bulgaria's foreign policy since the previous
party congress and presented it as a consistent implementation of the party's foreign policy line. Other Bulgarian
Politburo members such as Pencho Kubadinski, Peko Takov,
and Tsola Dragoycheva also made their contributions,
although in less important dailies than was the case with
the three examples cited. All in all, the entire Politburo
took an active part in the pre-congress campaign, trying

187

to intensify the population's political consciousness and
translate it into enthusiasm and support for party policy.

The political activization of party members and
ordinary citizens (within strictly prescribed limits, of
course) is one of the pre-congress campaign's main goals.
This "activization" can take various forms: participation
in pre-congress meetings and rallies, assuming new pledges
for working successes, and so forth. Sometimes even well-
controlled criticism of low-level party and state officials
is permitted, both as a means of letting off some steam and
as a demonstration of the democratic procedure involved in
the country's political life. Such was the case for a
3,000-word letter by a "nonparty member," Mincho Tanev,
published in Bulgaria on the eve of the 12th BCP Congress.[63]
Tanev severely criticized the party organization in his
(unnamed) industrial plant, accusing it of neglecting the
workers' needs, protecting its members even when they
violated working discipline and moral, and thus evoking
antagonism and dissatisfaction among nonparty members,
directed against the party organization of the plant.
Such letters are seldom (if ever) carried by the East
European daily press at times other than pre-congress
periods. Criticism of party leaders at any level is
exclusively reserved for the higher party officials and
control organs.

To conclude this part: the pre-congress campaign is
a "period of political and working upsurge," if we can
borrow a phrase extensively used in Eastern Europe during
this period. Although the campaign is essentially a
mobilization campaign to boost the population's productivity, political awareness, and party loyalty, it
also serves as a very good opportunity to thoroughly shake
up the entire party organization, review past activity
and elect new local leaders (and thus also get rid of a
certain percentage of old functionaries). With the
exception of the campaign preceding the Extraordinary 9th
PZPR Congress, the pre-congress campaigns are enveloped
in an aura of self-satisfaction and bright optimism, and
they provide a period to establish the proper mood for the
party congress itself.

THE MAIN EVENT

The congress itself lasts from three to six days.
During this period it is not just the major political
event of the country--it is the only event. The newspapers

and the radio report little else. Numerous related events
(concerts, meetings with foreign delegations, visits of
foreign delegations to various industrial and agricultural
plants where "friendship rallies" take place, etc.) magnify
the congress' proportions and turn it into a political
festival of tremendous dimensions.

The congress is attended by the delegates elected at
the pre-congress accountability-election meetings and
delegations of foreign communist and workers' parties and
"progressive" movements. The number of local delegates
depends on the size of the respective communist party and
the key for electing the delegates, but the number usually
is between 1,500 and 2,500 delegates. (Some 1,688 delegates attended the 12th BCP Congress,[64] 1,422 the 16th
CPCZ Congress,[65] 2,099 the 12th LCY Congress,[66] and so
forth.) In most East European congresses the local
delegates are divided into delegates with voting rights and
delegates with a consultative vote, the second group being
much smaller than the first.

The number of the foreign delegations to the East
European communist parties' congresses is also more or less
identical with the exception of the congress of the
Albanian Workers' Party. This party severed its relations
with the CPSU in 1961, and subsequently with almost all
other communist parties and movements throughout the world,
and branded them as "revisionists," "hegemonists," and so
forth. The 7th AWP Congress in November 1976 was attended
by thirty-two foreign delegations only, although they were
more than the number of foreign delegations attending the
5th and the 6th AWP Congresses. An official announcement
of Radio Tirana on a reception for the foreign delegations
attending the 8th AWP Congress in 1981[67] listed twenty-two
foreign delegations. For the sake of comparison, all other
East European communist parties' congresses that took place
in 1981 were attended by more than 120 foreign delegations,
Bulgaria leading the way with 126,[68] the GDR next with
125,[69] and the CSSR with 114.[70] The press of the country
in which the congress is taking place not only lists all
the delegations and their leaders (with full titles), but
also goes to great pains to indicate their status. Thus
the CSSR press divided the delegations attending the 16th
CPCZ Congress into the following categories: "The Congress
is being attended by foreign delegations of thirteen
fraternal socialist countries; twenty-eight communist and
workers' parties from the capitalist world; forty-seven
parties from the developing countries of Asia, Africa,
and Latin America; delegations from twenty countries of the

Third World already free from colonialism as well as from
national liberation movements; and six delegations from
socialist and social-democratic parties."[71]

With the exception of the Congress of the Albanian
Workers' Party, the rank and status of the Soviet delegation
to the congress determines the level of the party representatives of the other communist delegations. In the early
1970s the Soviet delegation was usually led by Brezhnev
himself, something that automatically obliged all other
East European communist parties to send their top leaders
to the congress. There were, however, exceptions. Thus,
although Brezhnev, Gomulka, Husak, and Zhivkov attended the
10th MSZMP Congress in 1970, Ceausescu remained in Bucharest. The 16th CPCZ Congress in 1981 was attended by
Brezhnev, but all other East European communist parties
sent very high-ranking officials who were not their top
leaders. Because nothing related to the congress is ever
left to chance, it seems that Brezhnev's presence at the
16th CPCZ Congress as the sole bloc leader (in addition to
the host Husak) was not a matter of protocol but one of
dramatic effect, designed to lend more authority to his
speech at the congress, which dealt, among other things,
with the situation in Poland. The usual situation, however, is that the rank of the leader of the Soviet delegation determines the rank of the leaders of all other East
European delegations. Thus the CPSU delegation to the 8th
PZPR Congress (February 1980) was led by the late Mikhail
Suslov, CPSU Central Committee secretary and Politburo
member. The rank of the leaders of the other East European
delegations (Grisha Filipov, Bulgaria; Miklos Ovari,
Hungary; Paul Verner, the GDR; Virgil Cazacu, Romania;
and so forth) was identical.

Sometimes the rank of the leader of the Soviet delegation is a sign of the CPSU attitude toward the party holding the congress. Thus, the CPSU delegation to the 12th
RCP Congress in November 1979 was led by the octogenarian
Avrid Pelshe. Although a member of the Politburo, he was
too old even by Kremlin standards to be a truly representative leading figure, especially when compared with the
leaders of the CPSU delegation to the 11th RCP Congress,
Andrey Kirilenko and Konstantin Katushev, both high-ranking
members (at that time) of the CPSU leadership. It seems
that the too-ordinary character of the CPSU delegation in
1979 reflected Moscow's displeasure with certain aspects
of Romania's foreign policy.

The congresses of the East European communist parties
all follow exactly the pattern of the CPSU Congresses.

More than sixty years of consistent use have turned this
pattern into a strict ritual to which all communist parties
everywhere adhere. This ritual includes even the AWP
Congresses and the Extraordinary 9th PZPR Congress (to be
examined later), which despite its heated debates did not
fail to observe the elements of the ritual: the Central
Committee report, read by the Central Committee first (or
general) secretary; the report of the Central Control-
Auditing Commission; and premier's report on the country's
economic situation; the report of the Congress Credentials
Committee on the credentials and various characteristics
of the delegates; the greetings of the leaders of the
foreign delegations; and the election of the congress'
organs (on the first day) and the party's top organs (on
the last day). Meaningless debates take place, repeating
parts of the Central Committee report and glorifying the
party. This is the sacred framework, which never changes.

The first session of the congress is usually chaired
by the oldest member of the Politburo. (Tsola Dragoycheva
chaired the first session of the 12th BCP Congress in
April 1981; Horst Sindermann the first session of the April
1981 10th SED Congress; and so forth.) He opens the
congress, greets the foreign delegations, reads the names
of those proposed as candidates for the congress organs
(presidium, secretariat, editorial commission, and mandate
commission), announces their (usually) unanimous election
(by acclamation), and reads the congress' agenda. The
reports cited above always figure in the agenda, and
additional items such as approval of the economic plan,
the amendment of party statutes, etc., may also appear
from time to time.

Having disposed of the procedural matters (which
seldom take more than 30-60 minutes), the chairman of the
session gives the floor to the party leader, who reads the
Central Committee report. This speech, based on the theses
(or the guidelines), which have been extensively discussed
during the pre-congress campaign, is the central event of
the congress and represents a substantial physical effort
for the aging East European party leaders. Enver Hoxha,
for instance, spoke for thirteen-and-one-half hours at the
7th AWP Congress![72] Other East European leaders, such as
Todor Zhivkov at the 12th BCP Congress and Janos Kadar
at the 12th MSZMP Congress, delivered extensive summaries
of the written report handed out to the congress dele-
gates--summaries that nevertheless lasted almost four hours.
Tito, on the other hand, by the time of the 11th LCY
Congress in June 1978, was not capable of any serious

physical effort. He read only a one-hour summary, and his
full 92-page report was distributed to the delegates in
written form.[73] In any event, all papers carry the full
text of the Central Committee report.

The speech of the leader, which as already stressed
covers the activity of the party in every conceivable area
since the previous congress, as well as the country's
economic situation, international policy, and scientific
and cultural successes, usually takes the entire first day
of the congress, or at least most of it. Then it is the
turn of the delegates and the leaders of the foreign delegations to take the floor. The delegates who are allowed
to speak (once again, the reader must understand that
everything is prearranged and rehearsed) are carefully
selected. They usually are outstanding workers, higher
party officials, leaders of artistic and creative unions
and mass organizations, and so forth. Their speeches follow
the same lines: a review of the successes of their
respective unions, plants, or organizations, giving credit
to the party for successes, admitting minor weaknesses,
and pledging new successes and unreserved loyalty to the
party and its policy. Very seldom are there unexpected,
or rather unrehearsed developments. One such known
incident in recent East European party congresses was the
speech of Constantin Pirvulescu at the 12th RCP Congress
in November 1979.

Pirvulescu was one of the founders of the RCP and one
of its top leaders until the establishment of the socialist
regime. Afterwards he was chairman of the RCP Central
Control Commission, playing an important role in purging
the Ana Pauker group, and he remained a Politburo member
until 1960. According to various Western news agencies'
reports, the 84-year old Pirvulescu was apparently given
the floor by Ceausescu, after complaining that he had not
been granted permission to speak. Pirvulescu then delivered what is generally regarded as the first oral attack
made on Ceausescu at an RCP Congress. In complete
dissonance with the other speakers, who lavishly praised
Ceausescu and his achievements in every area, Pirvulescu
accused the secretary general of placing his personal
interests before those of the country, attacked the congress
as passing over the country's problems while devoting its
energies to promoting Ceausescu's reelection, and declared
that he would not vote for the secretary general.[74]

Some of Ceausescu's supporters tried to drown
Pirvulescu's remarks with pro-Ceausescu chants, and
Ceausescu himself is said to have accused Pirvulescu of

being a "foreigner in Romania . . . who still wants the time when the fate of our country was decided not in our country but abroad."[75]

A motion from the floor resulted in Pirvulescu losing his delegate's status so that Ceausescu could be re-elected "unanimously," and although AGERPRES, the Romanian news agency, vaguely mentioned Pirvulescu's "provocative behavior," which prompted "strong displeasure and indignant reaction" from the delegates, nothing was mentioned by Romania's daily press or radio broadcasts.[76]

The 12th LCY Congress in June 1982 also had its "unrehearsed" moments. Rade Koncar, a delegate from Belgrade, proposed--apparently without consulting any party organs--that the "class elements of the party be strengthened at the expense of the national elements" and "at the expense of the overemphasized territorialization."[77] This in fact meant to abolish the federative structure of the LCY and turn it into a uniform organization like the other East European communist parties (with the exception of the CPCZ, which was also based on a federative division). The proposal was flatly rejected at the congress. "Categorically and very sharply" was the phrase used by the Yugoslav press.[78] However, the incident prompted the Yugoslav press to comment: "The discussion at the congress demonstrated quite clearly that, in the League of Communists, not all are of the same mind about everything and that there are minor or major differences in relation to certain specific and practical issues and topics. Naturally, this is in no way a sensational dis-covery. Differences of this kind have probably existed in the past also, the only difference here being that no such open discussions as held at this congress have been held at similar gatherings in the past."[79]

The cases of Pirvulescu and Rade Koncar are rare exceptions--in fact, the only known such incidents at East European party congresses. The statements of the congress' delegates as a rule are predictable. They are dull and monotonous, devoid of any spontaneity or originality, and consisting of the endless repetition of prescribed formulas and slogans and trite praise for the party and the leader.

The leader of the Soviet delegation is the first foreigner to greet the congress. He usually reviews the international situation and praises the achievements of the host party and its loyalty to the CPSU and to the prin-ciples of Marxism-Leninism and proletarian (or socialist) internationalism. (The Albanian Congress is an obvious

exception). The speeches of the leaders of the East
European delegations follow the same pattern, describing
their own successes, pledging loyalty to the CPSU and the
hallowed principles of Marxism-Leninism and proletarian
internationalism, and extolling their friendship with the
host country.

Leaders of the delegations of the national liberation
movements or communist parties from noncommunist countries
describe their struggle for national liberation, social
progress, human rights, democracy, etc., and express
gratitude for the support and solidarity of the USSR,
the host country, and the entire socialist community.

It is obvious that not all leaders can greet the
congress. Those who are not important enough to do so at
one of the congress' sessions get their opportunity to
speak at one of the congress' commissions or sections
(when there are any), or at one of the friendship rallies
held in the host country during the congress. It is also
obvious that only a small fraction of the delegates can
take the floor and speak. (Who is to do so is a matter
decided long before the beginning of the congress.) The
role of the overwhelming majority of the delegates comes
down to chanting exclamations of support and voting as
prescribed. Naturally the decisions are adopted unanimously.

Even the AWP Congresses, which otherwise differ in
their size, the number of foreign delegations, and the
villains attacked from the congress' rostrum, follow
exactly the same pattern. Thus the 8th AWP Congress in
November 1981 included a long Central Committee report
read by Enver Hoxha, a report of the Central Control-
Auditing Commission, statements of the ministers of
foreign trade, defense, and internal affairs, a report of
the Credentials Commission (including information on the
delegates' age, social composition, professional and
educational background, and even awards), a report on the
Five-Year Plan by the premier, the late Mehmet Shehu, the
adoption of directives for the seventh Five-Year Plan,
the greetings of the leaders of the foreign delegations,
and, of course, the election of the new top party organs.[80]

The 16th CPCZ Congress opened with the Central
Committee report, read by party leader Gustav Husak, which
was the only event on the first day. Brezhnev was the first
to greet the congress on the second day, as the ritual
demanded, making the widely quoted and analyzed statement
on Poland: "It may be presumed that the Polish communists,
with the support of all true patriots, are able to deliver

the necessary rebuff to the intentions of the enemies of
the socialist system, as well as to the enemies of independent Poland."[81]

Prime Minister Strougal of Czechoslovakia, as well as
the leaders of the East European delegations, also figured
among the second-day speakers. CSSR foreign minister
Chnoupek spoke on the third day, along with certain local
delegates and the leaders of more foreign delegations.
The congress continued along the well-established lines,
elected the leading party organs on the last day, and
adopted the following resolutions:

1. On the Main Guidelines of the Economic and
    Social Development of the CSSR in the 1981-
    1985 period [i.e., the party directives for
    the seventh Five-Year Plan period];

2. On the Activity of the Central Committee of
    the CPCZ in the Implementation of the Program
    Set by the Party's 15th Congress;

3. On the Activity of the Central Control and
    Auditing Commission;

4. On the Reports and Letters to the Delegates
    [supposedly received by the thousands during
    the congress and containing pledges for more
    and better work as well as salutary addresses];

5. On Suggestions, Recommendations, and Requests
    Concerning Internal Questions of the Party
    and Membership Affairs.[82]

Several of these documents are mandatory, i.e.,
they are adopted by all congresses (the Central Committee
report, the reports of the other commissions, the theses,
and so forth). Other documents (economic guidelines,
Five-Year Plan) are "optional." Other decisions or
resolutions may relate to specific and topical international developments. Thus the 12th LCY Congress,
which took place during the 1982 Lebanon crisis, adopted
a special resolution on the situation in Lebanon: "The
12th LCY Congress, expressing the mood of all working
people and citizens of the SFRY, most severely censures
Israel's aggression against independent and nonaligned
Lebanon and the genocide of the Lebanese and Palestinian
population. It calls most resolutely for the unconditional
withdrawal of the Israeli aggressor."[83]

Sometimes the congress amends or adds to the party
statutes. The 12th BCP Congress amended the statutes by
changing the official title of the party leader from "first

secretary of the Central Committee" to "secretary general of the Central Committee."[84] The 12th LCY Congress also amended the party statutes by incorporating the principles of rotation and limiting the duration of the term of an official post.[85]

The Extraordinary 9th PZPR Congress was a different matter, as was everything else in Poland in 1980-1981. The work of the congress started with a long and heated dispute about procedures and agenda. The dispute, which began even before the congress was officially opened and continued into its second day, focused on the issue of the timing and method of electing the new party first secretary. Reportedly about 800 of the 1,962 delegates proposed that the future party leader be elected directly from the floor at the beginning of the congress. Some 50 more, however, were said to have argued for electing the entire Central Committee first, which should then elect the first secretary from among its members.[86] The issue was finally resolved at a closed session: the delegates voted to elect first the new Central Committee, which would then nominate candidates for first secretary, who would be elected by the congress by secret ballot.[87]

Party leader Kania's speech, which did not represent anything more than the standard Central Committee report, was followed by the statements of twenty speakers during the first two days of the congress. There was no common denominator in their statements. Most of them voiced regional or occupational interests and directed harsh criticism at party organs. At another closed session on the evening of 15 July, the second day of the congress, the delegates adopted a decision to expel from the party former party boss Edward Gierek and five of his close associates, including former Premier Edward Babiuch.[88]

When the decision on the procedure for electing the party's first secretary was announced, another unprecedented development occurred: the congress nominating commission received the names of several candidates for the post, among them Kania, Olszowski, and Grabski, and intensive lobbying on the part of their respective supporters began.

The election issue completely dominated the third day of the congress. The nominating commission submitted the names of 618 candidates for the 430 seats of the Central Committee, Control Commission, and Audit Commission. The various candidates, or at least a part of them, were reportedly subjected to questioning by the delegates.[89] The actual election took place in the late evening of 16 July. The procedure: each delegate crossed out the names

of the candidates he did not want. Only those candidates
who polled at least 50 percent plus one vote were eligible
for election. The introduction of this new procedure
(unprecedented in any other Soviet or East European
congresses) overshadowed any other of the congress
activities during the third day, despite the fact that
statements from the floor continued and the Solidarity
trade union was repeatedly criticized.

On 17 July it became apparent that most of the
incumbent PZPR Central Committee members had failed to gain
reelection. Only 18 of the old 143-member Central
Committee remained in the new body. Most dramatic was
the fact that only four of the 11 members of the Politburo
gained a place in the new Central Committee: Jaruzelski
(1,615 votes), Kania (1,355), Barcikowski (1,269), and
Olszowski (1,090).[90] Only one out of every six voivodeship party first secretaries was elected. In the past
their election had been automatic. In short, about 91
percent of the new Central Committee members were newly
elected. For the sake of comparison, at the 8th PZPR
Congress in January 1980 the turnover was 32 percent.[91]

On 18 July, Kania was reelected first secretary of the
Central Committee following a secret ballot, in which 1,944
of the 1,955 delegates participated (11 abstained).
Kania outpolled Kazimierz Barcikowski, his only competitor,
by 1,311 to 568 votes; 60 delegates voted against both
candidates and five votes were ruled invalid.[92]

On 19 July, the newly elected Central Committee
elected the new Politburo and the Secretariat. Kania
proposed the names of 14 candidates for full membership
in the Politburo, two candidate-members, and seven members
of the Central Committee Secretariat. More names were
proposed from the floor. The candidates were questioned
by the Central Committee members, after which the new
organs were elected by secret ballot. All the elected
officials were proposed by Kania. None of those proposed
from the floor were elected.[93] Afterwards the members of
the Central Control Commission and the members of the
Central Auditing Commission elected their chairmen--
both by secret ballot.

The entire procedure was unprecedented. For the first
time in the history of the East European party congresses
the election of the top party organs was a real event, and
not merely the repetition of a well-rehearsed show. For
the first time the candidates really had to organize a mini-
election campaign and answer penetrating questions. However,
there were more unprecedented aspects. The discussions

reflected the turmoil within the party, as well as the existence of different factions within the party. Various social problems, such as wages, housing, environmental protection, women's rights, and so forth, were discussed in a manner previously unheard of at such a forum. Different opinions were voiced, leaders were criticized, and different ways of solving the crisis proposed. Finally, there were no final documents adopted. The congress served as a landmark of real democratic procedures. However, it is impossible at this point to evaluate its lasting effect. Several months after the congress Stanislaw Kania resigned and was replaced as party leader by Jaruzelski, who introduced martial law on 13 December 1981. One must wait for the next party congress or at least for some major party conference in order to establish whether the democratic spark kindled by the Extraordinary 9th PZPR Congress has been preserved as an integral part of the PZPR internal affairs.

It has already been pointed out that the report of the Central Committee is the focal point of the congress. The second highlight is the "election" of the Central Committee by the congress delegates, and of the Politburo and the Secretariat, including the election of the first secretary (or secretary general) of the Central Committee by the Central Committee itself at its first (closed) session. The secret election of the PZPR Central Committee at the Extraordinary 9th PZPR Congress was the only really democratic election at an East European communist Party congress since the end of World War II. In all other congresses the "election" of the Central Committee, like everything else that takes place during the congress, is something that has been decided long before the congress. The congress elects the Central Committee at a closed session, and nothing has ever been published about any discussion or debates. On the contrary, it has always been stressed that the "Central Committee has been unanimously elected." (At the 12th LCY Congress the members of the future Central Committee came to the party congress already elected by the congresses of the republican and provincial party organization, and the party organization in the army; thus even the pretense of "electing" the Central Committee was dropped.) After its election, the new Central Committee holds its own closed session, and again "unanimously" elects the Politburo and the Secretariat. On both occasions, the entire matter comes down to reading a list of names prepared in advance by the Politburo, and automatically approving it.

It seems that election to the Central Committee
depends--to a certain degree--on factors and personal relations at the top of the party leadership, which are not
always clear. However, in some cases at least it seems
that the Politburo members try to influence the election
(or rather inclusion in the list read at the congress) of
as many of their supporters as possible. Failure to do so
indicates a weak position of the Politburo feudal lord
himself and the inability to take care of his vassals in
the party. For instance, the 7th AWP Congress, also known
as "the Congress of the great purge," elected 43 new members
of the 77-member Central Committee (almost 60 percent).
Because several top Politburo members had been purged in
the two or three years preceding the congress, observers
interpreted the unusually high turnover in Central
Committee members as a reflection of the turbulance at the
top of the party. The Politburo, on the other hand,
already purged of "unwanted elements," remained unchanged.
Enver Hoxha, naturally, was reelected AWP Central Committee
first secretary.[94]

The usual rate of turnover is about 30 percent. This
is the more or less acceptable quota of "one-timers"--
various outstanding workers who were elected to the Central
Committee as a reward for working successes or services
rendered--or aging leaders or Central Committee members
whose political career is on the decline.

The case of the Extraordinary 9th PZPR Congress,
when only 18 of the old 143-member Central Committee gained
reelection has been examined. At the previous, 8th PZPR
Congress, however, despite the already tense political
and economic situation, the turnover the Central Committee
members did not differ much from the established quota.
Some 97 of the 135-member Central Committee were reelected,
34 were dropped, and four were transferred to the Central
Auditing Commission.[95]

It seems that the CPSU has a say in the composition
of the list of the East European communist parties' top
organs; in any event, it is at least informed about them
in advance. A typical example was the 16th CPCZ Congress,
which was attended by Leonid Brezhnev. The composition
of the Central Committee was officially announced by Gustav
Husak on the last day of the congress, 10 April 1981. The
vote, of course, was reported to be "unanimous." However,
on the previous night Radio Hvezda in the CSSR reported a
meeting of "leading CPCZ representatives" and the CPSU
delegation led by Brezhnev. All attending leaders were
named, and it was reported that "they were warmly

congratulated by Brezhnev on being elected at the just-
concluded CPCZ Central Committee plenum."[96] Thus, the Soviet
delegation was at least informed about the election results
a good deal earlier than the Czechoslovak public.

      Although the Central Committee always undergoes
changes at the congress, the Politburo and the Secretariat
only seldom do. The reason is simple. The members of the
Central Committee are not constantly active. There are
three or four Central Committee regular plenums a year,
and they usually last for a day. There is seldom any
urgent reason to expel somebody from this organ. The
Politburo, on the other hand, is the central political
body, a quasi-cabinet, which in fact manages the country.
Changes in its membership are very important and usually
indicate political disgrace, a struggle within the leadership, and so forth. Therefore, the party does not wait
until the congress in order to make changes in the Politburo
membership, if such changes are necessary. Only
occasionally are changes in the Politburo membership left
until the congress. Reasons are seldom given, but then it
is hardly necessary to explain. However, Communist leaders
do not regard old age or even poor health as legitimate
reasons for retirement, so that when "retirement" is reported
as the reason for someone's name not appearing on the new
Politburo list, the explanation should be accepted with
caution.

      On its final day, the congress also adopts a number of
decisions, economic guidelines or plans, approves the
reports of the Central Committee and the Control and
Auditing Commission, and the final text of the theses. All
of these become once again subject to public discussion
and are constantly referred to in any major speech or
article. "To implement the decisions of the congress,"
"introducing the congress' decisions in life," "putting
into effect the decisions of the congress," etc., are key
phrases that are repeated in any communique, public
address, and party publication until the next pre-congress
campaign begins five years later. In addition, ministries,
mass and sociopolitical organizations, economic organizations, industrial plants, and so forth hold special meetings to "evaluate" the congress' decisions. In all visits
of party leaders, they inform each other on the "implementation of the party congress' decisions" or praise each
other on "correctly implementing" these decisions. Because
the Central Committee report at the congress affects every
single area of life and the congress' decisions are all-
inclusive decisions of heavy propagandistic character, no

one is unaffected in some way or another by the congress'
decisions. It must be pointed out that the constant,
ritualistic, and automatic reference to the congress'
decisions never specifies which particular decisions are
to be "implemented," "put into effect," and "introduced in
life." The simple adherence to "the decisions" is enough
evidence that one subscribes. Only one example will
suffice.

After the 10th SED Congress, the leadership of the
GDR Army convened to "evaluate the decisions" of the party
congress. The communique adopted after the meeting was a
typical example of all other post-congress statements and
pledges:

> On 6 May 1981 a joint meeting of the Collegium
> of the Ministry of National Defense and the
> Secretariat of the Army Main Political Adminis-
> tration focused its attention on the tasks re-
> lated to evaluating the decisions of the 10th
> SED Congress, which affect the National People's
> Army, the border troops, and the civil defense
> on a long-term basis. The meeting was headed
> by Army General Heinz Hoffmann, SED Central
> Committee Politburo member and Minister of
> National Defense.
>
> The participants discussed and adopted a
> plan which demands all heads, commanders, chiefs,
> and political organs to creatively implement the
> decisions of the party congress. This above all
> included, in close connection with the study of
> the materials of the 26th CPSU Congress, to
> deeply penetrate the trend-setting ideas and
> the political and theoretical contents of the
> documents of the highest SED forum and to reach
> specific conclusions for the spheres of respon-
> sibility in the period of 1981-1985. . . . The
> main thing is to achieve high results in all
> fields by efficient communist education and by
> further intensifying combat training, for
> instance by improving the education and training
> methods, and to still more consistently measure
> one's own achievements by the yardstick of the
> Soviet comrades-in-arms. . . .
>
> The 10th SED Congress has provided all army
> members, border soldiers, and civilian employees
> of the army with a purposeful orientation toward
> the reliable protection of the further construction

of the developed socialist society, and toward
guaranteeing peace.[97]

One notices immediately that no specific decisions of
the congress have been mentioned in this statement of
pledges. "Intensifying combat training" and "improving
the education and training methods" are stock phrases used
by all East European armies on every occasion. Using them
in reference to the congress' decisions means simply that
the army leadership in the GDR subscribes to the decisions
adopted by the congress (whatever they are) and expresses
loyalty to the party leadership. This is actually the main
goal of the post-congress campaign in all East European
countries.

In conclusion, the East European communist parties'
congress is an exact copy of the CPSU Congress. It is
formally designated in party statutes as the supreme
authority within the party, empowered to define the party's
goals and the operational means of their attainment. It
does not, however, play any important role in the country's
decision-making process. In fact, all its functions are
post factum functions: it legitimizes a policy line that
has already been formulated by the party central leadership,
"elects" a Central Committee that has already been approved
by the Politburo (and probably the CPSU), and adopts
decisions that have mostly a propaganda character, and
that also have already been formulated by the relevant
organs and organizations before the congress convened.

The election of delegates to the congress is a matter
of rewarding loyal vassals and outstanding workers or
functionaries, and not a question of any specific
functional competence or executive capacity. Obedience,
loyalty, and adherence to the prescribed procedure are the
key concepts governing the election of the delegates. In
fact, those are the rules governing the work of the
congress. Subsequently, everybody knows in advance the
congress' ritual, and surprises are very rare. It seems
that the main function of the congress is to shake up party
ranks through the accountability-election meetings, conduct
a minor purge, intensify productivity, increase the
political awareness of the population, and extract
declarations of loyalty to the party and adherence to its
policy--in short, a regular propaganda campaign of
mobilization-organizational nature. If the congress has
any real significance, then it is related to serving as an
authoritative forum for declaring the party line, restating
it, or announcing marginal changes.

There is yet another forum, which one has to mention, namely, the party conference. National party conferences are a rather rare and irregular event. Article 35 of the BCP statutes provides for such conferences being convened by the BCP Central Committee in the periods between party congresses "to deliberate on important questions of party policy."[98] Similar provisions exist in the statutes of the other East European parties.

The conference usually focuses on some central economic issue, although it may also discuss international issues. Thus, the 7-9 December 1977 RCP National Conference, which served mainly to offer broad approval of the 1976-1980 supplementary economic plan, touched upon some international issues. In his closing speech on 9 December, Ceausescu spoke both on the general international situation and on Romania's relations with its neighbors.[99] Nevertheless, economic affairs are usually the focal point of the attention of the conference.

The procedure resembles to a large degree the procedure followed by the congress. The delegates are elected by accountability-election meetings, i.e., in the same manner as the congress delegates. There are usually no foreign delegations; but there may be "guests"--meaning that various dignitaries and the mass media are permitted to attend.

A typical national conference was the 20-21 April 1978 BCP National Conference on the theme "For Improving the Socialist Organization of Labor and the Planned Management of Economy." An extensive report on this topic was read by Todor Zhivkov on the first day of the conference; it was followed by statements on the same issue by various economic ministers and representatives of industrial plants and economic organizations.[100] The conference ended with the following decision, which was "unanimously adopted":[101]

> The national party conference approves and
> unanimously adopts the conclusions, evaluations,
> tenets, and tasks stemming from the report read
> by Comrade Todor Zhivkov, BCP Central Committee
> first secretary. The national party conference
> adopts the report as a practical party program
> for a consistent and comprehensive implementa-
> tion of its strategic line on high quality and
> great efficiency. The conference adopts the
> theses of the national party conference aimed
> at perfecting the socialist labor organization

and planned economic management. The conference
notes with satisfaction the tremendous efforts
devoted by the BCP Central Committee to the purpose
of expanding the efforts of the communists and
of the workers' class, the efforts of all working
people aimed at implementing the decisions adopted
by the 11th BCP Congress, so that the struggle for
high quality and great efficiency may become a
nationwide cause. The national party conference
expresses its high appreciation of the personal
example set by Comrade Todor Zhivkov, BCP
Central Committee first secretary, in working out
the problems of our development for their application in practical life.

The national party conference expresses sincere
gratitude to the communists, the united agrarians,
the Fatherland Front, and Komsomol members as well
as to the workers' collectives, to the agricultural
toilers, and to the creative intelligentsia and all
Bulgarian people for supporting the party policy
and its practical initiatives aimed at implementing
the decisions of the 11th BCP Congress and the
decisions adopted by the July plenum of the BCP
Central Committee and calls upon them to engage
in the nationwide struggle for a decisive improvement of the socialist labor organization and of
planned economic management, for the fulfillment
and overfulfillment of the Five-Year Plan for the
accelerated construction of a developed socialist
society in the People's Republic of Bulgaria.[102]

This short decision mentions twice the "implementation of
the decisions of the 11th BCP Congress."
Such decisions, of course, provide another key phrase
for all speeches and articles until the next congress,
namely, "strictly adhering to the decisions of the National
Party Conference," or "putting into effect the decisions
of the National Party Conference," and so on ad nauseam.
Organizational (personnel) matters usually are not
dealt with at such forums, and consequently there are no
sensational changes in the party top organs. The
conference is simply another party instrument for
injecting enthusiasm into the country's economic life and
delivering new and catchy phrases to be used as slogans
in urging the workers to improve their economic
performance.

NOTES

1. <u>Trybuna Ludu</u> (Poland), 20–21 October 1979.
2. <u>Borba</u> (Yugoslavia), 10 February 1978.
3. <u>Rabotnichesko Delo</u> (Bulgaria), 30 July 1980.
4. Belgrade TANJUG Domestic Service in Serbo-Croatian, 1926 GMT, 30 September 1981; <u>Daily Report</u> (FBIS), 1 October 1981.
5. <u>Politika</u> (Yugoslavia), 15 January 1975.
6. Radio Bucharest "Evening Chronicle," 1900 GMT, 26 February 1975.
7. Warsaw Domestic Service in Polish, 0100 GMT, 3 December 1980; <u>Daily Report</u> (FBIS), 3 December 1980.
8. Warsaw Domestic Service in Polish, 1700 GMT, 7 April 1981; <u>Daily Report</u> (FBIS), 8 April 1981.
9. Tirana Domestic Service in Albanian, 1900 GMT, 27 February 1981; <u>Daily Report</u> (FBIS), 2 March 1981.
10. Ibid.
11. <u>Buletinul Oficial</u> (Romania), 6 July 1979.
12. <u>Rabotnichesko Delo</u>, 30 July 1980.
13. RFE Situation Report, Bulgaria, 8 August 1980.
14. <u>Rabotnichesko Delo</u>, 30 July 1981.
15. Ibid.
16. Belgrade TANJUG Domestic Service in Serbo-Croatian, 1926 GMT, 30 September 1981; <u>Daily Report</u> (FBIS), 1 October 1981.
17. <u>Borba</u>, 9 April 1982; <u>Daily Report</u> (FBIS), 15 April 1982.
18. <u>Nepszabadsag</u> (Hungary), 9 December 1979.
19. <u>Rabotnichesko Delo</u>, 16 February 1981.
20. RFE Background Report, Hungary, 20 December 1974.
21. RFE Background Report, Hungary, 19 December 1979.
22. RFE Background Report, Hungary, 20 December 1974.
23. <u>Rabotnichesko Delo</u>, 16 February 1981.
24. Ibid.
25. RFE Situation Report, Bulgaria, 30 March 1976.
26. <u>Rude Pravo</u> (Czechoslovakia), 15 November 1975.
27. <u>Zivot Strany</u> (Czechoslovakia), no. 5, 1981, pp. 32–33.
28. Ibid.
29. <u>Borba</u>, 9 April 1982; <u>Daily Report</u> (FBIS), 15 April 1982.
30. <u>Neues Deutschland</u> (East Berlin), 31 May–1 June 1980.
31. Ibid.
32. Ibid.
33. <u>Partelet</u> (Hungary), October 1979 and February 1980,

in RFE Background Report, Hungary, 26 February 1980.

34. Partelet, November 1979, also RFE Background Report, Hungary, 26 February 1980.

35. Magyar Hirlap (Hungary), 22 January 1980.

36. Partelet, February 1980.

37. Sofia Domestic Service in Bulgarian, 1830 GMT, 17 March 1981; Daily Report (FBIS), 18 March 1981.

38. Radio Hvezda, Prague, 1900 GMT, 8 March 1981.

39. Belgrade TANJUG Domestic Service in Serbo-Croatian, 0932 GMT, 26 April 1982; Daily Report (FBIS), 27 April 1982.

40. RFE RAD Background Report, Yugoslavia, no. 118, 24 May 1982.

41. RFE RAD Background Report, Yugoslavia, no. 136, 16 June 1982.

42. Nepszabadsag, 14 February 1980.

43. Borba, 10 February 1978.

44. Komunist (Yugoslavia), 27 March 1978.

45. Belgrade TANJUG Domestic Service in Serbo-Croatian, 1926 GMT, 30 September 1981; Daily Report (FBIS), 1 October 1981.

46. RFE Situation Report, Hungary, 11 March 1980.

47. Sofia Domestic Service in Bulgarian, 1630 GMT, 18 February 1981.

48. Sofia Domestic Service in Bulgarian, 1830 GMT, 17 March 1981.

49. Sofia Domestic Service in Bulgarian, 1000 GMT, 11 March 1981.

50. Trybuna Ludu, 20 October 1979.

51. Ibid., 12 November 1979.

52. Ibid., 18 November 1979.

53. Ibid., 12 November 1979.

54. RFE Situation Report, Poland, 3 July 1981.

55. RFE Background Report, Poland, 10 July 1981.

56. Kania's speech was disseminated by PAP in English on 16 June 1981 and quoted by RFE Situation Report, Poland, 3 July 1981.

57. Moscow Radio at 1700 and 2000 GMT, 22 June 1981; TASS in Russian on 22 June 1981; RFE Situation Report, Poland, 3 July 1981.

58. AP, Reuter, and Radio Warsaw reports on 25 June 1981, quoted by RFE Background Report, Poland, 10 July 1981.

59. RFE Background Report, Poland, 10 July 1981.

60. Rabotnichesko Delo, 7 March 1981.

61. Ibid., 5 March 1981.

62. Otechestven Front (Bulgaria), 20 March 1981.

63. Rabotnichesko Delo, 20 March 1981.

64. Ibid., 1 April 1981.

65. Rude Pravo, 10 April 1981.

66. Belgrade TANJUG Domestic Service in Serbo-Croatian, 1926 GMT, 30 September 1981; Daily Report (FBIS), 1 October 1981.

67. Tirana Domestic Service in Albanian, 1330 GMT, 30 October 1981; Daily Report (FBIS), 2 November 1981.

68. Rabotnichesko Delo, 1 April 1981.

69. Neues Deutschland, 12 April 1981.

70. RFE Situation Report, CSSR, 30 April 1981.

71. Rude Pravo, 7 April 1981.

72. RAD Background Report, Albania, 9 November 1976.

73. RAD Background Report, SFRY, 21 June 1978.

74. RAD Background Report, Romania, 28 November 1979.

75. Ibid.

76. Ibid.

77. Nin (Yugoslavia), no. 1644, 4 July 1982; Daily Report (FBIS), 9 July 1982.

78. Ibid.

79. Ibid.

80. All listed speeches were printed in Zeri I Popullit of 1 to 10 November 1981 and published by FBIS in a special Daily Report, 7 December 1981.

81. RFE Situation Report, CSSR, 30 April 1981.

82. Ibid.

83. Belgrade Domestic Service in Serbo-Croatian, 0942 GMT, 29 June 1982; Daily Report (FBIS), 2 July 1982.

84. Rabotnichesko Delo, 5 April 1981.

85. Belgrade TANJUG Domestic Service in Serbo-Croatian, 1003 GMT, 26 June 1982; Daily Report (FBIS), 28 June 1982.

86. AP, UPI, and Reuter, 14 July 1981; N.Y. Times, 14 July 1981; RAD Background Report, Poland, 3 August 1981.

87. RFE RAD Background Report, Poland, 3 August 1981.

88. Trybuna Ludu, 16 July 1981.

89. N.Y. Times, 17 July 1981.

90. UPI, 17 July 1981; RAD Background Report, Poland, 3 August 1981.

91. PAP, 18 July 1981; RAD Background Report, Poland, 3 August 1981.

92. Radio Warsaw, 18 July 1981; Trybuna Ludu, 19 July 1981.

93. RFE RAD Background Report, Poland, 3 August 1981.

94. RFE RAD Background Report, Albania, 9 November 1976.

95. RFE RAD Background Report, Poland, 29 February 1980.

96. RFE Situation Report, CSSR, 30 April 1981.

97. *Neues Deutschland*, 7 May 1981; *Daily Report* (FBIS), 11 May 1981.

98. RFE Situation Report, Bulgaria, 16 December 1977.

99. RFE Situation Report, Romania, 23 December 1977.

100. Sofia BTA in English, 1430 GMT, 21 April 1978; *Daily Report* (FBIS), 24 April 1978.

101. Sofia Domestic Service in Bulgarian, 1630 GMT, 21 April 1978; *Daily Report* (FBIS), 24 April 1978.

102. Ibid.

7
The Leaders

    The three most important leadership posts in the East
European communist states are party leader, head of government, and head of state; that is, general secretary (or
first secretary) of the communist party Central Committee,
premier (or chairman of the council of ministers), and
president (or chairman of the state council). The most
important of these three is the post of party Central
Committee secretary general. Although it is frequently
the case in Eastern Europe that one man may wear two or
even three hats, the party leader and the head of state
being the same person (Romania, Bulgaria, and the CSSR,
for instance), or the party leader and the chairman of
the Council of Ministers being one person (Jaruzelski in
Poland), it is the party boss that is The Leader.
    Most of the first generation leaders, i.e., those who
were appointed immediately after the end of World War II,
came directly from Moscow where they had spent rather long
periods of their life during the pre-communist era of their
own countries. Thus they were Moscow's choice. Dimitrov
(Bulgaria), Gottwald (CSSR), Rakosi (Hungary), and
Ulbricht (the GDR) were actually "imported" from Moscow
by their respective countries. For the rest, Tito was the
undisputed leader of the partisan movement and party
leader, who had also spent a long time in Moscow earlier but
remained throughout the war in Yugoslavia; Gomulka (Poland)
was appointed by his party, apparently without Moscow's
consent; Gheorghiu-Dej (Romania) spent eleven years in a
Romanian prison until 1944 and proceeded straight from
prison to the party leadership; and Enver Hoxha (Albania)
was Belgrade's choice. Actually the entire Albanian
party formation was sponsored by Yugoslavia, which is
interesting when one considers the frosty relations today

between Albania and Yugoslavia.

The picture of the leadership in Eastern Europe during the first years after the war was rather confused. Although Tito, Dimitrov, and Hoxha were undoubtedly the number one men in their countries, in Romania, Gheorghiu-Dej was overshadowed for a while by Ana Pauker and Luca; in Hungary, Rakosi shared power with Gero and Revai; in Czechoslovakia, Slanski and Zapotocky enjoyed no lesser status than Gottwald; and finally, in the GDR, Pieck and Grotewohl were Ulbricht's equals. Since those days, however, the position of the party leader has consolidated and emerged pre-eminent, and today the party first secretary has no peers.

CHARACTERISTICS OF THE TOP POSITION

Several basic characteristics of the first secretary's post have asserted themselves since the end of World War II:

1. None of the East European communist parties' first secretaries has ever been elected by the entire population in a democratic way. None was the choice of the people (although pressure from below had some influence in the reappointment of Gomulka in Poland in 1956). None (with the exception of Stanislaw Kania at the Extraordinary 9th PZPR Congress) has been elected by democratic and secret elections, and only a few have been elected without the explicit consent of Moscow.

2. Succession is an unpredictable matter in Eastern Europe (see Table 7.1). Because the "election" of a new leader is a process that has nothing to do with fixed democratic procedures, it is also true that his expulsion, being ousted, or his "resignation" can (and does) take place unexpectedly. Even when there is no immediate indication of an imminent removal, it is impossible to determine the length of the party boss's term in office or the identity of his successor.

3. Because being ousted is an ever-present possi-bility, and because this is only done by or through the Politburo, the atmosphere in this leading party organ is rife with tension, mistrust, rumor, and suspicion. The communist leaders do not trust anybody, and especially not each other. One effect of this atmosphere of suspicion is the immediate removal of any potential rival for the post of party secretary general (the case of Boris Velchev in Bulgaria has already been examined) or the practical institutionalization of a constant shifting of

Table 7.1
Leadership Succession in Eastern Europe, Post-World War II Through 1984

Nation	Initial Leader	Leader's Fate	Successors and Their Fates	Present Leader	Years in Office (1982)
Albania	Hoxha	4		Hoxha	37
Bulgaria	Dimitrov	1	Chervenkov,[2] Zhivkov[4]	Zhivkov	27
CSSR	Gottwald	1	Novotny,[2] Dubcek,[2] Husak[4]	Husak	13
GDR	Ulbricht (with Grotewohl and Pieck)	3	Honecker[4]	Honecker	11
Hungary	Rakosi	2	Gero,[2] Nagy,[2] Kadar[4]	Kadar	25
Poland	Gomulka	2	Bierut,[1] Gomulka,[2] Gierek,[2] Kania,[2] Jaruzelski[4]	Jaruzelski	1
Romania	Gheorghiu-Dej	1	Ceausescu[4]	Ceausescu	16
Yugoslavia	Tito	1	Annual rotation of leaders since 1980		

1. Died in office without losing power.
2. Overthrown or eased out by his colleagues.
3. Retired peacefully.
4. Remains in office.

posts, with ranking cadres alternating between party and state posts, as is the situation in Ceausescu's Romania.

4. The East European leaders show a marked reluctance to leave office. In fact, usually the only possibilities for doing so are death or disgrace. Yet Kania in Poland resigned in 1981 in what seemed at the time to be a voluntary move, and he did not disappear completely from the political scene. On 26 May 1982 he was elected by the Polish Sejm to the Council of State,[1] which is unlikely to have pleased the powers in Moscow, considering the severe criticism leveled against him from that quarter in the autumn of 1981. However, Kania's case can be regarded as the exception that proves the rule. Normally any ousting, expulsion, or "resignation" of an East European Communist Party first secretary is actually a punishment for failing to implement the duties of the post as expected (usually by Moscow).

5. Sometimes the party leaders are also heads of state. Succession to the presidency or other high elective office adds to the party leader's prestige and enhances his position when visiting and receiving Western or other foreign heads of state, where international protocol gives pride of place to the head of state. Nevertheless, this is always a post factum assertion of status that already exists.

6. The East European party leaders, and especially those who have been in power for a long time, tend to develop a personality cult as a result of their absolute preeminence in their own society, and this sometimes, as in Ceausescu's Romania, borders on the ridiculous. The incessant glorification and even virtual deification of the party leader is often accompanied by unashamed nepotism—members of the leader's immediate family being appointed to high party and state positions—and at least in the case of Bulgaria's late Lyudmila Zhivkova and perhaps Romania's Elena Ceausescu, being mentioned as possible heirs of the leader.

These basic characteristics will now be explained and illustrated with specific examples.

ELECTION AND SUCCESSION OF LEADERS

The first secretaries (or general secretaries) of the East European communist parties are usually elected by the Central Committee on the last day of the party congress, at a closed (secret) session. Thus, each owes his post to a

relatively small group within a small elitist party, and
of course, to the consent of Moscow. Little if anything
is known about the procedure within the Central Committee
(the Extraordinary 9th PZPR Congress remaining an extraordinary exception), but it does not seem that there has
ever been more than one candidate. What is known very
well, however, is the fact that none has been elected in a
democratic, secret, nationwide election. Furthermore,
whatever other top posts they may hold (president, prime
minister, etc.), they derive their authority from their
position as party secretary, not from any other post to
which they have been elected or appointed in a constitutional procedure. As a rule when a state leader is being
reelected the entire procedure is a mere formality,
particularly in the case where the state leader is also the
party secretary. Thus in May 1980 Gustav Husak was reelected president of the CSSR for a second five-year term.
The entire process, including the "presidential campaign,"
lasted four days. It began on 19 May with a televised
commentary on the significance of the presidential office.
The next day a CPCZ Central Committee plenum adopted its
Presidium's proposal and unanimously "suggested" Husak as
the party's and the National Front's joint candidate for
the presidency. The motion was made by Prime Minister
Lubomir Strougal, who praised Husak's "wide knowledge,
education, theoretical erudition, experience, political
practice, prudence coupled with determination, his ability
to speak frankly and comprehensibly about complex topical
matters and to create a quiet atmosphere."[2]

The National Front immediately acted on the party's
suggestion and nominated Husak as the only candidate for
president. The formal proposal was conveyed to the
assembly on 21 May by Slovak Communist Party first secretary
Jozef Lenart.[3] On 22 May the Federal Assembly convened and
unanimously reelected Husak president of the CSSR.[4]
Throughout the four-day campaign the CSSR media reported
that the party Central Committee had been flooded with
telegrams and messages expressing popular joy over Husak's
nomination and extolling his virtues.

Short as it is, the presidential election campaign is
at least a constitutional process, which albeit nominal,
is incorporated in the law of the land. The election to
the post of party first secretary is an entirely different
matter. It is a nebulous, almost clandestine affair. One
can assume that the candidacy is proposed by the Politburo,
but one does not know whether any debates are involved.
Nevertheless, the procedure seems to be rather simple, in

fact as simple as the procedure employed to remove the
first secretary from his post. Thus, as already observed,
sudden transitions from power to prison (or at least
oblivion), or from prison to power are not unusual. Gomulka
(Poland), Kadar (Hungary), and other East European leaders
spent long periods of time in communist prisons prior to
their election as party leaders. In Gomulka's case, it was
a matter of top-bottom-top-out. Forced to resign once in
1948, he spent several years in the political wilderness
and about three years in prison. Released in 1954, he
emerged as the most sound alternative for party leader
after the October 1956 events in Poland. He remained party
leader until 19 December 1970, when he was more or less
forced to resign from the Politburo at a time of widespread
social upheaval, triggered by a massive workers' revolt
and the accompanying factional struggles and bitter
conflicts within the party. (Ostensibly, he was asked to
resign by other Politburo members, when following a heart
attack he appeared incapable of exercising his leadership
functions.)[5] Later on, the Polish press openly accused him
of "increasingly concentrating in his hands autocratic
power," "conducting an incorrect and unrealistic policy,"
and so forth.[6]

Gustav Husak spent even longer periods in prison. He
was purged from the party in February 1951 and sentenced to
life imprisonment in April 1954. He was pardoned in May
1960 and rehabilitated in April 1963. However, Husak
returned to active political life only in early 1968, as
Dubcek's deputy premier. On 17 April 1969 he was elected
party chief.[7]

Two important conclusions follow. The first is that
the leaders must realize that their position is impermanent
and transient. They all have learned (many of them from
personal experience) how easy and simple it is to remove
them. They know that there is no tenure in their post,
nor are there any fixed rules for removing them. It can
take place any day. By the same token, they know that
there is no legal or fixed limit to the length of their
tenure. In any event (except for leaders in Albania and
Yugoslavia), they know that their status depends to a large
degree on Moscow. Hence, they fell obliged to constantly
demonstrate their loyalty and to adhere publicly to any
political and ideological line issued by Moscow.

The second conclusion is that the leaders must realize
that the technical or rather mechanical procedure of their
removal will take place in the Politburo and will be conducted by the members of the Politburo. They also know

that their steps are being watched and often reported to
Moscow by various members of the inner circle, eagerly
awaiting a mistake on their parts to remove them. The result
is the already mentioned aura of suspicion and mistrust that
characterizes the East European Politburos. Yet despite
this heavy atmosphere, no East European first secretary has
ever resigned voluntarily (again, with the possible
exception of Stanislaw Kania).

The case of Gomulka has already been described. Most
of the accusations leveled at Gomulka were sponsored by his
successor Edward Gierek. Gierek's own turn came in 1980,
again in a period of social unrest and strikes. On 5
September 1980, during a special Central Committee plenum,
he was removed from all positions of political responsibility.
At that time some "health reasons" were also muttered sotto
voce by the Polish press.[8] However, on 2 December 1980, at
another Central Committee plenum, Gierek was charged with
"serious political responsibility" for mistakes in social
and economic policies. The PZPR Central Committee also
added that "Edward Gierek's most important mistake was to
have created a pattern of interrelations in and methods of
work for the leadership of the party that were contrary to
the party's principles. This (mistake) brought about an
atmosphere of underhand plotting and replaced true
democracy with (its) appearance."[9] Gierek himself sent a
letter to the Central Committee,[10] apologizing for some of
his mistakes and offering explanations for the others.

This was not the end of the problem. In May 1981
Gierek was summoned by a specially created Central
Committee commission headed by Central Committee secretary
and Politburo member Tadeusz Grabski and given another
opportunity to explain his mistakes. During the ensuing
meeting Gierek assumed responsibility for his mistakes.[11]

When Gierek "resigned" in September 1980, he was
replaced by Stanislaw Kania. Kania remained PZPR Central
Committee first secretary for only about a year. During
this time the situation in Poland continued to deteriorate,
with the Solidarity trade union gaining more influence and
the PZPR being subjected to severe criticism from inside
and outside (Moscow). After the September 1981 Solidarity
Congress, the criticism of Kania and his treatment of
Solidarity became an open matter. On 9 October 1981 the
PZPR Gdansk Executive Committee adopted a resolution
openly criticizing the party leadership, without mentioning Kania by name.[12] A plenum of the Warsaw city party
organization took place on 13-14 October 1980. The party
leadership was severely criticized once again, and although

Kania was not mentioned by name, "lack of leadership" was a phrase repeated by many participants.[13] The East European press also joined the campaign of hints and inferences. Berlin's Neues Deutschland of 16 October reported the Warsaw party plenum, and cited one of the speakers, Professor Jan Rychlewski, for the fact that "he was ready to fight for the party but under a different leadership."[14] In addition to all this, Moscow repeatedly criticized the PZPR leadership for its performance against Solidarity, following the direct challenge to the regime launched at the first round of the Solidarity Congress.

In this atmosphere a special PZPR Central Committee plenum convened on 16 October. On the third day of the plenum, after continuous attacks and criticism on the part of the participants, Kania resigned. His resignation was first reported in a dry and factual manner: "Stanislaw Kania resigned from the post of the PZPR Central Committee first secretary during the organizational part of today's debates. The resignation has been accepted."[15]

Later on PAP, the official Polish press agency, reported that "Stanislaw Kania requested that the plenum accept his resignation from the post of Central Committee first secretary. In a secret ballot, his resignation was accepted by 104 votes, with 70 against."[16] The candidacy of Prime Minister Wojcoech Jaruzelski was proposed by Central Committee secretary Kazimierz Barcikowski. The Central Committee conducted the vote by secret ballot. Jaruzelski was elected PZPR Central Committee first secretary by 180 votes, with four against.[17] Thus he concentrated in his hands the posts of PZPR Central Committee first secretary, premier, and minister of defense.

Kania was not subjected to malicious personal criticism, let alone charged with personal responsibility for the situation. There were no open and clear demands for his resignation. On the other hand, his resignation came only on the third day of the Central Committee plenum, when it became obvious that the majority of the Central Committee members did not support him. Therefore, it is doubtful whether even his resignation can be regarded as a voluntary one.

It has already been pointed out that there are normally only two ways out for the East European leaders: death or disgrace (accompanied by isolation and oblivion). However, sometimes even a leader's death is wrapped in mystery. On 18 December 1981 a terse official announcement on Tirana radio said that Premier Mehmet Shehu had "killed

himself in a moment of nervous crisis."[18] Shehu had been
Premier since 1954, was the party's ideologue, and had long
been considered the number two man in Albania, Hoxha's right
hand. The brief announcement was followed by a short and
rather dry obituary.[19] This was the last that was heard
of Shehu. There was no announcement about his funeral, no
further explanation, and no period of official mourning.
This complete failure to observe the usual niceties connected with the death of a prominent leader of long duration
prompted speculation in many Western newspapers (Paris
Le Figaro 21 December 1981, Turin La Stampa 3 January 1982,
and many others), and some Yugoslav sources[20] about the
nature of Shehu's death. Various theories about a violent
argument (in the true sense of the term) with Hoxha about
political doctrine and an opening to the West, about a
succession struggle, murder, and so forth were voiced, none
of them proved or even supported by any evidence. Shehu's
death remains a mystery. So far in Albania he has not
been accused of anything, nor has his name ever been
mentioned again in the media.

Sometimes, the party first secretary can be removed
as a result of "serious errors" without the errors ever
being specified. Such was the case with Bulgaria's
Vulko Chervenkov, who was ousted in 1956. Chervenkov was
one of the central figures in Bulgaria's communist party
before World War II. During the war he was the head of
the clandestine Khristo Botev radio station operating from
the USSR and a lecturer at the CPSU Lenin International
School. He was married to the sister of Georgi Dimitrov,
the undisputed leader of the Bulgarian communists.

After the establishment of the communist regime in
Bulgaria, Chervenkov became a member of the Politburo and
chairman of the Committee on Arts and Culture. In February
1950 he became chairman of the Council of Ministers and in
November 1950, secretary general of the BCP Central
Committee, a post he kept until the 6th BCP Congress in
February-March 1954, when Todor Zhivkov replaced him as
first secretary. Still, Chervenkov retained his prominence
until the April 1956 Central Committee plenum--the
Bulgarian repercussion of the 20th CPSU Congress--when he
was demoted to deputy chairman of the Council of Ministers.
His career continued to suffer one setback after another,
until the November 1961 Central Committee plenum accused
him of encouraging the personality cult and "mistakes and
vicious methods."[21] Chervenkov was ousted from the Politburo
and his post as deputy premier. Finally, at the 4 November
1962 Central Committee plenum he was again sharply

criticized and ousted from the Central Committee and the party itself, together with Premier Anton Yugov.[22] In 1969 his party membership was restored.[23] According to the 1969 Brief Bulgarian Encyclopedia "a BCP Central Committee plenum on 19 May 1969 revoked the penalty of expulsion from the party that had been imposed on Vulko Chervenkov, [evaluating it] as having played its role, and restored his membership in the party, recognizing his uninterrupted length of party service."[24]

Chervenkov died on 21 October 1980. Despite his restored membership in the party, he remained virtually a nonperson. He was never mentioned in the press and made no recorded public appearances. Still, Todor Zhivkov attended his funeral, carefully refraining from any eulogy.[25]

There is yet another category of removed party and state leaders, namely, those removed as a result of Moscow's direct intervention. Such were the cases of Alexander Dubcek in Czechoslovakia (1969) and Rakosi, Gero, and Nagy in Hungary (1956), who were removed on Moscow's orders. Dubcek and Nagy were abducted to Moscow, Nagy losing his life in the process. He was sentenced to death following the October-November 1956 uprising in Hungary and executed on 16 June 1958. An official communique issed on 17 June and printed in Nepszabadsag listed a whole page of various accusations against him.[26]

SELF-PROTECTION BY THE SUCCESSORS

Whatever the reasons for their withdrawal, East European party leaders have rarely fared well at the hands of their successors, generally being criticized, accused of various mistakes or even crimes, or at best ignored and neglected, to be remembered only on important anniversaries, if at all. Such has been the fate of Boleslaw Bierut, Wladislaw Gomulka, and Edward Gierek of Poland; Walter Ulbricht of the GDR; Klement Gottwald and Antonin Novotny of the CSSR; Matyas Rakosi and Erno Gero of Hungary; Vulko Chervenkov of Bulgaria; and Gheorghiu-Dej of Romania. (Bulgaria's Georgi Dimitrov, who was truly a major figure in international communist affairs, seems to be the sole exception to this practice.) One example will suffice to illustrate this point: Romania's Gheorghiu-Dej has never been officially castigated for any mistakes or ideological deviation. He died in office, and in generally good status. Although the 70th anniversary of his birth was noted in the RCP daily Scinteia by a long article with old photographs, the 80th anniversary on 8 November 1981 was completely ignored by the Romanian press.[27]

There seem to be two reasons for this general pattern of irreverent treatment. First, it enables the heir to make a new start, blaming his predecessor for all the negative aspects of the system and reserving praise of the positive aspects for the party. In this way, errors, deviations, mistakes, and shortcomings are always attributed to individual scapegoats, and the party and "the system" remain infallible and unblemished. The second reason is related to the very essence of the East European communist states. The party leader often considers himself threatened not only by the Politburo feudal lords, but also by the shadow of a powerful predecessor. If the new leader is to step out of the shadow of his predecessor and establish his own authority, almost everything related to the previous leader is to be underestimated or even completely negated.

At the same time they undermine the authority of their predecessors, the East European party leaders try to strengthen their positions and discourage potential opposition in the Politburo. One obvious way is winning Moscow's benevolence. The automatic and reflexive adherence to everything Moscow says or does, the annual meetings with the Soviet leaders, and so forth, are all examples of keeping Moscow happy in an attempt to keep themselves in office.

Controlling the Politburo is also a matter of personal safety. The basic principle is to prevent any member of the Politburo from appearing as the heir apparent. Romania's Ceausescu has become famous for the "Ceausescu shuffle," i.e., the frequent transfer of officials from party to state posts and vice versa so that no one has enough time to organize a power base in his post and thus turn into a political rival. The latest of these "Ceausescu shuffles" took place in May 1982, when several top officials were removed in what seemed at the time a major reorganization of the government and an additional attempt to blame individuals for the system's shortcomings. The most important changes were:

1. The replacement of economic administrator (and presumed relative of Ceausescu), Ilie Verdet, with political administrator Constantin Dascalescu as prime minister;
2. The removal of all eight deputy prime ministers (but none of the three first

       deputy prime ministers), including Ceausescu
clan member Cornel Burtica (who also lost his
position as minister of foreign trade), old
stalwarts Janos Fazekas and Ion Ionita (both
reportedly for reasons of health), and
trouble-shooter Emil Bobu, who was also
replaced as chairman of the National Council
of Agriculture, Food Industry, Forestry,
and Water Management;

3. The appointment of four new deputy prime
ministers, including one apparent ethnic
Hungarian, Ludovic Fazekas, and one reported
member of the Ceausescu clan, Gheorghe
Petrescu;

4. The dismissal of Aneta Spornic, Cornelia
Filipas, and Janos Fezekas from the Political
Executive Committee, and of Ionita as an
alternative member of that body.[28]

This reorganization of the Romanian government took
place on 21 May 1982 and was performed (as usual) by the
RCP Central Committee "at a working meeting on 21 May
1982,"[29] the actual decision then being adopted by the
Grand National Assembly "on the basis of a recommendation
made by the RCP Central Committee."[30]

Another way of dealing with potential competition is
simply to demote the official considered to be number two
at a given moment. Such was the case with former Bulgarian
Premier Stanko Todorov. Until 1977, whenever the members
of the Politburo were listed, his name appeared not in the
usual alphabetical order, but in second place, right after
Todor Zhivkov. This was a clear indication that Todorov
was number two in the Bulgarian hierarchy. After June
1977, Todorov's name was dropped from second place and
began to be listed in alphabetical order, along with other
Politburo members.[31] For Todorov and for the Bulgarians
that meant that whereas he had up to that point been clearly
identified as the number two man in the combined party-
state hierarchy (since 1971 when he was appointed chairman
of the Council of Ministers), he had now been relegated to
the rank of an ordinary Politburo member. The major step
in his political demotion came in June 1981, when following
the general elections in Bulgaria, he was removed from his
position as premier and appointed chairman of the National
Assembly.[32] Although he retained his membership in the
Politburo, Todorov was clearly no longer Zhivkov's heir
apparent. It is interesting to note that Todorov's

demotion coincided with the meteoric rise in the career of Todor Zhivkov's daughter, Lyudmila, whose case will be examined later in this chapter.

Although the East European communist parties' first secretaries are in a position to initiate transfers, demotions, promotions, and other maneuvers aimed at strengthening and securing their positions, the state leaders (in this sense the government leaders and heads of states, as opposed to the party leaders) have a serious handicap. They need the approval of the Central Committee (and, of course, the Politburo), for everything they do. But the party first secretary dominates these forums, so that the opportunity for impasse is clear. Stanko Todorov's case was only one example. There are many others of East European state leaders desperately clinging to the constitutional rules defining their terms of office and struggling against any attempt to remove them. Czechoslovakia's President Ludvik Svoboda was a typical example. He was first elected president on 30 March 1968.[33] On 22 March 1973 the aging and infirm Svoboda was reelected, although even then he did not have enough mental and physical energy to fulfill the purely representative and ceremonial duties of his office. During his second term he traveled abroad only twice: to the GDR in August 1973 for Walter Ulbricht's funeral, and to the USSR in September 1973 for a vacation. His 1974 New Year's message had to be read over the radio by another speaker, and his last public appearance was recorded on 7 March 1974, when he received Bulgaria's foreign minister Petur Mladenov.[34]

Immediately afterwards it became obvious that the aging president was obviously unfit to carry on but was reluctant to resign from his office. The CPCZ had no choice but to initiate an amendment to the Constitution to the effect that the Federal Assembly could elect a new president if the old one had been unable to execute his duties for "at least one year." This amendment became law on 28 May 1975, and the next day Gustav Husak, the party leader, succeeded Svoboda as president of the Republic.[35]

Svoboda appears to have been equally reluctant to resign from the Presidium of the CPCZ Central Committee, of which he had been a member since 31 August 1968. There, however, the case was simple. There are no constitutional provisions (or rules of any kind other than a post factum approval of the Central Committee) for changes in the Presidium, and no formal procedure is necessary. Svoboda was kept pro forma in the top party organ until the April 1976 15th CPCZ Congress, which then simply eased him out by reducing the number of the Presidium's full members from 12 to 11.[36]

The first secretaries, who have no protective constitutional brakes or checks, must rely mainly on themselves (and Moscow). The demotion of potential rivals and frequently shifts of other responsible officials are only two of their techniques of self-protection. Two additional techniques are intensive nepotism and personal glorification.

Nepotism is a favorite way of certain East European leaders to achieve relative security in their positions. First of all, blood is thicker than water, and second, members of the family know to whom they owe their posts. Subsequently, unconditionally supporting the party leader is not only a matter of gratitude, but simply a way of protecting their own offices. (They know that in most cases when the leader goes, they go as well.) There is one additional advantage to being surrounded by relatives. A ruling group composed of the members of the family could not lead to the creation of a clique Moscow could influence as it might wish. The result is that in certain East European countries members of the leaders' immediate families are usually Central Committee members and/or ministers and even Politburo members.

The Hoxha and Shehu clans in Albania have placed scores of their members in top positions; first of all the two wives, Nexhmije Hoxha (member of the People's Assembly, Central Committee member, Director of the Central Committee Institute for Marxist-Leninist Studies, and member of the Central Council of the Albanian Women's Union)[37] and Fiqrete Shehu (member of the People's Assembly, Central Committee member, Director of the Lenin Higher Party School, chairman of the Commission on Education and Culture, and member of the leadership of the Albanian Women's Union).[38] In addition to the two wives, other close relatives have also been placed in sensitive posts.

After the mysterious suicide of Mehmet Shehu, his wife's name disappeared completely from the Albanian media and she made no recorded public appearances afterward. Despite the fact that at the time there were no official announcements, it has been suggested that she apparently lost all her official functions.[39] Many high officials lost their positions in what seemed an obvious attempt to eliminate Shehu's base of power in the party and the country.[40]

In the GDR, Margot Honecker, wife of the party leader, is a member of the People's Chamber (GDR's parliament), a Central Committee member, and minister of public education.[41]

In Bulgaria, Todor Zhivkov's late daughter Lyudmila (whose
case will be described in detail), was not only a member
of the Politburo, National Assembly, and chairman of the
Committee on Culture, but also one of the most powerful
members of the BCP leadership, obviously being groomed
to be her father's heir.

However, all East European leaders could take
lessons from Romania's Nicolae Ceausescu. At one time,
in August 1977, the list of his prominent relatives was
published by a West German weekly.[42] It included the
following family members:

1. Nicolae Ceausescu, The Boss.
2. Elena Ceausescu, The Boss's wife.
3. Nicolae Ceausescu (Nicu), a son (secretary
   of the Union of Communist Youth).
4. Ion Ceausescu, a brother (deputy minister of
   agriculture and food industry).
5. Ilie Ceausescu, a brother (major general in
   the Romanian Army; deputy secretary of the
   Army Higher Political Council; member of
   the military academy).
6. Marin Ceausescu, a brother (counselor with
   the Romanian embassy in Vienna; chief of the
   Romanian trade mission in Vienna).
7. Florea Ceausescu, a brother (leading
   journalist; Scinteia editorial board member).
8. Nicolae Ceausescu, a brother (consul in Kiev).
   (The name "Nicolae" is correct; the leader
   and his brother share it.)
9. Elena Burbulescu, a sister (director of the
   highschool of The Boss's native village,
   Scornicesti).
10. Manea Manescu, a brother-in-law (prime
    minister).
11. Ilie Verdet, a brother-in-law (member of the
    Executive Political Committee; RCP Central
    Committee secretary; member of the Permanent
    Bureau).
12. Cornel Burtica, a nephew (member of the
    Executive Political Committee; member of the
    Permanent Bureau; RCP Central Committee
    secretary; deputy premier).
13. Gheorghe Petrescu, a brother-in-law
    (minister secretary of state at the ministry
    of machine building industry; on 21 May 1982,
    at one of the Ceausescu shuffles, he was

appointed a deputy premier).

14. Dumitru D. Petrescu, a brother-in-law (first deputy chairman of the Executive Committee of the Arges County's People's Council).

15. Ion Ionita, a nephew (deputy premier; member of the Executive Political Committee).

As in several other East European countries, it is Madame who carries many of the state and party responsibilities. Elena Ceausescu is a member of the RCP Central Committee Political Executive Committee (the Politburo), first deputy chairman of the Council of Ministers (since March 1980), member of the Grand National Assembly, chairman of the Institute for Chemical Research, and a member of the Romanian Academy of Sciences. Since 1979 she has also been the chairman of the powerful Central Committee commission for party and state cadres.[43] During the second half of the 1970s she started receiving foreign ambassadors, along with her husband, and insistent reports had it that she is strongly influencing the selection of party and state officials[44] and in general "keeps an eye on the cadres." When her 60th birthday was marked in 1979, she was referred to with such hyperbolic epithets as "the first woman of the country," "the legendary mother from the fairytales of our childhood," and "the most just woman on earth," who is "always active and in unison with Comrade Ceausescu's political genius."[45] On 7 June 1979 Elena Ceausescu was appointed to yet another important post, namely, chairman of the Romanian National Council on Science and Technology,[46] and finally, as already noted, in March 1980 she was appointed first deputy prime minister.

The presence of so many family members in high places has given rise to the joke that the difference between the Hohenzollerns and the Ceausescus is that the former ruled in succession, while the latter rule all together. What lends a measure of truth to this joke is the spectacular political career of yet another member of Ceausescu's family, his son Nicu. He entered the political scene at only 19 years of age, when on 13 January 1972 he was appointed chairman of the committee on organizing a symposium titled "The Union of Communist Youth, a School for the Communist Education of Youth."[47] In March 1973 he was elected vice chairman of the Council of the Union of the Romanian Communist Students' Association, a post he inherited from his sister Zoya.[48] Nicu Ceausescu began to travel extensively as a member of various delegations, and soon many new posts were conferred on him: In 1974

he was elected a member of the Socialist Unity Front
Council. In 1975 he became a member of the Bureau of the
Central Committee of the Union of Communist Youth (UCY),
and in 1976, secretary of the UCY Central Committee. In
August 1978 he was elected a member of the Executive
Bureau of the National Radio and Television Council, and
at the 12th RCP Congress in 1979, a candidate-member of
the RCP Central Committee.[49] Two additional posts
acquired in 1980 were member of the Executive Committee
of the Socialist Democracy and Unity Front, and member of
the Grand National Assembly.[50] In March 1981 he was
elected chairman of the Consultative Committee of the
United Nations for the International Year of Youth.[51] In
addition to all this, he made himself very busy inter-
nationally, visiting various countries as leader of a
Romanian youth delegation. Such was his May 1982 visit to
several countries in the Far East, including Japan,[52]
the Philippines,[53] and Thailand.[54]

As interesting as the meteoric career of Ceausescu's
son may be, it is eclipsed by the career of Todor
Zhivkov's late daughter, Lyudmila. Born in July 1942,
Lyudmila Zhivkova was educated in Bulgaria, Moscow, and
Cambridge. After a brief prelude as a Komsomol activist,
in 1971 she became first deputy chairman of the Committee
on Friendship and Cultural Relations with Foreign
Countries.[55] In March 1972 she became deputy chairman of
the important Committee on Art and Culture, in 1973 first
deputy chairman of the same committee, and in June 1975
its chairman.[56] At the 11th BCP Congress in 1976
Zhivkova became a full member of the Central Committee
(jumping over the stage of candidate-member) and in 1979 a
full member of the Politburo.[57] At the time, various
Western sources[58] considered her promotion unpopular and
premature. However, Zhivkova acclimatized herself quickly
to the atmosphere at the top and soon became very active
at the international level, leading Bulgarian cultural
delegations to every corner of the world, leading the
Bulgarian delegation to the 1979 UN General Assembly regular
session, and promoting her characteristic ideas about the
"aesthetic education" and applying the "laws of beauty" to
every aspect of human activity. She was considered the
"eminence grise" behind her father and was thought to have
influenced the appointment of many relatively young persons
to top positions--Aleksandur Fol, minister of education, and
Lyubomir Levchev, chairman of the Union of Bulgarian
Writers, being only two among many. Her husband, Ivan
Slavkov, also progressed quickly and became director general

of Bulgarian Television.[59]

 After the death of her mother in 1971 Lyudmila
Zhivkova acted as Bulgaria's first lady, taking part in
official state affairs alongside her father. She conducted
official visits to many countries, and observers started
viewing her as a possible political heir of her father.
When asked about this possibility by the Western press,
Lyudmila Zhivkova answered, "Why not? There is no sex
discrimination in Bulgaria."[60]

 But Zhivkova's glorious future was not to be. On
20 July 1981 she died of "brain hemorrhage, caused by over-
work."[61] The brief announcement of her death was followed
by extensive obituaries, which reviewed her career and
contributions to various areas of Bulgarian life. Her
husband was not mentioned at all. Even at the funeral he
remained in the background, most of the condolence messages
being addressed to her father and children.[62] In fact,
Ivan Slavkov sank into oblivion in Bulgaria. In March 1982
he was appointed chairman of the Bulgarian Olympic Committee
(relinquishing his previous post as director general of
Bulgarian Television), which meant a farewell to a
political career.[63]

 Zhivkova's memory was honored in numerous ways: an
international foundation named after her was established,
aiming "to promote studying, popularizing, and translating
into life Lyudmila Zhivkova's spiritual heritage"[64]; a
National Lyudmila Zhivkova Award was instituted, to be conferred on political and cultural figures who have contributed
to the development of their respective national cultures[65]
and so forth. On the first anniversary of her death many
Bulgarian streets, schools, and institutes were named after
her, and Sofia's Palace of Culture was also renamed
Lyudmila Zhivkova Palace of Culture.[66] One last observation: after Lyudmila Zhivkova's death, Vladimir Zhivkov,
her brother, became politically active. Very little has
ever been said about his professional background. However,
in October 1981 the party daily Rabotnichesko Delo reported
that Vladimir Zhivkov holds a university degree in law.[67]
He published several articles in the Bulgarian daily
press[68] and was appointed secretary general of the Banner
of Peace Children's Assembly.[69] (The Banner of Peace
Children's Assembly was one of Lyudmila Zhivkova's pet
projects. In essence this is a biannual gathering of
children from all over the world, at which peace, friendship, and various cultural issues are discussed. The first
gathering took place in 1980 and was chaired by Lyudmila
Zhivkova. The second gathering took place in August 1982,

and as noted, it was chaired by the new secretary general
of the enterprise--Zhivkova's brother Vladimir.)

PERSONALITY CULTS

Not only are members of the East European leaders'
families appointed to top posts, but sometimes their birthdays are celebrated with an exuberance that comes close to
the exultation with which the birthdays of the leaders
themselves are celebrated. The celebration of Elena
Ceausescu's 60th birthday in January 1979 has already been
mentioned. Soon it became apparent that this celebration
was to become an annual event, widely reported by the
Romanian mass media:

> On January 7 a festivity was held in celebration
> of the birthday of Elena Ceausescu, member of the
> Executive Political Committee of the Central
> Committee of the RCP, and first deputy prime
> minister of Romania. On the occasion Elena
> Ceausescu was conveyed a congratulatory telegram
> addressed to her by the Executive Political
> Committee of the CC of the RCP.
> President Nicolae Ceausescu, Premier Ilie
> Verdet, and the other members of the party and
> state leadership attending the festivity have
> congratulated Elena Ceausescu. On her birthday
> Elena Ceausescu received congratulatory messages
> from county, municipal, and town party
> committees, from mass and civic organizations,
> and from collectives of working people from
> all over the country.[70]

It need hardly be pointed out that the birthday of no
other leader (other than The Boss himself) is celebrated
in the same way. It is interesting to note that this
practice of celebrating the birthday of the leader's wife
is accepted even in rather puritanical Albania. On 7
February 1981 the 60th birthday of Enver Hoxha's wife
Nexhmije was pompously celebrated by all Politburo members.
She was awarded the title Hero of Socialist Labor with
the citation: "For her distinguished contribution as a
party leader and organizer in the struggle for national and
social liberation of the Albanian people and the construction
of the new socialist Albania; for her consistent revolutionary activity and the fulfillment of tasks entrusted to

her by the party in various sectors; for her merit in
developing education and culture and the progress of our
new science, particularly in the field of social studies;
for her unstinted effort in the communist education of
the masses, the strengthening of the people's unity around
the party, and the strengthening of the people's power;
and for loyalty to the cause of revolution and communism,
for her determined struggle in defense of the party's
line against the internal and external enemies of the party
and the people, and for her defense of Marxism-Leninism
against all trends of modern revisionism."[71]

Lyudmila Zhivkova's posthumous 40th birthday was also
celebrated as a state event of great importance, public
events being organized in Sofia and all Bulgarian cities,
and the major events in Sofia being attended by all party
and state leaders.[72]

However, nothing comes even close to the celebration
of the birthdays of some East European leaders themselves,
and foremost among them Nicolae Ceausescu and Todor
Zhivkov. In fact, the personality cult is inherent in the
East European regimes. Borrowed (like almost everything
else) from the USSR, the practice of deifying the leader by
attributing to him supernatural or at least unusual qualities and merits in every conceivable area of human life is
an integral part of East European daily life. Scores of
ousted East European leaders have been accused of
"personality cult," but their successors have actually
perfected this practice to a fine art.

Enver Hoxha and Tito (until 1980), as the senior East
European leaders, had enough time to consolidate themselves
as unquestionable leaders, and introduce a solid, almost
conservative type of personality cult. The "little
Stalins"--Rakosi, Chervenkov, Bierut, etc., have all been
found guilty by their successors of personality cults,
although their cults were short-lived and mostly sporadic.
However, the current champion in the area of the personality
cult is Romania's Nicolae Ceausescu.

On 26 January 1978 his 60th birthday was pompously
celebrated throughout Romania. For many days beforehand
the Romanian radio and press had described and glorified
every single aspect of the life of the "most prominent
statesman of our modern history."[73] The Central Committee
message of greeting, carried by all Romanian newspapers,
read: "We wish to express our most profound and reverent
admiration and appreciation of the brilliant work you have
done as head of the party and the state, of your invaluable
contribution to the creation of Romania's new socialist

destiny, to the cause of progress and civilization of our
era, an era that represents the most fruitful chapter of our
entire 1,000-year history, one rich in achievements and
great success."[74]

Ceausescu was awarded many Romanian and foreign medals
and orders, including the title Hero of the Socialist
Republic of Romania (for the second time) and the order
Victory of Socialism.[75] As for Ceausescu the communist
ideologist, the country's main seats of learning and
culture--the University of Bucharest, the Stefan Gheorghiu
Academy, the Central Institute for Economic Research, the
Polytechnic Institute, the Nicolae Balcescu Agricultural
Institute--held special meetings in his honor, at which his
contribution to the progress of Romanian science and learning over the years since his ascent to power was the main
subject under consideration.[76] On 24 January the Stefan
Gheorghiu Academy made him a doctor of political science,
and the Academy of Economic Research made him a doctor
of economics.[77] Hundreds of greetings messages were
received from foreign countries, and Ceausescu was also
awarded many foreign orders and medals, including the Soviet
Lenin order.[78]

Special attention was devoted to Ceausescu's native
village, Scornicesti. It was visited (a pilgrimage?) by all
Romanian leaders on 28 January 1978.[79] Many exhibitions
were organized in the village, including one on its part in
Romania's uprisings.

An unusual attempt was made to present Ceausescu as a
great thinker who had made original contributions to all
fields as a Marxist ideologist, an economist, a scholar,
an educator, a theoretician, and an international statesman
and strategist. The adulation was carried to the point
where Ceausescu was hailed as a man who had instilled a new
spirit into every field of human activity.[80]

The orgy lasted three weeks. Writers, poets, and
composers composed hyperbolic works of art in honor of
Ceausescu. For days the newspapers printed almost nothing
but materials related to Ceausescu's life and achievements.
Festive celebrations took place throughout Romania, at
which poets and artists recited poems eulogizing Ceausescu.
A delegation of Romanian writers visited Ceausescu's native
village and interviewed old people on the leader's childhood and early achievements. Afterwards they reported
significant facts, such as the story that "little
Ceausescu was never afraid of the wolf when going into
the forest," and that "in school he was always elected
leader of the game."[81] The veneration reached religious

proportions when Romania Libera printed a letter sent to Ceausescu by a 106-year-old peasant from Vrancea area: "In practically every house in Vrancea your portrait hangs beside that of the famous and courageous Prince Stephen the Great."[82]

Finally, Ceausescu was glorified as "the beloved, providential son of Romania and the world,"[83] "the golden apple of all the age-old struggles and fights in Romania,"[84] and so forth. His "eternal youth" was also frequently pointed out.

Ceausescu's birthday has become a major annual celebration in Romania. His birthdays in 1980[85] and 1981[86] were celebrated along the already established pattern. One final word on the subject of Ceausescu's personality cult: a high stage of such a cult is reached when a leader is compared with some historical hero and assigned some of that hero's qualities (even if it first means assigning some of his qualities to that hero). When the 500th anniversary of the death of the Romanian Medieval Prince Vlad the Impaler was marked in 1976, he was hailed as a "hero of the struggle for freedom and independence,"[87] a man with "clear-cut political goals in mind that justi-fied his actions,"[88] and finally--the unmistakable implication--that "considerable mobility of dignitaries [the Ceausescu shuffle] was one of the characteristics of his period."[89] Something similar happened also to the sixteenth century Walachian Prince Michael the Brave, with whom Ceausescu is frequently compared.[90]

Zhivkov's personality cult follows similar lines, although it lags behind the Romanian model in intensity and imaginativeness. Still, Zhivkov's 70th birthday in 1981 was celebrated in a way that was clearly molded after the Romanian pattern. A special album on Zhivkov's life entitled A Son of His People, a Son of His Time, containing 360 pages of pictures of his life, beginning as a schoolboy in his village school, was published and a film on his life entitled A Man of the People was shown throughout Bulgaria.[91] He was awarded various orders and titles (Hero of the People's Republic of Bulgaria, the Lenin order, etc.),[92] and his native village, Pravets, was in fact turned into a museum and a tourist attraction, in much the same way as Ceausescu's native village. All Bulgarian newspapers of 4-8 September 1981 were given over almost entirely to articles on Zhivkov's contribution to every conceivable area, his friends' memories about him, articles by his collaborators and assistants, pictures and reports on various celebrations of his birthday, poems in

his honor, and so forth. The weekly <u>Literaturen Front</u>
of 3 September 1981 was completely devoted to Zhivkov's
birthday and included, in addition to various poems and
eulogies, articles on Zhivkov's mother (Grandmother
Mavrutsa), his landlady ("very clean and orderly" is how
she described Zhivkov), young writers (Zhivkov encouraged
them to write), a mountaineer (Zhivkov immediately knew
how to orient himself in the mountains), and so forth.[93]
Nevertheless, despite all this, the Bulgarian celebrations
did not come close to the Romanian proportions. After all,
how can one top a statement such as "He (Ceausescu) is our
lay god, the heart of the party and the nation, the man of
history and eternity, whom we shall follow faithfully along
the way toward implementing the eternal ideals of Romania
and humanity!"[94]

Despite these extremes, and frankly, some ridiculous
overtones, the personality cult of the East European
leaders (and none of them is innocent in this aspect) has
obvious political purposes. Attributing various charismatic
qualities to the leader, describing him as irreplaceable,
unique, great, and so forth, aims not only at strengthening
the position of the leader inside the party leadership,
but also at guaranteeing the continuity of his policy and,
paradoxically, strengthening his country's (relative)
independence vis-à-vis Moscow. At least in the case of
Romania, observers perceived the stepping up of Ceausescu's
cult as a measure aimed at building up the self-confidence
of the Romanian people, following the Soviet invasion of
Afghanistan.[95]

The East European leaders (with the exception of the
Albanian and Yugoslav leaders) like to maintain close
contacts among themselves. They frequently visit each
other, congratulate each other on every possible occasion,
and in general like to maintain a picture of fraternal
benevolence and, more important, permanency. After all,
they know that being elected by nobody in particular, their
fate is in the hands of the Politburo and Moscow. The
sudden fall from grace can come any moment. There seldom
are any indications that it is coming. After the fall
there is only oblivion or disgrace, or both. Therefore,
a significant part of their efforts is aimed at prolonging
the present (as a means of postponing the future) and
guaranteeing themselves another period of prominence.

NOTES

1. Warsaw PAP in English, 2015 GMT, 26 May 1982; Daily Report (FBIS), 1 June 1982.
2. Radio Prague, 20 May 1980; Rude Pravo, 21 May 1980; RFE Situation Report, CSSR, 28 May 1980.
3. Radio Hvezda, 21 May 1980; Rude Pravo, 22 May 1980.
4. Rude Pravo, 23 May 1980.
5. RFE Situation Report, Poland, 6 February 1980.
6. Ibid.
7. RFE Situation Report, CSSR, 28 May 1980.
8. All Polish newspapers of 6 September 1980.
9. Nowe Drogi (Poland), December 1980, p. 57.
10. Ibid.
11. RFE RAD Background Report, Poland, 26 May 1981.
12. Glos Wybrzeza (Poland), 12 October 1981, Dziennik Baltycki (Poland), 13 October 1981.
13. Zycie Warszawy, no. 14, 15 October 1981.
14. Neues Deutschland, 16 October 1981.
15. Warsaw PAP in English, 1435 GMT, 18 October 1981; Daily Report (FBIS), 19 October 1981.
16. Warsaw PAP in English, 2114 GMT, 18 October 1981; Daily Report (FBIS), 19 October 1981.
17. Ibid.
18. Tirana Domestic Service in Albanian, 1900 GMT, 18 December 1980; Daily Report (FBIS), 21 December 1981.
19. Tirana Domestic Service in Albanian, 1903 GMT, 18 December 1981; Daily Report (FBIS), 21 December 1981.
20. TANJUG Domestic Service in Serbo-Croatian, 1835 GMT, 21 December 1981; Daily Report (FBIS), 22 December 1981.
21. RFE Situation Report, Bulgaria, 31 October 1980.
22. Ibid.
23. Ibid.
24. Brief Bulgarian Encyclopedia (Bulgarian Academy of Science, 1969), p. 445.
25. RFE Situation Report, Bulgaria, 31 October 1980.
26. Nepszabadsag (Hungary), 17 June 1958; RFE RAD Background Report, Hungary, no. 127, 15 June 1978.
27. RFE Situation Report, Romania, 3 December 1981.
28. RFE RAD Background Report, Romania, no. 120, 24 May 1982.
29. Bucharest AGERPRES in English, 1818 GMT, 21 May 1982; Daily Report (FBIS), 24 May 1982.
30. Bucharest AGERPRES in English, 1745 GMT, 21 May 1982; Daily Report (FBIS), 24 May 1982.
31. RFE Situation Report, Bulgaria, 23 June 1977.

32. All Bulgarian newspapers of 18 June 1981.
33. RFE Situation Report, CSSR, 25 September 1979.
34. Ibid.
35. Ibid.
36. Ibid.
37. Directory of Officials of the People's Republic of Albania (Washington, D.C.: National Foreign Assessment Center, December 1980).
38. Ibid.
39. RFE RAD Background Report, Albania, no. 140, 29 June 1982.
40. Ibid.
41. Directory of Officials of the German Democratic Republic (Washington, D.C.: National Foreign Assessment Center, April 1978).
42. Weltwoche (FRG), 10 August 1977.
43. RFE Situation Report, Romania, 18 January 1979.
44. Ibid.
45. Luceafarul, 6 January 1979; Tribuna, 4 January 1979; Contemporanul, 5 January 1979 all Romanian.
46. RFE Situation Report, Romania, 6 July 1979.
47. RFE Situation Report, Romania, 3 December 1981.
48. Ibid.
49. Ibid.
50. Ibid.
51. Bucharest Domestic Service in Romanian, 0500 GMT, 8 March 1981; Daily Report (FBIS), 9 March 1981.
52. Scinteia (Romania), 4 May 1982; Daily Report (FBIS), 7 May 1982.
53. Bucharest AGERPRES in English, 1733 GMT, 5 May 1982; Daily Report (FBIS), 6 May 1982.
54. Bucharest AGERPRES in English, 0900 GMT, 8 May 1982; Daily Report (FBIS), 10 May 1982.
55. RFE RAD Background Report, Bulgaria, no. 253, 27 October 1980.
56. Ibid.
57. Ibid.
58. International Herald Tribune, 24 August 1979; Die Presse, 3 September 1979; Der Tagesspiegel (West Berlin), 16 November 1979; Stern, 6 December 1979, etc.
59. RFE Background Report, Bulgaria, 27 October 1980.
60. The Observer, 29 February 1979; Die Presse, 3 September 1979.
61. All Bulgarian newspapers of 22 July 1981.
62. RFE Situation Report, Bulgaria, 29 July 1981.
63. RFE Situation Report, Bulgaria, 12 March 1982.
64. RFE Situation Report, Bulgaria, 24 March 1982.

65. Ibid.
66. Rabotnichesko Delo (Bulgaria), 27 July 1982.
67. Ibid., 1 October 1981.
68. Ibid., 30 September 1981 and 1 October 1981.
69. RFE Situation Report, Bulgaria, 24 March 1982.
70. Bucharest AGERPRES in English, 1830 GMT, 7 January 1981; Daily Report (FBIS), 8 January 1981.
71. Tirana Domestic Service in Albanian, 1900 GMT, 7 February 1981; Daily Report (FBIS), 10 February 1981.
72. Rabotnichesko Delo, 27 July 1982.
73. Radio Bucharest, 18 January 1978; RFE Situation Report, Romania, 9 February 1978.
74. Scinteia, 26 January 1978.
75. Ibid.
76. RFE Situation Report, Romania, 9 February 1978.
77. Ibid.
78. Ibid.
79. Scinteia, 29 January 1978.
80. Ibid., 26 January 1978.
81. Flancara (Romania), no. 3, 19 January 1978.
82. Romania Libera (Romania), 19 January 1978.
83. Scinteia, 27 January 1978.
84. Ibid.
85. RFE RAD Background Report, Romania, no. 34, 11 February 1980.
86. Bucharest AGERPRES in English, 1857 GMT, 26 January 1981; Daily Report (FBIS), 27 January 1981.
87. Romania Libera, 14 December 1976.
88. Nicolae Stoicescu, Vlad Tepes, Bucharest, 1976, p. 1,660.
89. Ibid., p. 1,666.
90. RAD RFE Background Report, Romania, no. 191, 1 September 1976.
91. RFE Situation Report, Bulgaria, 10 September 1981.
92. Ibid.
93. Literaturen Front (Bulgaria), 3 September 1981.
94. Saptamina (Romania), no. 477, 25 January 1980.
95. RAD RFE Background Report, Romania, no. 34, 11 February 1980.

8
Church and State

There are many reasons why religion--any religion--
and the East European political system are incompatible.
The East European socialist states have a totalitarian
political system that tolerates no competition and, in
particular, no factor that may represent an alternative
value system. The domination of the totalitarian system is
total, as the name implies. It engulfs every area of life,
controls every aspect of human activity, and refuses to
relinquish the slightest hold on supremacy. The result
in Eastern Europe is that there is no real or effective
political opposition and no organization, political or
social, whose existence does not serve the sole purpose of
facilitating the implementation of the regime's interests.
This, however, is not enough for the totalitarian regime.
Political and physical supremacy and lack of overt
opposition and competition are only a part of the goal.
Communist totalitarianism is a messianic political system,
which claims to have a message for the whole world and to
possess all the answers and solutions to all past, present,
and future problems. The success of the communist system
depends not only on its physical power, but also, and
perhaps mainly, on its ability to convince the world, and
first of all its own subjects, that its message is real,
applicable in every situation, and--most of all--that it is
the only correct message. This means that not only is it
the political opposition that must perish but also any
factor that is capable of presenting alternative solutions
and a competing set of values--thus capable of exercising
a certain spiritual influence on the people (at least those
who believe in the alternative set of values) and diminishing the effectiveness of the totalitarian message.
    Religion influences the mind, and it is the mind that

236

must first be neutralized and then subjugated to the
totalitarian state and thus eliminated as a realm of
resistance to the totalitarian (communist) ideology.
Consequently, long before there were any communist
regimes, the fate of religion under communism was predetermined.

TACTICS ADOPTED BY THE STATE TOWARD THE CHURCH

Immediately after the establishment of the East
European communist system the various regimes set out to
annihilate religion. In most cases, especially when the
Catholic church was involved, this was not only a question
of liquidating a potential competitor for the minds and
hearts of the people and exterminating an "obscurant" part
of the previous regime ("opiate of the people"), but also
a question of liquidating a social and political factor
whose spiritual center was located outside the geographic
borders of the country concerned--this being only one of
the reasons for this factor's (very) questionable loyalty.
Various means were employed by the socialist state,
physical pressure and persecution being only a part of the
thorough antireligious campaign. In one East European
state at least--Romania--the regime tried to form a
schismatic Catholic church, led by loyal priests and
bishops, and with no Vatican ties.[1]
Religious leaders were imprisoned (Cardinal Mindszenty
in Hungary and Archibishop Wyszynski in Poland were only
two prominent examples among thousands), some were
physically liquidated, and most of the Church's property
was nationalized. Nevertheless, it was clear that while
the Church as a material entity could easily be destroyed,
religion as a factor of spiritual power--exercising
considerable influence over the minds of the people--
would remain. Recognizing this fact, the socialist regimes
changed their tactics. When the attempt to exterminate
religion immediately and totally proved futile, the regimes
decided to subjugate religion, to channel its activity and
utilize it, as far as possible, for its own goals. Thus,
to a certain extent, the status of churches became
similar to that of other mass organizations: their
existence became tolerated as long as they could be used to
facilitate the implementation of the regime's goals. There
is, however, one essential difference: whereas all the
sociopolitical mass organizations in the East European
socialist countries have in fact been created by the

twentieth-century communist regime, and function as auxiliary organs of that regime, religion as such was in existence long before the establishment of the East European political system. Furthermore, even though it is allowed to exist so long as it pledges loyalty to the regime and constantly manifests its adherence to various initiatives and policies of the regime, the Church has never ceased to be a target of active and sometimes even violent propaganda, which has been institutionalized by various communist-inspired organizations such as institutes of atheistic research.

The regime encourages membership in its mass organizations and not only discourages religious belief but often denounces it as "antisocialist." One should never forget that the final goal--the eventual extermination of religion--has never been relinquished by the socialist countries. The result is that today, the situation of religion in all East European states is more or less similar, with two exceptions at either end of the scale: Albania, where the regime has refused to allow religion even the minimal opportunity for existence, and Poland, where the Catholic church has not only preserved a substantial part of its power, but after the election of Pope John Paul II and the Church's deep involvement in the activity of the Solidarity trade union actually became a political factor of considerable consequence in Poland.

In all other East European countries the Soviet model exists, i.e., a certain freedom of religion is tolerated (and incorporated in the Constitution, along with the regime's right to conduct antireligious propaganda), as long as freedom is not utilized as a political vehicle by the Church, and as long as religious factors publicly and unreservedly pledge and demonstrate in action their loyalty to the communist regime (whose final goal is to exterminate religion).

As already pointed out, the situation in Albania and Poland is somewhat different. Article 37 of the Albanian Constitution explicitly states: "The state recognizes no religion and supports and carries out atheistic propaganda to implant the scientific-materialistic world outlook in people." In 1967 Albania declared itself "the first atheistic state in the world."[2]

In addition to its official declarations the Albanian government is conducting a crusade against religion, compelling Albanian citizens to change their names, if these names have religious origin or sound,[3] urging "vigilance toward former clergymen, who secretly were

trying to influence others to take part in religious
rituals,"[4] and stressing the need "to bring the ideological
struggle into the family, where remnants of religious
ideology are often manifested,"[5] as well as "the need to
stop the influence of parents, contaminated by the spirit
of remnants of religious ideology, over their children."[6]
Nevertheless, occasionally the Albanian government admits
that despite its fierce anti-religious propaganda, various
religious customs still persist among vast segments of the
population. (Celebrating birthdays on the name day and
not on the date on which the person was born, observing
various religious rituals in commemoration of the dead,
etc., are examples frequently pointed out by the Albanian
regime to show that religion "is hard to eradicate from the
mentality of the citizens."[7])

All other East European states' constitutions guarantee
freedom of religion, usually qualifying this right as
excluding "illegal" (meaning antisocialist) activities.
Thus Article 32 of the Czechoslovak Constitution states:
"Freedom of religion is guaranteed. Anyone may adhere to
any religious faith, or be without a religious faith, and
conduct religious rites insofar as they do not conflict
with the law."[8]

Several articles of the Constitution of the Socialist
Republic of Croatia in Yugoslavia state:

Art. 4: Citizens may belong to any religious
community whatsoever, or may choose not to belong to any.
Art. 5: No one may legally be impeded in expressing
the rights to which he is entitled in the Constitution
because of his religious convictions or because of his
membership in a religious community.
Art. 17: Religious education may be given on the
same premises as those where other religious acts are
performed, and in other rooms, provided that legal and
other regulations are observed.[9]

Finally, the 1971 Bulgarian Constitution states:

Art. 52: The citizens may form organizations for
political . . . religious, sports, and other noneconomic
purposes.
Art. 53: 1. The citizens are insured freedom of
thought and religion. They may hold religious services or
engage in antireligious propaganda.
2. The church is separated from the state.
3. The law regulates the legal status,

> material support, and the right
> to internal organization and autonomy
> of various religious communities.
> 4. The misuse of church and religion for
>   political purposes and the formation
>   of political organizations on a
>   religious basis are banned.
> 5. Religion cannot serve as a grounds for
>   refusal to fulfill obligations imposed
>   by the Constitution or the laws.[10]

Various East European sources frequently publish
extensive numerical data and rosy descriptions aimed at
proving the freedom of religion, which they claim exists
in Eastern Europe. Thus, Bratislava's Rolnicke Noviny
stated in January 1982: "In Czechoslovakia there are
eighteen organized churches and religious societies that
have their own organizations and rules. To pursue their
activities, they have ten publishing houses. In all,
twenty-seven religious periodicals are published. In
accordance with Government Directive no. 112 (1950) of the
Collection of Laws and no. 123 (1950) of the Collection of
Laws, theologians have been trained at six divinity schools
since 1950. The state financially assists in the operation
of church facilities. In addition, it allocates money for
habilitation and renovation of church buildings. The
state also recognizes as paid holidays three days each
year, related to religious traditions."[11]

Another Czech source maintains that in 1980 in
Czechoslovakia there were "almost 5,000 clergymen, pastors,
preachers, and other persons for whom spiritual activity in
the church or in religious society is a profession. According to the law on the insurance of the economic basis of
churches of 1949, the state extends to them salaries,
differentiated according to the church office held.
Clergymen also have health and social insurance. . . .
The churches and religious societies have more than 8,000
churches, chapels, prayer halls, and other assembly
facilities. . . . Every year hundreds of millions of
korunas are earmarked from the state budget for the care
of cultural and historic monuments. A considerable part
of those funds is designated for maintenance and repair of
churches; in the year 1978, for instance, approximately
KSS164 million were spent for those purposes."[12]

In 1980 an official Yugoslav source claimed: "In
Yugoslavia there are about 20,000 professional religious
officers doing 'the work of the Lord' in about 20,000

churches, monasteries, mosques, and church homes. The impressiveness of this mosaic pattern of churches is an indication of the openness of society. . . . The religious communities are not hampered in disseminating their doctrine. According to data of the Catholic Church and the Islamic community, which are the only ones who keep records on this, half a million children receive Catholic religious instruction in a thousand lecture rooms, and there are about 100,000 students in a slightly smaller number of Islamic religious schools."[13]

The same source maintained that the "churches in Yugoslavia are financially independent aside from the aid of the government; they are supported by the offerings of their congregations, and they perform religious services."[14] To prove this, the newspaper printed a long list of religious property (churches, monasteries, and so forth).

Similar data on the number of churches and priests, governmental support in the form of wages for church officials, various social security benefits, etc., are often cited by all East European countries with the exception of Albania. This practice constitutes an obvious attempt to prove that there is freedom of religion in Eastern Europe. On other occasions the very same sources are not hesitant about publishing articles on the subject of the obscurantist and antisocialist nature of religion, the inevitability of its disappearance under communism, and, most of all, the prices the churches have to meet if they are to preserve their relative freedom of existence.

OFFICIAL STATE ATTITUDES TOWARD RELIGION

The usual explanation of the official attitude toward religion takes the following lines:

According to Marxism-Leninism, religion is a product of certain objective conditions and of certain socioeconomic situations that in the final account determine and limit decisively man's cognition and the potentiality of his spiritual life. Religion is an outcome of the 'limitations of all interhuman mutual relations and of relations between the people and the nature' (K. Marx) which stems first of all from underdeveloped or undeveloped forces of pro- duction in society and from the spiritual life

of people circumscribed by a narrow framework
of an underdeveloped or insufficiently in-
significantly developed process of material
production. In other words, it is an outcome
of a situation in which people find themselves
under the domination of arbitrarily acting
natural and especially social factors acting
against people as alien, hostile forces and
against which people are helpless because they
do not recognize their causes and their substance. Through the prism of such restrictions
the natural and social forces that the people
do not know and cannot control appear supernatural; the result is a fantastic, reversed
image of the world where erroneous figments
of human imagination are attributed an
independent, objective existence that is
elevated even above the objective, real,
natural world whose fantastic reflection had
produced religious illusions.

If we proceed from this Marxist, truly
scientific explanation of the origin and
substance of religion and if we explain its
social function on that basis in truly scientific
terms (that religion must objectively fulfill the
role of mystification and obscure reality and
real problems with which people must deal; that
it must play--whether anyone wants it or not,
or whether anyone desires it or not--the role
of the 'opiate of the people,' i.e., false
consciousness reflecting contortedly the real,
objectively existing world and the processes
occurring in it, including the movement of social
development), then naturally, Marxist atheism with
its principled critical attitude toward religion
appears in a totally different light than that in
which religious propaganda tries to present it.
It is axiomatic that this is not a question of
some arbitrary or self-serving negation of
religion that should 'take faith away' from the
people and assault their religious feelings,
but rather an integral part of the process of
emancipation where revolutionary action liberates
man not only from his economic and social shackles
but also from his spiritual shackles, opens him
to a straight, undistorted view of natural laws
governing the development of nature, society,

and thought, and thus, enables him to learn
these natural laws on the basis of their
objectively true cognition, and to use them
to his advantage.[15]

Having established the theoretical foundations of
religion's negative and obscurant character, the same
source goes on to describe the practical (and negative)
consequences of religious beliefs:

First: although many believers are subjectively,
sincerely convinced that religion and religious
world views are compatible with socialism and
do not preclude full identification with it,
objectively the influence and vestiges of religion
hinder total integration of the believers in a
socialist society, stymie the process of growth
of people's social awareness, their social
activity and involvement. Value orientation of
the believers and value orientation stemming
from the scientific world view often clash and
that is necessarily negatively reflected in the
consciousness of the believers; this in turn must
generate certain reservations against socialism
and doubts about it and in the end, also the
opinion that religious convictions and the
socialist world view are, after all, incompatible.
It goes without saying that this also leads to
adverse practical social consequences.
    Secondly: the influence and vestiges of
religion link the believers--consciously or un-
consciously, willingly or unwillingly--with the
world 'on the other side of the barricades.'
They serve as a kind of bridge to that world
which never ceases to be interested in liquidating
socialism and eliminating all the achievements
we have scored in the process of building
socialism. Religious awareness remains a
potential tool for manipulating the believers,
their social and political attitudes; it remains
a tool for using them against socialism and for
the abuse of socialism, as is now being
demonstrated so often and so very dramatically
by the events in neighboring Poland as well as
in other parts of the world where the imperialist
circles and the spokesmen of the hierarchy
ultimately use the religious convictions of the

working people and their feelings and manipulate
them in order to enforce interests profoundly
alien and hostile to the working man.
        For that reason we emphasize so vigorously
not only political vigilance and watchfulness
and we say bluntly that we shall not let anybody weaken, violate, and frustrate in any way
the building of socialism in our country, under
the guise of religion and the defense of the
freedom of religion.[16]

The article cited above deals only theoretically with
religion, but there are many others that discuss practical
sides of religious activities in the East European
countries and condemn religion in general, or at least
certain religious aspects or practices. Thus Zagreb's
Vjesnik, discussing various forms of opposition to the
socialist regime, lists "profascist elements in the
Catholic church"[17] influenced by "various traitors living
across the border."[18] CSSR sources frequently attack what
they call "political clericalism," "clerical anticommunism,"
and "antisocialist attitudes of believers in Czechoslovakia,"[19]
and so forth. Such and various other attacks and overt
persecution (to be described later in this chapter) place
the church in Eastern Europe always on the defensive.

TACTICS ADOPTED BY THE CHURCH TOWARD THE STATE

        To maintain any relative security at all, church
leaders constantly have to reiterate their loyalty to the
regime and pledge, and actively demonstrate, their support.
They have to endorse every initiative of the regime in
both international and domestic policies, join various
international propaganda campaigns sponsored by the USSR,
and in general pay a heavy price for the relative
toleration of their own existence.
        The "demonstrative obedience" begins by acknowledging
the role of the state in appointing (or rather tolerating)
church officials. One should not forget that although it
is the church that is responsible for the appointment of
priests, in Eastern Europe it is the state that pays their
salaries and in fact enjoys the right of veto over their
appointment. The following official Romanian announcement
is characteristic: "The president of the Socialist
Republic of Romania declares that Bishop-vicar Leonid
Plamadeala is recognized in the position of the Diocese of

Buzau, to which he was elected by the electoral college of
the Roman Orthodox Church on 9 December 1979. Archimandrite
Vasile Costiu is recognized in the position of Bishop-vicar
of the Romanian Orthodox Church on December 10, 1979."[20]

Although the announcement is purely factual, its
implication is unmistakable: until the elected official is
recognized by the state authorities, his election is not
legal. Or, even more briefly, a religious appointment is
void unless approved by the state.

Sometimes, this practice creates absurd situations.
Thus, when at the beginning of 1976 Laszlo Lekai was
appointed Archbishop of Esztergom--head of the Hungarian
church--he was interviewed by the Hungarian Press Agency
(MTI), the interview being published by all Hungarian
newspapers on 14 February 1976. In this interview he
expressed "personal gratitude" to the Pope for having
appointed him to the see of Esztergom and added his
"grateful thanks" to the Presidential Council for having
given prior consent to the appointment. . . . Lekai pledged
that he and his fellow bishops would do their best to
confirm Hungary's Catholics in their faith and to cooperate
conscientiously in the "peaceful and blessed" building of
"our Hungarian fatherland." He concluded by saying that
he would strive to justify the trust placed in him by the
Holy See and the Hungarian state.[21]

The selective freedom of religion in Eastern Europe
has its price, which has to be paid in full by the Church:
the complete depoliticization of religion (the exception of
Poland will be dealt with later in this chapter); demonstrative adherence to party policy and propaganda documents and
campaigns; the acceptance of the constant threat of becoming vestigial; compliance with the violent atheist
propaganda and with the persecution of priests who deviate
from the strict borders of their activity set by the government; and--above all else--the constant expression of
loyalty to and support for the regime, whose declared goal
it is, as earlier noted, to extinguish religion.

The loyalty pledge is usual whenever a church
official is appointed. Thus, when Hungarian Archibishop
Laszlo Lekai was elected Archibishop of Esztergon, he
lavishly praised "the place Church has found in the
socialist society" and urged Hungarian Catholics "to join
enthusiastically in the building of socialism," stressing
that "their conscience can rest untroubled in that case."[22]

Sometimes the head of a church pledges loyalty on
behalf of the entire clergy or brethren. Thus in June 1977
Justin Moisescu, metropolitan of Moldavia and Suceava, was

elected new Romanian Orthodox Patriarch by the Synod of the
Orthodox Church.[23] His election was recognized by the
political authorities on June 18 at a ceremony at the
State Council, at which Vice-president Stefan Voitec handed
Moisescu a presidential decree acknowledging him as
Patriarch of the Romanian Orthodox Church and Archbishop
of Bucharest. On the same day he was received by Nicolae
Ceausescu, RPC Secretary General and Romanian president.
During the reception Moisescu made a speech in which he
declared that the entire clergy "nurtures feelings of high
esteem for and warm gratitude to Ceausescu, who identifies
himself with the destiny of the Romanian people," and he
expressed thanks for the "freedom enjoyed by the Orthodox
Church and by the other denominations in Romania." He also
pledged that the Orthodox Church would actively support
"the building of socialism in Romania" (a promise made by
the Orthodox Synod in a telegram addressed to Ceausescu
and published by the party daily Scinteia.)[24]

On certain occations the loyalty pledge is taken en
masse, by all religious heads. Similar occasions are
usually covered by the entire daily press of the relevant
country. Thus in April 1981, all religious heads in
Czechoslovakia pledged their loyalty to the regime: "The
superintendent of the Methodist Church of Czechoslovakia,
Dr. Vilem Schneeberger; the chairman of the Inner Council
of the Union of Czech Brethren, Jindrich Halama; the Bishop
of Brno Diocese of the Czechoslovak Hussite Church, Dr.
Rudolf Medek; and the chairman of the Council of Jewish
Communities in Bohemia and Moravia, Dr. Dezider Galski,
were administered yesterday a loyalty oath to the
Czechoslovak Socialist Republic by the CSSR Minister of
Culture, Milan Klusak."[25]

The loyalty pledge can take the form of a long and
detailed document that analyzes the reasons for the
Church's loyalty to the socialist regime and touches upon
the entire subject of church-state relations under the
socialist regime. Such a document was issued in May 1981
by the GDR Protestant Church. In a 10,000-manuscript page
thesis entitled "Church in Socialism," the GDR Protestant
Church declared the following principles in its relations
with the socialist regime:[26]

1. In our view the socialist society in conformity
   with the laws of social development represents
   the historical locus where we are truly able
   to expose the cause of freedom and social
   justice.

Our standpoint, therefore, is as follows:
Our place is within real socialism. This
decision of ours is irreversible.

2. Recognizing the fact that our place is within
real socialism presupposes acknowledging the
leading role of the party of the workers' class,
the indestructible alliance of the community
of socialist states, and the firm and stead-
fast friendship with the USSR. It also presupposes that our social engagement lies
within the framework of the GDR National Front.
Our standpoint therefore, is as follows:
In preparation for the 10th SED Congress, we
place our entire creative power in the service
of strengthening the GDR internally, of
promoting its foreign policy of peace and
détente, and of continuing its social policy.
We heed with pleasure the new call of the 26th
CPSU Congress and welcome Leonid I. Brezhnev's
logical and realistic proposals.

3. The GDR's developed socialist society has
fraternal relations with all Third World
progressive forces fighting for social and
national liberation, especially with the new
countries that have overcome the legacy of
colonialism.
Our standpoint, therefore, is as follows:
By contributing to the strengthening of the
socialist state and by proclaiming our solidarity
with the peoples fighting for their freedom or
securing the results of their liberation
struggle, we set an example for development
in the context of social justice.

4. Christians in our country, who appreciate
the lessons of history in general, and church
history in particular, and who strive for the
fulfillment of Christian principles in the
social domain--love for peace, love for your
neighbor, justice, and brotherhood--have opted
for socialism.
Our standpoint, therefore, is as follows:
The firm place we have found within our
country's real socialist order is grounded
on the abovementioned decision and on our

partiality to our religious faith. By
acknowledging the unity of our spiritual
and social dispositions, and the harmony
between testimony and service, we help
strengthen our developed socialist society
while seizing the opportunities offered by
our socialist democracy. At the same time,
we fight for peace, détente and progress
within the world peace movement and the
Christian Peace Conference.

5. In a complicated process of learning and
reorientation, the Protestant churches in the
GDR have been evolving ever since 1969, and
especially in the 1970s, their position in
GDR society as a community of testimony and
service, as churches in socialism. This
position determines their specific place
within the ecumenical movement.

Our standpoint is as follows: By
continually cherishing the results of that
process and by confirming especially the
results of the 6 March 1978 talks, the churches
are able to perform within the ecumenical
community their testimonial duty in our
society and render service to others in the
freedom and commitment of our faith and in
continuation of the legacy of all Christians
who, within the context of their own time,
espoused the cause of humanity and progress.

Our journalistic work will continue to
be grounded on these five principles, which
constitute our very standpoint. We will be
guided by these principles in the conduct of
our spiritual debate, our theological discussions, in our evaluation of historical
processes and cultural achievements,
particularly in questions regarding our
legacy, in our promotion of social involvement
and pastoral activity of Christians as members
of our church and citizens of our socialist
state with equal rights.

The Church is expected to demonstrate its loyalty to
the socialist regime not only by issuing frequent loyalty
declarations, but also (and in fact, mainly) by taking part
in pro-government activity on the domestic and international

fronts. An obvious precondition of such activity is that the Church leaders are briefed on the regime's current needs and policies. In every East European country there are regular meetings between Church leaders and party and state officials, serving the sole purpose of briefing the Church leaders on topical developments and the ensuing party needs and goals. In Hungary, for instance, "It has become regular that the leaders of the Hungarian churches and denominations, several of whom are elected for posts in the Patriotic People's Front, meet and discuss international and internal issues that are of interest to every Hungarian citizen irrespective of ideological conviction. At their Budapest meeting on Thursday, which was attended by State Secretary Imre Miklos, chairman of the Hungarian State Office for Church Affairs, Istvan Sarlos, member of the MSZMP Political Committee and secretary general of the Hungarian Patriotic People's Front, delivered a lecture to church dignitaries. He spoke about the most important international issues, including the process of consolidation in Poland, and analyzed the tasks of the Hungarian economy."[27]

This particular meeting dealt primarily with the situation in Poland. It was reported that "several conferees stated that the most important church circles did not want to become means of Cold War beyond Hungary's borders, even on the pretext of the situation in Poland."[28] The issue of the Polish Church and the response of the East European churches to the Polish crisis will be described later in this chapter.

One of the most accepted and traditional political activities of the Church in Eastern Europe is participation in the election campaign. The East European churches usually participate willingly in the election campaign, because the entire election period is a period of relative relaxation of the state's atheist propaganda, and a period during which the churches are regularly given a breathing space. Of course, in return the regime expects (and receives) full cooperation and commitment.

A typical meeting was held by the "Christian circles" in Gera (the GDR) in June 1981. Otto Hartmut Fuchs, chairman of the Presidium of the Berlin Conference of European Catholics, said that "everyone who wants to support coexistence in the tested alliance of the GDR National Front" should elect the candidates of the National Front in the forthcoming elections.[29] He said further, "In our country the political and moral unity of our citizens, irrespective of different ideologies and

religious denominations, is, above all, proved by
determinedly realizing the common responsibility for
peace, security, and détente."[30]

Usually, the Church's efforts in the election
campaign are coordinated with the proper authorities.
Thus on 21 September 1976 CSSR Deputy Premier Matej Lucan
received representatives of all recognized churches in
Czechoslovakia, to discuss the preparations for the general
elections.[31] Since another loyalty pledge could do no
harm, the occasion was utilized by the Church dignitaries
to hand Lucan a lengthy declaration adopted at a meeting
of the Christian Peace Conference in Prague. The declaration stated that the CSSR clergy supported the election
program that the National Front had put before the
citizens, because "this is a program which guarantees a
peaceful development for our homeland, the general
prosperity of the republic, and growth in the standard of
living and the cultural standard of the people." Further
on, the declaration of the CSSR churches and religious
societies on the general elections emphasized the achievements of the party and government in building a socialist
society, as well as the decisive contribution of the
socialist community, with the USSR at its head, to the
struggle for worldwide peace.[32]

In addition to actively participating in the election
campaign by calling upon the believers to vote for the
National Front candidates, the East European Church is also
expected to take part in various festive domestic occasions,
such as the celebration of the socialist regime's high days
and holidays--for example, the anniversary of the October
Revolution.

On 10 November 1977 the official organization of the
CSSR Catholic clergy, Pacem in Terris, held a session of
its augmented federal plenum in Kosice, under the keynote
"Peace on Earth (is) the Desire of Nations." Reviewing
the meeting, Radio Hvezda reported: "Professor S. Soka,
dean of the St. Cyril and Methodius Theological Seminary
in Bratislava, discussed the importance and contribution
of the Great October Socialist Revolution to believers and
said that in the field of divinity its importance was
especially pronounced from the psychological, ethical,
and legal points of view. At the conclusion of the
conference, the Pacem in Terris members present approved
a declaration marking the 60th anniversary of the Great
October Socialist Revolution. This declaration reiterated
the importance of the epoch-making event in eliminating
social injustice in the world."[33] The amazing fact is that

while official party and state spokesmen continuously
stress that the October Revolution liberated mankind from
"religious backwardness," they nevertheless require the
East European Church to festively celebrate the revolution's
anniversary.

Having mentioned the CSSR Church organization Pacem in
Terris, one ought to explain the nature of it. Pacem in
Terris is in fact a governmental organization that was
created in 1971 in place of the former Peace Movement of
the CSSR Catholic Clergy.[34] It is one of the party's
auxiliary organizations, active in the social mobilization
process and facilitating the implementation of the regime's
goals. The organization's structure and daily activity
resembles that of all other sociopolitical organizations
in Eastern Europe. Thus in February 1980, Pacem in Terris
held a congress attended by religious delegations from the
socialist countries and the West. The great propaganda
value of the congress was underlined by the presence of a
governmental delegation headed by the deputy premier of the
federal government, Matej Lucan.[35] The two-day congress
was extensively covered by the CSSR media. Although there
was no mention of any religious services held during the
congress, there was plenty of purely political and
propaganda activity. It was reported that the organization
"will prepare preventive measures against the violators
of peace," and that "the Cold War could be no alternative
to détente in international relations."[36] U.S. President
Jimmy Carter was attacked by some of the congress participants: "On the one hand, he acts as if he was preaching
the Gospel, and on the other, he drives the world to the
brink of a world war."[37]

The highlight of the congress was the speech of
Federal Deputy Premier Matej Lucan, who began by reading
the delegates a letter from the Czechoslovak party leader
and president, Gustav Husak, to the congress. The president
of the Republic expressed his satisfaction with the Catholic
clergy's resolve to continue helping the progress of
socialist society and to work for good relations between
the Catholic Church and the state. He also said that he
"appreciated the work of the believers who fulfill all
their civic duties and thus contribute to the building of
socialism." In conclusion, Husak's letter praised the
clergy's efforts in support of the policy of peace pursued
by the Soviet Union and the socialist countries.[38] Lucan
himself continued in the same vein and praised the
organization members for "behaving like citizens of a
socialist state . . . who understand that it is not enough

to pray for peace, but that one must also actively fight for it."[39]

In conclusion, the delegates to the two-day congress approved a declaration in which they again confirmed the preservation of peace as being one of the main concerns of the organization; they also proclaimed their commitment to fight for a relaxation of international tension and an improvement of relations among nations.[40]

When in 1977 Charter-77 was published in the CSSR (a document demanding more human rights in the CSSR and protection of basic freedoms, or, in fact a call for those rights already embodied in the CSSR Constitution to be recognized and observed, signed by several Czechoslovak intellectuals), and the government began its anti-Charter-77 campaign, all CSSR churches and religious societies officially had to keep their distance from Charter-77 and were forced to make a statement to the effect that religious freedom was fully respected in Czechoslovakia. Special zeal in these efforts was displayed by the highest representatives of the Czechoslovak Church, Patriarch Miroslav Novak[41] and Prague Bishop Josef Kupka.[42]

Church officials are frequently asked to take part in various international propaganda campaigns conducted by the socialist world. When the propaganda campaign against the August 1981 decision of U.S. President Reagan to go ahead with the production of the neutron bomb began, the synods of all East European churches issued appropriate declarations. The declaration of the Bulgarian Holy Synod read: "The arms race, the stockpiling of nuclear weapons, the plans for deployment of new medium-range nuclear missiles in some countries in Western Europe and particularly the monstrous decision of the United States to produce the neutron bomb, place the people of Europe and the world before the danger of nuclear destruction."[43]

The declaration also pointed out that the U.S. president's decision contradicted the final act of the Helsinki Conference, international peace and cooperation, and concluded: "It is with a sense of civic duty that the Bulgarian Orthodox Church joins in the protest of the world peaceloving public against the production of the neutron bomb and insists on a total ban on it."[44]

A similar demand was issued by the August 1981 Dresden meeting of the Central Committee of the World Council of Churches. In addition to protesting against the production of the neutron bomb ("an enormous threat"), the declaration issued by the meeting appealed to all member-churches "to increase their support for peace," to contribute to "justly and peacefully solving the Namibian problem," and advocated renewing and intensifying disarmament negotiations. [45] The leaders of the World Council of Churches were received by GDR party and state leader Erich Honecker, who "acknowledged the numerous activities of the WCC and its member-churches in securing peace and in reducing the escalation in the arms race."[46]

Whatever the occasion, the East European churches are always alert and ready to echo the official policy of their government. Thus, already at the beginning of July 1982, long before the climax of the Israeli invasion of Lebanon, the GDR Christian Conference for Peace (another religious peace organization) sent a message to the PLO leadership in Beirut and assured the Palestinians of the "inseparable solidarity" of the GDR believers. "The constant aggression of the Zionist state against the Arab people of Palestine and the population of Southern Lebanon and Beirut fills us with resentment," the message stated. "One can destroy cities, villages, and refugee camps and kill and expel their inhabitants; but one cannot extinguish the claim of the Palestinian people before God and the world to a just peace in their own country. . . . We honor the courageous resistance of the armed forces of the Palestinian people who must fight for their existence not only against the Israeli aggressor but also against the biggest military power of the imperialist camp supporting Tel Aviv."[47]

Although on occasions the East European churches may support particular "peace initiatives" of their regimes, denounce specific aspects of U.S. foreign policy, or subscribe to specific initiatives of their governments (for instance, the Evangelical Church of the GDR supporting the "Berlin Appeal" of the GDR Government, calling for a "nuclear-free Europe and negotiations to this end between the two German states which ultimately are to lead to the withdrawal of the occupation powers"[48], as a rule their support is of larger scale, covering the entire foreign policy of their countries. To this end, frequent international conferences are organized, international meetings of various church delegations held, and so forth. Thus in February 1982 there was a meeting in Prague between delegations of the Berlin Conference of Catholics in the European countries, and the CSSR Christian Peace Conference. The delegations "condemned the militarist policy of the Reagan administration . . . which contradicts the principles of Christian ethics," "expressed their solidarity with the people of El Salvador in the fight for justice and their people's independence," stated "their opposition to the attempts to abuse the Madrid meeting," and expressed their readiness "to actively contribute to the preparations and the proceedings of the world all-religious conference against the threat of a nuclear war, which will be held on the initiative of the patriarch of the Russian Orthodox Church, Pimen."[49]

Incidentally, the CSSR Christian Peace Conference is another pseudo-religious organization founded in fact by the government, "fighting to promote the renewal of relations of trust and cooperation among the peoples, to ward off all attempts at abusing religion for antisocialist goals, and to lead believers toward more actively participating in building and developing our socialist fatherland."[50] It was the Christian Peace Conference that in March 1982 organized in Prague an international meeting of churches, attended by representatives of twenty-six countries, and aimed at supporting the various foreign policy initiatives of the Soviet Union. The meeting adopted a letter to Brezhnev expressing support for the unilateral moratorium on the deployment of medium-range missiles in the European Soviet Union . . . "a step that opened the path toward liberating Europe from nuclear danger"; denounced the Israeli policy in the Middle East, calling for the withdrawal of the Israeli troops from all Arab territories conquered in 1967 and the establishment of a Palestinian state; and condemned the U.S. policy in Central America "where the U.S. administration is constantly stepping up its military assistance to regimes that, for the sake of maintaining power, are violating basic human rights."[51]

A similar meeting of representatives of fourteen European countries took place in Prague in September 1979. The meeting, sponsored by Pacem in Terris, adopted a program entitled "The Responsibility of Catholics in the Political Process of Détente."[52] The usual topics--the Helsinki final act, SALT II, curtailing the arms race, the Madrid conference, etc., were dealt with along the officially established lines.[53]

From time to time Church leaders are asked to take part in foreign language broadcasts--within the framework of their propaganda efforts--in which they glorify religious freedom in their country. In January 1980 this was done by several Romanian Church leaders, who after participating in the Congress of the Socialist Democracy and Unity Front (and stating there, "we are partners in the goals of your political activities"[54]) told Western audiences about the "full freedom and rights enjoyed by all sects in Romania."[55]

The activities of the East European churches in support of their governments' policies carry certain rewards. First of all, as already stressed, this activity is to a large extent lip service, which has to be paid in order to preserve the delicate status quo in church-state relations and the selective freedom of religion. Then, there are the meetings between Church and state leaders, which--among other things--preserve the myth of freedom of religion in Eastern Europe, mark awards of decorations to Church activists, and so forth.

An appropriate occasion for decorating Church officials was the 36th anniversary of the Hungarian Catholic clergymen's peace movement, which was marked in September 1980. On this occasion the Hungarian Presidential Council "conferred high decorations on the leaders of the Catholic Church," and Premier Gyorgy Lazar received a delegation led by Cardinal Dr. Laszlo Lekai, Archbishop of Esztergom.[56] Again, in Hungary in February 1981 the Presidential Council awarded the Labor Order of Merit in gold to Karoly Prohle, secretary general of the Ecumenical Council of Hungarian Churches, "in recognition of his successful activity in forming good relations between the state and the protestant churches and on the occasion of his 70th birthday."[57]

Sometimes not individuals, but the Church as a whole, receives an award. Thus in Yugoslavia, in June 1981, the Federation of the Yugoslav Orthodox Clergy Association was awarded the Order of Merit for the People with golden star, on the occasion of "30 years of successful activity in Yugoslavia . . . its contribution to development of brotherhood and unity of all nations and nationalities, and the continued centuries-old freedom-loving orientation and commitment of patriotic priests."[58]

Finally, a further way of displaying satisfaction with the activity of the Church in Eastern Europe can be an interview with some state official in charge of relations with the church, in which he praises the church's activities. Thus in February 1982 Imre Miklos, Hungary's secretary of state and chairman of the State Office for Church Affairs, was interviewed by the party daily Nepszabadsag on church-state relations. Stressing that "defending peace is our common cause and task," Miklos positively evaluated the international propaganda activity of the Hungarian Catholic Church and "its contribution to promoting the realization of the party's policy."[59]

THE CONTINUING STATE STRUGGLE AGAINST RELIGION

It is an amazing fact that, despite the strictly
controlled "freedom" of religion, the obvious cooperation
between at least a substantial part of the Church and the
authorities, the Church's declarations and conferences
supporting various communist initiatives, the meetings between Church and state leaders, and the various awards
bestowed on Church leaders, the East European governments
have never ceased in their unrelenting struggle against
religion. As Ceausescu put it succinctly: "The freedom
for religious beliefs is one thing and the activities of
the party in promoting the revolutionary philosophy on
nature and society is another."[60]
The governmental antireligious campaign utilizes
direct and indirect means. The direct means, or rather
measures, are aimed against the Church as an institution,
and against the clergy, while the indirect ones involve
pressure on the believers, antireligious propaganda,
atheistic education, and so forth. The first type of
measures aims at curbing or even liquidating the activity
of the church by limiting the number of divinity schools
and students, accusing clergy of various kinds of criminal
and antistate activities, and restricting religious publications, and the second type of measures aims at "immunizing"
those who can even theoretically be "infected" by
religious beliefs.
Arresting members of the clergy and subjecting them
to physical pressure is one of the most radical measures
against religion. Arresting members of the clergy, simply
for being such, was the usual practice immediately after
the establishment of the East European socialist regimes,
when for a while the socialist regimes entertained the hope
of extinguishing religion quickly, partly by physical
measures. Today, the arrests continue (although on a smaller
scale), and the arrested clergymen are usually charged with
various criminal offenses. In August 1981 two Czechoslovak
Catholic priests, Jeroslav Kuka, a 38-year old Dominican
from Pilsen, and Josef Kordik, 33, a Jesuit incumbent at
Lipceves, were arrested. AFP (France Press) reported that
the arrests were a result of charges of running a
clandestine printing press that had produced religious
material in defiance of government regulations.[61] In the
CSSR in 1976, the Roznava District Court sentenced Stefan
Javorsky to eighteen months in prison on charges of working
among the intelligentsia and young people, and of having
recommended listening to Vatican Radio. The result of

Javorsky's appeal on the verdict was that the Kosice Regional Court increased the sentence to two years.[62] For one more example, in Bulgaria in 1979, six Pentecostalists were tried in Sofia for "violation of foreign currency laws and customs regulations."[63] The defendants were accused of having had clandestine contacts with representatives of religious groups abroad. One of the strongest arguments of the prosecution was that they helped distribute thousands of smuggled Bibles and other religious books, an act described by the Bulgarian press as "a provocation against our social system, against our laws, and against our national feelings."[64] The defendants were sentenced to three to six years imprisonment.[65] It must be pointed out that such trials of clergy for "having smuggled religious books" are frequent in all East European countries. In these countries officialdom equates religious literature with pornography and strictly restricts and even prohibits the import of Bibles.

A much more serious matter is when clergy are accused of maintaining contact with "antisocialist factors" across the border. This is often the case in Yugoslavia, where Catholic clergy are frequently accused of maintaining contact with various emigrant, dissident, and even fascist circles in Western countries. In November 1981 Ferdo Vlasic and Jozo Krizic, brothers in the Franciscan Monastery in Duvno, were accused of such contacts and sentenced respectively to eight and five-and-one-half years in prison.[66]

Sometimes, persecution is not aimed at individual members of the clergy but against the Church itself. Thus at the beginning of 1981 the Catholic Church of Croatia was subjected to bitter attacks for its alleged oppositional and nationalistic activities. On 29 January 1981 TANJUG reported the president of the Republic of Croatia, Jacob Blazevic, as saying: "A foreign nucleus in the Roman Catholic Church is waging a battle against the Croatian people . . . acting against the people and socialism, which has given them the greatest freedoms."[67]

In a speech made on the occasion of the publication of his memoirs, President Blazevic attacked both the late Catholic Cardinal Stepinac for collaborating with the German occupation forces during World War II, and the present Church hierarchy for cultivating Stepinac's memory.[68] In addition, the Catholic Church of Croatia (and other East European countries) has been accused of "trying to create a political confrontation between the Catholic Church and the Yugoslav state,"[69] and of "trying to turn the Church into a political organization."[70]

It should be pointed out that the Yugoslav authorities do not discriminate among the various Yugoslav churches. Thus in August 1981 several Serbian Orthodox clergymen were accused of and sentenced for "creating religious intolerance and acting from positions of religious nationalism."[71] The more specific accusation was "playing tapes containing messages with hostile content," originating from émigré circles abroad.[72] Several cases of such character, especially when the Catholic Church was involved, prompted the Yugoslav authorities to point an admonishing finger at the Church warning its clergy to refrain strictly from any political activity, and reminding them that in Yugoslavia the Church, any church, is subject to state jurisdiction and supremacy: "The principle of separation of state and church by itself cancels out any kind of partner-like equality in discussion. The bishops may not like the Constitution and the existing laws, but the Church has accepted them and, therefore, they are binding."[73]

After 1980, obviously following the events in Poland, where the Catholic Church did nothing to hide its sympathy and support for the Solidarity trade union, the East European socialist states intensified their anti-Church campaign. In Romania it was suddenly discovered that "religion is a result of the exploitation of man by man," that "religion still has an instrumental character, providing very easy and plausible explanations for people of little education and culture," and subsequently, "since the ideological struggle against religion is the task of the entire party, qualification as a communist is essentially incompatible with the attitude of concession or adherence to religion."[74]

Admitting that the Romanian Constitution guarantees the freedom of religion, the same source added: "But the guarantee of freedom of conscience gives no one license to exploit any citizens' religious feelings or to use those problems as a means of social-political diversion or interference in another country's internal affairs. . . . Religion cannot open or maintain educational institutions other than those specially intended to train their own personnel. It is also prohibited by law to disseminate religious propaganda outside the religious institutions and the authorized media."[75]

Finally, as if to disperse any doubt about what the Romanian government was talking about, the party daily Scinteia stated: "Religion must not and cannot interfere with politics; any attempt to do so must be fought against, because, willy-nilly, it thus turns into an instrument in the hands of reactionaries."[76]

In Czechoslovakia it was estimated that by the end of 1981 there were about 100 clergymen in prison, most of them Roman Catholics.[77] Western sources reported numerous cases of persecution aimed at curbing the church's activity and compromising its members.[78]

In Yugoslavia in 1981, the authorities began a propaganda campaign against clergymen suspected of cooperating with the Germans in World War II. Several priests were arrested and sentenced to long terms of prision.[79] Every church activity was viewed with apparent suspicion by the authorities. When in February-March 1982 the GDR Evangelical Church tried to organize several antiwar rallies and demonstrations (obviously without the official blessing of the authorities and outside the accepted "channels" or "frame" of such activity), the authorities swiftly moved to preclude any "unauthorized" pacifism.[80]

The East European countries are especially sensitive to "underground religious activity," i.e., religious services that do not take place within one of the recognized (and strictly controlled) churches. The situation in Czechoslovakia, where an "underground" Catholic church exists, has been most acute. According to Western sources[81] this church has been very active, holding services, Biblical seminars, and so forth. A special unit has been set by the CSSR secret policy to investigate and root out the underground church.[82]

Arrests, direct pressure, and persecution are only a part of the direct means of curbing the influence of the Church in Eastern Europe. There are more (and more sophisticated) means, including the premature pensioning of priests,[83] restricting the number of divinity students and the size of a faculty,[84] and similar steps aimed at reducing the number of clergy. Thus, although in 1960 in Hungary there were 3,722 Catholic clergymen, in 1979 their number had decreased to 2,790. The number of seminarians also dropped significantly.[85]

The second type of measures--the indirect ones--is directed against the believers. Again, as in the case of the clergy, pressure is one of the most widely used means. Reporting on religion in Czechoslovakia, the Vienna daily Neues Volksblatt described and illustrates the pressure against believers in the CSSR, citing examples to show how the political police routinely photograph believers who regularly attend religious services and send this photographic evidence to the management of enterprises, asking them to dismiss those concerned, albeit officially on other grounds.[86]

Party members are especially singled out for religious "deviations." Reporting the fact that several party members had sponsored a religious wedding, Bucharest's Munca de Partid added: "Unfortunately, we still find some party members who are 'flirting' with anachronistic, mystical practices, which are, obviously, diametrically opposed to the philosophy of the working class, a philosophy which, when they asked to be admitted to the ranks of communists, they solemnly pledged to embrace and cultivate."[87] The same source reported that one of those criticized by the newspaper was relieved of her position as a member of the enterprise's party bureau.[88] More such cases reporting the participation of communists in various religious rites are cited by the Romanian press.[89] Lamenting that the RCP city committee in Vatra Dornei city had not taken notice that a leader of an enterprise "was spending a good part of his free time in religious establishments,"[90] Munca de Partid tried to rationalize this with the "freedom of religion" in Romania: "Of course, our state guarantees freedom of religion and respects the religious beliefs of citizens, but membership in the Communist Party assigns to a party member and, especially, a cadre entrusted with leadership functions, the obligation of being guided in everyday life and activity by revolutionary ideology, by the scientific outlook of dialectical and historical materialism, affirming himself as an active propagandist of the programmatic principles of our party."[91]

Zagreb's Glas Koncila of 28 June 1981 reported similar cases in Yugoslavia, including the case of party members being expelled from the party because on one occasion they went to a church not to worship but to attend a concert of Bach music, no priest being present.[92]

In the CSSR (which is a leading state in the anti-religious propaganda), the authorities did not hesitate to quote the Constitution itself in order to disqualify "leading workers" because of their religious beliefs:

Religion for us is not the private affair of a party member. It is an affair for the entire party, the organs and organizations, which check the world view of the members. Nor is religion a private affair for those workers who have educational jobs in our country. This applies to a large group of teachers, educators, and cultural

workers. They are obligated by Article 16 of
the Constitution, which says: "The entire cultural policy in Czechoslovakia, the development
of education, training, and teaching are conducted
in the spirit of the scientific world view, i.e.,
Marxism-Leninism, and in close relationship with
the life and work of the people."

A similar demand is placed on leading workers.
According to the resolution concerning cadre and
personnel work, approved by the Presidium of the
CPCZ Central Committee on 6 November 1970, and
according to the subsequent directives given to
various state organs, only fully qualified workers
can be appointed to leading positions. Qualifications here is understood as a sum of technical
knowledge, moral qualities, political maturity,
and class consciousness. Political maturity and
class consciousness are directly related to the
scientific world view, i.e., to the materialistic
and thus also atheistic understanding of all
social phenomena and processes as well as active
everyday life and atheistic work. [93]

The Polish party daily Trybuna Ludu, shortly before
the imposition of martial law in Poland, presented a
similar view, although in a slightly different way. The
beginning sounds almost revolutionary: "It has been
stated hundreds of times--both in our party and other
communist parties throughout the world--that believers
may become party members, obviously full-fledged party
members, since party rules do not provide for any other
kind of membership."[94] The newspaper even quoted Marx
and Lenin on the existence of such a possibility: "Marx
often stated his opposition to making atheism a precondition of party membership. Lenin admitted the possibility of a priest's becoming a party member."[95] Then,
however, the newspaper explained that all this applies
only until the religious person joins the party. Afterwards "his specific duties with respect to political
questions," "Marxist-Leninist ideology," and the need to
"maintain a critical attitude toward statements of church
authorities and (struggle) against the propagation among
party members of those authorities' political views"[96]
clearly preclude any religious predispositions of party
members.

Atheistic propaganda is an integral part of education
in all East European states. Countless articles and

pamphlets published by the state authorities aim at countering religious influence: "The struggle against the
religious Weltanschauung is a complex task. It is being
carried on for the people and not against them. It is the
primary task of our schools, teachers, and young communists
to educate the young to be faithful to the idea of
socialism. Our main means of fighting down the religious
outlook is mass political education, the propagation of a
scientific Weltanschauung, and the consistent and high-
level profession of the ideas of Marxism-Leninism."[97]
Writers and poets are constantly urged to include antireligious themes in their works. In Romania, for instance,
the press frequently criticizes artistic and literary works
with religious overtones.[98]

A typical means of attack on religious traditions is
the replacement of religious holidays and rites with civil
ones. This involves the introduction of official civil
holidays near or on the day of the religious holidays,
enforcing state-sponsored civil ceremonies on occasions
that formerly required a religious service (weddings,
etc.), and so forth. The clear goal of this practice has
been expressed in the Hungarian press as follows:

"The propagation of civil ceremonies has become both
an important aim and instrument of ideological educational
work, as well as a public device to persuade people of all
age groups to turn away from the churches."[99]

According to the Hungarian daily Magyar Hirlap, "today
an increased number of people are calling for civil
ceremonies to mark family events."[100] Other Hungarian
newspapers maintain the opposite, namely, that most of the
people still prefer religious ceremonies to the civil
ones.[101]

Bulgaria dealt with the whole practice of replacing
religious holidays and rites by civil ones by legislative
decree. On 12 April 1978 the State Council issued a
document designed to encourage the process of substituting
new "socialist" holidays and rites for all religious
occasions and ceremonies.[102] This was the fifth such
document issued by the Bulgarian authorities, following two
BCP Secretariat decisions of 1966 and 1971[103] and two
decrees of the Council of Ministers.[104] The 1978 decision
stated that socialist holidays, ceremonies, and symbols
will serve to spread the ideas of Marxism-Leninism, socialist
ideology, patriotism, and internationalism more rapidly
and effectively. It defined the basic goals of introducing
civil holidays and rites at length, including the following:

o to strengthen socialist relations and improve the
  socio-psychological climate;
o to consolidate communist ideals and the BCP's
  policies;
o to foster love and devotion to socialist Bulgaria;
o to advance the feelings of fraternal friendship
  with and loyalty to the USSR and the CPSU;
o to maintain class solidarity with the world's
  working people;
o to stand up for socialist moral values.[105]

Does the Church protest against the official attitude
toward religion in Eastern Europe? The answer is yes, but
very seldom--and mostly pianissimo. Too strong a protest
would only cause a further deterioration in the church-
state relations and result in even greater restriction on
religious freedom. Still, from time to time, the Church
lets its voice be heard. Thus in his 1980 Easter message
Msgr. Fanjo Kuharich, Archbishop of Zagreb and secretary of
Yugoslavia's Catholic Bishops' Conference, complained that
official atheistic propaganda was eroding the moral
foundations of the young generation: "A systematic atheiza-
tion is also present in our country in all spheres of
instruction and education, from kindergarten to the university. This is a fact. It is not even necessary to prove
it. However, we should repeatedly state that this is a
violation of the fundamental right of parents who are
believers, when their children are educated in a materialistic ideology that leads them to atheism, and all this is
done in schools which are the property of the people."[106]
The official Yugoslav press immediately rejected the
Bishop's complaint.[107]
    Still, the Yugoslav Catholic Church continues to issue
infrequent protests, some of which even have the character
of official statements. Such was the official protest of
the Yugoslav bishops on 8 October 1981, which consisted of
four points: The Yugoslav Catholic Church rejected the
official notion of the SFRY government that it engages in
political activity while preaching the gospel; regret was
expressed "that Marxist atheism is being presented to young
believers in primary, secondary, and higher educational
establishments as the only scientific world view"; protest
was voiced against attacks on religious employees by
journalists; and finally, belief was expressed that "love
is the only constructive way for our social community to
progress."[108] This protest was also rejected by the
official press, which used the protest itself as a proof of

the Church's political activity.[109]

On some extremely rare occasions, some East European churches have registered their differences with some aspects of their respective government's policy in the international arena. Thus, although the GDR Protestant Church expressed its support for various aspects of the GDR foreign policy in 1975 (for instance, support for the final act of the Helsinki Conference and participation in the 1975 Moscow Peace Conference), it also registered its protest against the resolution of the UN General Assembly denouncing Zionism as a racist movement.[110]

POLAND--THE CHURCH AND SOLIDARITY

Throughout this chapter it has been pointed out that the Polish Catholic Church represents a special case that does not fit into the East European regular model of church-state relations. It is much more than a misfit. It is a unique phenomenon, a non-Marxist institution whose traditional influence affects almost the entire population of a country that since 1945 has been subjected to a totalitarian regime of a Marxist character.

It is not our intention to survey here the history of the Polish Catholic Church since the end of World War II. However, it must be stressed that it has always been an institution closely linked with the history of the Polish nation and has served as a symbol of national unity and identity. The Polish Communist government, although committed to the Marxist-atheist ideology and forced to adopt at least partially the Soviet model of church-state relations, realized that no social transformation or even statehood was possible without the cooperation of the Church. This gave rise to a certain ambiguity in the attitude of the communist leaders toward the Polish Catholic Church; they have alternately dispensed terror and compromise agreements (which were not painstakingly adhered to). In September 1953 Stefan Wyszynski, Primate of Poland, was arrested and imprisoned for three years, but the Catholic Church as an institution still enjoyed relative freedom and was even allowed to continue its religious publications. From time to time antichurch campaigns flared up, such as the 1965-1966 Gomulka-inspired campaign, which culminated in 1966 when Gomulka denied the Pope an entry permit for a visit to Czestochowa on the occasion of the 1,000th anniversary of Poland's Christianization. Still, as it preserved its overwhelming influence,

the Polish Catholic Church was not active in political
opposition. One must not forget that since 1957 Catholic
Church activists have consistently been elected to the Polish
Sejm, without exercising any lasting effect on Poland's
political life.

The election of Cardinal Karol Wojtyla as Pope (16
October 1978), the growing unrest of the Solidarity trade
union, and the Church's profound involvement in the subsequent conflict, turned the Polish Catholic Church into a
political factor of tremendous importance, closely involved
in Poland's daily developments. By then, the Church had
already formed many divisions, to use Stalin's celebrated
question about the Pope's divisions. Between 1945 and mid-
1981 the number of Polish clergy had doubled. There were
about 20,000 priests and eighty bishops. Poland's twenty-
seven dioceses were divided into 7,600 parishes, each
serving 4,300 faithful on the average. Children received
religious instruction in 21,000 catechism classes.[111]
In 1980, nearly 6,300 seminarians were studying in the
forty-six seminaries in Poland.[112] The only Catholic university between the Elbe River in the West and Vladivostok in
the East is located in Lublin.[113] In short, few Catholic
countries, let alone any other East European country, can
boast of such dynamic religious activity.

The election of Cardinal Wojtyla boosted the confidence
of the Polish Church. By the end of the 1970s, it did not
hesitate to openly state its antigovernmental position on
some issues and thus align itself with various forces and
groups in Poland that demanded internal reforms as prerequisites for improving conditions of life in the country.
Thus in December 1979 a general assembly of the Catholic
bishops in Poland openly charged the authorities with
responsibility for the "rapidly deteriorating economic,
moral, and social situation in the country."[114]

Until 1980, when Solidarity was formed, the Polish
Catholic Church was the only organized force in Poland that
cut across all social groups and confronted the government
when the latter abused the civil rights of separate groups.
The strikes of 1980 and the emergence of the Solidarity
movement as a third political force in Poland transformed
the role of the Church from major adversary of the regime
to a much-needed mediator between the regime and Solidarity.
Thus on 21 October 1980 there was a meeting in Warsaw
between Stefan Cardinal Wyszynski, the Primate of the
Polish Catholic Church, and Stanislaw Kania, then first
secretary of the PZPR Central Committee. The formal
communique on the meeting stated that the two had "discussed

matters of great significance for the internal peace and development of the country. A common view was expressed that constructive cooperation between the Church and the state serves well the interests of the nation, and that is why it will be continued in the name of Poland's well-being and security."[115]

On the following day, 22 October, Warsaw's Catholic Bishop Bronislaw Dabrowski met with several representatives of the Solidarity trade union.[116] If nothing more, those meetings at least symbolized the growing involvement of the Polish Catholic Church in the internal political develop-ments and a willingness to act as arbiter or mediator be-tween different forces and groups. On at least one occasion (at his famous August 1980 sermon), Cardinal Wyszynski urged the Solidarity activists to adopt a more cautious and restrained approach,[117] thus establishing a substantial degree of credibility in the eyes of the authorities. He frequently met the communist leaders (with Kania on 25 August and 21 October 1980 and February 1981, and with General Jaruzelski on 26 March 1981)[118] in an obvious effort to achieve some sort of modus vivendi between the government and Solidarity. Still, the growing ties with and support of Solidarity gradually became evident. By mid-1981 Wyszynski's successor, Archbishop Jozef Glemp, could openly state: "For the Church the emergence of Solidarity as a power which has moved to the forefront of society, came as a big surprise, but acceptance of Solidarity as a free trade union did not confront us with any problems. . . . The Church is supporting Solidarity not as an ally but as a defender of human rights in the spirit of the Gospel. . . . We do not want to dominate Solidarity, but we are ready to defend it if human rights are violated."[119]

And indeed, on 28 December 1981, two weeks after martial law was announced in Poland and all Solidarity activists had been interned, the primate sent General Jaruzelski a long letter, asking the authorities to revoke the measures and the sackings from work they caused. Archbishop Glemp pointed out that these measures were "discriminatory" because they were founded on "the idea that any member of Solidarity is an enemy of order," which according to him was a "fundamental mistake."[120] Still, true to its role as arbiter and mediator, the Polish Catholic Church expressed its support for the government in condemning the sanctions announced by Western govern-ments--sanctions "which mean that it is considerably more difficult to overcome the crisis and which curb the return to full realization of the renewal process in the spirit of the social agreements."[121]

There is no doubt that in 1982 the Polish Catholic Church consolidated even further its unique position as the only really independent social force in the communist world. What was the reaction of the other East European churches to this development? In most cases, apparently under governmental pressure, they condemned both Solidarity and the attitude of the Polish Catholic Church. Thus, Hungary's Cardinal Lekai said: "Even the Pope realizes that the Polish way is not the only one leading to salvation. Being Hungarians, Hungarian Catholics, we have to go our own way. Conditions in Hungary are different from Poland."[122]

The much more sweeping condemnation of the Polish Church was reserved, however, for the communist authorities. Commenting on Walesa's trip to the Vatican, CSSR Radio stated: "This is not coincidental that the activization of the anticommunist and antisocialist forces had a precise date--the return of Lech Walesa from Rome, where he had deliberations with the Pope and other Vatican represen-tatives. . . . It is clear that the Vatican gave Walesa instructions and that the Catholic fifth column in Poland is to help the leader of the so-called new trade unions in the implementation of these directives."[123]

In May 1981 Bratislava's Pravda sharply attacked the attitude of the Polish Catholic Church toward the socialist revolution: "For some time prior to the strikes the activity of the Catholic hierarchy in Poland reached far beyond the framework of a mere satisfaction of the religious needs of members of the Catholic Church. The Church became increasingly active as a political force, and at present it is heading the clerical movement which has antisocialist features. Its goal is to eliminate the socialist system and to effect a return to capitalism. . . . The present course of the Catholic hierarchy in Poland represents a political risk in which the fate of the Polish people is the object of ruthless gamble."[124] After the announcement of martial law, the same Slovak newspaper attacked the Polish Church in a much harsher language: "The so-called patriotic stances of the church hierarchy concealed a carefully thought out, precisely prepared and dosed anticommunism, unambiguously aimed at utilizing every suitable opportunity for gaining official recognition and support of its world-outlook and of political pluralism, combined with a denial of the leading role of the Marxist-Leninist party and a renewal of all former

privileges."[125] The same newspaper accused the Polish
Catholic Church of actually "helping the birth of
Solidarity," and "advising Solidarity throughout its
activity."[126]

In March 1982 Bratislava's _Pravda_ (which seemed to be
a leading source of antireligious propaganda) went as far
as accusing the Pope of supporting the "Polish counter-
revolution."[127]

During 1980 and 1981 the East European regimes were
engulfed in fear, most of them realizing that the developments in Poland could be contageous. Thus the GDR
authorities stated: "The imperialist forces keep trying
to affect citizens with religious ties and religious
communities in the GDR through anticommunist agitation in
'Christian' garb and ideological diversion, so as to push
them into opposition to the socialist state and to socialist
development."[128] And the CSSR made its contribution:
"In the countries of real socialism in which united trade
unions exist and act, clerical tendencies objectively have
no place. . . . The latest example of such a course is the
activity of political clericalism in connection with the
establishment and the activity of Solidarity in the Polish
People's Republic. Experience shows that there have [also]
been attempts from outside to revive clericalism in our
country."[129]

In conclusion, the Polish example, too, merely highlights by partial contrast that religion is permitted to
exist in Eastern Europe only so long as its officials
refrain from any form of antigovernmental activity
("political clericalism") and issue regular and consistent
pledges of loyalty. The Church is assigned a role that
resembles closely the roles of the mass and public organizations in Eastern Europe, namely, to function as an
auxiliary organization of the communist party and participate
in various internal and international campaigns organized
and sponsored by the communist party. The threat of
persecution hangs constantly over the heads of the church
officials, and indeed is often translated in practice,
in order to keep them away from any thought of political
activity. If the Church is allowed to be active within
strictly prescribed limits, and in fact exists under
"controlled conditions," the regimes go further in their
pointed atheist and anticlerical propaganda and openly
state that religion has no place in the socialist society.

NOTES

1. H. Gordon Skilling, The Governments of Communist East Europe (New York, 1966), p. 205.
2. Tribuna E Gazetarit (Albania), July-August 1980, pp. 29-32.
3. Tirana Domestic Service in Albanian, 21 January 1976; Zeri I Popullit, 29 February 1976.
4. Tribuna E Gazetarit, July-August 1980, pp. 29-32.
5. Ibid.
6. Bashkimi (Albania), 11 August 1980.
7. Shqiptarja E Re (Albania), no. 4, April 1982, p. 18; FBIS East European Report, no. 2037, 26 July 1982.
8. RFE RAD Background Report, CSSR, no. 115, 21 June 1977.
9. Glas Koncila (Yugoslavia), 23 March 1978.
10. Rabotnichesko Delo (Bulgaria), 9 May 1971.
11. Rolnicke Noviny (CSSR), 28 January 1982; FBIS East European Report, no. 1987, 10 March 1982.
12. Tribuna (CSSR), no. 10, 5 March 1980, pp. 8-9.
13. Nedeljne Informativne Novine (Yugoslavia), no. 1549 7 September 1980, pp. 16-19.
14. Ibid.
15. Tribuna (CSSR), no. 35, 2 September 1981; FBIS East European Report, no. 1938, 5 November 1981.
16. Ibid.
17. Vjesnik (Yugoslavia), 19 February 1981; FBIS East European Report, no. 1859, 18 March 1981.
18. Ibid.
19. Rude Pravo (CSSR), 27 March 1980.
20. Buletinul Oficial (Romania), Part I, no. 107, 25 December 1979, p. 4.
21. Nepszabadsag (Hungary), 14 February 1976.
22. Ibid., 15 February 1976.
23. RFE Situation Report, Romania, 22 June 1977.
24. Scinteia (Romania), 15 June 1977.
25. Prace (CSSR), 29 April 1981.
26. Standpunkt (GDR), vol. 9, no. 4, April 1981, p. 85.
27. Budapest MTI in English, 1022 GMT, 29 January 1982; Daily Report (FIBS), 1 February 1982.
28. Ibid.
29. Neues Deutschland (East Berlin), 4 June 1981; Daily Report (FBIS), 8 June 1981.
30. Ibid.
31. Rude Pravo, 22 September 1976.
32. Radio Prague, 21 September 1976, in RFE Situation Report, CSSR, 23 November 1977.

33. Radio Hvezda, 10 November 1977, in RFE Situation Report, CSSR, 23 November 1977.

34. Katolicke Noviny (CSSR), 27 January 1980.

35. Radio Hvezda, 5 February 1980, in RFE Situation Report, CSSR, 13 February 1980.

36. Ibid.

37. Radio Prague, 5 February 1980, in RFE Situation Report, CSSR, 13 February 1980.

38. Radio Hvezda, 6 February 1980, in RFE Situation Report, CSSR, 13 February 1980.

39. Ibid.; Lidova Demokracie, 7 February 1980.

40. Radio Hvezda, 11 February 1980, in RFE Situation Report, CSSR, 13 February 1980.

41. Kostnicke Jirsky (CSSR), no. 5, 2 February 1977.

42. Lesky Zapas (CSSR), no. 4, 23 January 1977.

43. Sofia BTA in English, 1830 GMT, 5 February 1981.

44. Ibid.

45. Neues Deutschland, 25 August 1981; Daily Report (FBIS), 31 August 1981.

46. East Berlin ADN International Service in German, 1554 GMT, 28 August 1981; Daily Report (FBIS), 31 August 1981.

47. Neues Deutschland, 7 July 1982; Daily Report (FBIS), 9 July 1982.

48. Frankfurter Rundschau (FRG), 17 February 1982, Daily Report (FBIS), 22 February 1982.

49. Rude Pravo, 12 February 1982; Daily Report (FBIS), 18 February 1982.

50. Ibid., 17 February 1982; Daily Report (FBIS), 23 February 1982.

51. Rude Pravo, 27 March 1982; Daily Report (FBIS), 30 March 1982.

52. RFE Situation Report, CSSR, 25 September 1979.

53. Ibid.

54. Biserica Ortodoxa Romana (Romania), nos. 1-2, January-February 1980, p. 8.

55. RFE Situation Report, Romania, 29 January 1980.

56. Budapest MTI in English, 1716 GMT, 23 September 1980; Daily Report (FBIS), 25 September 1980.

57. Budapest Radio in Hungarian to Europe, 2100 GMT, 20 February 1981; Daily Report (FBIS), 24 February 1981.

58. Belgrade TANJUG in English, 1618 GMT, 19 June 1981; Daily Report (FBIS), 22 June 1981.

59. Nepszabadsag, 20 February 1982; Daily Report (FBIS), 25 February 1982.

60. Scinteia, 7 July 1979.

61. AFP in English, 1013 GMT, 19 August 1981;

Daily Report (FBIS), 20 August 1981.
    62. Pravda (CSSR), 26 January 1977.
    63. Otechestven Front (Bulgaria), 31 October 1979, in
RFE Situation Report, Bulgaria, 13 November 1979.
    64. Anteni (Bulgaria), no. 44, 31 October 1979.
    65. RFE Situation Report, Bulgaria, 13 November 1979.
    66. Oslobodjenje (Yugoslavia), 21 November 1981;
FBIS East European Report, no. 1593, 24 December 1981.
    67. Belgrade TANJUG in English, 1614 GMT, 29 January
1981; Daily Report (FBIS), 30 January 1981.
    68. RFE RAD Background Report, SFRY, no. 237,
21 August 1981.
    69. Vjesnik (Yugoslavia), 6 March 1981.
    70. Zagreb Domestic Service in Serbo-Croatian, 1400
GMT, 31 March 1981; Daily Report (FBIS), 1 April 1981.
    71. Politika (Yugoslavia), 5 September 1981; FBIS
East European Report, no. 1933, 26 October 1981.
    72. Ibid.
    73. Borba (Yugoslavia), 27 May 1981; Daily Report
(FBIS), 18 June 1981.
    74. Era Socialista (Romania), no. 6, 20 March 1982,
p. 25; FBIS East European Report, no. 2033, 13 July 1982.
    75. Ibid.
    76. Scinteia, 7 May 1982.
    77. The Times (London), 18 December 1981.
    78. These sources included the Times (London), already
cited; the Frankfurter Allegmeine Zeitung, 10 April 1980;
Reuters, 15 October 1981; Agence France Press, 30 September
1981; and Newsweek, 15 February 1982.
    79. RFE RAD Background Report, Yugoslavia, no. 269,
17 September 1981.
    80. RFE RAD Background Report, GDR, no. 94,
20 April 1982.
    81. Stutgarter Zeitung (FRG), 12 March 1981, in RFE
Situation Report, CSSR, 26 March 1981.
    82. Ibid.
    83. Katolicke Noviny (CSSR), no. 9, 1 March 1981,
p. 3; RFE Situation Report, CSSR, 26 March 1981.
    84. Novy Zivot (Rome), no. 11, 1977.
    85. RFE RAD Background Report, Hungary, no. 204,
16 July 1981.
    86. Neues Volkblatt (Austria), 10 June 1977.
    87. Munca de Partid (Romania), March 1980, pp. 90-91.
    88. Ibid.
    89. Ibid., December 1980, pp. 85-86; March 1980,
pp. 90-91; December 1979, pp. 114-115, etc.
    90. Ibid., December 1980, pp. 85-86.

91.   Ibid.
92.   Glas Koncila, 26 June 1981.
93.   Rolnicke Noviny, 28 January 1982; FBIS East European Report, no. 1987, 10 March 1982.
94.   Trybuna Ludu (Poland), 10 November 1981; Daily Report (FBIS), 19 November 1981.
95.   Ibid.
96.   Ibid.
97.   Zoltan Kovacs, "Topical Questions of Atheistic Education," in Ifji Komunista (Hungary), September 1976; RFE RAD Background Report, Hungary, no. 219, 27 October 1976.
98.   Revista de Pedagogie (Romania), March 1980, pp. 39-41.
99.   Partelet (Hungary), January 1978; RFE Situation Report, Hungary, 15 March 1978.
100. Magyar Hirlap (Hungary), 10 July 1976.
101. Magyarorszag, 12 January 1976; Csongrad Megyei Hirlap, 30 December 1973; Veszprem Megyei Naplo, 15 August 1975; RFE Situation Report, Hungary, 1 September 1976.
102. Rabotnichesko Delo, 23 May 1978.
103. Narodna Mladezh (Bulgaria), 26 September 1970; Rabotnichesko Delo, 10 March 1973.
104. Rabotnichesko Delo, 8 April 1969; Narodna Mladezh, 26 September 1970.
105. Rabotnichesko Delo, 23 May 1978.
106. Glas Koncila, 9 March 1980.
107. Vjesnik, 25 March 1980.
108. Glas Koncila, 25 October 1981, FBIS East European Report, no. 1948, 4 December 1981.
109. Vjesnik, 1 November 1981; FBIS East European Report, no. 1948, 4 December 1981.
110. RFE RAD Background Report, GDR, no. 240, 8 October 1980.
111. J. Nowak, "The Church in Poland," in Problems of Communism, January-February 1982, p. 3.
112. Polish Episcopate Press Office Bulletin no. 7, 1981.
113. Nowak, "The Church in Poland," p. 3.
114. Communique of the 14 December 1979 171st Plenary Conference of the Polish Episcopate, RFE Situation Report, Poland, 20 December 1979.
115. Radio Warsaw, 22 October 1980, in RFE RAD Background Report, Poland, no. 262, 30 October 1980.
116. RFE RAD Background Report, Poland, no. 262, 30 October 1980.
117. Nowak, "The Church in Poland," p. 14.

272

118.   Ibid.

119.   Tygodnik Powszechny, 21 June 1981, reported in Nowak, "The Church in Poland," p. 14.

120.   Le Monde (Paris), 19 January 1982; Daily Report (FBIS), 4 February 1982.

121.   Le Figaro (Paris), 21 January 1982; Daily Report (FBIS), 4 February 1982.

122.   Die Welt (Bonn), 14 November 1980.

123.   Prague Domestic Service in Czech, 1730 GMT, 28 January 1981; Daily Report (FBIS), 29 January 1981.

124.   Pravda (CSSR), 23 May 1981; Daily Report (FBIS), 2 June 1981.

125.   Pravda (CSSR), 5 March 1982; Daily Report (FBIS), 9 March 1982.

126.   Pravda (CSSR), 5 March 1982; Daily Report (FBIS), 9 March 1982.

127.   Pravda (CSSR), 25 March 1982; Daily Report (FBIS), 29 March 1982.

128.   Neue Zeit (GDR), 3 January 1981.

129.   Pravda (CSSR), 29 December 1980, Daily Report (FBIS), 5 January 1980.

9
The Judiciary

Like the structure of the East European parliaments
and electoral systems, the formal structure of the East
European judicial system is its least important feature.
Without any real independence from, or power vis-à-vis,
the other branches of the political system (and above all
the communist party), the judicial system of the East
European countries acts as a subordinate organ of law, in
charge of protecting the interests of the communist party
and the political system. Indeed, the constitutions of most
of the East European states contain special articles articu-
lating the duty of the courts to protect the country's
socialist system. Thus, the 1960 CSSR Constitution
reads: "The courts of law and the procurators' offices
protect the Socialist State, and its social system."[1]
The Bulgarian Constitution of 1971 states in similar vein:
"The courts dispense justice in the People's Republic of
Bulgaria. They protect the state and social system
established by its Constitution, the socialist property, the
life, freedom, honor, rights, and legitimate interests of
citizens, [and] the rights and legitimate interests of
socialist organizations."[2]
These (and other) East European constitutions also
have special clauses on the duty of the judicial system to
"educate the population," that is, its obligation to serve
as an instrument of political indoctrination. In this
respect the CSSR Constitution reads: "By all their actions,
the courts and the procurators' offices educate the
citizens toward loyalty to the country and to the cause of
Socialism, toward the observance of the law and of the rules
of Socialist coexistence, and to honest fulfillment of
their obligations toward the State and the community."[3]
The Bulgarian Constitution uses almost the same words:

"The courts consolidate socialist law and order, assist in the prevention of crime and other violations of law, and educate the citizens in a spirit of devotion to the motherland and the cause of socialism, labor discipline, conscientious fulfillment of the laws, and respect for the rules of the socialist community of people."[4]

It is interesting to point out that while the Romanian, Albanian, GDR, and Hungarian constitutions have similar clauses, the 1974 Yugoslav Constitution does not mention the indoctrinational duties of the judicial system. It is also interesting to note that in 1977 Jan Nemec, the Czech minister of Justice, defined "protecting the socialist state and its socialist system, and relations with the international socialist system" as "the basic task of the CSSR courts."[5] Asked to outline other differences between the socialist and the bourgeois courts, the minister pointed out three basic aspects: the "class composition" of the socialist courts ("judges chosen from among citizens loyal to our social system"); "the fundamental difference . . . that the bourgeois courts are instruments of oppression used by the ruling class against broad sections of the people, against the majority of the population, . . . [whereas by] contrast, the courts in the socialist state system are instruments of building a socialist society and protecting the rights and interests of the citizens of this society"; and finally, "While in bourgeois societies the role of the courts in penal cases is suppressive and repressive, in that they impose punishment, in a socialist society enforcement . . . [although] also a part of court activity . . . is neither the sole nor the main one . . . [because] the law also lays down the duty of prevention and of reeducation of persons who have committed an offense, and also determines the role of education in the work of all courts."[6]

STRUCTURE OF THE COURT SYSTEM

An area in which the socialist courts resemble the "bourgeois" ones is their structure. The structure of the East European judicial system (like many other aspects) is almost an exact copy of the Soviet system. In each country there is a supreme court appointed by the national assembly (Albania, Bulgaria) or the council of state (Poland), for a period of four or five years, and consisting of professional and "lay judges" or "lay assessors." The rest of the judicial hierarchy corresponds more or less to the country's

administrative structure. Thus in Albania, the Supreme
Court judges are elected by the National Assembly at its
first session after the general elections, and the lower
courts are similarly formed by the corresponding people's
councils.[7]

Bulgaria has a Supreme Court elected for a four-year
term by and accountable to the National Assembly and the
State Council, plus okrug (region) courts, rayon (district)
courts, and courts-martial.[8] Juries (or "people's
assessors") are also elected for four-year terms, to
participate "in the dispensation of justice."[9]

In Hungary, the Supreme Court is elected for five
years by the State Council, and the lower courts are
appointed by the minister of justice.[10] In fact, the
principle of a Supreme Court plus two or three tiers of
local courts (according to the administrative division of
the country) applies to all East European countries. The
judges, both professional and lay, are subject to recall
before the end of their term. Although the language of the
law usually is very dry ("Judges and members of the jury
may be recalled prior to the expiration of the term for
which they have been elected"[11]), it means indeed that the
national assembly (or actually the communist party) can
readily replace judges who do not act according to the
regime's expectations.

The only significant difference among the East
European countries is the existence of Constitutional
Courts in the CSSR (since 1968) and Yugoslavia (since
1964). The 1974 SFRY Constitution devotes more place to
the Constitutional Court (the highest one) than to the
rest of the judicial system. Its prerogatives are defined
as: deciding whether the laws are in agreement with the
SFRY Constitution; deciding whether local laws and regulations are in agreement with federal laws and acts of the
federal authorities; settling disputed rights and duties
between the federation and the republics or the autonomous
provinces, between the republics and the autonomous provinces
and among other sociopolitical communities; deciding conflicts of competency among the republican and provincial
constitutional courts; assessing the constitutionality of
the laws and the constitutionality and legality of the
regulations and general acts of organs of the sociopolitical communities; controlling phenomena pertaining
to implementing constitutionality and legality; submitting
opinions to the Federal Assembly, and so forth.[12] It
consists of a president and thirteen judges elected by the
SFRY Federal Assembly. Two members from each republic and

one member from each of the autonomous provinces are elected
to the Constitutional Court of Yugoslavia.[13] The members
of the SFRY Constitutional Court cannot be "recalled," as
the judges of all other courts in Eastern Europe can be.
According to Article 382 of the SFRY Constitution: "The
president and the judges of the Constitutional Court of
Yugoslavia may be relieved before the expiration of their
term only if they themselves ask to be relieved, if they
are sentenced to imprisonment for a criminal act, or if
they suffer a permanent loss of their ability to perform
their function."[14] Their unique (for a single-party
dictatorship) status stems also from the fact that they
provide an outlet for popular dissatisfaction caused by
inefficiency and arbitrariness on the part of the
bureaucratic apparatus.

The GDR judicial system includes not only the regular
courts of law, but also "social courts." According to the
Law on the GDR Social Courts, signed on 25 March 1982 by
Erich Honecker, chairman of the GDR State Council,[15] "the
social courts make a great contribution to strengthening
state security, preventing crimes and other law violations,
and educating citizens. . . . They make a specific contribution to further shaping our society."[16]

In practice, the GDR Social Courts deal with plain
civil suits among citizens, settling monetary claims of up
to DM1,000. They can impose fines to a maximum of DM500
and/or require the citizens who have committed law violations to perform "acts of public benefit during their
leisure time."[17] Most of all, however, the Social Courts
"promote public activity and enforce socialist legality
and ensure order, discipline, and security in the combines,
enterprises, towns, and communities. Their activity is
aimed at protecting the socialist state and social order
and socialist property . . . [and] reinforcing the citizens'
socialist state and legal consciousness, encouraging their
readiness to abide by socialist law voluntarily, and
strengthening their intolerance toward conduct that is
socially inappropriate."[18]

These courts exist in plants, enterprises, and
organizations where more than fifty workers are employed.
The members of the courts are "citizens who are models of
public and personal conduct . . . older than 18 years of
age." They are elected by "citizens or the organs of local
government"[19] (most often by the workers of the plant in
which they function). They too can be recalled,[20] so that
it does not seem that the existence of the Social Courts in
the GDR alters the nature of that country's judicial system.

Two other structural or rather procedural characteristics of the East European courts lie in the "expediency"
of their activity. The cases seldom last more than one to
three sittings. Appeal is usually restricted to one
instance only. All this makes the dispensation of justice
a rather quick process in Eastern Europe.

THE PROSECUTOR GENERAL'S OFFICE

The office of the prosecutor general (or procurator
general) is another characteristic specific to the East
European judicial system. Once again it is a Soviet feature,
transplanted into the East European judicial (and, in
fact, political) system. The office of the prosecutor
general overshadows in importance and authority the
regular courts. His duties involve not only the prosecution of criminals, but also the vaguely defined task of
"safeguarding the rule of law." In the words of an official
Polish source: "The establishment of the Prosecutor's
Office of the Polish People's Republic . . . is a result
of the recognition that the task of his office is not only
to prosecute perpetrators of crimes, but also to safeguard
the rule of law by assuring the protection of social
property and the observance of civil laws."[21]
Although in some East European countries (Bulgaria,
Albania, Romania, etc.) the prosecutor general is appointed
by the national assembly, and in others (the CSSR) by the
president, the prosecutor general is always responsible to
the national assembly. His duties are defined in almost
the same terms in all East European countries: in
Albania, ". . . To exert control through a strict and equal
observance of the law . . . to veto illegal documents . . .
to submit to the National Assembly laws and regulations
that are not in conformity with the Constitution," etc.[22];
in Bulgaria, the prosecutor general "Supervises the precise
and equal compliance with the laws by ministries and other
bodies of central administration, by local state organs,
economic and public organizations, and by officials and
the citizens . . . protects the rights and the legitimate
interests of the citizens . . . repeals illegal acts and
restores violated rights . . . and is especially vigilant
and presents for trial and punishment those who commit
crimes that violate the independence and sovereignty of
the Bulgarian People's Republic and its political and
economic interests"[23]; and in the CSSR, "The Prosecutor
General of the CSSR exercises supreme control over the

consistent execution and observance of laws and other rules
of law by all Ministries and other offices, courts of law,
National Committees, organs, institutions, and officials
as well as by individual citizens."[24]

What all this means in practice is that the prosecutor
general in Eastern Europe (whose office has local branches
at each administrative level, which are independent of the
municipal authorities), is a combination of district
attorney, ombudsman, and a mini-supreme court, who supervises the observance of laws by officials, organs, and
citizens, enforces "socialist legality," protects the
country's interests, and facilitates the implementation of
party policy. This is how Lucjan Czubinski, Poland's
prosecutor general, defined the duties of his office in
August 1981: "Obviously the role of the prosecutor's
office in a socialist government is different from that in
a capitalist government. The prosecutor is not only or even
primarily an accuser but first of all the guardian of law
and order in its broadest sense. There is no sector in
which the prosecutor general would not have to be active.
Prosecution is just one of the many less pleasant though
necessary duties. The basic responsibility is the supervision of law enforcement by government and social organs,
as well as the enormous civil law department. . . . We
serve the government, party, and society."[25] Dr. Jaroslav
Krupauer, prosecutor general of the Czech Socialist
Republic, summarizes all this in one sentence: "We are
conducting a struggle against everything that hampers a
more successful progress toward an advanced socialist
society."[26]

The close connection between the office of the
prosecutor general and the communist party is no secret.
In June 1981 Dr. Josef Streit, member of the SED Central
Committee and GED prosecutor general, defined "conducting
the party's political work with the masses"[27] as one of
his office's main functions. In addition, he stated that
"the decisions adopted by the 10th SED Congress, aimed at
further constructing the developed socialist society in
the GDR, will continue to guide our work."[28]

The aforementioned example is not unique. Various
East European sources frequently stress the importance of
party decisions and instructions for guiding the activity
of the prosecutor general. Usually, the decisions of the
most recent party congress (without specifying what
decision) are invariably pointed out as the "guiding light"
of the prosecutor general's activity. Occasionally, even
the party leader is credited with guiding the activity of

the prosecutor general's office. Thus, in a March 1980
interview, Florin Dimitriu, assistant chief prosecutor in
the municipality of Bucharest, especially underlined the
importance of the instructions of the 12th RCP Congress
and in particular the instructions of Nicolae Ceausescu,
for improving the work of the prosecutor general's
offices.[29]

Occasionally, the prosecutor general openly reports
to the communist party. In May 1982 a national symposium
on violations of law was held in Bucharest. The symposium
was sponsored by the prosecutor general's office. All
speakers (among them RCP Central Committee secretary Ion
Coman) stressed "Ceausescu's contribution to promoting the
'working class' concept of truth and justice, as well as of
equality and ethics."[30] The symposium ended with a telegram
to Ceausescu, in which the participants emphasized their
resolution to combine the concepts of socialist humanism
with revolutionary intransigence in their efforts to
combat crime.[31]

East European authorities see nothing unusual in the
fact that the activity of their judicial system is openly
and officially "guided" and "instructed" by the communist
party. Each and every party congress reviews the performance of the respective country's judicial system and
issues praise, admonition, and instructions as appropriate.
This is usually a routine matter, involving standard
phrases such as: "The socialist legal order and the
activities of the court and prosecutor's organs must be
developed and improved further. . . . The court and
prosecutor's organs . . . must increase their intolerance
of crimes. They must intensify their preventive efforts in
order to protect the legal order and socialist property."[32]
Occasionally however, the reference is more specific, as
at the 12th RCP Congress in 1980, when specific decisions
related to the judicial process were adopted by the party
forum.[33]

It is not unusual for other party organs, or even a
special Central Committee plenum, to deal with judicial
matters. Such was the May 1956 plenum of the CPCZ Central
Committee, which concerned itself with "serious shortcomings" in the CSSR judicial system and resolved "to take
measures to correct them with the greatest possible speed
. . . in a way that will guarantee the maximum enforcement
of socialist justice."[34]

SPECIAL COURT CONCERNS

In addition to subjugation of the judicial system to
the political needs of the regime, there are other
characteristics of the East European judicial system that
must be underlined, namely, the special concern with
political and economic crimes, and the specific interpretation of the human rights issue. Two main categories of
offenses focus the attention of the East European courts:
crimes against the socialist political system and against
the socialist economic order, or in short--political and
economic crimes.

The very nature of the socialist regime vastly
increases the potential for the commission of political
offenses. Let us ignore the notorious political trials of
the late 1940s and early 1950s, when communist leaders
such as Traycho Kostov (Bulgaria), Laslo Rajk (Hungary),
Rudolf Slanski (Czechoslovakia), and many others were
sentenced to death for imaginary antiparty and antistate
conspiracies. Such trials were a part of the Stalinist
epoch and are not in evidence today. However, there are
numerous other cases that fall into the category of
political trials only because of the special interpretation
of citizens' basic rights. Freedom of speech in the
socialist countries is not an absolute right. On the
contrary, indiscriminate use of this right might be
considered sedition, which is a grave political offense.
The East European constitutions guarantee freedom of
speech, thought, press, and public assembly, but only as
long as "they do not serve as a pretext for undermining
the constitutional order and disturbing the peaceful
construction of the socialist society."[35]

It has been officially explained that "the free
flow of ideas to which humanity owes its most beautiful
achievements, might become as harmful as fire, which gives
us light and heat, but if unattended and running wild often
becomes the cause of great disaster, destitution, and
devastation. . . . The more high-soaring the spirit that
pervades the perception of government and legislatures,
the more cautious and different must they be in drawing
the line that divides criminal intent or prohibited
information from that which is admissible."[36]

What this means in practice is that in the East
European countries the right to free speech (and all other
basic rights) is a conditional right that can be used only
prudently, i.e., not critically toward the socialist regime.
When one does so (misinterprets the right to free speech as

a right to say anything), it is the state itself (or the party) that decides whether the misuse of the right to free speech has harmed the system. The result, in most cases, is the criminalization of the use of a right conditionally guaranteed by all East European constitutions.

Sometimes, specific political developments sharply increase the rate of "political crime" in some East European countries. Thus, following the unrest among the Albanian population of the Yugoslav province of Kosovo, "political crimes in that province increased almost 65 percent."[37] Another result of the Kosovo events was the fact that according to Yugoslav sources 64.98 percent of the "political offenders" in Yugoslavia in 1981 were of Albanian origin (albeit Yugoslav citizens).[38] The accusation in almost all cases was "provoking national and religious hatred."[39] Another Yugoslav source reported that during 1980 "93 percent of the political cases involved verbal misdemeanor of a slight nature."[40] The offenders obviously misunderstood the freedom of speech granted by the Yugoslav Constitution. Other East European countries, although admitting that political crime exists, very seldom if ever publish statistics on the rate of this particular crime. When such statistics are published, absolute figures are seldom given, percentages being the usual way of reporting these crimes. Thus in 1977 the Hungarian press reported that "offenses against the state, peace, or humanity amounted to less than 2 percent of the total."[41] Other East European countries deny outright the existence of any political prisoners. Thus in 1979 Romania's President Ceausescu claimed that Romania had no political prisoners.[42] Independent Western sources, however, disclosed that not only are there still political prisoners in Romania, but that now they are also illegally confined in psychiatric hospitals.[43]

It is obvious that the entire issue of human rights is interpreted in Eastern Europe in a somewhat different way from the one accepted in the West. Furthermore, official East European sources even claim that in the socialist countries there is no need to protect many of the human rights that the citizens of the Western countries claim for themselves: "In the West more than a few legal experts and politicians are of the view that the real objective in the national codification of human rights is to defend the citizens against their own state (which was true in the feudal state and can be true even today in some capitalist countries). Against this attitude, we assert that in the socialist countries there is no need for

such protection because, in addition to the generally and
fundamentally positive relations between the state and the
individual, a host of valid statutory rules provide
adequate guarantees to the citizen against possible abuse of
power by the state."[44]

A typical example of the official treatment of human
rights was the harassment of the Charter-77 activists in
Czechoslovakia. The Charter-77 movement, which basically
demanded more human rights for CSSR citizens and issued a
petition to this effect (Charter-77), demanded no more than
what--theoretically--had been guaranteed by the CSSR
Constitution. Yet its activists were subjected to cruel
persecution and harassment, some of them were imprisoned,
and others were forced to seek refuge in other countries.
Characteristic of the whole affair was the case of two of
the movement spokesmen--former Foreign Minister Jiri Hajek
and philosophy professor Jan Patocka. On 29 January 1977
they were called to the office of the CSSR prosecutor
general in Prague and told that their Charter-77 activities
were illegal. The officials with whom the two men spoke
did not deny the constitutional right of CSSR citizens to
petition their government, but argued that this right "has
to be applied in harmony with the interests of the socialist
state." Hajek and Patocka had also violated another
constitutional article, the official said, by denying the
leading role of the CPCZ.[45]

The least familiar feature of the East European
judicial system to many Westerners is its preoccupation
with offenses against the countries' economic order. These
offenses can encompass almost anything--from petty felonies
and minor infractions that would hardly qualify even as
misdemeanors in the Western democracies, to theft and
embezzlement of national funds. The width of the range
places economic crime in one of the first places in the
socialist countries. In Czechoslovakia in 1981 economic
crime accounted for more than 23 percent of all crimes
committed.[46] In the past, mostly during the Stalin era,
economic crimes of a trivial character were punished
cruelly. Falsification of food ration cards and conceal-
ment of property from governmental authorities were often
punished by death.[47] Even today death sentences for severe
economic crimes are not unheard of. Certain high-ranking
officials have even been severely punished for economic
violations, apparently in an attempt to turn the cases into
cautionary examples. Thus in March 1982 in Bulgaria,
several officials including former deputy minister of
foreign affairs and BCP Central Committee candidate-member

Zhivko Popov were put on trial for "misappropriation and transgression of the hard currency regulations."[48] Zhivko Popov was sentenced to twenty years of imprisonment, confiscation of his entire property (including the property of his wife and daughter, "acquired with the money he misappropriated"), and loss of his right to hold official posts or to live in Sofia for a period of twenty-three years. Similarly severe verdicts were imposed on the others.[49] As usual in trials involving high-ranking officials, as well as political trials, the official announcement explicitly stated: "The sentence is final and not subject to appeal."[50]

Economic crimes in particular frequently occupy the attention of the East European political authorities as they try to deal with the effectiveness of their judicial systems. Thus on 30 March 1982 the Bulgarian National Assembly devoted a substantial part of its regular session to discussing various judicial bills for amendments and addenda to the Criminal Code, to the Criminal Procedure Code, and to the Law on the Execution of Sentence.[51] Although according to the official announcement, the amendments were "prompted by the wish to simplify and step up both the judicial inquiry and the legal procedure, and by the wish to overcome a certain formalism and bureaucracy as practised by the investigation, the prosecution, and the court authorities,"[52] the announcement also stressed that "the amendments have been prompted by the need to step up efficiency in combating economic crimes."[53] Incidentally, the amendments expanded the prerogatives of the district courts and the prosecutor's office, and simplified some procedural matters.[54] Similar issues (simplifying procedures, increasing prerogatives, and combating economic crimes) were also discussed by the Hungarian National Assembly[55] and other East European parliaments. The Romanian National Assembly announced its intention of enacting a new economic code in 1976,[56] but as late as 1982 there still was no new legislation in this area. Romania has frequently announced in the past grandiose new programs and reforms that have seldom materialized. The various legal reforms announced in the mid-1970s also failed to materialize. On the other hand, and perhaps because of it, several justice ministers have lost their positions: Constantin Statescu was appointed minister of justice in 1977 and removed in 1979.[57] He was followed by Justin Grigoras, from October 1977 through March 1980[58]; Grigoras was replaced by Ion Ceterchi.[59] All this does not prevent the Romanian authorities from preparing a new

"legislative Five-Year Plan" for each broader Five-Year
Plan period, stipulating new judicial reforms and the
impending introduction of new Codes.[60]

The judicial organs of the socialist countries are in
fact auxiliary organs of the communist parties. As such,
along with all other auxiliary organs, they are not only
expected to serve the party interest but also to engage in
intensive propaganda. Their duty to popularize the law and
educate the citizens has been incorporated in the East
European constitution. In addition, East European jurists
often join various international propaganda causes of the
regime and issue resolutions, declarations, and appeals
condemning various aspects of the U.S. and other Western
countries' foreign policy, and expressing support for
foreign policy initiatives of the USSR and other socialist
states. (Protests against the decision of the U.S.
administration to produce the neutron bomb, and against
the Israeli invasion of Lebanon are two recent examples of
political declarations issued by all East European
judicial organs.)

The occasional amnesties for citizens who have left
the country illegally (providing that they return within a
short period) also belong to the category of judicial
documents of apparent propaganda nature. Such amnesties
were announced by the CSSR in May 1980[61] and Bulgaria in
1981.[62] The introduction of both amnesties was accompanied
by an extensive campaign in the newspapers on the abundance
of basic freedoms and rights in the socialist countries,
and the humane attitude of the authorities toward citizens
"lured by foreign propaganda."[63]

THE JUDICIAL MANDATE--PARTY NEEDS

The overriding aspect of the East European judicial
system is its total subjugation to party needs. In fact,
in Eastern Europe the judiciary is a subordinate organ of
law enforcement, which has no possibility of actually
controlling and checking the other branches of the government, let alone the party. Furthermore, the party can
overrule the entire judicial system and divert its
activity toward a goal or into a channel supervised by the
party. A typical example was the introduction of martial
law in Poland. Only the day after the imposition of
martial law was announced, the Polish Council of State
published a "decree on the Transfer of Cases Involving
Certain Crimes to the Jurisdiction of Military Courts and

on Changes in the Organizational Structure of Military
Courts and Military Organizational Units of the Prosecutor
General's Office of the Polish People's Republic During a
State of Martial Law."[64] The decree actually subjugated
the entire judicial system to the military courts (in
fact, to the martial law authorities), transferred almost
all offenses and crimes to the authority of the military
courts, significantly increased the authority of the
military prosecutors, and accelerated the judicial
procedure. It goes without saying that the Sejm was not
consulted on the aforementioned decree, nor were there any
provisions enacted as to the rights of the accused while
being tried by the military courts.

In conclusion, the East European judicial system
resembles the Western model only in its structure. Its
functions are completely different from those of the
Western courts, and the traditional roles of judge,
prosecutor, and attorney are nonexistent. Not only are
the powers of the prosecutor much more extensive than anywhere else in the world, but in most political cases the
defendants cannot expect much legal assistance. (Many
jurisprudence books, dealing with this particular aspect of
the East European judiciary, mention the case of the
Bulgarian communist leader Traycho Kostov, accused of
"Titoism," spying for the West, etc., in the late 1940s,
who was attacked much more viciously by his attorney than
by the prosecutor.)

The East European courts are responsible for ensuring
"socialist legality." The constitutions explicitly define
their main function as serving the interests of the
socialist system. Consequently, certain crimes (political
and economic violations) are attributed exceptional
importance, and other issues, related to human rights, for
instance, are subjugated to specific interpretation, which
serves the goals of the regime. The ideological functions
of the courts have also been incorporated in the constitutions, which articulate the courts' duty to "educate the
citizens in devotion and loyalty to the party and the
regime and in the orderly observance of the socialist
norms of life." All this turns the East European courts
into another instrument of the regime, charged with the
responsibility (within a specific area) of protecting
the regime and facilitating the implementation of its
political goals.

286

NOTES

1. CSSR Constitution, Ch. 8, Art. 97 (1), in Rude Pravo, 19 April 1960.
2. Bulgarian Constitution, Ch. 8, Art. 121 (1), in Rabotnichesko Delo, 30 March 1971.
3. CSSR Constitution, Ch. 8, Art. 97 (2), in Rude Pravo, 19 April 1960.
4. Bulgarian Constitution, Ch. 8, Art. 121 (2), in Rabotnichesko Delo, 30 March 1971.
5. Tvorba (CSSR), no. 51, 15 December 1976; interview with Jan Nemec.
6. Ibid.
7. Verfassung der Sozialistischen Volksrepublic Albanien, Tirana, 1977, Art. 101, p. 52.
8. Bulgarian Constitution, Ch. 8, Art. 122, 124, 128, in Rabotnichesko Delo, 30 March 1971.
9. Ibid., Art. 123.
10. R. Staar, Communist Regimes in Eastern Europe (Stanford, California, 1977), p. 111.
11. Bulgarian Constitution, Ch. 8, Art. 124 (2), in Rabotnichesko Delo, 30 March 1971.
12. SFRY Constitution, Ch. 7, Art. 375-379, in Borba, 9 June 1973, and in Narodna Armija, 21 February 1974; Daily Report (FBIS), 17 April 1974.
13. Ibid., Ch. 7, Art. 381.
14. Ibid., Ch. 7, Art. 382.
15. Gesetzblatt der Deutschen Demokratischen Republic, Part I (13), 6 April 1982, p. 269.
16. Neues Deutschland (East Berlin), 26 March 1982.
17. Ibid.
18. Gesetzblatt der Deutschen Demokratischen Republic, p. 272.
19. Ibid., p. 274.
20. Ibid.
21. Preglad Morski (Warsaw), no. 10, October 1980, pp. 77-80.
22. Albanian Constitution, Ch. 8, Art. 104-105.
23. Bulgarian Constitution, Ch. 8, Art. 104.
24. CSSR Constitution, Ch. 8, Art. 104.
25. Granica (Warsaw), no. 8, 2 August 1981, pp. 4,5; FBIS East European Report, no. 1928, 15 October 1981.
26. Prague Domestic Service in Czech, 1430 GMT, 19 February 1982; Daily Report (FBIS), 23 February 1982.
27. Neue Justiz (East Berlin), vol. 35, no. 6, January 1982; FBIS East European Report, no. 1999, 15 April 1982.

28. Ibid.

29. Pentru Patrie (Romania), no. 3, March 1980, p. 6; East European Report, no. JPRS L/9096, 19 May 1980.

30. RFE Situation Report, Romania, 21 May 1982.

31. Ibid.

32. Theses of the 12th BCP Congress, in Rabotnichesko Delo, 10 April 1980.

33. RFE Situation Report, Romania, 30 May 1980.

34. Rude Pravo, 11 May 1956.

35. Magyar Kozloni (Hungary), no. 92, 31 December 1978; RFE Situation Report, Hungary, 8 May 1981.

36. Magyar Jog (Hungary), February 1981; RFE Situation Report, Hungary, 8 May 1981.

37. Politika (Yugoslavia), 21 March 1982; Daily Report (FBIS), 24 March 1982.

38. Ibid.

39. Ibid.

40. Belgrade TANJUG Domestic Service in Serbo-Croatian, 1335 GMT, 21 April 1981; Daily Report (FBIS), 22 April 1981.

41. Magyar Nemzet (Hungary), 26 February 1977; RFE Situation Report, Hungary, 19 April 1977.

42. Scinteia (Romania), 21 March 1979; RFE Situation Report, Romania, 30 May 1980.

43. Amnesty International Documents on Romania, as reported in DPA from Hague on 23 December 1979; RFE Situation Report, Romania, 30 May 1980.

44. Nepszabadsag (Hungary), 14 August 1977.

45. RFE Situation Report, CSSR, 3 February 1977.

46. Bratislava Domestic Service in Slovak, 1730 GMT, 22 March 1982; Daily Report (FBIS), 24 March 1982.

47. Rude Pravo, 13 July 1951 and 30 April 1952.

48. Sofia Domestic Service in Bulgarian, 1830 GMT, 23 March 1982; Daily Report (FBIS), 24 March 1982.

49. Ibid.

50. Ibid.

51. Sofia BTA in English, 1447 GMT, 30 March 1982; Daily Report (FBIS), 31 March 1982.

52. Ibid.

53. Ibid.

54. Ibid.

55. RFE Situation Report, Hungary, 13 October 1977.

56. Revista Romana de Drept (Romania), no. 1, 1976; RFE Situation Report, Romania, 12 June 1981.

57. Scinteia, 26 January 1977 and 25 October 1979.

58. Ibid., 25 October 1979 and 29 March 1980.

59. Ibid., 30 March 1980.

288

60. RAD RFE Background Report, Romania, no. 18,
27 January 1978.
61. Rude Pravo, 9 May 1980.
62. Rabotnichesko Delo, 8 July 1981.
63. Ibid.
64. Dziennik Ustaw (Poland), no. 29, 14 December 1981,
pp. 321-322; FBIS East European Report, no. 1990,
22 March 1982.

10
The Ritual

There are several reasons why one may properly ask if it is advisable to present the East European communist regimes as one uniform political system. After all, there are a number of fundamental differences among the East European states. Albania has its unadulterated anti-Soviet, anti-Chinese, anti-imperialist, and anti-nearly-everyone line. Yugoslavia is not a member of the Warsaw Pact and its foreign policy frequently deviates from the uniform Soviet model, not to mention its position as a founder member of the nonaligned movement. In addition, its internal characteristics (federalism, periodic and institutionalized change of party and state leadership after Tito's death, and so forth), set it further apart from the other East European states. Romania's foreign policy also differs on occasions from the Soviet model (it is the only East European state to maintain diplomatic relations with Israel and the only Warsaw Pact member not to permit Soviet troops to be stationed on its territory). Finally, Poland of 1980-1981 was one great exception to the rule in almost every area, although as far as one may judge, after the announcement of martial law on 13 December 1981, in many respects things have returned to "normal," at least on the surface.

In spite of all this, it can be said that most of these differences are of a nature that does not affect the essence of the regime or the quality of public life. In everything connected with party structure, party activity, total domination of all areas of life by the communist party, the political process, and the constitutional and legal system, there are no substantial differences. That is why these regimes have been treated as one uniform political system.

This chapter deals with yet another common denominator
of all East European states, namely the ritual related to
many aspects of political life. This is a ritual that
is strictly followed by all East European countries and
that fits both the definition of religious ritual (the
form of conducting a devotion service, established by
tradition or by sacredotal prescription) and that of
secular ritual (any practice done or regularly repeated
in a set precise manner so as to satisfy one's sense of
fitness, and often felt to have a symbolic significance).
Any deviation from the established pattern, any substitu-
tion of words or events does not merely mean an alteration
of that established pattern but can be reliably expected to
be an indication that things are afoot, politically or
ideologically, to cause the change, and that further changes
may well be heralded politically.

As is the case with other characteristics of the East
European system, the ritual has been created and perfected
by the Soviet Union. Closely following the rules of the
ritual is another way of adhering to the Soviet political
system and manifesting loyalty to the world communist movement. Nevertheless, one should remember that in many
respects the communist regime's ritual closely follows
normal diplomatic protocol, especially where visits are
concerned. Where it differs is in the glosses caused by
party life, and in the absolute invariability with which
one event in the scheme follows another where two
communist sides are involved.

One final word: the ritual is not a part of the real
political game, which takes place behind closed doors in
the Politburo or the Central Committee. However, it is
closely related to the political process, and as already
stated, any changes in the form, words, or events that
constitute the ritual indicates or reflects significant
developments in official policy.

Some aspects of the ritual have already been
described. The procedure at the party congress or at the
congresses of the auxiliary organizations is a significant
part of it. Other aspects of party life (admission
procedure, routine party activity at the local level, and
so forth) belong to the same category. Many aspects of
the East European cultural life (creative unions, the
themes used by the writers, painters, and other artists,
and even their style) are a part of the ritual. These and
other topics have already been dealt with. Now let us look
at the specific ritual that accompanies visits, official
statements, joint communiques, and declarations and related

matters.

OFFICIAL VISITS AND COMMUNIQUES

Official visits are an integral part of the East
European political system. It seems that party secretaries,
prime ministers, other ministers, Central Committee delegations and "working groups," friendship delegations, and so
forth, are constantly on the move, and the East European
leaders are forever visiting each other or hosting leaders
and delegations from the Third World. The rules of the
ritual are always the same: the visiting leader is greeted
by his counterpart and other top officials. If it is a
visit by a head of state, he is given the full military
honors prescribed by protocol. When the visitor comes from
a socialist state, or a state ruled by a "friendly" party
(meaning a socialist party), the official reports describing the visit invariably use both the party and state
titles (in that order) of the host and the visitor. ("On
8 September Todor Zhivkov, BCP Central Committee first
secretary and State Council chairman, gave an official
dinner in Sofia in honor of Samora Machel, Frelimo chairman
and president of Mozambique."[1]) On the other hand, when the
visitor comes from the West, or from a nonsocialist country
of the Third World, only state titles are used to indicate
that this is a state and not a party affair.

From the airport, the visitor and the hosts proceed
to the official residence of the guests. If it is a visit
by a head of state, then the two leaders take part in a
short ceremony at the airport (which is invariably decorated
with the portraits of the two leaders, the two countries'
flags, and friendly slogans), after which they drive together toward the official residence, "enthusiastically
greeted" along the streets (as the official announcement
always points out) by the citizens of the capital.

The visit can be "official and friendly," (socialist
countries, friendly Third World regimes), "friendly,"
(short unofficial visits of socialist or pro-socialist
leaders), "official" (Western leaders), or "businesslike"
or a "working" visit—usually a short visit by a premier
or a minister, related to one specific economic or
political matter. Finally, when the leader of an East
European socialist country is the visitor, he usually
comes as a leader of a "party-state" delegation, indicating
that both relations between the two states and the two
parties will be discussed.

A few hours after the arrival (unless, of course,
it is an unusual late night arrival), the guest visits the
hosting counterpart. A short announcement invariably issued
after that reports the meeting, the participants, the
topics discussed (in very general terms, no details), and
the atmosphere in which the talks took place. Expectedly,
the reference to the atmosphere is also a matter of
ritual. "Warm, cordial, exceptionally friendly and
fraternal" (or at least two of those) is the accepted
formula for socialist states' visits, and "open" or
"frank" atmosphere (sometimes also "sincere") usually
indicates that there have been some differences of opinion,
usually or always with visitors from Western or pro-
Western states. If the visitor is not a head of state,
but nevertheless has a high rank (premier or an important
minister), he is usually received by the party leader or
head of state (when different) of the host country.

The official talks usually consist of two or three
rounds, a short announcement being published after each
round, again using broad terms and generalization to
describe the issues discussed. The beginning of the
official talks is followed by an official dinner given by
the host, at which the guest and the host toast each other.
If the visitor comes from a Western or pro-Western country,
the toasts are usually short, describing the mutual
pleasure with the visit, relating the areas of agreement,
expressing support for peace (obligatory, but sticking to
most general terms), praising bilateral relations, and
studiously omitting any area of disagreement. However,
if the visiting delegation comes from a socialist or pro-
socialist country, the toasts are long, setting out the two
countries' position on all important international issues,
and containing a condemnation of imperialism, colonialism,
Zionism and reaction, a denouncement of U.S. foreign
policy, and a declaration of adherence and friendship with
the USSR and the CPSU. Both speakers praise the successes
of the counterpart country in socialist construction
("building successfully the developed socialist society"
being the accepted formula), and each one reports on the
implementation of the decisions of the most recent party
congress. The importance of meetings and talks "at the
highest level" is invariably stressed (meaning that personal
meetings between the leaders are instrumental to solving
problems), and the Soviet foreign policy line is precisely
echoed. When the visitor comes from a country that has
taken part (or is taking part) in what is described as a
"national liberation struggle" (which can mean a struggle

against a colonial country, or simply a struggle against the lawful nonsocialist regime), the East European host expresses obligatory support both for the struggle for national liberation in general, and the struggle of the particular country (or movement) of the guest. The support of the entire socialist community is also stated.

For certain visits--usually involving non-European Third World states--there is usually a "friendship rally" on the second day of the visit. The rally can take place at a public hall or at an industrial plant. The leader of the visiting delegation and the host read speeches, which in fact are expanded versions of their toasts, although there are more details about the countries' economic successes. Sometimes the guests also visit sites in the capital or elsewhere in the country (more friendship rallies are possible). In recent years in Romania and Bulgaria (where the personality cults of Ceausescu and Zhivkov have reached unprecedented dimensions), foreign visitors are also taken to the native village of the leader, which in both countries has become a village-museum. A standard feature of the ritual in Bulgaria is to visit the mausoleum of Georgi Dimitrov and lay a wreath and "pay respect to his sarcophagus" (the phrase invariably used to describe the paganish ceremony at the mausoleum).

The visit ends with an official communique (which may also be called "joint statement") and, possibly, with a "joint declaration." (A "declaration" is different from a "communique" or an "announcement" in that it is usually a recitation of certain principles followed by some state-ments of intention, as opposed to a "communique," which is essentially an official report on specific talks.) When a relatively newly established pro-socialist regime is involved, other documents may also be signed at the end of the visit, such as a friendship treaty, cooperation agreement, and so forth.

The communiques always follow the same line: they describe the nature and length of the visit, list the members of the guest delegation as well as the names of the host country officials that participated in the official talks, enumerate the activities in which the visitors have taken part, and list the agreements and other documents that have been signed.

Another part of such a communique deals with bilateral matters: expanding relations, intensifying cooperation, increasing the level of bilateral contacts, etc. The part dealing with the international situation, which usually follows the internal affairs part, is the most important.

Although the essence of it has already been stated in the
toasts, it is nevertheless the most recent statement of the
countries' position on all important international issues.
Still, most of it is predictable: the old enemies are
condemned, and "unity and cohesion" (being the accepted
formula) is invariably presented as a precondition for increasing the strength of the socialist bloc. In the case
of a developing pro-socialist country, solidarity with the
struggle of the relevant national liberation movement is
expressed. The support of the USSR and the entire socialist
community is also pointed out. The importance of the
cooperation of the "progressive and revolutionary forces
throughout the world" is also stressed. (This, of course,
means support for the USSR and its foreign policy on the
part of the mentioned forces.)

The last part of the communique usually states that a
delegation of the hosting country has been invited to visit
the guests' state. The invitation is always "accepted
with pleasure."

Of course, when the visitor is a leader of a Western
or pro-Western state, the communique is much shorter and
deals primarily with the importance of expanding mutual
relations and protecting peace. Sometimes, when a minister
comes on a "business visit," there might be no communique
at all, but just a short announcement on the visit, the
activities, and the documents that have been signed.

One should never expect an East European communique
to refer to the real problems that have been discussed, or
to reflect differences (if any) between the two sides. On
the contrary, the areas of agreement (no matter how narrow)
are the ones that are stressed. The other areas are un-
mentioned or are included in the formula describing the
two sides' opinions as "close" or "similar." (The formula
for socialist countries' visits is "total identity" or
"total unanimity of views on all discussed questions,"
or "complete unity of thought and action.")

These are the most important general points of the
ritual related to foreign visits. They shall now be
illustrated by several specific examples.

VISITS AND COMMUNIQUES AS REPORTED

The first group of examples relates to visits by
nonaligned countries' delegations. In August–September
1980 Zambia's President Kenneth Kaunda visited Bulgaria,
the GDR, the CSSR, Yugoslavia, and other countries. His

schedule in all countries he visited was absolutely identical. Comparison of the toasts exchanged at the official dinners (say, the dinners in the GDR[2] and the CSSR[3]) shows not only that the form and style were identical, but also that the standard and routine formulas were used in both countries, such as: "all peace-loving forces must unite their efforts and struggle for international security and stopping the arms race, and for disarmament"; "the aggressive forces of imperialism are preventing a peaceful settlement and elimination of existing centers of tension"; "the plans of imperialist and hegemonist circles must be thwarted"; and so forth. In addition there were identical references to South Africa's "aggressive policy and racism," "the struggle of the national liberation movements," and of course, references to the solidarity of the relevant country with the struggle of Namibia, and to the friendship with the USSR and the entire socialist community. The toasts in Bulgaria[4] and Yugoslavia[5] followed the same pattern. When Kenneth Kaunda, speaking at East Berlin's Humboldt University, permitted himself a slip of tongue, mentioning the unmentionable wall ("your little [sic] wall is the perfect symbol of Europe's dangerous partition"), the East German interpreter faltered, and the statement made waves throughout Europe.[6] Such "violations" of the ritual do not happen often.

When at about the same time Mozambique's President Samora Machel visited Bulgaria,[7] Romania,[8] and the GDR,[9] the "African toast" was pulled out and used again: identical references in the three toasts to the fond memories of former visits of Zhivkov, Ceausescu, and Honecker to Mozambique, enthusiasm over the working successes of Mozambique, identical evaluation of the international situation, similar description of the host countries' working successes, etc., appeared in all toasts. One could substitute Kaunda for Machel, and use the Zambian toast, or vice versa.

The same phenomenon can be observed when the communiques ending such visits are compared. This can be illustrated best by simply presenting the communiques on Kaunda's visits to the GDR[10] and the CSSR[11] and demonstrating their common (ritualistic) sources. If further evidence is needed, there are the communiques on the visits of Angola's President Dos Santos to the CSSR,[12] Bulgaria,[13] the GDR,[14] and Hungary,[15] which read like the same communique over and over again. (See appendixes.) Finally, to dispel the notion that this is a phenomenon reserved for communiques with African countries only, there

are the communiques on the visit of Hun Sen, Kampuchea's
premier and foreign minister, to the CSSR[16] and Bulgaria[17]
(see appendixes), which once again prove the same point.

In the case of a joint communique on a visit of one
East European leader to another, such as the visit of
Gustav Husak to Romania,[18] Gierek's visit to the CSSR,[19]
Kadar's visit to the GDR,[20] and Husak's visit to Hungary,[21]
as well as any other similar visit, one notices immediately
the common denominatos: adherence to the official East
European (USSR) position on every significant international
issue (identical), references to the importance of détente,
disarmament, and peace; references to the importance of
increasing the strength and cohesion of the international
communist and workers' movement, and so forth. Naturally,
the communiques are all abundantly sprinkled with repeating
references to the almost kabalistic (in the communist
religion) concepts of Marxism-Leninism and socialist internationalism, which in effect mean strict adherence to the
Soviet model of socialism (Marxism-Leninism) and the right
of the USSR and/or other East European countries to defend
the socialist regime of any East European country (socialist
internationalism). When a reference is to rendering
assistance to a national liberation movement or a movement
struggling against a nonsocialist regime, then the ritualistic concept is "proletarian internationalism."

The visits of prime ministers tend to have a business
character (dealing primarily with economic matters) and
are frequently defined in the communiques as "businesslike
and friendly" or "friendly and working,"[22] "friendly,"[23]
or "official and friendly."[24] However the visit may be
officially described, this does not alter its procedure:
official talks, meeting with the party leader, official
dinner, toasts, a friendship rally (optional), and the
final communique. The communique is usually shorter than
the one following the visit of a party leader but touches
upon the same matters (bilateral relations, mutual
admiration of each other's successes, briefing on the
tasks solved since the last party congress, and the common
position on various international issues, cum adherence
to every point of the USSR policy on the same issues).
The only difference is that communiques following the
visits of prime ministers tend to stress more the economic
relations and agreements between the two countries. The
"total identity of views" on all discussed issues is
usually stressed, although on occasions it must not be
mentioned, as in the case of the visit of CSSR Prime
Minister Strougal to Romania in November 1980, when the

official communique stated that "the talks took place in a friendly atmosphere of mutual understanding and respect."[25] This might have meant that there was a certain measure of disagreement on some of the issues, because the usual formula is different, as the following example of a CSSR-GDR communique indicates: "The talks between the CSSR premier and the chairman of the GDR Council of Ministers took place in a cordial and fraternal atmosphere and confirmed full unanimity of views on all questions under discussion."[26] Exactly the same formula was repeated on the visit of Strougal to Bulgaria in November 1980: "The talks proceeded in a cordial and friendly atmosphere as well as in full unanimity of views on the topics discussed."[27]

The absence of "cordial" and "full agreement of views" in the case of Strougal's visit to Romania indicates disagreement. Whether it was Poland, bilateral economic relations and payments, or other issues is open to different interpretations. The fact is, however, that by deviating from the ritualistic formula, the sides implied their differences in a "semi-official" but fully accepted manner. Thus, paradoxically, the rules of the sacrosanct ritual, intended to demonstrate agreement and uniformity, were used in order to imply disagreement.

A word of caution to the reader who remains skeptical: we are dealing with a ritual. Any deviation--even by a letter--implies not only diversion from the ritual, but a deviation from what stands behind it--in this particular case, the monolithic and uniform position of most East European countries on most issues of importance. Therefore, when two East European prime ministers describe their talks as "friendly" only (omitting the obligatory "cordial") and abstain from any reference to unanimity of views (also obligatory), they imply differences of opinion by violating or rather diverting from the accepted ritual. Or do they? Is not even this a ritualistic way of expressing differences? After all, one cannot expect them to list the subject of difference, let alone specify their specific (and different) positions. Therefore--in a ritualistic way--understandable by all observers of East European politics, they semi-officially tell everybody that there were some differences of views, which turned the talks into something less than cordial. This can also be an alibi for future reference.

Yugoslavia, which so often is the exception to the rule, sometimes also departs from the ritual in order to infer a different interpretation of the dogmas represented by the ritual. Thus, instead of the otherwise mandatory "socialist internationalism" or "proletarian internationalism,"

Yugoslavia prefers the use of "voluntary international cooperation"--one of the formulas adopted by the East Berlin Conference of the European communist parties.[28] Incidentally, in 1976 Aleksandr Grlichkov, member of the LCY Central Committee Executive Committee, writing in the party daily Borba,[29] maintained that the Yugoslav formula ("international voluntary cooperation") should permanently replace "proletarian internationalism." His proposal has not been adopted.

Another common characteristic of the communiques is the uniform way in which the sides refer to each other's leaders. They enthusiastically call each other "a prominent figure of the international communist and workers' movement," and never anything else. Thus, Georgi Dimitrov, the leader of the Bulgarian Communist Party until his death in 1949, is always referred to as "the great leader and teacher of the Bulgarian people and a prominent figure of the international communist and workers' movement." No deviation from this formula is permitted. When the centennial of his birth was marked in Bulgaria (15-17 June 1982), by an International Theoretical Conference, attended by representatives from more than 100 countries, all speakers, without exception, used the accepted formula. Some added other (permitted) compliments such as "the great son of the Bulgarian people," or "heroic fighter against fascism," but none omitted the ritualistic "great leader and teacher . . . ," and "the prominent figure. . . ."[30]

The last stage of visits involving East European leaders takes place at the relevant Politburos. Several days after the visit, the Politburo convenes to "hear the report" of the leader and "approve the results of the visit." This is the formula used throughout Eastern Europe. Needless to say, the exact "results" are never published.

THE RITUAL DURING OTHER EVENTS

The ritual and its rigid formulas govern other areas of public life. Thus, the ousting of leaders is always a matter of "expediency" (disgrace), "transfer to another post" (if unspecified--demotion), "transfer to another responsible position" (probably true), "reasons of health" (occasionally true, but often a formula intended to save face). Although second-rate officials are often accused of various economic or administrative violations, the main leaders are never ousted for specific mistakes, crimes, or

deeds. One is never accused of anything specific. The
system simply pronounces the appropriate formula--and then
the guessing game can begin. In the chapter dealing with
the East European leaders, the case of Bulgaria's Vulko
Chervenkov was described. Despite the fact that he was
expelled from all posts and severely criticized, his
"mistakes" and "errors" were never specified.

The appearances of the leaders at parades, demonstrations, and receptions also have a deep significance. The
physical distance from the leader indicates the current
status of the political hierarchy. Even the order and
manner of listing the leaders' names has a ritualistic
meaning. As noted in an earlier chapter, former Bulgarian
Premier Stanko Todorov was always listed second, after the
party and state leader Todor Zhivkov, and then the other
Politburo members followed in alphabetical order. The first
indication of the demise of Todorov's political fortunes
was the fact that his name began to appear in alphabetical
order, and not as number two. Soon afterwards, he was
appointed chairman of the National Assembly and had to
relenquish his post as chairman of the Council of
Ministers.

The ritual is evident whenever East European delegates
attend congresses of communist or socialist parties. Their
delegations are an exact copy (number and rank) of the
Soviet delegation to the same event. It is the USSR that
determines whether the East European delegations will be
led by the Central Committee secretary general, a secretary,
or a member of the Politburo. (Brezhnev's participation
in the May 1981 Congress of the CPCZ was considered an
exception, related to the situation in Poland and the
CSSR's having been the object of "socialist internationalism"
in the past). When Brezhnev regularly used to attend the
congresses of the East European communist parties, the
participation of all other East European leaders was
mandatory.

The greetings messages of the East European communist
parties to the various congresses of fraternal parties could
have been written by the same hand. A single example
suffices. The 10th Congress of the Spanish Communist Party
was held in July 1981. An examination of the greetings
messages of the BCP,[31] the RCP,[32] and the SED[33] Central
Committees reveals not only that they dealt with the same
issues, in the same order, but that they even used identical
phrases and formulas such as "the traditional relations of
lasting friendship and cooperation between (the relevant
party) and the Spanish Community Party . . .," "solidarity

with the struggle of the Spanish communists to defend and
develop democracy," and so forth. The sacred formulas of
"Marxism-Leninism" and "proletarian internationalism"
in relation to the Spanish Communist Party were con-
spicuously absent from the greetings messages of all East
European countries, because the Spanish Communist Party
tends to have a different view on those issues.

The same similarity of text and identity of content
is evident in greetings messages on all other occasions,
or even in condolences messages. Comparison of greetings
messages on national holidays, elections, international
events, and other occasions shows that they invariably
follow the basic rules of the ritual in everything
connected with style, content, and degree of cordiality.
Thus the greetings messages of the GDR,[34] Romania,[35]
and other East European countries[36] to Iraq on its national
holiday in July 1981 all included a sentence on the
importance of "further developing the two countries'
cooperation in the interest of the two peoples and the
struggle against imperialism, Zionism, and reaction."
(In similar messages to countries that are not a part of
the Middle East conflict, "Zionism" is omitted. In
messages to African countries "struggle against racism,
colonialism, and neocolonialism" is the mandatory formula.)

The ritual dictates the greetings messages and the
orders bestowed on East European leaders on their birthdays.
Every greetings message to a party and state leader in
Eastern Europe has three mandatory parts. The first part
announces on whose behalf the greetings message is being
sent. The invariable formula: "on behalf of the (relevant
party) Central Committee, the State Council, and the
Council of Ministers, all communists and the entire working
people of (the relevant state), and on my (our) personal
behalf. . . ." The second part extolls the merits of
the relevant official whose birthday is being celebrated,
as well as the successes achieved under his rule. The
last part of the message expresses wishes for long life
and personal happiness, "and more and even greater
successes in your highly responsible activity, for the
benefit of your people and the entire socialist community."
Hope is always expressed that the relations between the two
countries will continue to develop, again "in the benefit
of the two peoples and the entire socialist community."

These three integral parts are evident in the greetings messages of Todor Zhivkov (Bulgaria),[37] Ceausescu
(Romania),[38] Dragosavac (Yugoslavia),[39] Husak (CSSR),[40]
and other leaders to Hungary's Janos Kadar on the occasion

of his 70th birthday in May 1982, and all of them read as a carbon copy of the greetings message of Brezhnev on the same occasion.[41] Furthermore, because the USSR Supreme Soviet awarded Kadar with the highest Soviet order, namely, the Lenin Order,[42] all other East European countries were obliged (by the ritual) to award him with their highest orders: "On the occasion of the 70th birthday of Janos Kadar, first secretary of the Hungarian Socialist Workers Party Central Committee--in recognition of his merits acquired in deepening internationalist cooperation between the socialist countries--the State Council of the Bulgarian People's Republic has awarded the 'Georgi Dimitrov Order'; the president of the Czechoslovak Socialist Republic the 'Klement Gottwald Order'; the Council of State of the Republic of Cuba the 'Jose Marti Order'; the Council of State of the Polish People's Republic 'The Great Ribbon of the Order of the Polish People's Republic'; the Presidium of the People's Great Hural of the Mongolian People's Republic the 'Suhe Bator Order'; the Council of State of the German Democratic Republic, the 'Karl Marx Order'; the president of the Socialist Republic of Romania, the first class of the ribbon decorated 'Star Order of the Socialist Republic of Romania'; the Council of State of the Socialist Republic of Vietnam . . . the 'Golden Star Order,' to Janos Kadar."[43]

Three months later, in August 1982, Erich Honecker, SED Central Committee general secretery and chairman of the GDR State Council, celebrated his 70th birthday. The entire show surrounding Kadar's birthday (including the same greetings messages and the same orders) was repeated, strictly following the rules of the ritual.[44]

Ritual is manifested not only in communiques and greetings messages, or reference to leaders and the order of their appearance, but also in the celebration of international communist holidays (notably the October Revolution anniversary, 1 May). The festive meetings marking the events, the official slogans (reflecting the Soviet position on every issue of importance) published on the eve of these special days, the parades and manifestations, and the speeches of the leaders are a part of the ritual, and thus subject to elaborate coordination and synchronization. The annual "vacations" of the East European leaders in the Crimea, where they meet the really vacationing Soviet leader, are also mainly a ritualistic matter. They last for about forty-eight hours (or even less) and are followed by a brief communique, which as usual does not reveal anything. These visits ("vacations at the invitation of the CPSU Central

Committee") are so traditional that even their dates seem
to be reserved in advance. Thus Zhivkov's visits to the
Crimea in recent years were on the following dates: 1978,
11-14 August; 1979, 7-9 August; 1980, 6-9 August; and
1981, 6-8 August.[45] Despite their obviously ritualistic
nature, these meetings are also followed by an "announcement" on the visit (or rather "vacation") and a Politburo
session, at which the "results of the meeting" are
approved.[46]

Incidentally, some of the East European leaders hold
an annual mini-court of their own, i.e., they invite second-
league communist leaders (usually from the developing
countries) to spend a brief vacation in their country.
Bulgaria's Todor Zhivkov, who spends most of the summer
at the Varna Black Sea resort, receives many (secondary)
foreign dignitaries invited to vacation in Bulgaria. In
August 1982 he met (among others) Muhamed Harmel, first
secretary of the Communist Party of Tunisia[47]; Luis Corvalan
secretary general of the Communist Party of Chile[48];
Oliver Tambo, chairman of the African National Congress of
South Africa[49]; and Rodney Arismendi, first secretary of
the Central Committee of the Communist Party of Uruguay.[50]
The lengthy communiques that followed those obviously short
meetings touched upon every topical international issue,
using exactly the same words and phrases. They all
condemned "the barbarous Israeli aggression against
Lebanon" and the "genocide conducted by Israel against the
Palestinian people." They all praised "the heroic and brave
struggle of the Palestinian people." "Warm gratitude" was
expressed to the BCP for its support of the relevant
struggle of each party. The usual villains were denounced,
the danger of a nuclear war pointed out, and the USSR
"peaceful foreign policy and initiative" praised.

Another aspect of the ritual has been the constant
reference to the words of the relevant party leader and,
until his death, Leonid Ilich Brezhnev. There has been
absolutely no difficulty in finding an appropriate quota-
tion from a recent speech (preferably the speech at the
most recent party congress), thus lending more authority and
weight to the words of the speaker, and testifying to his
ideological erudition and his ability to keep abreast with
topical party instructions. Consequently, phrases like
"as our leader says," and "our leader stated at the last
party congress" embellish the speeches of every East
European political figure. "Effectiveness and quality--
quality and effectiveness" in Bulgaria, "preserving the
independence of every country" in Romania, and so forth--

are obligatory phrases in every major public address. Of course, they are attributed respectively to Zhivkov and Ceausescu.

Despite the rigid rules of the ritual, it can be swiftly and uniformally changed when necessary (i.e., when the needs of Soviet foreign policy demand this). After the fall of the Shah of Iran, all East European states denounced him in univocal terms as a "usurper," "dictator," "lackey of imperialism," "tyrant," and so forth. Not so long before, however, he was a persona grata in Eastern Europe, whose friendhip (and oil) were sought, and to whom warm hospitality was given. During his visits to Eastern Europe in 1977-1978 he was awarded doctor's degrees in jurisprudence and philosophy in the CSSR, as well as orders and medals.[51] In his toast at the official dinner, Husak declared that "there was a broad identity of interest in mutual relations and identical or very close stands on many basic issues of current world developments."[52] Bulgaria, Poland, and Hungary[53] used the same formulas.

Apropos of Husak, when the East European laws of uniformity demanded, he was also very quick in changing his views and adapting them to the rules of the ritual. In August 1968, at the extraordinary Congress of the Slovak Communist Party in Bratislava, commenting on the invasion of the CSSR by the Soviet and Warsaw Pact troops, Husak stated: "Armies of five socialist states have entered our territory. It is necessary to say that the leading organs of our party and our state did not ask for this entry, did not invite their armies on our territory. A tragic misunderstanding, a tragic miscomprehension, has occurred. In this context, the question of who invited the armies arises. The CPCZ Central Committee Presidium . . . [has] issued a declaration that neither the Presidium, the government, nor the party leadership extended such an invitation. . . . I do not know a single leading personality in Czech or Slovak political life about whom one could safely say that he took such a step."[54]

Precisely ten years later, greeting Leonid Brezhnev in the CSSR, Husak paid the ritualistic lip service to "socialist internationalism," saying "The historic decision to heed innumerable requests from Czechoslovak communists and noncommunists for the salvation of the revolutionary achievements of our people was an expression of loyalty to socialist internationalism, of a determination to defend jointly the sacred cause of socialism. This helped save our country from a counterrevolutionary reversal and its tragic effects on the life of the working people."[55]

SANCTITY OF THE RITUAL

Communism has often been compared to religion. After
all, it too has its saints, holy scriptures, holy places,
prescribed prayers, "anti-Christs," sworn enemies, and many
other common aspects. As in religion, uniformity is an
essential part of communism, or at least of Moscow's socialism.
Subsequently, other forms of socialism are deemed anathema--
the false religion. One way of guarding the true religion
against anathema and its enemies is by strictly adhering
to the rules of behavior prescribed by the highest authority,
which guarantee uniformity. Hence the great importance of
uniformity in East European political life, and hence the
significance of the ritual as a reflection of this uniformity. One must remember that the ritual governs every
area of public life (including many areas that have not
been dealt with in this chapter, such as the national
assembly sessions, elections, and so forth, subjects that
have been discussed in separate chapters).

The ritual has many additional functions. It is a
criterion for evaluating the loyalty of the East European
regimes to Moscow, to Marxism-Leninism, and to the current
line of the CPSU, as well as a demonstrative means of
proving the cohesion of the East European political system.
Because of the strictness of the rules, and because of the
inherent importance of the ritualistic uniformity, any
deviation has a special meaning. Constant and repeating
differences, especially in the accepted concepts indicating adherence to Soviet foreign policy, imply a
different interpretation of some aspects of it (Yugoslavia,
Romania), or a different interpretation of the entire notion
of socialism (Albania). However, the fact that those
countries (and especially Yugoslavia and Romania) use the
ritual themselves in order to demonstrate their differences
(changing exactly those concepts whose implied meaning has
such overwhelming importance) actually underlines the
significance of the ritual in the East European political
system.

NOTES

1. Rabotnichesko Delo (Bulgaria), 9 September 1980;
Daily Report (FBIS), 18 Se;tember 1980.
2. Neues Deutschland (GDR), 23-24 August 1980;
Daily Report (FBIS), 27 August 1980.
3. Rude Pravo (CSSR), 27 August 1980; Daily Report

(FBIS), 29 August 1980.

4. Rabotnichesko Delo, 31 August 1980; Daily Report
(FBIS), 5 September 1980.

5. Belgrade TANJUG in Serbo-Croatian, 1925 GMT,
3 September 1980; Daily Report (FBIS), 8 September 1980.

6. Frankfurter Rundschau (FRG), 26 August 1980;
Daily Report (FBIS), 28 August 1980.

7. Rabotnichesko Delo, 9 September 1980; Daily Report
(FBIS), 18 September 1980.

8. Scinteia (Romania), 14 September 1980; Daily Report
(FBIS), 18 September 1980.

9. Neues Deutschland, 18 September 1980; Daily Report
(FBIS), 2 April 1980.

10. Neues Deutschland, 25 August 1980; Daily Report
(FBIS), 27 August 1980.

11. Rude Pravo, 30 August 1980; Daily Report (FBIS),
4 September 1980.

12. Rude Pravo, 13 October 1981; Daily Report (FBIS),
16 October 1981.

13. Rabotnichesko Delo, 7 October 1981; Daily Report
(FBIS), 14 October 1981.

14. East Berlin ADN International Service in German,
1802 GMT, 14 October 1981; Daily Report (FBIS), 15 October
1981.

15. Nepszabadsag (Hungary), 10 October 1981; Daily
Report (FBIS), 15 October 1981.

16. Pravda (CSSR), 16 July 1981; Daily Report (FBIS),
20 July 1981.

17. Phnom Pehn SPK in French, 0435 GMT, 19 July 1981;
Daily Report (FBIS), 23 July 1981.

18. RFE Situation Report, Romania, 1 July 1977.

19. RFE Situation Report, CSSR, 30 January 1980.

20. RFE Situation Report, Hungary, 29 March 1977.

21. RFE Situation Report, Hungary, 26 September 1977.

22. Communique on L. Strougal visit to Bulgaria, in
Rabotnichesko Delo, 12 November 1980; Daily Report (FBIS),
18 November 1980; communique on L. Strougal visit to
Romania, in Scinteia, 23 November 1980; Daily Report (FBIS),
26 November 1980.

23. Communique on Willi Stoph visit to CSSR, in Rude
Pravo, 4 December 1980; Daily Report (FBIS), 10 December
1980.

24. Communique on Ilie Verdet visit to the GDR,
Neues Deutschland, 13 March 1981; Daily Report (FBIS),
18 March 1981.

25. Scinteia, 23 November 1980; Daily Report (FBIS),
26 November 1980.

26. Communique on Willi Stoph visit to CSSR, Rude Pravo, 4 December 1980; Daily Report (FBIS), 10 December 1980.

27. Communique on L. Strougal visit to Bulgaria, Rabotnichesko Delo, 12 November 1980; Daily Report (FBIS), 18 November 1980.

28. RFE Situation Report, Romania, 10 December 1976.

29. Borba (Yugoslavia), 28, 29, and 30 November 1976.

30. FBIS East European Report, no. 2031, 9 July 1982, carried all important speeches at the Dimitrov Conference, based on various East European sources.

31. Rabotnichesko Delo, 29 July 1981; Daily Report (FBIS), 3 August 1981.

32. Bucharest AGREPRES in English, 1812 GMT, 29 July 1981; Daily Report (FBIS), 30 July 1981.

33. Neues Deutschland, 28 July 1981; Daily Report (FBIS), 31 July 1981.

34. Neues Deutschland, 17 July 1981; Daily Report (FBIS), 21 July 1981.

35. Scinteia, 17 July 1981; Daily Report (FBIS), 21 July 1981.

36. Sofia BTA in English, 1832 GMT, 16 July 1981; Daily Report (FBIS), 17 July 1981.

37. Sofia Domestic Service in Bulgarian, 1730 GMT, 25 May 1982; Daily Report (FBIS), 27 May 1982.

38. Bucharest AGERPRES in English, 1822 GMT, 26 May 1982; Daily Report (FBIS), 27 May 1982.

39. Belgrade TANJUG Domestic Service in Serbo-Croatian, 1234 GMT, 25 May 1982; Daily Report (FBIS), 27 May 1982.

40. Prague Domestic Service in Czech, 1630 GMT, 25 May 1982; Daily Report (FBIS), 26 May 1982.

41. Moscow Domestic Service in Russian, 1100 GMT, 25 May 1982; Daily Report (FBIS), USSR, 26 May 1982.

42. Ibid.

43. Budapest MTI in English, 1748 GMT, 25 May 1982; Daily Report (FBIS), 26 May 1982.

44. East Berlin ADN International Service in German, 0202 GMT, 26 August 1982.

45. RFE Situation Report, Bulgaria, 14 August 1981.

46. Sofia BTA in English, 1842 GMT, 9 August 1981.

47. Sofia BTA in English, 1430 GMT, 25 August 1982.

48. Sofia BTA in English, 1440 GMT, 26 August 1982.

49. Sofia BTA in English, 1430 GMT, 27 August 1982.

50. Sofia BTA in English, 1430 GMT, 28 August 1982.

51. RFE Situation Report, CSSR, 7 September 1977.

52. Ibid.

53.   RFE Situation Report, Hungary, 6 July 1978.

54.   _Pravda_ (CSSR), 29 August 1968; RFE Situation Report, CSSR, 5 June 1978.

55.   RFE Situation Report, CSSR, 5 June 1978.

11
The Auxiliary Organizations

It has already been stressed that one of the basic characteristics of the East European political system is the state of permanent mobilization in which the population is kept. What this means in practice is that the people are constantly in the process of implementing specific and urgent tasks set by the party, participating in various demonstrative campaigns organized by the regime, and as a result are preoccupied with various organized and orchestrated economic and political activities that leave little or no time for uncontrolled behavior. This state of permanent mobilization is achieved and maintained through a network of public organizations or mass organizations, as the bloc media like to call them, such as the trade unions, the youth organizations, the creative unions, women's organizations, and above all--the so-called National Fronts.

THE NATIONAL FRONTS

The National Fronts exist under different names in all East European countries. In Albania it is the Democratic Front; in Bulgaria, the Fatherland Front; in Hungary, the Patriotic People's Front; in Romania, the Front of Socialist Democracy and Unity; in the SFRY, the Socialist Alliance of the Working People; and finally, in the GDR, Poland, and the CSSR--the National Front. The fronts are the earliest form of communist-sponsored mass organizations, and in fact they preceded the establishment of the socialist regimes. The idea of creating the "united," "national," or "people's" fronts is usually attributed to Georgi Dimitrov, and dates back to the late

1920s and the early 1930s, when he was in charge of the
West European Bureau of the Comintern (1929-1933), and
more specifically to April 1934, when Dimitrov became
secretary-general of that body (until its dissolution in
May 1943). At the Seventh Congress of the Comintern (July-
August 1935), Georgi Dimitrov presented the tactics and
strategy of the "united fronts." Based on Dimitrov's
report, the congress adopted a resolution that detailed
the tactics of the world's communist movement for achieving its ultimate goal: setting up proletarian dictatorship
under the disguise of a common front against fascism.

In that early stage it was clear that the communists
were not able alone to oppose the rising fascism, Nazism,
and other radical rightist forces. They ostensibly
abandoned their slogan of "class struggle" and looked for
prospective allies among all political parties to the left
of the center and among some bourgeois democratic parties
as well. Thus, the fronts were founded as coalitions of
antifascist and antirightist forces. Although communist-
sponsored, the fronts were not themselves communist organizations. The communist parties were only one of the
elements composing the national fronts, although usually
the most powerful one. It was mostly through the national
fronts that the communist parties in Eastern Europe
established their domination after World War II. These
fronts were instrumental in establishing and consolidating
the East European communist regimes. Once this original
goal was fulfilled, they became umbrella organizations,
uniting all the public organizations in the socialist
countries (youth, trade unions, paramilitary organizations,
creative unions, and so forth), and they assumed a new
role. It is the national fronts that mobilize the public
to "elect" the candidates of the regime's choice in the
elections, and to implement the party's tasks, plans, and
goals (usually under the all-embracing term of "congress'
decisions"); it is the national fronts that organize the
big propaganda campaigns and the demonstrations in support
of the regime's foreign policy, to denounce the U.S.
policy or the policy of any factor considered a "class
enemy" or just a hostile element at a given moment. If all
this could be summarized in one Leninist phrase, then the
national fronts are the transmission belt conveying the
party orders and activating all social segments.

In addition, the national fronts serve as a useful
and accepted framework for the surviving noncommunist
parties (the Czechoslovak Socialist Party, the Czechoslovak
People's Party, the Slovak Freedom Party, and the Slovak

Renaissance Party in the CSSR; the Christian Democratic
Union and the Liberal Democratic Party in the GDR; the
United Peasants' Party, the Democratic Party, and the
Catholic Znak Group in Poland; the Bulgarian Agrarian
National Union in Bulgaria, etc.).

The organizational structure of the national fronts
resembles the structure of the communist party to a large
degree. Their supreme organ is the congress, which
follows the party congress by several months. The national
front congress is preceded by the election of delegates at
the village, district, city, and county levels. At the
election meetings the national front local committees submit reports on their activity since the previous congress,
list the tasks for the future, and stress the significance
of the most recently adopted party decisions of propagandistic character (usually adopted by the most recent party
congress or Central Committee plenum). These pre-election
meetings also examine the implementation of the economic
plan, the Five-Year Plan, and various local affairs. In
fact they are used both as a means of gathering information
about the prevailing mood of the population and letting off
some social pressure, while allowing the participants to
freely voice (restrained) complaints about some weaknesses
and shortcomings at the respective local level. Thus
during the election campaign preceding the 6th Congress
of the Patriotic People's Front in Hungary in 1976, the
local pre-congressional meetings discussed, among other
things, the inadequacies of supplies and lack of scope in
life of the small villages.[1]

The pre-congressional meetings, which at the region
and big-city levels are usually attended by Politburo
members,[2] also deal with the resolution of the forthcoming
national front congress. The draft resolution is regularly
published in advance and subjected to broad public debate.
The proposed amendments and addenda are then taken into
consideration in the preparation of the final draft, which
is ultimately adopted by the congress.

The pre-congress campaign in Hungary in 1976 lasted
more than three months. During this period, 4,165 new
committees were elected, with 101,354 members and 800
delegates to the congress. The most widely discussed
subjects during the campaign were "the complete development
of socialist national unity," "the Patriotic People's Front
educational tasks," "strengthening the economy for the
benefit of the people," "the Front's legal activity," and
"the Front's role in developing socialist democracy."[3]

Because the national fronts have no independent

political role, one cannot expect anything unusual to happen during the congress. The report of the Central Committee and the debates echo the most recent party congress, glorify the successes of the party and the country, make the obligatory expression of loyalty to the USSR, the Warsaw Pact, and CEMA, and denounce the perennial enemies of socialism.

Implementing party policy in every area of life is the essence of the national fronts' goals and tasks. Thus the 7th Congress of the Hungarian Patriotic People's Front in March 1981 listed the following as being the most important tasks for the organization: struggling for peace (supporting the peace program of the 26th CPSU Congress), strengthening national unity (church-state relations, expanding ties with Hungarians abroad, combating signs of nationalism, etc.), promoting the unity of socialist and democratic forces, providing the public with topical information, intensifying public participation in various campaigns and plans of the regime, promoting various cultural activities, and so forth.[4] Similar tasks were also listed at the 8th Fatherland Front Congress in Bulgaria in June 1977. Stressing that "the program of the 11th BCP Congress laid down the place, role, and tasks of the Fatherland Front in building a developed socialist society," and that "all Fatherland Front activities are carried out in accordance with party decisions,"[5] Pencho Kubadinski, chairman of the Fatherland Front's Central Council, listed the following topical tasks of the organization: strengthening socialist democracy, intensifying the patriotic and international education of the entire population, countering "religious anachronisms," introducing new civil rites and holidays, promoting ideological and educational activities as well as voluntary work, and facilitating the implementation of the state plan.[6]

Similar if not identical tasks are usually listed by all National Fronts' congresses. This is not the only aspect of these congresses that is similar. They all have the same agenda, which consists of listening to the report of the front's leadership, approving the statements of various party, state, and front's leaders, listening to the greetings of the foreign delegations, and electing the front's leading organs. One notices immediately the similarity between the congresses of the front and the party, which actually follow the same procedure. In fact the congresses of all auxiliary organizations in Eastern Europe are modeled on the party congress and copy its agenda and procedure.

The party leaders invariably attend the National Fronts' congresses. In three East European countries-- Albania, the CSSR, and Romania--the party leaders are also leaders of the National Fronts, while in other countries the National Front leaders are usually members of the party Politburo (Pencho Kubadinski in Bulgaria, Istvan Sarlos in Hungary until June 1982, and so forth). The leader of the GDR National Front, Lothar Kolditz, is a member of the State Council only, and the status of Todo Kurtovic in the SFRY is similar.

The structure of the National Fronts' leading organs also resembles the structure of the party leadership. Thus the 2nd Congress of the Romanian Socialist Unity and Democracy Front elected Ceausescu as President of the Front; Constantin Arseni, an academician, was elected chairman of the Executive Board (nineteen members, clearly modeled on the party Politburo); and a 209-member Central Committee (modeled on the party Central Committee) was also elected.[7] The 7th Congress of the Hungarian Patriotic People's Front elected Gyula Kallai as its president (nominal head), Istvan Sarlos as secretary general, the National Council of 271 members, seven deputy presidents, four secretaries, and the fourteen-member national secretariat, as well as the 45-member Presidium of the National Council.[8] The 8th Fatherland Front Congress in Bulgaria reelected Pencho Kubadinski as its chairman and elected a 369-member National Council and a 64-member Presidium, one first deputy chairman (Sava Dulbokov), seven deputy chairmen, five secretaries, and five bureau members.[9]

The most important practical task of the National Fronts (aside from supporting the regime's propaganda campaigns and facilitating plan implementation and ideological indoctrination) is to organize the national elections. The election mechanism and the extensive National Front involvement in the campaign has been examined in the chapter dealing with the elections. Therefore, it will only be mentioned briefly here.

The National Front's involvement in the election campaign begins with a special plenum of its Central Committee (or Central Council), usually attended by all party and state leaders.[10] This plenum sets the tone of the entire campaign, adopting a decision on the elections, and publishing a declaration on the same topic, as well as the list of candidates. Those documents have a mostly propagandistic character, surveying the country's working successes, glorifying the party policy in every area of life, and pledging loyalty to the party on behalf of the entire population.

Thus the plenum of the Bulgarian Fatherland Front of 23 April 1981 adopted a resolution whose main points are summarized below:

1. Basic guidelines on the organization's activity during the election campaign were adopted. The BCP Central Committee accountability report read by Todor Zhivkov at the 12th BCP Congress and the congress' decisions were adopted as the political platform of the forthcoming election campaign.
2. The decision was made to intensify the people's sociopolitical and labor activities for implementing the national plan, the decisions of the 12th BCP Congress, and the April plenum of the BCP Central Committee.
3. Joint candidates on behalf of the Fatherland Front were proposed for election as candidates for National Assembly deputies, people's councillors, mayors, judges, and jurors.
4. The list of Fatherland Front's candidates for National Assembly deputies to the Eighth National Assembly was approved.
5. The okrug Fatherland Front committees, together with the other social organizations and movements, were entrusted with organizing the discussions with candidates.
6. The Fatherland Front National Council Bureau was entrusted with making amendments to the list of candidates for National Assembly deputies, if in the process of debates such amendments became necessary.[11]

In his concluding speech, Kubadinski made the obligatory reference to the "peace program of the 26th CPSU Congress" and denounced the policy of "U.S. imperialism, European warmongers, and Beijing leaders," who were accused by him of "trying to implement an openly hostile anti-Soviet and antisocialist policy."[12]

A reference to the "Soviet peace program," the relevant country and party, the USSR, the Warsaw Pact, and CEMA is an indispensible part of all National Fronts' election declarations.[13] And of course, they all appeal to the population to vote for the National Front (communist party) candidates.

The meetings of the National Fronts' Central Committees are frequently attended by the party and state leaders, who

closely supervise the organization's activities. Such
meetings (when not dealing with the election campaign) are
usually devoted to plan implementation or mobilizing the
public for the current propaganda campaign sponsored by
the regime. Such a session took place in Prague on
18 April 1978. It approved some personnel changes in the
Central Committee, heard a report of Gustav Husak on the
economic and political situation, and adopted a resolution
denouncing the neutron bomb.[14] The resolution condemned
the intention to deploy the neutron bomb in Europe,
demanded the condemnation of "this barbaric weapon" by the
UN General Assembly, declared the desire of the CSSR
citizens to live in peace, and endorsed "the recent USSR
peaceful proposals."[15]

Such declarations and resolutions are an important
and integral part of the National Fronts' foreign policy
activity. This aspect of the fronts' activities was
compressed in one sentence of the report of the Hungarian
Patriotic People's Front to its 7th Congress: "The
Patriotic People's Front contributes to attaining the
foreign policy objectives of the Hungarian People's
Republic, strengthens the unity of the socialist countries,
aids the struggle of revolutionary and progressive movements in the developing countries and the coming together
with the socialist countries, and strives to strengthen
cooperation with progressive forces and personages in
capitalist countries."[16] Toward these purposes it was
reported that the Patriotic People's Front maintains working relations with 48 partner organizations and democratic
parties, and 238 peace organizations in 128 countries.
From January 1977 to March 1981 it had hosted 58 foreign
delegations and sent 64 delegations abroad.[17]

Topical propaganda campaigns of the East European
regimes invariably enjoy the National Fronts' support. Thus
in 1981 they all issued declarations condemning the neutron
bomb. Some of the declarations dealt with the neutron
bomb only, as in the Bulgarian declaration,[18] whereas
others, such as the declaration of the CSSR National
Front, took the opportunity of the neutron bomb issue to
take a swipe at "Walesa's trade unions" and other topical
issues.[19]

The National Fronts are also a useful instrument for
conducting relations with national liberation movements.
On occasions, most of the East European governments have
preferred to conduct business with many such movements
through the National Fronts. Such was the case with the
relations between these countries and the PLO. Even today,

when the PLO enjoys official status in all East European
states, its close relations with the National Fronts are
still evident. Thus in 1981 a PLO delegation led by
Faruq Qaddumi, chairman of the PLO Executive Committee
Political Department, visited Bulgaria,[20] the CSSR,[21]
and other countries at the invitation of the respective
national fronts and signed cooperation agreements with the
host organizations.

The East European National Fronts serve as models
for similar organizations in other countries dominated by
the Soviet Union. (Because the Soviet Union has no
similar organization, it cannot serve as an example in
this area.) When the Afghan National Fatherland Front was
established in June 1981, the new organization was immediately greeted by the East European counterparts. The messages
expressed "solidarity with the efforts of the Democratic
Republic of Afghanistan, its government and people, to
defend the national independence and the territorial
integrity of the country and to preserve and protect the
acquisitions of the April Revolution."[22] Soon afterwards
a delegation of the newly created front visited several
East European states "to study from the experience of the
National Fronts . . . in mobilizing the progressive and
democratic forces . . . and building the socialist
society."[23]

TRADE UNIONS

Despite the fact that the East European trade unions
are only the second mass organization in Eastern Europe to
be dealt with--several more will follow--it is already
time for an apology and a caution. First the apology:
the reader will inevitably find this chapter repetitious.
The reason is simple: no matter how many mass-public
organizations exist in Eastern Europe, the only difference
among them is their name. Everything else--role, tasks,
structure, organizational procedure, party control, and so
forth--hardly vary from one organization to another. This
should not be surprising; they all spring from the same
source--the party needs and interests. First is the need
to maintain the population in a state of permanent
mobilization, to enhance the people's enthusiasm and
intensify their labor production and loyalty to the regime;
to this end the trade unions all copy the party's organizational structure (centralist democracy, strict
discipline, etc.) and in the final account, they all

exist in order to serve the party. Therefore, despite
the fact that different mass organizations will be examined
in this chapter, the reader will find much common ground
among them, and thus, inevitable repetition.

Now for the caution: East European trade unions are
not the same as those that exist in every democratic
society.   The latters' purpose can be summarized in one
basic sentence: to represent the workers' interests vis-
à-vis their employers, to negotiate on the part of the
workers, and, essentially, to strive to improve their labor
and social conditions. Thus, the trade unions most
familiar to the reader actually become a natural venue
of popular participation in every democratic-industrial
society. This is not the function of the East European
trade unions. (Once again, the specific case of Poland
in 1980-1981 and its ramifications will be discussed
later in this chapter). No organization in Eastern Europe
is allowed to challenge the policies and decisions of the
party. Furthermore, no organization is ever permitted to
ask questions that can embarass the authorities. After
all, there can be no conflict of interests when the party
of the working people is the ruling party. Consequently,
the party itself represents the interests of the workers.
"Logically" there is no need for trade unions if the
workers' interests are already represented by the party.
How can the workers oppose themselves by making demands
on the party? How can they negotiate better contracts
with the party, which represents their interests? Subsequently, because there is no need (or rather room) for
regular trade union activity, the East European trade
unions concentrate on implementing the specific tasks
assigned to them by the party.

The primary task of the East European trade unions
is to organize the labor force to increase production
efforts and fulfill various national goals. First among
them is the successful implementation of the national
economic plan. The trade unions are expected to stir up
general working enthusiasm and facilitate the implementation of the plan, and failure to achieve this inevitably
calls for some explaining on the part of the trade union
leaders. Thus, Harry Tisch, chairman of the FDGB (the
GDR trade union) and member of the SED Central Committee
Politburo, stated at a 1980 meeting of the GDR trade
union National Executive Committee: "We are conscious of
our responsibility for the required greater rise in the
performance of the national economy. We regard the
fulfillment and overfulfillment of the 1980 economic plan

as a fighting task."[24]   In a similar vein, Karel Hoffmann,
CPCZ Central Committee Presidium member and chairman of
the CSSR trade union, analyzing the responsibility of the
trade union for plan implementation, stated: "The results
which we achieved in the past Five-Year Plan are not as
good as we had wished, among other things because the
necessary conditions for adopting the exacting socialist
pledges, oriented to our economy's key problems, had not
been created everywhere, and because the responsible
managers and trade union bodies and organization did not
always pay enough attention or give enough help to those
who were competing."[25]

        This particular task (plan fulfillment) is implemented
by the East European trade unions through "acting as a
motivating power in the drafting of counterplans and
making a high contribution to the socioeconomic development of the country,"[26] "mobilizing the workers for an
exemplary achievement of economic tasks and production
indicators,"[27] "better organizing and conducting the
socialist competition,"[28] "better utilization of time and
power,"[29] "better use of fuel and raw materials,"[30] and
so forth.

        During the early 1980s, apparently under the influence
of the social unrest in Poland, many East European countries
concluded that one way of encouraging the trade unions'
help in insuring the implementation of the national economic
plan was to involve them in the very process of planning,
by incorporating their proposals and comments in the final
draft of the plan. This novelty, announced as "fully
independent planning by the trade unions,"[31] or planning
"from the bottom up,"[32] appears to be an instrument of
demonstrating the trade unions' involvement in national
economic planning.

        The fact that the East European trade union leaders
are usually members of their respective parties' Politburos
or the Central Committee Secretariat (Harry Tisch in
the GDR, Petur Dyulgerov in Bulgaria, Karel Hoffmann in
the CSSR, Rita Marko in Albania, Emil Bobu in Romania,
etc.) is not accidental. Their post is a testimonial to
the party-trade union alliance and to the essential trade
union function--promoting party interest. This vital
connection is frequently and openly pointed out by many
East European sources. Thus, in February 1982 an Albanian
official source stated: "As revolutionary political
organizations of the masses the trade unions of Albania
have and had in the foundation of their activity the
political and ideological line of the Albanian Workers'

Party, the permanent leadership of the party, the implementation of its directives and the teachings of Comrade
Enver Hoxha, which are the greatest guarantee that the
trade unions of Albania successfully perform their role and
tasks."[33]

Usually, the party-trade union affiliation is pointed
out by stressing the trade union role in implementing the
decisions of the most recent party congress. The number
of the congress and the country may be different, but the
relationship is always identical: "The 12th Congress of
our party formulated realistic aspirations and attractive
goals, goals for which it is worthwhile to struggle, and
the trade union movement will work with its creative
strength for the realization of these goals."[34] Or, "In
the words of the FDGB chairman Harry Tisch, the GDR's
9 million trade unionists will devote themselves whole-
heartedly to the fulfillment of the historic 10th SED
Congress decisions."[35] Or, "The Albanian trade unions
will mobilize the working people to carry into effect the
tasks of the 8th Congress of the party, and will increase
their enthusiasm to fulfill them to a letter."[36]

A necessary precondition of implementing the economic
plan and fulfilling the decisions of the recent party
congress is the development of successful ideological-
indoctrinational activity, or in other words, the
ideological mobilization of the workers. Presented as
"political education,"[37] "enhancing the socialist awareness of the workers,"[38] and "educational work,"[39] it usually
involves clarification of relevant party decisions, study of
party history and Marxism-Leninism, and so forth. In the
GDR alone in 1980 "some 150,000 schools of socialist labor
disseminated Marxist-Leninist knowledge."[40] In 1982 in
Romania, 2.6 million workers attended political courses
organized by the trade union.[41] On certain occasions the
communist party Central Committees held special plenums
devoted to intensifying the ideological activity of the
trade unions.[42] In addition, sometimes specific working
successes were attributed to successful indoctrinational
activity on the part of the trade unions.[43]

In addition to the ideological aspect of the indoctrinational activity, the trade unions in Eastern Europe
are also expected "to join the effort of giving all
educational-formative activities a rich political-
ideological content filled with the principles of socialist
humanism, promoting the spirit of right, respect for the
truth, honesty, modesty, and correctness, comradely relations
of trust, mutual esteem and mutual assistance, and the

combating of expressions that fail to consider the general interests of society."[44] What is meant here is that the East European trade unions should act as indoctrinators, educators, mentors, and censors of the workers.

The three trade union tasks mentioned so far--facilitating socialist construction by assisting in fulfilling the national plan, implementing topical decisions of various party organs, and finally, ideological indoctrination, are the basic and most important trade union tasks. There are, however, several additional tasks worth mentioning. One of them is providing the party leaders with information on the mood and attitudes of the workers. Although not a primary task (there are other means of obtaining the same information), this task is nevertheless frequently mentioned by official spokesmen. Thus, Ferenc Roland, deputy head of the Hungarian Trade Union Central Council Agitprop section, said in 1978: "The National trade union Council, the supreme directing organization of the trade unions, attaches great importance to receiving sufficient information from the enterprises about the mood and attitude of the workers. . . . The aim of the monthly 'duty report' is to ensure that leading bodies are aware of the workers' mood. This is essential for the higher authorities to be able to take suitable measures at the proper time."[45]

The East European trade unions also perform various international tasks. Two of the most important ones are supporting the party foreign policy and participating in various international propaganda campaigns (in fact, the two standard international duties of all auxiliary organizations). The statement of the CSSR trade union leader Hoffmann on this matter is characteristic of the position of all East European trade unions: "We regard the full support for the foreign political line of the 16th CPCZ Congress and all the noble initiatives of the 26th CPSU Congress, again conveyed by Comrade Leonid Ilich Brezhnev in his greeting message to the 16th CPCZ Congress, to be of vital importance. From our international standpoint arises the need to develop specific forms of cooperation with the trade unions of the socialist countries, particularly with the Soviet trade unions, and to learn from their experience."[46]

The support of the party foreign policy is usually expressed by official declarations and statements of the trade union leaders, or by expressing the trade union positions on various international issues in joint communiques, following the visits of trade union delegations.

Thus, the joint communique issued at the end of the visit of the Bulgarian trade union delegation to Hungary in 1981 confirmed the determination of the two countries' trade unions "to continue to resist and unmask the anti-Soviet, antisocialist, and anticommunist propaganda."[47] "Concern with the situation in Poland" was expressed, and finally, "the NATO plans for deploying middle-range missiles in Western Europe and Washington's decision to produce the neutron bomb" were condemned.[48]

The trade unions (as well as the National Fronts) provide the party with a useful and unofficial channel of contact with nonsocialist countries' clandestine movements and organizations, or national liberation movements. It must be stressed again that the initial relations between the East European countries and the PLO were usually at trade union level.[49]

The establishment of the Polish independent Solidarity trade union in 1980 activated a red light in all other East European countries. Even before 1980 the East European trade unions had occasionally deviated from their traditional role and voiced mild and well controlled criticism of some weaknesses and shortcomings of local character. These "deviations" were usually prompted by the party and were used as a valve for letting off some pressure. Thus in 1978 in Yugoslavia, the trade unions were assigned the task of finding out the reasons for the strikes in Croatia.[50] Shortly afterwards, the Yugoslav press even urged the trade unions to assume the role of "spokesman of conscience and of the opposition in the Yugoslav system."[51] However, when this really happened in Poland, and the Solidarity trade union turned into "a spokesman for conscience and opposition to the system," the East European regimes immediately took urgent measures to prevent the "contamination" of their own trade unions, first of all by condemning the very notion of trade union independence: "The slogan about the 'independence of the trade unions,' no matter how well meant--but about which one can have doubts, of course, after our own experience and after the experience of the comrades from fraternal Poland--is always reactionary. It is, in fact, aimed at weakening the main instrument for building the advanced socialist society--the socialist state--by making trade unions oppose it. The slogan is also aimed at weakening trade unions by reducing their real tasks as coparticipants in the working people's construction feat."[52]

The Hungarian trade union leader Sandor Gaspar used

almost the same words to condemn the notion of trade union
independence. It was quite understandable, he said, that
under capitalist circumstances, where several parties
operate, the trade unions were anxious to safeguard the
working class's freedom of action, although they were not
always successful in doing so. Under socialist conditions
a trade union could be less free, because it would otherwise isolate itself from the struggle led by the communist
party for the prosperity of the entire society. A slogan
of independence would be tantamount to opposing the
interests of the working class and society.[53] Similar
statements were voiced by Romanian authorities[54] and, in
fact, by all East European countries, although Albania has
its own version of the forces behind the Solidarity trade
union. On 6 June 1982, at the opening session of the 9th
Congress of the Albanian trade union, Rita Marko, president
of the Central Council of the Albanian trade union, stated:

> The events in Poland are undeniable proof of the
> rootlessness of the revisionist system. The
> revisionist course steered by the 20th Congress
> of the Soviet revisionist party, the savage
> oppression and exploitation of the working class,
> the neo-colonialist Soviet plunder and dictate,
> the opening of doors to Western capital--all this
> led to the outbreak of class conflict between the
> working people and the revisionist regime in
> power. Convinced that it was reduced to an
> oppressed and exploited class, the Polish working
> class has risen in revolt. But it lacks a leading
> political force and its revolt is exploited by
> the Catholic Church and reaction. The offspring
> of their activity is the so-called independent
> "Solidarity" trade union, which is for capitalist
> relations, the further political and economic
> penetration of Western imperialism, and the re-
> placing of the rule of Moscow with the yoke of
> Western imperialism. This is the real reason
> why the statesmen of the imperialist countries,
> the Vatican, the bosses of the American
> reactionary trade-unions AFL-CIO, etc., support
> it by all means. [55]

Whatever the reason, Albania fully agrees with the
other East European states: independent trade unions
are a negative phenomenon. The unanimous denunciation of
the Solidarity trade union by all East European states was

accompanied by expressions of support for the official, communist party-controlled, branch trade unions: "In accordance with the character and goals of the revolutionary trade union movement, we fully support the branch trade unions of the Polish People's Republic and their coordination committee in their difficult struggle for the renewal and consolidation of the country's socialist order, for the fundamental interests of the working people. The workers' trade unions in the Polish People's Republic, which are genuinely class and socialist trade unions, can continue to count on our solidarity and active assistance."[56] It was also frequently stressed that "to make use of the right to strike means to threaten with an extreme measure, which reflects real hostility."[57]

Along with the attacks on Solidarity, the East European countries took urgent measures to increase the involvement of their trade unions in political life and in the decision-making process. Numerous meetings were held at which the question of improving various aspects of the workers' life was discussed. For example, a plenum of the CSSR Trade Unions Central Council in February 1982 dealt with improving the working conditions of women and developing free-time artistic ability of the workers, along with improving the ideological work.[58] While continuing to condemn strikes, the press urged the workers to "use their rights" to improve labor conditions and social benefits,[59] or even their "right to veto" certain decisions affecting their activity.[60] Funds were allocated for various cultural and social enterprises, improving the quality of the workers' lives, and so forth.[61] Certain trade union leaders were ousted (in Bulgaria, for instance, Misho Mishev was replaced by Petur Dyulgerov), and various mistakes admitted. Romania went as far as to pledge full autonomy for its trade unions while admitting a whole series of past errors and deficiencies in the activities of the unions, including failure to defend the interests of the workers.[62]

In Hungary the press reminded the workers of Part II, Art. 14 (3) of the Labor Code, which states that "labor union local within the enterprise has the right to object to any action by the enterprise that infringes upon the regulations relating to employment or to treatment offending against socialist morality. The practice to which objection is taken may not be instituted until a decision thereon is reached by the appropriate body."[63] The press called this right "one of the most important interest-protecting devices of the trade unions."[64]

The entire campaign was well synchronized, conducted by similar means by all East European countries, and demonstrated the concern of these regimes to avoid the Polish infection and to prevent the existing dissatisfaction with the activity of the trade unions from turning into opposition to party policy.

The organizational structure of the East European trade unions reflects the structure of the communist party (and the National Fronts). It is based on the principle of democratic centralism, its main organ being the congress (same frequency as the party congresses), a Central Council (or Central Committee) directing the trade union activities between congresses, and a bureau, which manages the daily affairs. As already pointed out, the chairman of the trade union Central Council is usually a Politburo member or a Central Committee secretary, who serves as a visual link between the trade unions and the party, or as a symbol of their common leadership.

The trade union congress is preceded by local accountability-election conferences, first at the places of work, then advancing according to the geographic-municipal-administrative structure of the country, and concluding with the conferences of the branch unions. At each of these conferences accountability reports are read by the respective leaders, and new organs are elected, along with delegates to the nationwide trade union congress. The entire procedure takes several months. Thus, the Bulgarian Trade Union Central Council decided on 12 January 1982 to hold its congress in April.[65] By the end of March all local and branch conferences and congresses had taken place, and 2,997 delegates to the trade union congress had been elected.[66] The entire pre-congressional procedure involves hundreds of thousands of meetings (during the 1976-1977 pre-congressional campaign that preceded the 9th Congress of the CSSR trade union, some 250,000 local trade union pre-congressional meetings were held).[67] This is a long campaign, designated to keep the workers in a state of mobilization.

The congresses of the East European trade unions follow the party congresses. In April 1982 the Bulgaria, CSSR, and GDR trade unions held their congresses precisely one year after the congresses of their respective communist parties. The trade union congress is attended by all party and state leaders (including the entire Politburo at the opening session) and many foreign delegations. (The 9th trade union congress in Bulgaria was attended by 67 foreign delegations.)[68] In similarity to the party congress, it has

two major highlights--the report of the trade union leader
and the election of the trade union organs. The report
of the trade union leader is predictable, devoid of any
surprises. He usually surveys the trade union's activity
since the last congress, reviews its tasks and goals,
reiterates the connection with the communist party and
pledges new successes, and admits minor weaknesses and
shortcomings. Thus, Petur Dyulgerov's report at the 9th
Congress of the Bulgarian trade unions (exactly like the
report of his predecessor Misho Mishev at the 8th Congress),
consisted of five parts: fulfilling the economic tasks
set by the 12th BCP Congress; increasing the standard of
living as a part of the trade union social policy; intensifying the trade union ideological activity (he reported
that some 1,300,000 trade union members were attending
ideological courses sponsored by the trade unions[69]);
organizational matters; and finally, the international
activity of the trade unions. (In this context Dyulgerov
enumerated the following tasks: enhancing the cooperation
with the Soviet and socialist countries' trade unions;
promoting further cooperation with the trade unions in Asia,
Africa, and Latin America; strengthening the solidarity with
"the struggle of the working people of the capitalist countries"; and increasing the "multilateral contacts" with the
Balkan countries' trade unions.[70]) Precisely the same
subjects were covered by the trade union leaders' reports
to the April 1981 Congress of the Romanian trade unions
and the December 1980 Congress of the Hungarian trade
union.[71]

     Another common denominator of these reports at the
time was the preoccupation with expanding the trade
unions' role in social life, while denouncing the activity
of the Solidarity trade union in Poland. Thus at the 24th
Congress of the Hungarian trade union (12-14 December 1980),
Sandor Gaspar, dealing with the "events in Poland,"
declared solidarity with the Polish party, government, the
official branch trade unions and workers. He took pains
to explain why the trade unions could not act as an
oppositional force in a socialist society, and denied the
usefulness of strikes, "which can only make us poorer,
not richer."[72]

     Usually the party leader also has a major speech at
the trade union congress, at which he repeats what he had
already said at the party congress, the National Front
congress, the youth league congress, and so forth. His
address sometimes follows the report of the trade union
leader at the afternoon session of the first day (as with

Husak at the April 1982 10th Congress of the CSSR trade union[73]) or represents one of the last day's highlights, as with Zhivkov's speech at the April 1982 9th Congress of the Bulgarian trade unions.[74]

Other events at the congress include the statements of the leaders of the foreign delegations, the greetings message of the party Central Committee, usually read by a Politburo member, and statements of local delegates. On the last day of the congress the Central Council (200-300 members) and the Bureau of Executive Committee (30-40 members) are elected, and in their turn elect the chairman or secretary general of the trade union. The final session is used to adopt a message to the party Central Committee (pledging loyalty and new successes) and various declarations and resolutions. Thus the June 1982 9th Congress of the Albanian trade unions adopted a resolution on agriculture; a resolution on social sectors; a resolution on construction, communications, and communal economy; and a resolution on the tasks of industry.[75] On the other hand the 10th Congress of the GDR trade unions adopted a "Peace Statement"[76] and a letter to party leader Honecker.[77]

In conclusion, the trade unions of the East European states are auxiliary organizations of the communist parties. They are officially assigned two basic tasks, which are contradictory and mutually exclusive: to help with fulfillment of the national economic plan and defend the workers' interests. In fact, however, they serve as an additional "transmission belt" of the communist party, facilitating the implementation of various party goals and strengthening the grasp of the communist parties over the population.

YOUTH ORGANIZATIONS

All East European countries have a youth organization, which under whatever name is an exact copy of the Soviet Komsomol. In Bulgaria it is the Dimitrov Komsomol; in the CSSR, the Socialist Youth Union; in Romania, the Union of Communist Youth; in Hungary, the Communist Youth League; in the GDR, the Free German Youth; in Albania, the Union of Working Youth; in Poland, the Union of Socialist Polish Youth; and in the SFRY, the Socialist Youth Federation. The youth unions are one of the most important mass organizations in the East European bloc, structured to carry out political socialization and Marxist indoctrination among the youth, and serve as a recruitment agency for the communist party. In a certain way, the East European youth organizations are apprentice organizations of the communist party, which prepare the politically active youth for their future tasks as party members, and in the meantime carry out various political, ideological, and cultural-social tasks outlined by the communist party.

Joining the youth organization is a relatively easy and uncomplicated matter, especially when compared with the rigid procedure for joining the communist party. Despite the fact that a candidate needs the recommendation of two Komsomol members of good standing, and in some East European states the recommendation of a party member, admission is usually collective (whole school classes join the organization en masse). The procedure usually involves a ceremony at which members of an already established Komsomol[78] unit ask the candidates short questions related to current events, party history, etc., and vote on the candidacy. In the specific case of this book's author, the admission ceremony took place at a military unit near the school, the questions revolving around the national elections then taking place and the future plans of the 14-year old candidates. The soldiers were supplied in advance with the names of the candidates to be admitted to the meeting and directed their questions personally to the potential new members. About half of the class was admitted, while the second half (mostly children of non-proletarian families, nonparty members, and so forth) had to participate in another meeting of similar character later on.

Despite the fact that admission to the Komsomol is almost automatic, that future admission to the university depends to a large degree on a positive record as a Komsomol member, and that there is usually social pressure to join, it would be wrong to assume that all eligible youth (15-25) are members of the youth organizations. Usually the membership is about two-thirds of the eligible youth.[79] The percentage varies among the various educational groups. Because Komsomol membership is a sine qua non for admission to higher educational establishments, naturally the percentage of students among its members is 100 or almost 100 percent. Thus at the 2nd Congress of the CSSR Socialist Youth Union in 1977 it was reported that the organization's membership included 47.6 percent of the CSSR apprentices, 69.1 percent of its secondary school pupils, and 96.9 percent of the college students.[80] (In 1976 the Hungarian youth organization reported 56 percent of the high school students and 96 percent of the university students as members.)[81]

It is interesting to note that despite the fact that
membership in the Komsomol is a matter of a temporary
nature (the age factor), purges among the members are not
unheard of. They can involve both the leadership and the
rank-and-file members. For example, at the 11th BCP
Congress in 1976 the Komsomol leadership was severely
criticized. The result was a speedy dismissal of its
Central Committee first secretary Encho Moskov, along with
other high officials. Incidentally, the specific accusation voiced at the 11th BCP Congress was that the Komsomol
leaders "indulged in heavy drinking and attended drunken
parties."[82]

In 1975 the Hungarian youth organization decided to
screen its rank-and-file members on the basis of the
system of personal tasks and duties introduced in 1974.
In accordance with this system, every member of the youth
organization was expected to make a pledge to help fulfill
the union's action program, and then be judged by the end
of the year on how well he had helped to implement it.
The extent to which the youth league's member had fulfilled his or her pledge was decided at the membership
meeting during the evaluation of the leaders and of the
individual members. Following this evaluation, the
membership meeting usually decided by open vote whether
the person deserved to remain a member.[83]

There are several basic tasks that the East European
youth organizations are expected to implement.

1. The most important task is to facilitate the
implementation of decisions, resolutions, and instructions
of the most recent party forum (congress, conference,
Central Committee plenum, and so forth), as well as the
implementation of the national economic plan. In fact,
every East European article or document dealing with the
tasks of the youth organizations lists this as the
organization's most important function. Furthermore,
very often it is stressed that facilitating the implementation of party decisions and policy is the sole criterion
for evaluating the effectiveness of the youth organizations' activity.[84] In order to increase the Komsomol
members' awareness of the importance of this fact, between
June 1976 and March 1977 all members of the Romanian
youth organization were asked to sign a solemn pledge
affirming their "boundless" attachment to the domestic and
foreign policies of the Romanian Communist Party and the
Romanian state, "something which was expected to have a
beneficial effect on their behavior."[85]

2. The youth organizations' members are expected to

take an active part in the "construction of the socialist society." This means direct participation in various construction, agrarian, and industrial enterprises, often serving as an example to other workers, or fulfilling the function of a "front-line" unit.

A catalogue of the industrial enterprises in Hungary sponsored by the Komsomol reads like a list of the major industrial development programs of the country. In recent years the organization has been involved in completing the second phase of the building programs at the Danube River power plant and the Danube oil refinery. They completed the first phase of the building programs at the Szeged oil and natural gas plant and the Tisza River chemical combine. Other projects included the first phase of the Tisza River Locks II construction, the Orenburg Friendship gas line, and the Ust-Ulims celluloid combine, the latter two in cooperation with similar Komsomol groups from the Soviet Union. The Hungarian Communist Youth League's sponsorship also played a role in work done at the Lenin metallurgical plant in Diosgyor, the cooperative efforts of the socialist countries to meet delivery deadlines and increase efficiency in work for the Moscow Olympic Games, and so forth.[86]

Usually, during the summer months (and whenever else it is necessary), members of the youth organizations join special voluntary labor camps, in which they assist agricultural workers. In 1975 it was reported in Hungary that during the previous seventeen years some 500,000 students had spent two weeks in 121 camps.[87] And in 1981, again in Hungary, it was reported that some 100,000-150,000 members participate annually in various industrial activities, and that during the five previous years almost 300,000 students had participated in the voluntary construction camps sponsored by the Communist Youth League.[88]

How to intensify the participation of youth in the country's economic enterprises also focused the attention of the Extraordinary 3rd Congress of the Union of Socialist Polish Youth, which took place in May 1981. In a program declaration adopted by the congress it was explicitly stated that the organization's members had a duty to facilitate the implementation of various industrial and agricultural tasks.[89]

3. The members of the youth organizations are expected to participate in various ideological activities and thus become an integral part of the party's mobilizational apparatus. Their activity extends to cover the entire population. During 1978-1979, 48.8 percent of all CSSR permanent propagandists were members of the Socialist

Youth Union.[90] The ideological activity of the youth
organizations is considered to be "an important factor in
gaining youth's active support for the communist party
policy."[91] Consequently, the effectiveness of the youth
organizations' ideological activity is closely watched and
evaluated by the appropriate organs of the communist party,
with the Central Committee itself occasionally dealing with
the effectiveness of the Komsomol's ideological activity.
Thus on 20 February 1980 the LCY Central Committee had a
plenum that dealt exclusively with the effectiveness of
the youth organization's Marxist education.[92] Often party
leaders, and even the Central Committee secretary general,
take part in a plenum of the Komsomol Central Committee
dealing with its ideological activity. On 15 January 1981,
Todor Zhivkov, BCP Central Committee first secretary, and
Georgi Atanasov and Milko Balev, Central Committee secretaries, took part in a plenum of the Komsomol Central
Committee, that dealt with improving the Komsomol's political and ideological activity.[93] Such plenums often discuss
a specific program on the Komsomol ideological activity
that has previously been adopted by the party Central
Committee. One such plenum in Romania in January 1977
adopted a telegram to Nicolae Ceausescu, expressing the
members' determination "to apply the party's ideological
program by making youth competition a political instrument
and the participation of young people engaged in patriotic
work on major construction sites a 'genuine revolutionary
school for the youth.'"[94] The same plenum appointed
Ceausescu's son Nicu as a secretary of the Union of
Communist Youth Central Committee.[95]

The ideological activity of the youth organization
is closely connected with training, or "bringing up" as
the communist media like to call it, the ideal member of
the socialist society. One German source points out that
the most important aspect of their ideological activity is
"to prepare the youth for their communist future and teaching them to understand and master the shaping of the
developed socialist society as a historical process of
penetrating political, economic, social, and intellectual-
cultural changes . . . to teach them to work, to fight,
to dedicate themselves to socialism, to the victory of
our just cause all over the world. Communist education
aims at instilling revolutionary characteristics in
youth such as respect and love for people and life, strength
of will, discipline, comradeship, and humility."[96]

This task of the youth organizations is also closely
linked with controlling the children's organizations (the

pioneers), whose activity is completely directed by the
youth organizations.

    4. The youth organizations are a recruiting field
for party members. In fact, leadership of the youth
organizations is one of the best jumping boards for the
party leadership itself. Usually, when Komsomol leaders
complete their term--if they have not been dismissed in
disgrace--they join the party Central Committee or may
even be directly promoted to a higher position, as was the
case with Jindrich Polednik in the CSSR, who was elevated
to the post of CPCZ Central Committee secretary at the
end of his term as Komsomol leader.[97]

    On the other hand, the opposite can sometimes
happen, namely, parachuting a member of the Central
Committee to the post of Komsomol leader. Thus on 1
December 1980 Gyorgy Fejti was appointed first secretary
of the Hungarian Communist Youth League Central Committee,
after serving for years as deputy head of one of the MSZMP
Central Committee departments.[98] It is not unusual for the
youth organizations' leaders to hold another high party or
state position. Thus Egon Krenz, leader of the GDR youth
organization FDJ, is also a candidate-member of the SED
Central Committee Politburo, and the leader of the Bulgarian
Komsomol, Stanka Shopova, is also a candidate-member of the
BCP Central Committee and member of the State Council.[99]
The leaders of the East European youth organizations travel
frequently abroad. Although usually they head delegations
of their respective organizations, on occasions they join
official party-state delegations led by the party leader.
Thus Jerzy Jaskiernia, chairman of the Union of Socialist
Polish Youth Main Board Presidium, was one of the members
of the Jaruzelski-led Polish party-state delegation that
visited Romania in June 1982.[100] The close connection
between the communist parties and youth organizations
is further manifested by the frequent party decisions and
resolutions involving the activity of the youth organizations, as well as the direct meetings between party and
Komsomol leaders and the personal messages of the party
leaders to their Komsomol counterparts.

    In December 1967 the BCP Central Committee published
"Theses on Youth."[101] This document meted out the most
severe criticism to which the Komsomol had been subjected
since its founding. According to it, the Komsomol was
"devoid of content," "inactive in daily life," "uninvolved
in sociopolitical, economic, state, and cultural life,"
and so forth. Since then, similar documents continued to
be issued from time to time, the climax being a letter from

Todor Zhivkov to the Komsomol Central Committee "on some
topical problems in the life, activities, and role of youth
and the Komsomol,"[102] dated 18 July 1978. A plenum of the
Komsomol Central Committee met on the following day to
discuss the letter, defined as "a new expression of care
and trust in youth," "a scientifically-founded operative
program for the development of youth," "a remarkable
historic document of intransient significance," and so
forth.[103] Zhivkov himself appeared at the plenum, and
while admitting that great work of positive activity had
been done since the publication of the "theses," he
subjected the Komsomol leadership to serious criticism for
their "incapability," "formalism," "uninspired and un-
imaginative work," and so forth. Naturally, the plenum
adopted pledges on improving the Komsomol activity and
declared Zhivkov's letter "a program for the development
of the Komsomol."[104]

On the occasion of the 40th anniversary of the
Organization of the Albanian Communist Youth (the Labor
Youth of Albania), Enver Hoxha sent the organization a
greetings message in which he stressed the organization's
role in mobilizing the population, implementing the
decisions of the 8th Congress of the Albanian Workers'
Party, and constructing socialism in Albania. Throughout
the message Hoxha reiterated the close connection between
the party and the youth organization, which was repeatedly
called "a loyal auxiliary of our party."[105]

Finally, on 15 February 1982 Erich Honecker, SED
secretary general, greeted Free German Youth leader Egon
Krenz and the Free German Youth Central Committee on their
successes in implementing the decisions of the 10th SED
Congress and other "important projects of socialist
construction, transferred to the FDJ by the party."[106]

5. As with all other auxiliary organizations,
participation in various propaganda campaigns of the regime
is an important task of the East European youth organizations. These organizations are instrumental in organizing
mass rallies and demonstrations, expressing support for
various aspects of their country's foreign policy (and of
course, the Soviet "peace initiatives"), and denouncing
U.S. and NATO policy. Thus at a Free German Youth peace
rally on 22 August 1981 in Halle, the GDR, Egon Kranz reminded the huge audience that "the FDJ members had resolutely opposed all imperialist threats as early as in the
1940s, 1950s and the 1960s."[107] The Bulgarian youth daily
Narodna Mladezh of 4 May 1982 printed a protest letter to
NATO headquarters, which the readers were supposed to cut

out and mail. Similar campaigns are one of the important
aspects of the East European youth organizations' activity.
　　6. Strengthening relations with affiliated organizations abroad is another important task of the youth organizations. It aims at improving the country's relations
with other countries, coordinating the activity of the
youth organizations in the world arena, and combining the
efforts in various international propaganda campaigns.
The framework for this task is usually a long-range
cooperation agreement, signed during a youth delegation
visit, and it encompasses mutual visits, participation in
international congresses, conferences and rallies, and
initiating various declarations or resolutions related to
current international developments. One such bilateral
agreement was the cooperation agreement signed between
the Free German Youth and the delegation of the Syrian
Union of Youth of the Revolution on 3 February 1981 in
Berlin. It provided for expanding the cooperation between
the two organizations, stressed their "fundamental agreement on important questions," and announced that a "friendship week" between the two organizations would be held in
Syria.[108] A similar document was signed in January 1981
between the CSSR Socialist Union of Youth and the
National Union of Algerian Youth. It also provided for
expanding cooperation, exchanging delegations, and
coordinating their international activity.[109]
　　Especially important is the coordination of the
activity of the different socialist countries' youth
organizations. For this purpose, their leaders maintain
constant contacts. At such meetings (such as the meeting between Soviet and Romanian youth leaders of August
1976[110] and the meeting between Polish and GDR youth
leaders in February 1982[111]), the coordination efforts
usually follow specific party instructions and touch upon
current events. The meeting between the Polish and the
GDR youth organizations, which took place shortly after
the declaration of martial law in Poland, stressed the
fact that "forces of imperialism and foreign propaganda
did not succeed in setting the two unions against one
another in the period before 13 December 1981."[112]
　　7. Finally, the youth organizations promote various
patriotic initiatives of internal character, such as
strengthening their relations with army units, recruiting
youth for military training, and so forth. This task is
usually implemented by holding rallies at which internal
politics and recent party decisions are discussed.[113]
Whenever such rallies are held, imperialism, reaction, and

other permenant "enemies of socialism" are usually denounced. Thus an East Berlin rally of GDR youth, aimed at
"winning the best GDR FDJ members for the military profession and strengthening the willpower of the youth,"[114]
in February 1980, took place under the slogan of "realizing
the continuous threat on peace on the part of imperialist
aggression."

It must be pointed out that the activity of the
youth organizations is constantly supervised, controlled,
and criticized by the communist parties. Zhivkov's
criticism of the performance of the Bulgarian Komsomol
has already been mentioned. Such criticism is frequently
expressed by all other East European parties. Thus in 1976
in Albania, Agim Mero, the first secretary of the Albanian
Union of Youth, was ousted for allegedly failing to be re-
educated. Zeri I Popullit of 18 March 1979, mentioning the
case, voiced more criticism of the youth organization's
"ineffective class education," "poor use of leisure time,"
and so forth. During 1979 the Yugoslav press also carried
many articles criticizing various aspects of its youth
organization's activities.[115]

The organizational structure of the youth organizations is an exact copy of the communist parties' structure,
i.e., the hierarchy starts with basic organizations and
moves through the geo-administrative layers to the top
organs (Central Committee, Secretariat, bureau, and auditing commission) elected by the congress, which is the
organizations' supreme organ.

As in the case of the communist parties' congresses,
the congresses of the youth organizations are preceded by
accountability-election meetings, held at the different
levels, at which local leaders report past activities,
present future plans, and stand for reelection. Delegates
to the upper level conferences and the congress are also
elected. Thus, the 29 September-2 October 1977 2nd
Congress of the CSSR Socialist Youth Union was preceded by
district conferences in April, and regional and municipal
conferences in May.[116]

The congress itself takes place along lines which by
now should be familiar to the reader. The opening meeting
is attended by all party and state leaders and the foreign
delegations to the congress. (The absence of Boris Velchev,
BCP Central Committee Politburo member and Central Committee
secretary, from the opening session of the 11th Congress of
the Bulgarian Komsomol on 9 May 1977 was clarified soon
afterwards, when it was announced that he had been removed
from all his posts.[117]) The most important highlights of

the congress are the report of the youth organization's
Central Committee, the speech of the party leader, and the
election of the organization's leading organs. The report
of the youth organization's Central Committee, read by its
leader, resembles the Central Committee report at the party
congress. It surveys the organization's successes, admits
some weaknesses and shortcomings, adheres to every single
detail of the party's domestic and international policies,
in this context condemns imperialism, reaction, colonialism,
racism, and Zionism, praises the USSR foreign policy,
quotes various statements of the party leader, and ends by
pledging loyalty to the party, the CPSU, socialism, and the
party leader personally.[118]

The greetings message of the communist party Central
Committee and the speech of the party leader follow the
same lines. Janos Kadar's speech at the 10th Congress of
the Hungarian Communist Youth League in May 1981,[119]
Honecker's speech at the 11th Parliament of the FDJ (as the
FDJ congress is officially called) in June 1981,[120] and
Zhivkov's speech at the 14th Congress of the Bulgarian
Komsomol in May 1982[121] were in fact summaries of their
speeches at the party congresses (held as usual shortly
before the congresses of their respective countries'
auxiliary organizations). They surveyed party policy,
stated their country's position on every important international issue, praised (lavishly) and criticized (mildly)
aspects of the youth organizations' activities, and wished
them successes in implementing the decisions of the most
recent party congress, as well as the decisions of their
organization's congress.

The party leaders usually receive the leaders of the
foreign delegations. As in all other areas of public life,
there is a special ritual, which is meticulously followed.
The leader of the Soviet delegation is received separately,
before anybody else.[122] On the following day the leaders
of the "fraternal" youth organizations of the socialist
countries are received,[123] and finally (but not obligatory),
there is a reception for the leaders of all the foreign
delegations.

As in the case of the party congresses, some delegates
and the leaders of some of the foreign delegations take the
floor to address the congress. However, as in the case of
the party congresses, the Komsomol congresses are
attended by more than 100 foreign delegations (the 11th
FDJ Parliament was attended by 131 delegations from 101
countries,[124] and the 14th Congress of the Bulgarian
Komsomol by "more than 120 foreign delegations"[125]; hence,

many of the leaders of the foreign delegations (obviously
the less important ones) speak at various friendhip rallies
and not at the congress. Then, on the last day, the first
secretary, the Central Committee, and the other leading
organs are "unanimously" elected.[126]

The newly elected (or reelected) leader concludes
the congress' work with a short speech in which he outlines
the organization's immediate tasks. Gyorgy Fejti, who was
elected first secretary of the Hungarian Communist Youth
League Central Committee at the 10th Congress of the organization, listed the following four tasks: supporting the
party's economic policy; holding more open and active
political discussion coupled with commitment to the policies
of the party; engaging in more work with youth and especially
with teenagers whose values have been affected by "unfavor-
able influences;" and making work "more democratic and
lively."[127]

It seems that at least some of these tasks were
strongly influenced by the situation in Poland at that
time, and particularly by the Extraordinary 3rd Congress
of the Union of Socialist Polish Youth, which took place
at the beginning of May 1981. Although that Congress'
procedure was conventional, some of the debates were rather
open, and various aspects of party life and policies were
criticized. Furthermore, in its Program Declaration the
Polish Youth Organization stated: "We declare cooperation
with the trade unions of the Independent Self-Governing
Trade Union Solidarity, branch unions, and autonomous
unions. We seek our ally in the trade unions, in the
fight for interests of youth and a partner for initiatives,
which serve the social good and improvement of living
conditions."[128]

In conclusion, it seems that the only characteristic
specific to the East European youth organizations is the
age of the members. In all other aspects of their
activity or structure they resemble all other auxiliary
organizations and are likewise completely dominated by
the communist parties, to whose interests and goals they
devote their entire activity.

THE PRESS

Although not an auxiliary organization, the East
European socialist countries' press is an auxiliary
instrument of the communist parties that has the same
basic goals as the auxiliary organizations, namely, to

promote the party's interests. In the words of Zdenek
Cermak, chairman of the CSSR Federal Press and Information
Office:

> Today the news media are again firmly under party
> control and are helping the party to implement its
> policy. They again are serving the working class,
> the interests of socialism and of its further
> development on a national and international scale.
> And as Comrade Vasil Bilak said about the news
> media in his report at the 15th plenum of the
> CPCZ Central Committee in March of 1980: "On the
> whole we may say that our news media are function-
> ing from a clear stand in support of socialist
> class interests, of Marxism-Leninism and socialist
> internationalism, speaking out for the interests
> and will of our people. The party regards the
> press, radio and television workers as its support
> and immediate aktiv. [129]

In addition to their officially declared affiliation
with the communist party, East European journalists are
organized in their Union of Journalists, which exists in
every East European state, along with the creative unions
(writers, painters, composers, etc.), and represents a
typical auxiliary organization, which is another plausible
reason for dealing with the East European press in this
context.

It was Lenin who defined the socialist press as "a
mass propagandist and agitator and a mass organizer."
It was also Lenin who defined news as "agitation by
facts," thus actually pointing out both the tasks and the
essence of the socialist press. In addition to these
basic features of the socialist press, there are several
specific differences between it and the Western press.

1. There is no private ownership of newspapers in
Eastern Europe. The overwhelming majority of the newspapers belong to the communist parties and their auxiliary
organizations, such as the youth organizations and the
trade unions. The few exceptions are the newspapers of
the church or the noncommunist parties, which are strictly
controlled by the official censorship.

2. The East European press is not concerned with the
two major functions of the Western press--providing
information and entertainment. Its main goal is to further
the interest of the communist party. Subjected to the
notion of purposefulness, the East European newspapers

carry only such information as suits the party goals and
policies at a given moment. This means that a large part
of the information can be suppressed, ignored, changed,
or even invented. It would be unrealistic to assume that
there is no bias behind many of the Western newspapers,
and that the information they carry does not serve somebody's interest. However, nowhere else but in the communist
countries is the entire press subjected to one monolithic
interest.

    3. The need to promote the party interests determines
the contents of the East European newspapers. They cannot
include material that is not sound from a Marxist-Leninist
point of view and that does not echo the party line. News
is presented in a heavily censored form so as to exclude
any information unpleasant to the USSR or to the socialist
system, and anything that is complimentary to the West.
Long and boring speeches, toasts, documents, etc., are duly
reported at length by all dailies, something that evokes
the impression that the title is the only difference among
the newspapers. This is especially the case at times of
congresses, conferences, and official visits.

    4. There are many subjects that are considered
important news in the West, but that are as a rule tabu in
Eastern Europe. These include the private lives of the
leaders, their state of health, natural disasters, or
catastrophes (in most cases). On the other hand, there
are other subjects, which no Western newspaper with an eye
on sales would publish because of the risk of boring the
readers to tears or sending them straight to sleep, such
as news on working successes and plan implementation, which
occupy a substantial part of the East European newspapers.

    5. All East European journalists, commentators, and
other newspaper workers are in fact state employees. They
know very well that their jobs depend on their servility.
In most cases they do not have to be told how to write.
Each of them carries a built-in highly sensitive self-
censorship mechanism that tells them what is acceptable and
what is not. In times of doubt, there are other instrumental devices, which help them to see the light.

    Control is the key concept characterizing the East
European press. There are several ways in which this
control is manifested in addition to the journalists'
own self-censorship:

    1. Supervising editors. These editors are on the
editorial board of every East European newspaper. They
are actually censors, whose job is to watch over both the
style and the content of what is written. They (in

addition to the authors, of course), are responsible for
the ideological purity and purposefulness of the material
published.

2. <u>The Central Committee press department</u>. The
Central Committee of each East European communist party has
a press department, subdepartment, or section. This department evaluates the performance of the press and the
individual journalists from the point of view of party
interest. It issues frequent instructions and directives
as to what must occupy the attention of the journalists
at a given moment and disseminates party decisions and
related material.

3. <u>News agencies</u>. In each East European country there
is a news agency (BTA in Bulgaria, CTK in the CSSR, TANJUG
in Yugoslavia, ATA in Albania, AGERPRES in Romania, ADN
in the GDR, and MTI in Hungary) that serves as the main
source of information for the newspapers. This means that
most of the stories and the news items the newspapers get
have already been censored by the press agencies themselves.

4. <u>Summonses to appear before the Central Committee
press supervisors</u>. The editors and the most important
journalists are frequently summoned to the Central
Committee press department, where they are informed on
the current party line and decisions for whose implementation the press is to be involved. It must not be forgotten that most of the press leading personnel are party
members, which provides yet another channel for controlling
their activity.

5. <u>Party and state conferences</u>. There are frequent
conferences and meetings at which the journalists are
briefed by party and state leaders on the international
situation, the party positions on various issues, and other
similar matters. There are subsequent meetings on lower
levels, at which journalists from the major newspapers
and local party leaders brief representatives of the local
press on the same subjects.

6. <u>The Union of Journalists</u>. Finally, there is the
Union of Journalists, whose organizational structure
(accountability meetings, congresses, etc.) serves one main
goal--improving party control over the press.

All this leaves very little freedom of action to the
journalists. In fact, very little of what the East
European newspapers publish consists of original contributions on the part of their staff. According to a
Hungarian newspaper[130] 20 percent of the material it
carries comes from the Hungarian Telegraph Agency (MTI) and
some 20 percent from Centropress (an information pool of

the Hungarian newspaper). About 10 percent of the newspaper space is devoted to advertisement, and 15 percent is allocated to contributions and articles by nonstaff members. Thus only 35 percent remains for the newspaper staff.

Despite this elaborate mechanism of control, in some East European countries there is yet another organ that serves as an overall censorship body. In Romania this body is the Council of Socialist Culture and Education, charged with "guiding the publishing houses and exerting control over their output." This organ is directly responsible for the import of any books and magazines, issues journalist cards, exercises censorship prior to the publication of anything written, and has the right to suspend the dissemination of any publication. In general it "encourages the education of the working people in the spirit of international solidarity with all people building the new order, and with the communists and progressive militants everywhere."[131]

A similar organ--the Federal Press and Information Office--was established by the CSSR in January 1981, on the basis of a CPCZ Central Committee resolution. Its main tasks, as defined by CSSR sources, are: "to assist the CPCZ in providing optimal conditions for the information policy of the mass media, especially so far as the uniform implementation and coordination of this policy is concerned, to ensure good publishing conditions for the newspapers and magazines, to organize and coordinate press conferences, seminars, and training for journalists, to ensure contact between the state administration and the public, to analyze for the needs of responsible organs the activity of selected newspapers, magazines, and radio and television series. It has also been commissioned to register periodicals significant from the viewpoint of entire society, to ensure safeguarding of important state interests in the press and other news media, and to decide on the import and circulation of foreign periodicals in Czechoslovakia."[132]

Despite the tight control and censorship, sometimes unorthodox material still slips through the fingers of the various censors and editors. In such cases there are usually unpleasant consequences for all persons involved.

In December 1976-January 1977 the Bulgarian youth daily Narodna Mladezh carried a discussion on the attitude of young people to physical labor and on various educational matters. On 20 January 1977 the participants in the discussion were Radoy Ralin, a controversial satirist,

and the caricaturist Boris Dimovski. Apparently both
expressed unorthodox opinions, because according to the
Austrian press[133] this particular issue of Narodna
Mladezh was confiscated and six editors, among them
Gencho Abadzhiev, editor-in-chief, were dismissed. One
must note that Radoy Ralin and Boris Dimovski did not
attack the Bulgarian government or the communist party.
They only spoke against the prevailing negative attitude
toward physical labor and the difficulty of gaining
admission to the universities if one is not well connected,
or does not enjoy special status.[134]

When a journalist is found guilty of contributing to
or publishing what is considered an "antigovernmental"
publication across the border, the punishment is much
harder. Thus the Czech journalist Jiri Lederer was
sentenced in October 1977 to three years imprisonment
for allegedly "subverting the country" by conducting a
series of interviews with CSSR writers and sending these
interviews, as well as his manuscripts, to "foreign
addresses."[135]

Senior appointments in the East European newspapers
are strictly party business, the appointees usually being
members of the party Central Committee. For example, in
Bulgaria in July 1977 Yordan Yotov replaced Petur Dyulgerov
as editor of the party daily Rabotnichesko Delo. Petur
Dyulgerov returned to the Central Committee (from where
he had come to Rabotnichesko Delo) and within two years
became a secretary of the BCP Central Committee. Yotov
himself also came from the Central Committee.[136]

Everything that has been said about the East
European press applies equally to the radio and television
services of these countries. They, as well as the press,
are frequently subjected to various party decisions and
resolutions of instructional character, aimed at improving
their performance in order that they may better serve the
party needs. On 8 September 1979 a special plenum of the
RCP Central Committee dealt with the performance of
Romanian Radio and Television. Nicolae Ceausescu, who
chaired the plenum, heavily criticized Romanian Radio and
Television for "formalism" and "superficiality," pointing
out that many television programs were not fulfilling their
role in the revolutionary education of the masses and that
this had to be changed. He called for effective measures
and more stress on ideology in order to form the socialist
consciousness of the Romanian people.[137] Several weeks
later it was announced that Valeriu Pop, the director
general of Romanian Radio and Television, and four of his

deputies had been replaced.[138]

The East European journalists, like all other auxiliary organs of the party, are required to join various propaganda campaigns of the regime, denouncing NATO and U.S. policies and glorifying various aspects of their countries' policies, or even joining campaigns involving a former colleague. When in July 1977 the BTA correspondent in France, Vladimir Kostov, decided to remain in France with his family (he subsequently revealed much information on the functioning of the East European press), the Bulgarian authorities tried to create the impression that he had been kidnapped or brainwashed. The Union of Bulgarian Journalists "appealed to the world public" to help the Kostovs return to Bulgaria. The appeal reiterated the kidnapping-brainwashing theme: "We cannot exclude the possibility that the Kostovs might have been coerced into dubious behavior . . . that he (Kostov) might have been forced into acting in a manner contrary to his convictions and traitorous to his homeland."[139]

All other aspects of the activity of each East European Union of Journalists resemble the activity of the other auxiliary organizations. They too hold a congress (every four or five years) at which the familiar ritual repeats itself. Party and state leaders attend, the union leader reads the accountability report, a Central Committee greetings message is read, the party leader greets the congress, and leading organs are elected. Pledges of loyalty to the party and its line are expressed by all speakers. The greetings message of the Central Committee is a very important component of the congress' work. It usually includes some greetings and much criticism of the journalists' work. In some cases, the congress usually decides to incorporate the Central Committee message in its final resolution and adopt it as "binding guidelines for the future activity of the Union."[140]

Members of the Union of Journalists may be ousted from the union, or their membership cards may simply be revoked or not renewed, which of course represents another form of control over their performance. Following the Soviet invasion of Czechoslovakia in August 1968, some 40 percent of the members of the Union of CSSR Journalists had to leave the union. During the 1970 exchange campaign (membership cards of the union members were "reviewed" and exchanged), the Czech Journalists' Union lost 1,212 members, and the Slovak union 368.[141] On the other hand, servility is rewarded. Better jobs, trips abroad, a permanent job as a representative of some East European newspaper in a Western capital--those are the accepted

rewards. The newspapers themselves are also the
recipients of state awards. Each East European newspaper
proudly shows its medals on the first page, next to the
newspaper's title.

One way of avoiding unpleasant consequences and to
guarantee rewards is constantly to reiterate the leading
role of the party. Rude Pravo Editor Zdenek Horeni,
speaking at the 1977 7th Congress of the CSSR Journalists,
pointed out: "Journalists must consider themselves
fighters for the socialist cause . . . and for the ideal
and goals of the party."[142] In its resolution the congress
pledged "to concentrate in a more powerful, convincing,
and profound way on the advantages of the socialist
system and the socialist way of life, on a more effective
struggle for the ideas of communism, against bourgeois
ideologists, revisionism, and anti-Sovietism."[143]

In the same vein Veselin Yosifov, chairman of the
Union of Bulgarian Journalists, stated at the 5th Congress
of the Bulgarian Journalists (13-14 December 1976): "All
Bulgarian journalists are convinced communists, no matter
if they are party members or not."[144] That statement
summarizes precisely the essence of the East European press.

ARTS AND CULTURE

In Eastern Europe the communist party regards the
arts, or "socialist culture" as it would say, as a most
useful area for reaching the population at large and thus as
a most important instrument for molding a conformist way
of life among the public, in the sense of instilling in the
people a specific attitude toward the party and the
socialist system, to work, to the enemies of socialism,
and indeed to life in general. One could even say that
in the East European socialist countries "culture" is
assigned the task of strengthening the socialist system by
means of indoctrinating the people and instilling in them
a specific set of values. In the words used by the SED
Central Committee: "In the framework of our ideological
tasks, the question of art and literature occupies a very
important place. The many-faced cultural work, carefully
conducted under the direction of our party, exerts a great
deal of influence on the formation of socialist consciousness and a new socialist way of life. Without the profound
educational impact of art, literature, and cultural mass
activities, the socialist education of our working class
and the development of a new relationship of man toward

work and life would be unthinkable."[145]

In particular, this means that arts in the East European political system are required "to spread the ideas of peace and the people's friendship, and contribute to our vigilance and readiness to protect our socialist accomplishment";[146] "to clarify the policies of the party and the socialist state, as well as the policy of the communist and the revolutionary movement throughout the world . . . to introduce to the people specific expressions of patriotism and internationalism . . . to teach them about the role and position of the USSR, its communist party, its peoples, and its efforts to preserve peace. This is not all. With socialist culture and arts we may open an offensive and convincingly introduce socialism in any country abroad";[147] "to enhance continuously the advantages of socialism and its moral criteria in the consciousness of the people . . . to mobilize our forces . . . to become more militant in terms of ideology in struggling against the vestiges and drawbacks in the development of socialism";[148] "to struggle against the cultural aggression of the bourgeoise and the two super-powers"[149] (unmistakably Albanian); and so forth.

The entire point of arts as a party instrument of ideological value was clearly stated by Vasil Bilak, member of the CPCZ Presidium (Politburo) and Central Committee secretary, at the June 1982 2nd Congress of the Czechoslovak Fine Arts Union:

> The party is aware of the invaluable role played by culture and arts in our life. You, sculptors and painters, depict the simple and heroic life of our people, their work as the source of all progress, nature and homeland in its beauty, dramatic expression and historic veracity. The party respects the fact that you are helping to enhance the active attitude of each of our citizens to the ideals of socialism and communism. . . .
> This is why we are striving to make the arts as effective as possible in the service of the noble socialist and communist goals. . . . The communist party and the socialist state are convinced that true artists can only live up to their humanitarian mission when they stand on the side of the workers' class and working people and take part in building the gigantic edifice of a new human civilization. . . .

We cannot tolerate anything that harms socialist
art and society, anything that runs counter to
the ideals of socialist humanism. We will not
allow anyone to sling mud at our people's work,
at either our revolutionary past or socialist
present. . . .
The most important yard stick in evaluating
works of art remains their artistic power, their
ability to enrich the life of man, to teach him to
appreciate the values of life and the fruits of
human work, to value progressive traditions and
the history of the nation, and to help the party
and the socialist community to advance.[150]

What this means in fact is that all forms of cultural
expression in the East European political system must be
ideologically sound, party oriented and controlled, and
free from any "bourgeoise" influence. They must be
permeated by "party-mindedness," which means that the
artist "openly and consistently advocates the ideas of
scientific socialism, agrees with the goals and tasks of
the Marxist-Leninist party as laid down in its programs
and resolutions, and through his personal involvement and
artistic means actively takes part in the shaping of
socialism. . . . Artistic freedom in socialism lies in
the fact that the artist finds himself in full agreement
with what is historically necessary."[151]
It must be pointed out that those principles affect
every means of artistic expression. Articles dealing with
"the effectiveness of music as an instrument of propaganda,
its role in the struggle for peace and in strengthening
the socialist way of life"[152] are nothing unusual in
Eastern Europe. Thus, the artists in the East European
political system are "cultural propagandists," "fighters
on the ideological front," "the party's assistants in instilling socialist values," etc.--phrases frequently used
by the communist parties to describe East European artists.
They also mean that these artists' creativity is limited
to certain specific patterns and directed to serve party
goals, as the Czechoslovak party daily Rude Pravo put it
so tellingly: "In our life there is no place for art that
meets with the sympathy of our ideological enemies, art
that is indifferent to the endeavors of our socialist
state, that estranges man from reality and distorts that
reality. There is no place . . . for works that elicit
bad qualities in people, that lead to hopelessness,
cynical views of the world, pessimism, and admiration of

violence."[153]

In Eastern Europe cultural activity is evaluated and
judged by its ideological and indoctrinational effectiveness and impact. There is little doubt that intellectual
and artistic output that lacks a clear-cut indoctrinational
purpose and does not openly militate for party policy cannot be tolerated. The party makes every effort to neutralize
the influence of "hostile culture": "The struggle to block
the path to the degenerate capitalist, bourgeois and revisionist culture, and preserve the national character and
ideological purity of our proletarian culture and art
contributes an important aspect to the work of the party
and its levers directly connected with the protection of
the moral and political purity of our new man and with the
conception of the correct implementation of the struggle
against foreign manifestations and liberal attitudes toward
them. . . . The party recommends that a critical revolutionary attitude be maintained toward foreign culture."[154]

An absolute precondition for guaranteeing the proper
functioning of art is tight party control of all forms of
artistic expression. This control is exercised through
frequent decisions of leading party organs and forums, in
the form of instructions, specific directives to the
artistic or creative unions, constant contact between these
unions and party bodies in charge of culture and ideology,
and finally--through the system of the stick and the carrot--
awards and prizes for the obedient, and punishment, including arrest (and in the past, also death), for the dis-
obedient.

As is every other area of life in Eastern Europe,
the arts are also subjected to the national annual
economic plan and Five-Year Plan.[155] In these plans "the
general goals of the arts for the relevant period, according to uniform principles and relevant party and state
documents,"[156] are articulated. With regard to the national
plans, it must be pointed out that the arts are assigned
various economic tasks in Eastern Europe. Stressing that
"culture and the arts are inseparable from economic and
social policy," the SED theoretical organ Einheit declared
in June 1981: "It is imperative to strengthen and deepen
the understanding of the creators of art and culture of the
requirements of our party's economic strategy for the
1980's. . . . Advances in culture and the arts affect the
tempo of our economic performance improvement."[157] In yet
another article, Einheit spoke of the role of the arts in
"boosting labor productivity and high labor efficiency"
and "stimulating the workers' readiness for achievement

and creativity."[158]

In their efforts to prevent the publication or release of any artistic works that do not reflect the official ideology and serve the goals of the communist party and the socialist system, the GDR authorities went as far as preparing a "Law for the Protection of the Professional Designation of Writers."[159] The law was intended to designate as criminals any politically embarrassing or anti-doctrinaire authors because of "antisocialist tendencies," and even provide legal justification for jailing and "re-educating" them.[160]

Decisions dealing with culture and the arts are fre-quently issued by the East European communist parties' Central Committees, which often devote special plenums to these issues. Every party congress analyzes the country's cultural activity since the previous congress, criticizing shortcomings and issuing specific redommendations and instructions.

A characteristic approach was that in Ceausescu's report at the 12th RCP Congress in November 1977. He had few words of praise for the literary and artistic efforts or Romanian artists and writers since the 11th RCP Congress. His speech provided both prescriptions for artistic work and an attempt to dictate the life-style of artists. The "constant presence of writers and artists in the whirlpool of constructive life and work" was said to be of "decisive importance." Writers and artists must not only use the work of socialist construction as their primary source of inspiration, but must "themselves participate in the heroic work of building the new society." The type of literature and art required were clearly defined: "Litera-ture is called upon to reveal in convincing fashion the new human conditions of our society, the ideals, worries, and aspirations of the new man, his ever richer spiritual universe, his progressive moral virtues and characteristics. Literature must militate for the triumph of (all that is) new, for the ideals of justice and social freedom. While castigating negative aspects and backward ideas, literature must develop man's confidence in his strength and in the superiority of the noble revolutionary ideals, while emphasizing the superiority of the socialist society."[161]

However, the East European communist parties do not wait five years for their congresses in order to issue instructions, criticism, or praise to the arts. As already mentioned, the parties' Central Committees, and even Politburos, frequently devote plenums and meetings to cultural and artistic matters. To cite only one character-istic example (among many), the 15th plenum of the CPCZ

Central Committee in August 1980 dealt with one subject only--the Ideological Functions of Literature and Art-- and placed "particularly high demands"[162] on this area.

It is not unusual for some party organ, or even the Central Committee, to deal thoroughly with one particular artistic branch, or even with a single work of literature or art. The Albanian party daily Zeri I Popullit of 26 September 1981 reported a plenum of the Union of Artists and Writers, at which two recent novels--Under the Burning Arches and Typhoon on the Sea Coast--were criticized for their "schematic construction, implausible presentation of the struggle of the class enemies, and inaccurate picture of political situations."[163]

The outstanding books of the Bulgarian novelists Dimitur Dimov (Tobacco) and Dimitur Talev (Prespa's Bells, Ilinden), were at first severely criticized by the official circles (and critics), but later lavishly praised after the BCP Central Committee had declared them masterpieces. The case of the film A 33-Year Old Woman was reversed. This Bulgarian film, released in 1982, deals with the fate of a divorced mother who has to cope with harassment, blackmail, and sexist attitudes on the part of her male colleagues, and ends up using exactly the same methods against them. The film, which included a scene in which a fox is devoured by dogs (apparently a comparison between the cruel laws of the animal world and the norms of the socialist society), was first acclaimed by the film critics.[164] Then on 7 May 1982 the organ of the Bulgarian Communist Party--Rabotnichesko Delo--denounced the makers of the film, accusing them of distorting socialist reality and deviating from the artistic line and instructions of the party. With reference to the film's epilogue, which implies that the story was based on fact, the BCP daily stated: "It might be so, but realistic art is not subject to the facts, and it is not the facts that play the most important role in art, but their artistic generalization."[165]

The entire Macedonian film industry was severely criticized at a plenum of the Presidium of the Central Committee of the Macedonian Communist Party in May 1981. The Macedonian film makers were accused of "passivity," and "unmotivated work," and it was pointed out by the party that "more effective work by the communists is needed in the film industry."[166] The film industries in Romania[167] and the GDR[168] were also criticized by these countries' respective communist parties for "ideological and political deficiencies" and other similar weaknesses.

The leaders of the East European communist parties

often consider themselves connoisseurs of the arts and maintain close contacts with artists and writers. When meetings
between the leaders and the artists take place, they usually
follow somewhat informal lines and involve both paternal
criticism and authoritative instructions. A meeting between
young Bulgarian writers and Todor Zhivkov took place on
2 December 1977. Trying to connect the party slogan of "high
quality and effectiveness" with artistic productivity,
Zhivkov expressed satisfaction with the work of Bulgaria's
young writers, dwelt on party policy in the area of literature and other areas, discussed the interrelationship between "politics and poetry, politics and literature, and
politics and the arts," refuted half-jokingly the existence
of dissidence in Bulgaria, and elaborated on the political
role of literature.[169]

A similar meeting between the entire CPCZ leaderhip
and the "foremost Czech and Slovak artists" took place on
24 April 1978. The assembled artists were greeted by Gustav
Husak, who stressed the party's appreciation of the artists'
"political commitment" and their contribution to the CSSR's
socialist construction. He stressed that the party was
deeply interested in developing socialist art and outlined
some of this art's characteristics.[170]

Sometimes the meetings between artists and party or
political organs have a more specific character. Thus on
10 May 1982 a meeting took place between the Bulgarian
Union of Composers and the leadership of the Main Political
Administration of the Bulgarian Army, at which a protocol
on cooperation between the two organs was signed.[171] Hard
as it may be to imagine a baton-wielding gunner, such agreements are a common phenomenon in all East European countries.

Each sphere of the arts in Eastern Europe--literature,
music, painting, etc.--has its own "creative union."
Membership in the writers' union, composers' union, and so
forth, is in fact a precondition of creating (or at least
publishing, exhibiting, etc.). Each union has its own
party organization, which holds frequent meetings and
serves as a constant liaison between the communist party
and the respective union. Thus on 14 April 1977 the party
organization of the Union of Bulgarian Writers reviewed
the output of Bulgarian writers. It repeatedly referred
to the "spirit of the BCP Central Committee July 1976
plenum" (whose proceedings, incidentally, have never been
published) and discussed the "alarming question of the
ideological richness and power of contemporary Bulgarian
literature, which is lagging behind in its political
zeal."[172]

Not only does each artistic union hold conferences and congresses that are attended by the party leaders, but there are the infrequent overall congresses of culture dealing in general terms with the ideological contents, goals, and tasks of culture. The 3rd Congress of Bulgarian Culture, which took place from 18 to 20 May 1977, was attended by 1,800 delegates and guests from 41 countries. BCP Politburo member Aleksandur Lilov read the party message to the congress, and the late Lyudmila Zhivkova, then chairman of the Committee on Culture, read the main report entitled "Dimensions of Culture," stressing that the arts were one of the regime's main instruments in the struggle against imperialist ideological subversion.[173]

A similar congress took place in June 1982 in Romania. Called "The 2nd Congress of Political Education and Socialist Culture," it was attended by 6,000 delegates and many foreign guests. Elena Ceausescu ("Academician Dr. Eng, RCP Central Committee Political Executive Committee member, and first deputy chairman of the Council of Ministers"--to mention only her important titles) read the main report, which dealt with subjecting more closely Romania's cultural life to the decisions and guidelines issued by the 12th RCP Congress.[174]

Then there are the "Fine Arts Conferences" or congresses of the "Art Workers' Union," where again art is discussed as a subject in itself. The procedure is familiar--report, party leaders present, Central Committee greetings message, and a resolution usually calling for "the more active implementation of the party instructions in the area of the arts." Romania's Fine Arts Conference of 22-23 June 1978, at which Ceausescu demanded from the artists "a stronger commitment to party needs and goals,"[175] was one such conference.

Finally, the congresses of the individual artistic unions also follow the established pattern of the mass organizations' congresses. All are attended by the party and state leaders, the top leader frequently speaking at the congress; the union's leader presents the report on the union's activity (admits shortcomings, reviews successes, pledges new successes and loyalty to the party line), the greetings message of the Central Committee is read, local and foreign delegates greet the congress, and a new leadership is elected or reelected. There is nothing unusual in a congress of sculptors adopting a resolution expressing "determination to do everything possible in the field of the arts, in order to implement the cultural-political program of the most recent party congress,"[176]

or a congress of musicians pledging "new and creative
works in the name of socialism and activity that are in
harmony with the principles of the party cultural policy
and the decisions of the 15th CPCZ Congress."[177]

Josef Havlin, CPCZ Central Committee secretary,
speaking at the 1978 Congress of CSSR Composers, listed the
following tasks of the union:

1. Composing works instrumental in the formation
   of the socialist way of life and aiding the
   education of man;
2. Focusing works on optimistic subjects, because
   life in socialist society is not dominated by
   fear of the future;
3. Exploiting to a greater extent the wealth of
   music created over thirty years of socialism
   in the CSSR and the other socialist states;
4. Concentrating innovative efforts on content
   rather than form.[178]

Even congresses of dramatic artists' unions are not
devoid of ideological content. Thus, the 25-26 April 1977
Congress of Czech and Slovak Dramatic Artists pointed out
that the "repertoire of theater must be inspired by the
ideals of socialism, and the creative interests of the
artists must turn toward party-oriented art."[179]

The most important congress is the Congress of the
Writers' Union. After all, the written word is one of the
main propaganda instruments and therefore the loyalty of the
writers is not to be underestimated and, in fact, must be
constantly enhanced and demonstrated. It is the writers
who more frequently than anyone else are reminded of the
party demands "to put the emphasis on the image of the
communist . . . the main hero of our time. The communist
. . . should reign over the entire territory of literature."[180] At their congresses the union's tasks are
usually related to implementing the overall decisions of the
most recent party congress, and thus the organic unity
between literature and party needs is reiterated.

Sometimes the artistic unions are called upon to
participate in the regime's propaganda campaigns. Thus in
October 1981 the GDR Writers' Union initiated a "meeting
of FRG and GDR writers for peace"[181] and the Union of CSSR
Writers published an "open letter to Western writers" asking
them to intensify their struggle for peace.[182] On other
occasions writers are briefed on recent and topical
international developments affecting their country. Thus

on 19 March 1982 an extended plenum of the Albanian Union
of Writers and Artists was addressed by Ramiz Alia, member
of the Albanian Workers' Party Politburo and Central
Committee secretary, who briefed them on the Albanian-
Yugoslav relations following the events in the Kosovo
province in Yugoslavia and on "foreign propaganda"
related to that issue.[183]

The artistic unions of the socialist countries maintain close contacts and hold frequent meetings at which
they exchange experience and coordinate their efforts.
On such occasions the main speakers are the representatives
of the Soviet creative unions, who usually are in charge
of the coordinating activity.[184]

Deviation from the party line is a serious matter,
the consequences of which may vary from a more or less
mild rebuke to something much more severe. It is not unusual for a party daily (like Belgrade's Borba of 8 December
1979) to describe the exhibition of a painter as a "malicious
diletantist, pretentious, and manipulative attempt at influencing politics." (The exhibition depicted the bitter
existence of the Yugoslav workers employed in Western
Europe and included portraits of several Serbian dissidents.)

A more serious consequence may simply be a ban on
creating. Both Letteres Francoises of 10 February 1971 and
Vienna's Die Presse of 11 March 1971 carried a list of
banned CSSR books--literature written for the drawer.

Many CSSR movie directors found themselves unable to
work in the CSSR after the 1968 Soviet invasion. Some of
them (Milos Forman) left and started a new career abroad,
while others (Elmar Klos, Jan Kadar) were simply silenced.[185]

Arrests are rare today, but not unusual. On 23 October
1974 the List Publishing House in Munich revealed that the
Hungarian writer Gyorgy Konrad had been arrested in his
home the previous day. A spokesman for the firm further
disclosed that the sociologist Ivan Szelenyi and the poet
Tamas Szentjoby had also been arrested a few days earlier.
In all cases smuggling uncensored manuscripts to the West
were involved.[186]

In 1976 in the CSSR, a group of CSSR rock musicians
were arrested and sentenced for "spreading decadent
nihilistic and antisocialist concepts through unauthorized
performances and organized hooliganism."[187] The trial,
which captured international attention, was held under
strict security provisions, with police guards and dogs
sealing off the court building.[188]

One should remember that despite all this, today

dissidents are treated somewhat better than they were in the past. In Czechoslovakia in 1952, twenty-five noncommunist poets, writers, essayists, and literary critics were put on trial and convicted. Some were executed; others were sentenced to life imprisonment or long-term sentences. The party organ Rude Pravo of 22 and 27 April 1952 called them "a group of spies and saboteurs . . . who prepared a conspiracy against the republic under the direction of the Wall Street agency, the so-called Green International."[189] Those who remained alive were released following an amnesty in 1960.[190] This was the stick. The carrot works at least as effectively. It consists of large salaries and commissions for the members of the unions, and various privileges, awards, and medals, most of which carry financial and social benefits. The Kossuth Prize in Hungary, the Dimitrov Award in Bulgaria, and similar awards in all other East European countries aim at rewarding not only artistic excellence, but also loyalty, dedication to the cause of socialism, and servility. There are extraordinary awards indeed for the most outstanding artists and writers, such as membership in the party Central Committee and the national assembly. There are also special titles such as People's Artist, Eminent Artist, and others, which provide the regime with yet another means of showing appreciation and rewarding artistic loyalty and dedication.

In conclusion, there is one main difference between the East European artistic unions and the other auxiliary organizations of the communist parties. While the activity of the other auxiliary organizations focuses on topical, short-range goals, culture and the arts serve long-range goals related to indoctrination, spreading communist ideology, and educating the new man, the ideal member of the socialist society, by instilling in him a set of values formulated by the regime. Nevertheless, because this activity has an obvious mobilizational character whose nature is determined by the needs and goals of the regime, culture and the arts in Eastern Europe serve as another auxiliary instrument of the communist parties.

OTHER AUXILIARY ORGANIZATIONS

This chapter has dealt with the most important auxiliary organizatins and instruments. The list has not been exhausted, and a few more will be mentioned briefly.

Women's Organizations

Women's organizations exist in every East European country. They are associated with the World Federation of Democratic Women (a pro-Soviet front organization) and their activity is directed by the communist party. It comprises mostly of taking part in various propaganda campaigns, participating in the mobilizational effort of the regime, "assisting the participation of women in work and social life,"[191] and "increasing the fervor and revolutionary drive of the women."[192]

The eighth day of March is International Women's Day. It provides an occasion for a mass rally, and there is one in all East European countries. The event is usually attended by at least some of the party and state leaders, who also express the party's gratitude for the organization's auxiliary activity. In the words of Vasil Bilak, member of the CPCZ Presidium and Central Committee secretary: "I want to express our profound gratitude to and sincerely thank the Czechoslovak women for their self-less, conscientious work in the factories and in the fields, in the services and in trade, in education, the health services and culture--everywhere where they are contributing with their work to the fulfillment of the goals adopted by the 16th CPCZ Congress--and for their concern for a satisfied and happy life for their families."[193]

This occasion is also considered an appropriate opportunity for holding "an objective and cordial talk on the present and future of the country and on the everyday joys and worries of women."[194] The leadership of the women's organization usually pledges more efforts in their activity and in the struggle for peace. Greetings messages are often sent to the party Central Committee and the World Federation of Democratic Women. For example, at the 8 March 1982 celebration in Sofia (attended by the entire Politburo), telegrams were sent to the World Federation of Democratic Women and to the UN secretary general, "appealing for peace and for nuclear disarmament, as well as for cooperation in Europe and throughout the world."[195]

On Women's Day the East European parties award outstanding members of the women's organizations for their contributions to implementing party and state goals: "On the occasion of the International Women's Day the Presidential Council of the Hungarian Republic awarded high decorations to those who exert outstanding work in the construction of Hungary's socialist new order, improving the working and living conditions of working women. The

Order of Labor, Golden Category, was awarded to six, the
Silver to forty-nine, and the Bronze to fifty-three
persons."[196]

The women's organizations hold conferences and congresses that are no different from those of other auxiliary
organizations; i.e., they have delegates from the country
and from abroad, the party and state leadership attend, there
is an accountability report, a Central Committee greetings
message, an election of the new leadership, and resolutions
of propaganda character. The party leader usually also
speaks at the session and greets the women. His speech
invariably touches upon the domestic and international
situation and elaborates on "the women's role in the
socialist society."[197]

Sports Unions

Sports unions not only manage the country's sports
life, but also engage in party-oriented activity of
mobilizational character. The importance of sports in the
socialist world is exceptional. Being one of the most
important areas of demonstrating the supremacy of the
socialist social system (implying that the system that
produces better athletes is superior in other areas, too),
sports are considered an area of extreme political importance
for the party and the state. Therefore it is not unusual
for the party Politburo to have sessions devoted exclusively
to sports. On 16 November 1976 the RCP Central Committee
Political Executive Committee held a special meeting on
sports matters. It "criticized various aspects of sport,
its organization and leadership, and the training of
sportsmen and sports cadres, calling for a strengthening
of discipline and order throughout sport, and avoiding any
tolerating of unwarranted features, including the immoral
behavior of sportsmen."[198] The RCP Political Executive
Committee approved guidelines for physical education and
sports, as well as a concomitant program for the following
five years with emphasis on mass sports activities.[199] On
other occasions the RCP leadership has dealt with separate
sports branches, often making operative decisions, such as
the decision to order the Romanian soccer coach Stefan
Covac, who had previously served as trainer of the French
national team, to whip the Romanian national soccer team
into shape.[200]

The East European sports unions also hold congresses
and conferences, which follow the pattern of those of the
auxiliary organizations. It is usually the Central

Committee greetings message to these congresses that reveals
the auxiliary-mobilizational nature of the sports unions.
Thus the Central Committee greetings to the 25-26 February
1977 Congress of the Bulgarian Sports Union reminded the
delegates that the organization and management of sports
must be improved "in the spirit of the 11th BCP Congress
and July 1976 Central Committee plenum." Then the message
went on: "Today, when the ideological duel has become the
main battlefield in the struggle between the two world
systems, international sports competitions more than ever
acquire a political character. . . . Therefore it is a
standing obligation for sports trainers, managers, and
sportsmen systematically and perseveringly to master the
fundamentals of Marxism-Leninism, to build up in themselves
a scientific world view, and to live with the problems of
the country."[201]

We have dealt with only a few (but important)
auxiliary organizations, which are only a small part of
the existing network of such instruments and organizations.
The list is long. It includes all professional associations (teachers, scientists, etc.) the Union of Lawyers,
the Political Science Association, the Union for Cooperation
with the Army, and many more. They differ more in their
names than in anything else. Their organizational structure,
pattern of activity, and goals are identical. Each and
every one of them serves its country's communist party
(and the world communist movement) in its own way, its
activity being closely controlled and evaluated by the
party. Their existence has one supreme goal: to further
the interests of the communist party by mobilizing the
population to greater efforts in implementing party
decisions and enhancing their loyalty to the party and
the socialist system.

NOTES

1. Nepszabadsag (Hungary), 22 April 1976.
2. Budapest MTI in English, 1734 GMT, 24 January
1981; Daily Report (FBIS), 26 January 1981.
3. RFE Situation Report, Hungary, 29 September 1976.
4. Budapest Domestic Service in Hungarian, 1730 GMT,
14 March 1981; Daily Report (FBIS), 18 March 1981.
5. RFE Situation Report, Bulgaria, 23 June 1977.
6. Ibid.
7. RFE Situation Report, Romania, 29 January 1980.

8. RFE Situation Report, Hungary, 25 March 1981.

9. RFE Situation Report, Bulgaria, 23 June 1977.

10. Prague Domestic Service in Czech, 1630 GMT, 24 April 1981; Daily Report (FBIS), 27 April 1981.

11. Rabotnichesko Delo (Bulgaria), 24 April 1981.

12. Ibid.

13. See GDR National Front Appeal, in Neues Deutschland, 28 April 1981; Daily Report (FBIS), 30 April 1981; Poland's National Unity Front Declaration, in Trybuna Ludu, 27 February 1980; FBIS East European Report, no. 1782, 30 April 1980; etc.

14. Prague Domestic Service in Czech, 1130 GMT, 18 April 1981; Daily Report (FBIS), 19 April 1981.

15. Prague Domestic Service in Czech, 1730 GMT, 18 April 1981; Daily Report (FBIS), 19 April 1981.

16. Magyar Nemzet (Hungary), 14 March 1981; Daily Report (FBIS), 23 March 1981.

17. Ibid.

18. BTA in English, 1830 GMT, 20 August 1981; Daily Report (FBIS), 21 August 1981.

19. Pravda (Bratislava), 17 September 1981; Daily Report (FBIS), 21 September 1981.

20. Sofia BTA in English, 1345 GMT, 5 May 1981; Daily Report (FBIS), 6 May 1981.

21. Prague CTK in English, 2009 GMT, 2 May 1981; Daily Report (FBIS), 3 May 1981.

22. CSSR--Kabul Bakhtiar in English, 0420 GMT, 6 July 1981; Daily Report (FBIS), 8 July 1981; Bulgaria--BTA in English, 1840 GMT, 15 June 1981; Daily Report (FBIS), 17 June 1981; etc.

23. Sofia BTA in English, 1835 GMT, 14 September 1981; Daily Report (FBIS), 17 September 1981.

24. Tribuene (East Berlin), 4 November 1980, p. 3.

25. Prace (CSSR), 12 May 1981, p. 3; Daily Report (FBIS), 18 May 1981.

26. Sofia BTA in English, 1335 GMT, 11 December 1981; Daily Report (FBIS), 15 December 1981.

27. Munca de Partid (Romania), February 1981, pp. 27-31.

28. Ibid.

29. Ibid.

30. Ibid.

31. Trud (Bulgaria), 26 August 1981.

32. Ibid., 27 August 1981.

33. Tirana ATA in English, 1000 GMT, 11 February 1982; Daily Report (FBIS), 12 February 1982.

34. Interview of Sandor Jakab, first deputy secretary

of the Hungarian Trade Union National Council, <u>Nepszabadsag</u>, 20 April 1980.

35. East Berlin Voice of the GDR Domestic Service in German, 1700 GMT, 25 May 1981; <u>Daily Report</u> (FBIS), 13 May 1981.

36. Tirana ATA in English, 1000 GMT, 11 February 1982; <u>Daily Report</u> (FBIS), 12 February 1982.

37. <u>Zivot Strany</u> (CSSR), no. 20, 22 September 1980.

38. <u>Munca de Partid</u>, February 1982, p. 45; FBIS East European Report, no. 1995, 2 April 1982.

39. <u>Pruga e Partise</u> (Albania), no. 5, May 1980, p. 76.

40. <u>Tribuene</u>, 4 November 1980, p. 4.

41. <u>Munca de Partid</u>, February 1982, p. 45; FBIS East European Report, no. 1995, 2 April 1982.

42. <u>Pruga e Partise</u>, no. 5, May 1980, p. 76.

43. Ibid.

44. <u>Munca de Partid</u>, February 1982, p. 45; FBIS East European Report, no. 1995, 2 April 1982.

45. RFE Situation Report, Hungary, 27 June 1978.

46. <u>Prace</u>, 12 May 1981; <u>Daily Report</u> (FBIS), 18 May 1981.

47. Sofia BTA in English, 1850 GMT, 27 August 1981; <u>Daily Report</u> (FBIS), 28 August 1981.

48. Ibid.

49. B. Hazan, "Involvement by Proxy--Eastern Europe and the PLO," in <u>The Palestinians and the Middle East Conflict</u>, ed. Gabriel Ben-Dor (Tel Aviv: Turtledove, 1978), pp. 321-322.

50. RFE RAD Background Report, SFRY, no. 166, 26 July 1978.

51. <u>Vecernje Novosti</u> (Yugoslavia), 3 October 1978, reporting a speech of Jure Bilic, Central Committee member and president of the Croatian National Assembly.

52. <u>Prace</u>, 27 January 1982; <u>Daily Report</u> (FBIS), 3 February 1982.

53. <u>Nepszabadsag</u>, 19 October 1980.

54. <u>Scinteia</u> (Romania), 16 November 1980.

55. Tirana ATA in English, 1135 GMT, 6 June 1982; <u>Daily Report</u> (FBIS), 8 June 1982.

56. <u>Prace</u>, 12 May 1981; <u>Daily Report</u> (FBIS), 18 May 1981.

57. <u>Rude Pravo</u> (CSSR), 8 December 1980.

58. Prague Domestic Service in Czech, 1430 GMT, 25 February 1981; <u>Daily Report</u> (FBIS), 26 February 1981.

59. <u>Prace</u>, 29 July 1981; <u>Daily Report</u> (FBIS), 3 August 1981.

60. <u>Nepszabadsag</u>, 19 October 1980.

61. Rude Pravo, 8 December 1980.

62. Scinteia, 16 November 1980.

63. RFE RAD Background Report, Hungary, no. 243, 10 October 1980.

64. Magyar Hirek (Hungary), 24 September 1980.

65. Trud (Bulgaria), 13 January 1982.

66. Ibid., 9 April 1982.

67. RFE Situation Report, CSSR, 1 June 1977.

68. Trud, 9 April 1982.

69. Ibid.

70. Ibid.

71. Bucharest AGRERPRES in English, 1120 GMT, 7 April 1981; Daily Report (FBIS), 9 April 1981; Budapest Domestic Service in Hungarian, 1100 GMT, 12 December 1980; Daily Report (FBIS), 15 December 1981.

72. RFE Situation Report, Hungary, 13 January 1981.

73. Prague Domestic Television Service in Czech and Slovak, 1240 GMT, 15 April 1982; Daily Report (FBIS), 16 April 1982.

74. Sofia Domestic Service in Bulgarian, 0600 GMT, 10 April 1982, Daily Report (FBIS), 12 April 1982.

75. Puna (Albania), 10 June 1982; FBIS East European Report, no. 2031, 9 July 1982.

76. East Berlin ADN International Service in German, 1720 GMT, 23 April 1982; Daily Report (FBIS), 26 April 1982.

77. East Berlin ADN International Service in German, 1741 GMT, 23 April 1982; Daily Report (FBIS), 26 April 1982.

78. After the Soviet Konsomol, the name Konsomol will be used for all these youth organizations, although only one of the East European countries--Bulgaria--actually uses it.

79. Iwe Tagesdienst (Bonn), no. 40, 12 March 1980.

80. RFE Situation Report, CSSR, 5 October 1977.

81. RFE Situation Report, Hungary, 18 May 1976.

82. RFE Situation Report, Bulgaria, 9 February 1977.

83. RFE Situation Report, Hungary, 18 February 1975.

84. Mlada Fronta (CSSR), 12 February 1980.

85. Scinteia Tineretului (Romania), 31 May 1976.

86. RFE Situation Report, Hungary, 21 March 1980.

87. Ibid., 2 September 1977.

88. Report of the KISZ Central Committee at the 10th KISZ Congress, Budapest Domestic TV Service in Hungarian, 1900 GMT, 29 May 1981; Daily Report (FBIS), 4 June 1981.

89. Wolka Mlodych (Poland), 10 May 1981.

90. Mlada Fronta, 12 February 1980.

91. Ibid.

92. RFE RAD Background Report, SRFY, no. 43, 26 February 1980.

93. Sofia Domestic Service in Bulgarian, 1430 GMT, 15 January 1981; Daily Report (FBIS), 16 January 1981.
94. RFE Situation Report, Romania, 20 January 1977.
95. Ibid.
96. Einheit (East Berlin), vol. 35, no. 3, March 1980.
97. RFE Situation Report, CSSR, 8 December 1977.
98. Ifju Kommunista (Hungary), no. 1, February 1981, p. 1.
99. Otechestven Front (Bulgaria), 18 June 1981.
100. Sztandar Mlodych (Poland), 16 June 1982; FBIS East European Report, no. 2034, 16 July 1982.
101. Rabotnichesko Delo (Bulgaria), 1 December 1967.
102. Sofia Domestic Service in Bulgarian, 1930 GMT, 19 July 1978; Daily Report (FBIS), 21 July 1978.
103. Rabotnichesko Delo, 21 July 1978.
104. RFE Situation Report, Bulgaria, 27 July 1978.
105. Tirana ATA in English, 0700 GMT, 24 November 1981; East European Report, no. 1952, 23 December 1981.
106. Neues Deutschland, 17 February 1982; Daily Report (FBIS), 22 February 1982.
107. Neues Deutschland, 24 August 1981; Daily Report (FBIS), 26 August 1981.
108. East Berlin ADN International Service in German, 1749 GMT, 3 February 1981; Daily Report (FBIS), 4 February 1981.
109. Prague CTK in English, 1734 GMT, 14 January 1981; Daily Report (FBIS), 15 January 1981.
110. Scinteia, 2 through 8 August 1976.
111. Sztandar Mlodych, 22 February 1982.
112. Ibid.
113. Neues Deutschland, 30 January 1981; Daily Report (FBIS), 4 February 1981.
114. Junge Generation (East Berlin), vol. 34, no. 2, February 1980.
115. Polet (Yugoslavia), December 1979, p. 17.
116. RFE Situation Report, CSSR, 5 October 1977.
117. Rabotnichesko Delo, 10 May 1977.
118. See Egon Krenz report to the 11th FDJ Parliament, East Berlin TV Service in German, 0753 GMT, 2 June 1981; Daily Report (FBIS), 18 June 1981.
119. Budapest Domestic Service in Hungarian, 1630 GMT, 29 May 1981.
120. East Berlin TV Service in German, 0800 GMT, 5 June 1981; Daily Report (FBIS), 18 June 1981.
121. Narodna Mladezh (Bulgaria), 28 May 1982.
122. Sofia Domestic Service in Bulgarian, 1500 GMT, 25 May 1982; Daily Report (FBIS), 27 May 1982.

123.   Sofia BTA in English, 1315 GMT, 26 May 1982;
Daily Report (FBIS), 27 May 1982.
124.   East Berlin ADN International Service in German,
1523 GMT, 5 June 1981; Daily Report (FBIS), 18 June 1981.
125.   Narodna Mladezh, 25 May 1982.
126.   East Berlin International Service in German,
1523 GMT, 5 June 1981; Daily Report (FBIS), 18 June 1981.
127.   RFE Situation Report, Hungary, 15 June 1981.
128.   Walka Mlodych (Poland), 10 May 1981; FBIS East
European Report, no. 1954, 29 December 1981.
129.   Nova Mysl (CSSR), no. 4, March 1982, p. 25;
FBIS East European Report, no. 2024, 22 June 1982.
130.   Naplo (Veszprem), 12 May 1970.
131.   RFE Situation Report, Romania, 19 January 1978.
132.   Nova Mysl, no. 4, March 1982, p. 25; FBIS East
European Report, no. 2924, 22 June 1982.
133.   Die Presse (Vienna), 21 February 1977.
134.   Narodna Mladezh, 20 January 1977.
135.   RFE Situation Report, CSSR, 16 January 1980.
136.   RFE Situation Report, Bulgaria, 5 August 1977.
137.   Scinteia, 9 September 1979.
138.   Buletinul Oficial (Romania), no. 85, 2 November
1979.
139.   BTA in English, 11 July 1977, and all Bulgarian
dailies of 12 July 1977.
140.   Congress of the CSSR Union of Journalists, June
1977; RFE Situation Report, CSSR, 22 June 1977.
141.   Novinar (CSSR), no. 3, March 1972, and no. 5,
May 1972; RFE Situation Report, CSSR, 22 June 1977.
142.   Rude Pravo, 19 June 1977.
143.   Ibid.
144.   RFE Situation Report, Bulgaria, 17 December 1976.
145.   E. Schubbe (ed.), Dokumente Zur Kunst Literatur
and Kulturpolitik der SED (Stuttgart, 1972), p. 814.
146.   Einheit, vol. 36, no. 1, January 1981, p. 58.
147.   Josef Havlin, CPCZ Central Committee secretary,
in Rude Pravo, 5 December 1981; FBIS East European Report,
no. 1968, 28 January 1982.
148.   Havlin, Rude Pravo, 5 December 1981; FBIS East
European Report, no. 1968, 28 January 1982.
149.   Pruga e Partise (Albania), November 1980,
p. 50; FBIS East European Report, no. 1850, 18 February
1981.
150.   Pravda (Bratislava), 10 June 1982; Daily Report
(FBIS), 16 June 1982.
151.   Einheit, no. 2, February 1981, pp. 169-175.
152.   Ibid., no. 4, April 1982, pp. 48-50.

153. Rude Pravo, 6 November 1980.
154. Pruga e Partese, November 1980, p. 51; FBIS East European Report, no. 1850, 18 February 1981.
155. Rude Pravo, 24 April 1976.
156. Nepmuvelas (Hungary), no. 10, 1980, p. 4; FBIS East European Report, no. 1838, 5 January 1981.
157. Einheit, no. 6, June 1981, pp. 587-588; FBIS East European Report, no. 1916, 8 September 1981.
158. Einheit, no. 7, July 1981, pp. 688-689; FBIS East European Report, no. 1921, 23 September 1981.
159. Die Presse (Vienna), 15 January 1982.
160. Ibid.
161. Scinteia, 20 November 1979.
162. Rude Pravo, 6 September 1980.
163. Zeri I Popullit (Albania), 26 August 1981; FBIS East European Report, no. 1940, 12 November 1981.
164. Narodna Kultura, 16 April 1982; Filmovi Novini (Bulgaria), 3 March 1982.
165. Rabotnichesko Delo, 7 May 1982.
166. Borba (SRFY), 25 May 1981; FBIS East European Report, no. 1894, 1 July 1981.
167. Era Socialista (Romania), no. 20, 20 October 1981, pp. 22-25.
168. Neues Deutschland, 12 February 1982.
169. RFE Situation Report, Bulgaria, 24 February 1978.
170. Prague Domestic Service in Czech, 1730 GMT, 24 April 1978; Daily Report (FBIS), 26 April 1978.
171. Sofia Domestic Service in Bulgarian, 1300 GMT, 10 May 1982.
172. Literaturen Front (Bulgaria), no. 16, 21 April 1977.
173. Rabotnichesko Delo, 19-21 May 1977.
174. Bucharest Domestic Service in Romanian, 0700 GMT, 24 June 1982; Daily Report (FBIS), 24 June 1982.
175. Scinteia, 24 June 1978.
176. Resolution of the Congress of CSSR Sculpters, Rude Pravo, 15 April 1977.
177. Congress of CSSR Composers, Rude Pravo, 18 January 1978.
178. RFE Situation Report, CSSR, 25 January 1978.
179. Rude Pravo, 26 April 1977.
180. Pantaley Zarev at the 3rd Congress of the Bulgarian Writers, in Literaturen Front, no. 42, 14 October 1976.
181. Der Spiegel (Hamburg), vol. 35, no. 44, 26 October 1981, p. 23.
182. Tvorba (CSSR), no. 46, 18 November 1981; FBIS East European Report, no. 1960, 13 January 1982.
183. Tirana ATA in English, 0730 GMT, 21 March 1982;

Daily Report (FBIS), 23 March 1982.
   184.   RFE Situation Report, Hungary, 4 May 1977.
   185.   RFE Situation Report, CSSR, 8 December 1976.
   186.   RFE Situation Report, Hungary, 16 November 1974.
   187.   UPI Prague, 23 September 1976; RFE Situation
Report, CSSR, 29 September 1976.
   188.   Ibid.
   189.   RFE Situation Report, CSSR, 7 July 1977.
   190.   Ibid.
   191.   Tirana ATA in English, 0900 GMT, 25 March 1981;
Daily Report (FBIS), 26 March 1981.
   192.   Tirana Domestic Service in Albanian, 2100 GMT,
7 March 1978; Daily Report (FBIS), 8 March 1978.
   193.   Rude Pravo, 10 March 1982; Daily Report (FBIS),
15 March 1982.
   194.   Trybuna Ludu, 6 March 1980.
   195.   Sofia Domestic Service in Bulgarian, 1600 GMT,
8 March 1982; Daily Report (FBIS), 11 March 1982.
   196.   Budapest MTI in English, 1704 GMT, 8 March 1982;
Daily Report (FBIS), 10 March 1982.
   197.   Nicolae Ceausescu's speech at the 21-22 April 1978
National Congress of Romanian Women, in RFE Situation
Report, Romania, 5 May 1978.
   198.   RFE Situation Report, Romania, 2 December 1976.
   199.   Ibid.
   200.   Ibid.
   201.   RFE Situation Report, Bulgaria, 10 March 1977.

12
Conclusions

The East European political system is essentially the
Soviet political system. It was transplanted after World
War II--some thirty years after the October Revolution (in
other words, after the system had been perfected in the
USSR), by the Soviet Army, Soviet agents, or by-products
of the Soviet political system. The first generation of
East European leaders were by-products. Many of them spent
years and even decades in Moscow, and some, such as Georgi
Dimitrov (Bulgaria), even became a part of the Soviet
political apparatus. All the characteristics of the East
European partiocracy, and above all the eminent distinction
between power and authority, or rather between format and
substance, originated in the USSR and were successfully
transplanted in Eastern Europe. This is a self-evident
fact.

The extensive Soviet influence in Eastern Europe is
another self-evident fact. Although Albania and Yugoslavia
succeeded in breaking away from the Soviet sphere of influence, Bulgaria, the German Democratic Republic,
Czechoslovakia, Hungary, Poland, and Romania, bound together in the Warsaw Pact and CEMA, clearly belong to the
Soviet bloc. Even though Romania displays some different
nuances in its foreign policy, and Hungary initiated
certain economic reforms whose relation to hard-core
Marxism is questionable, political life in these countries
is controlled and to a large extent directed by the USSR.

The third self-evident fact is that even the two countries that succeeded in "emancipating" themselves--Albania
and Yugoslavia--have preserved the basic characteristics
of the partiocracy. When after the death of Tito the
Yugoslav League of Communists, saying it was impossible
to fill the shoes of that political colossus, introduced a

system of rotating all leading party and state posts—a practice unique in Eastern Europe—this change of format did not change the substance of the system. Yugoslavia is a partiocracy like all the other East European countries. All important decisions, including the matter of rotation, are taken by the party leadership. Albania, which not only broke away from the Soviet sphere of influence but has declared the USSR (along with the USA, China, and almost everybody else) as an enemy, did not find it necessary to change anything in its political system. All the fine points of the partiocracy were meticulously preserved.

All this inevitably leads to the first conclusion:

1. <u>Although changes in the format of the partiocracy may be introduced from time to time, the substance of the system does not change</u>. The reason is simple: any significant change in the substance would inevitably undermine the absolute supremacy of the communist party and thus immediately jeopardize the existence of the system itself.

The political interest of the East European leaders is no different from that of their Western colleagues. Their basic instincts dictate the essential goal of political survival. In most cases this survival depends to a large extent on Moscow's will, but the perseverance of the partiocracy is a vital precondition of endurance. Major changes of substance in the system, say the introduction of really free elections, plurality, free political debate, and so forth, would immediately preclude the system of partiocracy, and consequently, its political and physical survival. Therefore, one should not expect any moves to introduce substantial changes in the East European system to come from the leaders. On the other hand, changes of format, such as the official name of the communist party, the fixed period between general elections (four or five years), the number of seats in the parliament, or even the introduction of some kind of rotation (as long as it is communist leaders who rotate) hardly affects the system and thus are permitted.

2. <u>The existence of the partiocracy is not only a precondition of the East European leaders own existence and tenure, but also a guarantee of preserving Soviet influence in Eastern Europe</u>. Consequently the interest of the East European leaders and the Soviet leaders is identical, namely, to preserve the substance of the system. Any change of substance in any East European country is considered dangerous for the existence of the entire socialist community. This is the basis of the Brezhnev doctrine, according to which the East European countries,

bound by the principles of Marxism-Leninism and socialist internationalism, are obligated to assist the USSR in removing the danger. The Soviet leaders have not hesitated to prove the seriousness of their intentions in this area. The cases of Hungary (1956), Czechoslovakia (1968), and even Poland (1980-1982) testify to the importance given by the USSR to substantial changes in the principles of partiocracy. In the latter case, the fact that the rise of Solidarity and the Polish government's accommodation of it did not actually result in an armed Warsaw Pact intervention can probably be put down to two reasons. First, at no time in the political developments were there any calls to replace "the leading role of the community party" or to pull out of the Warsaw Pact. These are the two pillars of the Soviet system. Second, the purely logistical aspects of administering a hungry and rebellious population of 35 million people were probably instrumental in holding the Soviet military machine in check. In addition, of course, there was the fact that a pro-Soviet government existed in Poland throughout the Solidarity events, while the loyalty of the Hungarian (1956) and even Czech (1968) governments was questionable. Nevertheless, it was clear that the Soviet Union was gravely concerned about the threat to the partiocracy in the period leading up to the imposition of martial law in Poland on 13 December 1981.

The 1968 Prague spring did represent an exception to our first conclusion. Although the influence of the intellectuals was evident in the political reforms, some of the reforms were initiated or at least sanctioned by Dubcek and several other top leaders. Nevertheless, the USSR did not allow the reforms to reach the stage of changing the substance of the system, and even those Czechoslovak leaders who supported the reforms (the political survival instinct of many leaders dictated that they adopt a negative attitude toward the reforms) maintained that they did not aim at changing the principles of the socialist society. Thus, to a certain extent, the Prague spring was an exception (some partiocracy leaders supporting substantial reforms), although the end product (armed Soviet intervention, greeted by some Czechoslovak leaders) supports our conclusion.

3. Under certain circumstances, the USSR may tolerate or even sanction some changes of substance, so long as they are introduced by the communist party and presented as changes of format. Obviously, such changes must not jeopardize the general character of the system and the supremacy of the communist party. There must be some

pragmatic advantages for the USSR in their introduction, and they must not involve major changes in format, and especially not in the daily ritual of East European political life. It has already been pointed out that Romania'a foreign policy often differs from the accepted line of the Warsaw Pact member-countries (i.e., the CPSU foreign policy), the most notable differences being the maintenance of diplomatic relations with Israel, a somewhat more even-handed position on matters of disarmament and security, or even some differences in the ideological interpretation of Marxism. None of these differences changes anything in Romania's political system. Romania is a rigid partiocracy, and the existence of the system is not jeopardized by Ceausescu's eccentricity. Furthermore, in maintaining diplomatic relations with Israel, Romania has afforded the USSR a secondary channel of communication and a measure of variety in its Middle Eastern policy.

The economic reforms in Hungary were clearly not taken from Das Kapital. Encouraging private initiative and lending a measure of flexibility to the socialist principles of economy are diametrically opposed to pure Marxism. On the other hand, the reforms have strengthened Hungary's economy, improved the living standard, and in the final analysis strengthened the party rule by releasing some social pressure. Therefore the economic reforms were sanctioned by the USSR, and other East European countries were encouraged to apply them. Needless to say, Hungary's economic reform did not alter the principles of the partiocracy, nor did they jeopardize the supremacy of the communist party or Soviet influence.

4. Because the existence of the system itself is all-important, a basic rule of the partiocracy is that the system never errs. It must never be forgotten that communism is a messianic movement, bringing a message to the entire world. Its state system—the East European political system—is presented as the most democratic and elaborate political system, an ideal to which all other states must aspire. Consequently, it is obvious that such a system can never be wrong. (In the introduction to this book it was pointed out that a monopoly on the truth is an inherent characteristic of the East European political system). This means that when grave mistakes are made, the accepted procedure is to accuse individual leaders of violating the principles of the system and thus (single-handedly) causing the calamity. In every case the system itself is exonerated.

This is the reason why so many East European political leaders die twice: once physically, and soon afterwards

politically. What could be easier than to blame a dead
leader for the shortcomings of the system? Why not explain
present difficulties as being the result of mistakes made
by the former leaders? The direct responsibility for a
particular offense can seldom be established--the accusations are usually vague or simply insinuated, and formulated
in the accepted ritualistic terms such as "deviation" from
the party line, "personality cult," etc.

Even East European leaders who died in office,
ostensibly unblemished, died a second time when various
economic or political mistakes were attributed to them. At
the present there is no former Polish, Romanian, or Hungarian
leader who still has a good reputation. The GDR's Ulbricht
and Pieck are seldom mentioned. The CSSR's Gottwald is
mentioned only infrequently. Only Bulgaria's Georgi Dimitrov
and Yugoslavia's Tito have preserved their reputation after
death, and it could still be too soon to say this of Tito.

Naturally, this is also the reason that so many of the
East European leaders are ousted from their positions. Most
of them are sacrificed on the altar of the system's in-
fallibility. Thus precisely as the East European leaders
strive to preserve the system (and thus protect themselves),
the system itself sacrifices them--in life or post mortem--
in order to protect itself and preserve its infallible
image.

5. Under the present circumstances there is no chance
of significantly changing the East European system. It
has already been stated that the East European leaders are
vitally interested in preserving the partiocracy. The
Polish example of 1980-1982 showed that the Soviet Union
will not tolerate a change caused by social unrest or
prompted at the demand of the population. A revolution
seems unlikely and in fact impossible, as any kind of antigovernmental organization in a totalitarian regime runs into
socialist internationalism. Any armed interference by the
West, aimed at changing the East European system, can be
ruled out. Given that it would almost certainly lead to
the outbreak of a world war, and given the tremendous
development of the two superpowers' potential to annihilate
the world many times over, it seems absolutely inconceivable.

Only one other possibility is left, namely, a change
initiated by the USSR itself. There is no question about the
USSR's ability to initiate and implement such a change.
Nevertheless, ability alone does not make even this
possibility a plausible one. The past record shows that
the USSR was ready to accept (reluctantly, of course) a
change in a country's attitude toward the USSR, as long as

the system preserved its essence and characteristics.
The anti-Soviet attitude of Albania and Yugoslavia did not
prompt an armed Soviet interference. (Naturally, the lack
of common borders contributed to the decision to refrain
from interference.) On the other hand, attempts to change
the system, even when there were no overt anti-Soviet
connotations (Czechoslovakia, Poland), were curbed by the
USSR. Still, the theoretical possibility, unlikely as it
is at present, remains. Only the USSR can initiate and
implement a modification of the East European political
system. This, however, would involve first a change in
the Soviet system, something that also seems unlikely at
the present. Perhaps there is another angle of this
theoretical possibility, namely, that the USSR could use
Eastern Europe as a laboratory for certain cautious changes
or modifications, which could then be applied later in the
USSR and in other East European countries. The example of
the Hungarian economic reform indicates that this possibility can develop into a careful process, especially if
the Hungarian reforms succeed in other East European
countries, but do not result in a significant or at any
rate sudden modification of the partiocracy. No matter how
theoretical and remote, at the moment this seems the only
more or less plausible scenario for gradually modifying
the East European partiocracies.

List of Acronyms

ADN	German General News Service
AGERPRES	Romanian Press Agency
APN	Novosti Press Agency
ATA	Albanian Telegraph Agency
AWP	Albanian Workers' Party
BANU	Bulgarian Agrarian National Union
BCP	Bulgarian Communist Party
BOAL	Basic Organizations of Associated Labor
BTA	Bulgarian Telegraph Agency
CEMA	Council for Economic Mutual Assistance
CPCZ	Communist Party of Czechoslovakia
CPSU	Communist Party of the Soviet Union
CSSR	Czechoslovak Socialist Republic
CTK	Czechoslovak News Agency
FBIS	Foreign Broadcast Information Service
FDGB	GDR Trade Union
FDJ	GDR Youth Organization (Free German Youth)
GDR	German Democratic Republic
LCY	League of Yugoslav Communists
MTI	Hungarian Communication Agency
MSZMP	Hungarian Socialist Workers' Party
PAP	Polish Press Agency
PPF	Patriotic People's Front
PZPR	Polish United Workers' Party
RAD	RFE Research and Analysis Department
RCP	Romanian Communist Party
RFE	Radio Free Europe
SED	GDR Socialist Unity Party
SFRY	Socialist Federative Republic of Yugoslavia
TANJUG	Telegraph Agency of New Yugoslavia
TASS	Telegraph Agency of the Soviet Union
UCY	Romanian Union of Communist Youth
USSR	Soviet Union

Index

Abadzhiev, Gencho, 341
Aczel, Gyorgy, 28(table),
  144
ADN. See German General
  News Service
Afghanistan, 24, 231, 316
Afghan National Fatherland
  Front (1981), 316
AFP. See France Press
African National Congress
  of South Africa, 302
"African toast," 295
AGERPRES (Romanian news
  agency), 192, 339
Agitation and propaganda.
  See Propaganda campaigns
Agricultural labor camps,
  329
Albania, 1, 6
  arts and culture, 348, 352
  church-state relations,
  25, 237-238, 240
  Constitution, 34, 237
  elections, 17
  Five-Year Plan (1981-
  1985), 174, 193
  judiciary, 274, 275, 277
  leadership, 209, 210.
  See also under Albanian
  Workers' Party
  mass media, 217

news agency. See Albanian
  Telegraph Agency
People's (national)
  Assembly, 34, 54, 274, 275,
  277
People's Assembly
  Presidium, 36
and Poland, 322
political regime, 2
and Soviet Union, 2, 54,
  322, 365, 366, 370. See
  also under Albanian Workers'
  Party
and Stalinism, 1
trade unions, 318, 319,
  322, 326
Union of Artists and
  Writers, 348, 352
Union of Working Youth,
  326, 332, 334
and Yugoslavia, 209-210, 352
See also Albanian Workers'
  Party; Democratic Front
Albanians, in Yugoslavia,
  281, 352
Albanian Telegraph Agency
  (ATA), 339
Albanian Workers' Party (AWP),
  289, 318-319
  Central Committee, 115, 124,
  125, 143, 198

(AWP) continued
Central Committee member-
  ship composition,
  127-128
Central Control and Auditing Commission, 162, 174,
  193
decision making, 157-158
8th Congress (1981), 62,
  124, 173-174, 188, 193,
  319, 332
leadership, 124-125, 128,
  198, 211(table), 216-217,
  222, 227-228, 313, 318
membership composition,
  62, 63(table)
9th Congress, 125
organization levels, 95
Politburo, 125, 150,
  157-158, 198
press. See Zeri I Popullit
primary party organiza-
  tion, 95
Secretariat, 125, 160, 161
7th Congress (1976), 128,
  188, 190, 198
and Soviet Union, 188,
  190, 214, 289, 304
and state system, 36
women in, 62, 75, 128
Aleksandrov, Chudomir, 161
Algeria, 333
Alia, Ramiz, 352
Amnesty, 284
Andreev, Veselin, 11
Andropov, Yuriy, 2
Angola, 295
Apro, Antal, 143
Arismendi, Rodney, 302
Arms race, 251, 253, 321
Arseni, Constantin, 313
Arts and culture, 342-353.
  See also Creative
  unions; Sports unions
Art Workers' Union, 350
ATA. See Albanian Telegraph
  Agency

Atanasov, Todor, 330
Avramov, Ruben, 133
AWP. See Albanian Workers'
  Party
Axen, Herman, 161

Babiuch, Edward, 147, 148, 195
Bakaric, Vladimir, 151
Balev, Milko, 92, 93, 161,
  330
Balevski, Angel, 49
BANU. See Bulgarian
  Agrarian National Union
Baranyai, Tibor, 144
Barcikowski, Kazimierz, 127,
  196, 216
Baryl, Jan, 145
BCP. See Bulgarian Communist
  Party
Bednarski, Commission
  Chairman, 126, 127
Belchev, Belcho, 146
Belovski, Dimce, 151
Berecz, Janos, 144
Berlin Conference of European
  Catholics, 248, 252
Bierut, Boleslaw, 211(table),
  218, 228
Bilak, Vasil, 120, 337, 344,
  354
Bilic, Jure, 151
Birthday messages, 300-301
Blazevic, Jacob, 256
BOAL. See Yugoslavia,
  Basic Organizations of
  Associated Labor
Bobu, Emil, 220, 318
Bonev, Vladimir, 49, 51
Borba (LCY), 298, 352
Bosnia-Herzegovina
  (Yugoslavia), 182,
  183(table)
Bourgeois societies, 274
Bozhinov, Todor, 146,
  152-153, 161
Brabec, Antonin, 145
Brethren Church (CSSR), 26, 245

Brezhnev, Leonid Ilich,
185, 189, 193, 198, 199,
253, 299, 301, 302, 303,
320
Brezhnev doctrine, 366
Brief Bulgarian
Encyclopedia, 218
Brutyo, Janos, 98, 144,
145, 163-164
BTA. See Bulgarian
Telegraph Agency
Buc, Jerzy, 142
Budgets, 43, 44, 45, 46, 48
Bulgaria, 1, 6
Academy of Sciences, 49
and Angola, 295
arts and culture, 11,
12(table), 37, 348, 349,
350, 353
and CEMA, 2
church-state relations,
238-239, 256, 261-262
Committee on Science and
Technological Progress, 49
Constitution (1971), 34,
42, 238-239, 273, 274
cosmonaut, 11
Dimitrov Komsomol, 103,
160, 326, 328, 330,
331-332, 334-335
diplomatic corps, 101
economic crime, 282-283
elections, 12, 17, 24, 28
judiciary, 273, 274, 275,
277, 283, 284, 285
and Kampuchea, 296
leadership, 209, 210. See
also under Bulgarian
Communist Party
Legislative Commission, 50
mass media, 51-52, 156,
186, 230, 231, 256, 342,
343
and Mozambique, 295
National Assembly, 11, 12,
34, 35, 40, 42, 43, 44,
47, 49-51, 52, 56, 274,

275, 277, 283
news agency. See Bulgarian
Telegraph Agency
noncommunist party. See
Bulgarian Agrarian
National Union
scientific cadres, 49
and Soviet Union, 24, 365
Sports Union, 356
State Council, 36, 37, 47,
101, 261, 275, 331
trade unions, 321, 323, 324,
325
and Warsaw Pact, 2
and Zambia, 295
See also Bulgarian Communist
Party; Fatherland Front;
under Czechoslovakia;
Yugoslavia
Bulgarian Agrarian National
Union (BANU), 12, 37, 61,
311
Bulgarian Communist Party
(BCP), 302
age distribution, 133,
135(table)
and army, 84, 186
Cadres Abroad department,
116
card exchanges, 92-94, 176
Central Committee, 24, 45,
49, 92, 103, 115, 116, 118,
119-120, 173, 174, 203, 217,
225, 299, 331, 348, 349
Central Committee Mass-
Information Media Depart-
ment, 116
Central Committee membership
composition, 132-135, 143,
146, 147
Central Committee Military-
Administrative Department,
116
Central Committee Transportation and Communication
Department, 116
Conference (1978), 202-203

(BCP) continued
conferences, 202
Central Control and
  Auditing Commission,
  162, 163
decision making, 156,
  157, 160, 261
education, 134
8th Congress (1962), 133
11th Congress (1976), 92,
  132, 133, 161, 174, 176,
  203, 225, 312, 328, 356
Five-Year Plan, 203
leadership, 100, 101,
  102-103, 119, 183, 186,
  194-195, 210, 211(table),
  212, 217-218, 220, 223,
  225-227, 228, 230-231,
  293, 298, 299, 313, 318,
  369
membership composition,
  62, 64(table), 84, 132
and Mozambique, 291
and National Assembly, 12
organization levels, 95,
  100-101, 102-103, 183
personality cult, 119
Politburo, 10, 49, 50,
  146, 150, 152-153, 155,
  156, 157
press, 92, 116, 157, 332,
  340-341
primary organization, 93,
  95
Secretariat, 81-82, 160,
  161, 162, 261
7th Congress (1958), 133
6th Congress (1954), 133,
  217
and Soviet Union, 262, 314
and state system, 36, 45
12th Congress (1981), 35,
  62, 132, 147, 153, 173,
  174-175, 176, 186, 187,
  188, 190, 194-195, 314,
  325
women in, 62, 133

Bulgarian Orthodox Church,
  251
Bulgarian People's Army, 84,
  186, 349
Bulgarian Telegraph Agency
  (BTA), 339, 342
Bulgarian Union of
  Composers, 349
Bulgarian Workers' Party, 92
Burbulescu, Elena, 223
Burtica, Cornel, 220, 223

Capka, Miroslav, 163
Carter, Jimmy, 250
Catholic Activists (Poland),
  13(table)
Catholic Bishops' Conference
  (Yugoslavia), 262
Catholic Church, 236, 237,
  243, 244, 248, 249, 250,
  254, 255-256, 257, 258,
  262, 263-267
Catholic parties, 3, 6,
  13(table). See also Pacem
  in Terris
Catholic Znak Group (Poland),
  311
Cazacu, Virgil, 189
Ceausescu, Elena, 212, 223,
  224, 227, 350
Ceausescu, Florea, 223
Ceausescu, Ilie, 223
Ceausescu, Ion, 223
Ceausescu, Marin, 223
Ceausescu, Nicolae
  and arts and culture, 347,
    350
  and church, 245, 255
  family, 223-224
  and foreign leaders, 155,
    158, 189, 300, 303
  and mass media, 341
  and national front, 313
  personality cult, 227,
    228-230, 231, 293
  and RCP, 55, 86, 90, 91, 126,
    161, 191-192, 202, 211(table),
    212, 219, 279, 281, 368

Ceausescu, Nicolae (cont.)
  and youth organizations,
  330
Ceausescu, Nicolae
  (brother), 223
Ceausescu, Nicolae (Nicu),
  223, 224-225, 330
Ceausescu, Zoya, 224
CEMA. See Council for
  Economic Mutual Assistance
Censorship, 338-341
Centralism, 76. See also
  Democratic centralism
Central planning, 55
Centropress (Hungary),
  339-340
Cermak, Zdenek, 337
Ceterchi, Ion, 283
Charter-77 (CSSR), 53-54,
  251, 282
Chervenkov, Vulko, 119, 120,
  211(table), 217-218, 228,
  299
Children's organizations.
  See Pioneers
Chile, Communist Party of,
  302
Chnoupek, Bohuslav, 54
Christian Conference for
  Peace (GDR), 252
Christian Democratic
  Union (GDR), 37, 311
Christian Peace Conference
  (CSSR), 25, 247, 249,
  252, 253
Church-state relations,
  235, 236-237, 240-243,
  247-248, 254, 255, 267
  propaganda, 25, 26, 238,
  250, 251, 260-261
  See also under individual
  countries
City party organizations,
  95, 96, 97, 181, 183
Ckrebic, Dusan, 151
Cold War, 250
Coman, Ion, 162, 279

Comintern, 310
Commune party organizations,
  95, 96, 97
Communism, 1
Communist parties, 1, 172
  admission, 82-87
  age minimum, 82
  and army, 7, 77, 79, 84
  bureaus, 96, 97-98
  card exchanges, 87-95
  central committees, 18, 20,
  21, 22, 44-45, 48, 78, 87,
  95, 97, 103, 109-127,
  142-149, 150, 154, 160,
  171, 172-173, 177, 190,
  198, 199, 212-213, 221,
  355-356
  central committees members,
  123-127
  central committees plenums,
  116-123
  central committees press
  departments, 339
  central committees
  secretaries general, 209,
  210-218, 221, 222
  central control commissions,
  109, 162-164, 171, 190, 199
  conferences, 95, 96, 202-203
  congresses, 10, 95, 109,
  123, 142, 171-203
  control and auditing
  commissions, 149
  decision making, 96, 115,
  154, 199-200
  general assemblies, 80
  hierarchy, 61, 76, 77, 81,
  83, 95-103, 109, 142
  indoctrination, 78, 79, 81,
  97, 116, 319-320
  leadership, 3, 6, 98, 99,
  100, 155-156, 189, 209-231,
  298-299, 348-349, 368-369.
  See also Personality
  cults
  legitimacy, 4-5, 7, 9
  and mass media, 78, 82, 116

Communist parties (cont.)
membership, 61, 62, 74-75,
84-85
from noncommunist
countries, 193
Politburos, 20, 21, 22,
95, 103, 109, 115,
149-159, 171, 190, 198,
199, 213, 219, 221, 298,
355
political opposition to,
4, 7, 79, 280-284
politicization, 5-6
presses, 99
primary organizations,
77-82, 83, 95, 96, 97,
182
purges, 62, 74, 87, 88,
94, 172
recruitment, 78. See also
Youth organizations
ritual, 290-304
Secretariats, 95, 96, 97,
103, 109, 115, 149,
159-162, 171, 199
size, 61, 62, 75
and Soviet Union, 10, 74,
82, 123, 201, 213,
214-215, 218, 219, 284,
290, 292, 294, 296, 299,
304, 366, 367-370
and state system, 3-4,
36, 37, 39, 40, 49-53, 55,
56, 97, 115, 142, 146-147,
150, 209, 212, 291. See
also National assemblies
structure, 75-82, 95-103,
180-181
and succession, 6, 210,
211(table), 218-227.
See also Elections
total rule of, 3-4, 9, 17,
19-20, 61, 75, 76, 366.
See also Partiocracy
See also individual
communist parties
Communist Party of

Czechoslovakia (CPCZ),
29, 192
admission, 86-87, 90
arts and culture, 348
cadres, 99
card exchanges, 89-90
Central Committee, 20, 21,
26, 89, 115, 116, 120,
143, 145, 156, 177, 194,
199, 213, 221, 260, 279,
337, 348
Central Control and Auditing
Commission, 162, 163, 194
decision making, 156
federation minicongresses,
181
15th Congress (1976), 89,
156, 177, 194, 221, 351
leadership, 198-199,
211(table), 213, 218,
221-222, 313, 318, 331, 369
membership composition,
62-63, 65(table), 74, 86,
87
political organization
department, 116
Presidium (Politburo), 149,
150, 156, 222, 303
press. See Rude Pravo
purges, 94
Secretariat, 160-161
16th Congress (1981), 22,
62, 177-178, 181, 188,
193-194, 198-199, 299,
320, 354
and Soviet Union, 121, 177,
198, 218, 249, 320
and state system, 36
and U.S., 120-121, 250, 253
women in, 63
See also under Polish United
Workers' Party
Communist Party of the Soviet
Union (CPSU), 77, 82, 192,
201, 292, 304, 368
Central Committee, 2

(CPSU) continued
congresses, 24, 171, 174,
189-190, 217, 312, 314,
320
election rules, 102
Community party organiza-
tions, 95
Congress of Bulgarian
Culture (1977), 350
Congress of CSSR Composers
(1978), 351
Congress of Czech and
Slovak Dramatic Artists
(1977), 351
Congress of Political
Education and Socialist
Culture (Romania), 350
Constitutional Courts,
275-276
Constitutions, 4, 6, 9, 17,
33, 39, 213, 237, 273,
280, 285. See also
under individual
countries
Construction camps, 329
Corvalan, Luis, 302
Costiu, Vasile, 244
Council for Economic
Mutual Assistance
(CEMA), 2, 312, 365
Council of Jewish Communi-
ties in Bohemia and
Moravia, 245
Council of ministers
chairman. See Premier
Covac, Stefan, 355
CPSU. See Communist Party
of the Soviet Union
CPCZ. See Communist Party
of Czechoslovakia
Creative unions, 309, 337,
349-353
Crime, 280-284, 285
Croatia (Yugoslavia),
183(table), 238, 256,
321
CSSR (Czechoslovak Socialist

Republic). See
Czechoslovakia
CTK. See Czechoslovak News
Agency
Cuba, 301
Cuic, Dane, 151
Culafic, Dobroslav, 151
Cypryniak, secretary, 127
Czechoslovak Fine Arts
Union, 344-345
Czechoslovak Hussite Church,
245
Czechoslovakia (CSSR), 1
and Angola, 295
arts and culture, 344-345,
349, 351, 352, 353
and Bulgaria, 297
and CEMA, 2
Chamber of Nations, 26, 34
Chamber of People, 34
church-state relations,
25-27, 238, 239, 243, 245,
249-251, 253, 255-256,
258, 259-260, 267
civil rights, 53-54
Constitution (1960), 18,
221, 238, 251, 259, 273
elections, 17, 18, 19, 25,
28, 29
ethnic composition, 41(table).
See also Czechs; Slovaks
Federal (National) Assembly,
18, 34, 41(table), 43, 44,
47, 53-54, 213, 221, 277
Federal Assembly Presidium,
36, 47
Federal Press and Information
Office, 337, 340
Five-Year Plan (1981-1985),
43, 194
and GDR, 297
human rights, 251, 282
judiciary, 273, 275, 277,
278, 279, 282, 284
and Kampuchea, 296
leadership, 209, 210, 213.
See also under Communist
Party of Yugoslavia

(CSSR) continued
mass media, 213, 239,
  266, 340, 341, 342
meat shortage (1971), 43
news agency. See
  Czechoslovak News Agency
noncommunist parties,
  310-311
and Romania, 296-297
Socialist Youth Union,
  326, 327, 329-330, 331,
  333, 334
and Soviet Union, 29, 303,
  342, 352, 365, 367, 370
standard of living, 26
trade unions, 318, 320,
  323, 324, 326
and Warsaw Pact, 2, 303
women, 354
and Zambia, 295
See also Communist Party
  of Czechoslovakia;
  National Front (CSSR)
Czechoslovak News Agency
  (CTK), 339
Czechoslovak People's
  Party, 310
Czechoslovak Socialist
  Party, 310
Czechs, 34, 36, 41(table),
  177
Czubinski, Lucjan, 278

Dabrowa, secretary, 127
Dabrowski, Bronislaw, 265
Dakov, Mako, 147
Danube oil refinery
  (Hungary), 329
Danube River power plant
  (Hungary), 329
Dascalescu, Constantin,
  219
Decision making, 33. See
  also under Communist
  parties; individual
  parties
Democracy, 4-5, 9, 10, 37,

76, 180. See also
  Socialist democracy
Democratic centralism, 75,
  76-77, 96
Democratic Front (Albania),
  18, 309, 313
Democratic Party (Poland),
  13(table), 37, 61, 311
Détente, 250, 253, 296
Developed socialism. See
  Socialist society
"Dimensions of Culture"
  (BCP), 350
Dimitriu, Florin, 279
Dimitrov, Georgi, 209, 210,
  211(table), 293, 298,
  309-310, 369
  Award, 353
  Order, 301
Dimitrov, Lalyu, 116
Dimov, Dimitur, 348
Dimovski, Boris, 341
Disarmament, 2, 296, 368
Dissidents, 353. See also
  Communist parties, political
  opposition to
Districts, 95, 275
Djuricin, Marko, 151
Dobieszewski, Adolf, 76
Dolhus, Horst, 88, 89
Dos Santos, Jose Eduardo, 295
Double candidacy, 20
Doynov, Ognyan, 146
Dragosavac, Dusan, 151, 300
Dragoycheva, Tsola, 133, 186,
  190
"Driving Forces and Brakes"
  (Buc), 142
Dubcek, Alexander,
  211(table), 214, 218
Dulbokov, Sava, 147, 313
Dunavska Pravda (Bulgarian
  daily), 92
Duparinova, Margarita, 11
Dyulgerov, Petur, 318, 323,
  325, 341
Dzhagarov, Georgi, 37

Dzhurov, Dobri, 146, 186

East Berlin Conference of
  the European communist
  parties, 298
Eastern Europe
  concept, 1
  political regimes, 1-3,
    4-5, 7, 9-11, 61,
    235-236, 289-290, 365
  press. See Mass media
  See also Communist
    parties; individual
    countries
Ecumenical Council of
  Hungarian Churches, 254
Einheit (SED), 346
Elections, 4, 5, 6, 9
  candidates, 11, 12-14,
    18, 19-22
  and church, 248-249
  committees, 18, 19, 21
  functions, 10-11
  national assemblies, 3,
    56. See also under
    individual countries
  and national front
    organizations, 313
  and noncommunist parties,
    11, 13-14
  periods, 17-18
  proxies, 27
  rallies, 22-27
  results, 27-30
  stages, 18-27
  terms, 20
  See also under
    individual countries
Electoral registers, 18
"Electoral System as a
  Mechanism for Turning
  Over Authority in the
  Party" (Erazmus), 102
El Salvador, 252
"Emissaries," 17
Engels, Friedrich, 1
Erazmus, Edward, 102

Ernst Thaelmann Organization
  of Young Pioneers (GDR),
  179
European Economic Community,
  2
Evangelical Church, 252

Fatherland Front (Bulgaria),
  10, 12, 18, 28, 51, 203,
  309, 313, 314
  8th Congress (1977), 312,
    313
Fatherland front organiza-
  tions, 3, 11
Fazekas, Janos, 220
Fazekas, Ludovic, 220
FDGB. See German Democratic
  Republic, trade union
FDJ. See German Democratic
  Republic, Free German Youth
"FDJ Central Council
  Resolution on Tasks for the
  10th SED Congress," 178
Federal Republic of Germany
  (FRG), 156, 351
Federation of the Yugoslav
  Orthodox Clergy Association,
  254
Fejes, Jan, 54
Fejti, Gyorgy, 331, 336
Filipas, Cornelia, 220
Filipov, Grisha, 47, 189
Finance ministers, 43-44, 45
Fine Arts Conferences, 350
Fiszbach, Tadeusz, 127
Fojtik, Jan, 20
Fol, Aleksandur, 225
Foreign policy, 56. See also
  Communist parties, and
  Soviet Union; individual
  communist parties and
  countries, and other
  countries
Forman, Milos, 352
France Press (AFP), 255
Franciscans, 256
FRG. See Federal Republic of
  Germany

Friendship rally, 293
Front of National Unity
  (Poland), 14, 18
Fuchs, Otto Hartmut, 248

Gabrielski, Secretariat
  member, 127
Galski, Dezider, 245
Gaspar, Sandor, 28(table),
  143, 321-322, 325
Gazeta Olsztynska
  (Polish newspaper), 127
GDR. See German Democratic
  Republic
GDR Writer's Union, 351
Georgiev, Khristo, 101
Germach, Manfred, 37
German Democratic Republic
  (GDR), 1
 and Angola, 295
 arts and culture,
   346-347, 348, 351
 and CEMA, 2
 church-state relations,
   245-247, 248-249, 252,
   263
 Council of Ministers, 157
 elections, 17, 21, 28, 29
 Five-Year Plan (1981-1985),
   157
 Free German Youth (FDJ),
   157, 178, 179, 326, 331,
   332, 333, 334, 335
 and FRG, 156, 351
 judiciary, 276, 278
 leadership, 209, 210. See
   also under Socialist
   Unity Party
 and Mozambique, 295
 National People's Army,
   200
 news agency. See German
   General News Service
 noncommunist parties, 37,
   311
 People's Chamber
   (Volkskammer) (national
 assembly), 34, 44, 47
 schools of socialist labor,
   319
 and Soviet Union, 365
 State Council, 37, 47, 313
 trade union (FDGB), 317, 319,
   324, 326
 and Warsaw Pact, 2
 and Zambia, 295
 See also National Front
   (GDR); Socialist Unity
   Party; under Czechoslovakia
German General News Service
  (ADN), 339
Germans
 in CSSR, 41(table)
 in Romania, 130
Gero, Erno, 210, 211(table),
  218
Gheorghiu-Dej, Gheorghe, 129,
  209, 210, 211(table), 218
Gierek, Edward, 45, 122, 147,
  148, 183, 184, 195, 211
  (table), 214, 218, 296
Glas Koncila (Zagreb), 259
Glemp, Jozef, 265
Gligorov, Kiro, 27
Goetting, Gerald, 37
Golden Star Order, 301
Gomulka, Wladyslaw, 189, 209,
  210, 211(table), 214, 215,
  218, 263
Gottwald, Klement, 177, 209,
  210, 211(table), 218, 369
Order, 301
Grabski, Tadeusz, 122, 127,
  195, 215
Green International, 353
Greetings messages, 299-301
Grigoras, Justin, 283
Grlichkov, Aleksandr, 298
Grotewohl, Otto, 210,
  211(table)
Gyenes, Andreas, 119, 144
Gyorgy, Imre, 144

Hadzhivasilev, Kiro, 151

Hajek, Jiri, 282
Halama, Jindrich, 245
Harmel, Muhamed, 302
Hasani, Sinan, 151
Havasi, Ferenc, 119
Havlin, Josef, 351
Helsinki Conference, 251,
  253, 263
Herljevic, Franjo, 151
Heroes of Socialist Labor
  (Bulgaria), 135
Herrmann, Joachim, 161
Hoffmann, Heinz, 200
Hoffmann, Karel, 318, 320
Homann, Heinrich, 37
Homogeneous management, 76
Honecker, Erich, 21, 156,
  161, 179, 211(table),
  252, 301, 326, 332, 335
Honecker, Margot, 222
Horeni, Zdenek, 343
Hoxha, Enver, 124-125,
  127-128, 158, 160, 173,
  190, 193, 198, 209, 210,
  211(table), 217, 228,
  319, 332
Hoxha, Nexhmije, 222,
  227-228
Hruza, Karel, 25-26
Human rights, 251, 280-282
Humboldt University
  (East Berlin), 295
Hungarian Communication
  Agency (MTI), 244
Hungarians
  in CSSR, 41(table)
  in Romania, 130, 220
Hungarian Socialist
  Workers' Party (MSZMP),
  173
  Agitation and Propaganda
  Committee, 112, 144
  card exchanges, 94, 98-99
  Central Committee, 23,
  38-39, 94, 110-115,
  118-119, 143, 331
  Central Committee Foreign

  Affairs Department, 144
  Central Committee membership
  composition, 130-132,
  143-145
  Central Control Committee,
  112, 118, 144-145, 163-164
  Committee on Economic
  Policy, 112
  Conference (1977), 202
  11th Congress (1975), 52,
  66, 94, 98, 130, 143,
  173, 175-176
  leadership, 131, 164,
  211(table), 214, 218, 313
  membership composition,
  66, 67(table)
  organization levels, 114,
  118, 181
  and Poland, 248
  Politburo, 14, 111, 112,
  113, 114, 150
  publications, 132, 144,
  163, 180
  Secretariat, 111, 112, 113,
  161, 162
  and Soviet Union, 218
  and state system, 38-39,
  118, 132
  10th Congress (1970), 66,
  143, 189
  3rd Congress (1954), 143
  12th Congress (1980), 110,
  130, 131, 132, 143, 175,
  179-180, 181, 190
  women in, 131
Hungary, 1
  and Angola, 295
  arts and culture, 352, 353
  and CEMA, 2
  church-state relations,
  236, 244, 248, 254, 258,
  261, 312
  Communist Youth League,
  326, 327, 328, 329, 331,
  335, 336
  Council of ministers, 118
  economic reforms, 2, 23,
  365, 368, 370

Hungary (continued)
  elections, 12-14, 17,
    18, 19, 20, 23, 28
  industrial enterprises,
    329
  judiciary, 275, 283
  leadership, 209, 210.
    See also under Hungarian
    Socialist Workers' Party
  mass media, 261, 323,
    339-340. See also
    Hungarian Communication
    Agency
  multiparty system, 12
  National Assembly, 12, 34,
    38, 42, 44, 47, 52-53,
    283
  noncommunist parties, 13-14
  political crime, 281
  Presidential Council, 36,
    38, 42, 244, 254, 275
  and Soviet Union, 24,
    365, 367, 368
  standard of living, 23,
    368
  trade unions, 320, 321,
    323, 325
  and Warsaw Pact, 2
  Western press in, 7
  women, 354-355
  See also Hungarian
    Socialist Workers' Party;
    Patriotic People's Front
Hun Sen, 296
Husak, Gustav, 21, 26, 62,
  156, 160, 181, 189, 193,
  211(table), 213, 214, 221,
  250, 296, 300, 303, 315,
  326, 349
Hussites, 245
Huszar, Istvan, 143

Information. See Mass media
Inokai, Janos, 52-53
International peace
  movement, 24, 251-253,
  312, 315, 332

International Women's Day
  (March 8), 354
Interpellation, 46, 47, 56
Ionita, Ion, 220, 224
Iran, 303
Iran-Iraq war, 158
Iraq, 158, 300
Israel, 194, 252, 253, 284,
  302, 368
Ivanov, Georgi, 11

Jablonski, Henryk, 127
Jagielski, Mieczyslaw, 127
Jakab, Sandor, 99, 144
Jakes, Milos, 145
Jaroszewicz, Piotr, 122, 148
Jaruzelski, Wojciech, 127, 146,
  149, 155, 158, 185, 196,
  209, 211(table), 216, 265
Jaskiernia, Jerzy, 331
Javorsky, Stefan, 255-256
Jews, 245
John Paul II (pope), 237, 267
Joint declaration, 293, 320
Jordan, 158
Judiciary, 273-285

Kadar, Janos, 23-24, 28(table),
  38, 131, 143, 161, 190,
  211(table), 214, 296,
  300-301, 335, 352
Kallai, Gyula, 143, 313
Kampuchea, 296
Kania, Stanislaw, 121-122,
  127, 147, 149, 155, 161,
  185, 186, 195, 196, 210,
  211(table), 212, 215, 216,
  264, 265
Kardelj, Edvard, 152
Katushev, Konstantin, 189
Kaunda, Kenneth, 294-295
Khaytov, Nikolay, 11
Kirilenko, Andrey, 189
Kisiel, Henryk, 45
Kiss, Karoly, 143
Klassa, Josef, 154
Klos, Elmar, 352

Klusak, Milan, 245
Kociolek, first secretary, 127
Kokanava, Nevena, 11
Kolditz, Lothar, 313
Komsomol, 12(table), 85, 103, 157, 160, 178, 326, 359(n78). See also Youth organizations
Koncar, Rade, 192
Konrad, Gyorgy, 352
Konvit, Jan, 26
Kordik, Josef, 255
Kosovo (Yugoslavia), 181, 183(table), 281, 352
Kossuth Prize (Hungary), 353
Kostov, Traycho, 280, 285
Kostov, Vladimir, 342
Krenz, Egon, 331, 332
Krizic, Jozo, 256
Kruszewski, Krzysztof, 48
Kruk, Wladyslaw, 127
Krupauer, Jaroslav, 278
Krzak, Marian, 45
Kubadinski, Pencho, 10, 186, 312, 313, 314
Kucan, Milan, 151
Kuharich, Fanjo, 262
Kuka, Jeroslav, 255
Kupka, Josef, 251
Kurdzhali Okrug (BCP), 103
Kurowski, Zdzislaw, 127
Kurtovic, Todo, 313

Labor order of Merit (Hungary), 254
Lakatos, Erno, 144
"Law for the Protection of the Professional Designation of Writers" (GDR), 347
Lazar, Gyorgy, 28(table), 254
LCY. See League of Yugoslav Communists
League of Yugoslav

Communists (LCY)
admission, 83
age composition, 72, 136(table)
and army, 84, 151, 152, 183(table)
Central Committee, 71, 115, 119, 121, 122, 123, 125, 126, 173, 175, 182, 197, 330
Central Committee membership composition, 136, 166(n74)
Central Control Commission, 163
democracy, 153
education, 136(table)
8th Congress, 83
11th Congress (1978), 152, 173, 182, 183(table), 190
federation minicongresses, 181-182
and Israel, 194
leadership, 123, 125-126, 195, 211(table), 289, 366, 369
and Lebanon, 194
membership composition, 71-74, 75, 84, 125, 183(table)
and MSZMP, 173
organization levels, 182, 183(table)
Presidium (Politburo), 36, 37, 149, 150-151, 153-154, 161, 197
Presidium secretary, 161
press. See Borba
purges, 72, 73(table)
resignations, 72
Secretariat, 161
and Soviet Union, 214, 289, 304
and state system, 151, 183(table), 365-366
12th Congress (1982), 122, 166(n74), 173, 175, 181, 188, 192, 194, 195, 197

(LCY) continued
 women in, 72, 73(table)
 See also Socialist
 Alliance of the Working
 People of Yugoslavia
Lebanon, 194, 252, 284, 302
Lederer, Jiri, 341
Legitimacy. See under
 Communist parties
Lekai, Laszlo Cardinal,
 244, 254, 266
Lenart, Jozef, 213
Lenin, V. I., 1, 76, 77,
 260, 337
Lenin metallurgical plant
 (Hungary), 329
Leninism, 93
Lettres Francoises, 352
Levchec, Lyubomir, 225
Liberal Democratic Party
 of Germany, 37, 311
Lilov, Aleksandur, 101,
 350
List Publishing House
 (Munich), 352
Literaturen Front
 (Bulgarian weekly), 231
"Little Stalins," 228
Losonczi, Pal, 28(table),
 143
Loyalty pledge, 245-248,
 249
Luca, 210
Lucan, Matej, 249, 250
Lukanov, Andrey, 146
Lukaszewicz, Jerzy, 147,
 148

Macedonia (Yugoslavia),
 181-182, 183(table),
 348
Macedonian Communist Party,
 348
Machel, Samora, 291, 295
Madrid conference, 253
Magyar Hirlap (Hungarian
 daily), 47, 261

Manescu, Manea, 223
Man of the People, A (film),
 230
Marinc, Andrej, 151
Marko, Rita, 318, 322
Markov, Sekul, 11
Markovic, Dragoslav, 27, 151
Markovski, Krste, 151
Marti, Jose, Order, 301
Marx, Karl, 1
 Order, 301
Marxism-Leninism, 1, 53, 78,
 81, 97, 110, 185, 240, 260,
 261, 296, 300, 304, 319,
 337, 338, 345, 356, 367,
 368
Mass media, 6-7, 47, 78, 121,
 153, 187-188, 336-343. See
 also individual communist
 parties, press; under
 individual countries
Mass mobilization, 172, 175,
 178, 309, 310, 316, 355,
 356
Mass organizations, 18, 175,
 309, 316, 350
Matic, Petar, 151
Mature socialism. See
 Socialist society
May 1 holiday, 178, 301
Medek, Rudolf, 245
Mero, Agim, 334
Methodist Church of
 Czechoslovakia, 245
Michael the Brave (prince
 of Romania), 230
Mikhaylov, Stoyan, 146, 161
Miklos, Imre, 248, 254
Milatovic, Veljko, 151
Mindszenty, Joseph Cardinal,
 236
Mishev, Misho, 161, 323,
 325
Mittag, Guenter, 117
Mladenov, Petur, 146, 186,
 221
Mlynczak, Tadeus, 37

Moczar, Mieczyslaw, 127
Moisescu, Justin, 244–245
Mokrzyszczak, Wlodzimierz, 67
Mongolian People's Republic, 301
Montenegro (Yugoslavia), 183(table)
Moscow Olympic Games, 329
Moscow Peace Conference (1975), 263
Moskov, Encho, 328
Mozambique, 291, 295
MSZMP. See Hungarian Socialist Workers' Party
MTI. See Hungarian Communication Agency
Munca de Partid (Bucharest) 259

Nagy, Imre, 12, 211(table), 218
Namibia, 295
Narodna Mladezh (Bulgarian youth daily), 332, 340–341
National assemblies, 4, 9, 17–18, 40–49, 55–56
    and foreign policy, 56
    legislation, 42
    members, 11, 39–40
    role, 33, 35, 43
    sessions, 34–36, 40, 43, 56
    special state organs, 36–39, 40, 42
    structure, 34–39, 55
    See also Communist parties, and state system; under Elections; individual countries
National Democratic Party (GDR), 37
National Front (CSSR), 18, 19, 22, 25, 26, 28, 29, 213, 249, 309, 313, 315
National Front (GDR), 18, 21, 28, 29, 246, 248, 309, 313
National Front (Poland), 309
National front organizations, 11, 19, 20, 27, 178, 309–316, 321
National liberation movements, 193, 292–293, 294, 315, 321
National Union of Algerian Youth, 333
National unity, 30, 312
"Nationwide discussion," 51
NATO. See North Atlantic Treaty Organization
Navratil, Gejza, 26
Nemec, Jan, 274
Nemeth, Karoly, 28(table)
Nepotism, 162, 222–227
Nepszabadsag (MSZMP publication), 132, 144, 163, 180, 218, 254
Neues Deutschland (Berlin), 216
Neues Volksblatt (Vienna), 258
Ney, Roman, 122, 127
Nikiforov, Veselin, 146
Nikolov, Krustyu, 101
Nonaligned countries, 294–296
Noncommunist parties. See under Elections; individual countries
North Atlantic Treaty Organization (NATO), 321, 332
Noszkay, I., 20
Novak, Miroslav, 251
Novotny, Antonin, 211(table), 218
Nuclear weapons, 251
Nyers, Rezso, 143

Official visits and communiques, 291–298, 320–323, 335–336
Ogherlaci, Vasilie, 145

Okrug, 95, 97, 100-101,
102, 275, 314
Olszowski, Stefan, 122,
127, 195, 196
Ondrej, Josef, 54
"On Further Strengthening
the Role of the Secretaries
of the Basic Party
Organizations" (BCP), 160
"On Increasing Rabotnichesko
Delo's Role in the Build-
ing of the Developed
Socialist Society" (BCP),
157
"On Results of Fulfilling
the Conclusions of the
15th CPCZ Congress and
on Further Action on Their
Implementation," 156
Order of Labor (Hungary),
355
Order of Merit for the
People (Yugoslavia), 254
Orenburg Friendship gas
line (Hungary), 329
Orthodox Church, 244, 245,
251, 254, 257
Otechestven Front
(Bulgarian daily), 116
Ovari, Miklos, 189

Pacem in Terris (CSSR),
26, 249, 250, 253
Palestine Liberation
Organization (PLO),
315-316, 321
Palestinians, 194, 252,
253, 302
Palin, Velko, 116
PAP. See Polish Press
Agency
Papazov, Nacho, 49
Parliament. See
National assemblies
Parliamentarians, 39-40
Partiocracy, 4, 5, 6,
365, 366-367, 368,
369-370

"Party Leadership is the
Foundation of the Army's
Cohesion and Power"
(Dzhurov), 186
Patocka, Jan, 282
Patriotic People's Front
(PPF) (Hungary), 13, 18,
28, 52, 248, 309, 313
National Council, 38, 52
7th Congress (1981), 312,
315
6th Congress (1976), 311
Pauker, Ana, 191, 210
Peasants' parties, 3, 6,
13(table). See also
Bulgarian Agrarian
National Union; United
Peasants' Party
Pelshe, Avrid, 189
Pendelashki, Lyudmil, 101
Pentecostalists, 256
People's committees, 97
People's councils, 23, 97,
101
People's democracies, 4
People's Front, 11, 13
Peristeri, Pilo, 174
Personality cults, 119, 143,
212, 227-231, 293, 369
Petrescu, Dumitru D., 224
Petrescu, Gheorghe, 220, 223
Petrov, Georgi, 103
Pieck, Wilhelm, 210,
211(table), 369
Pinkowski, Jozef, 146, 149
Pioneers, 179, 330-331
Pirvulescu, Constantin, 191-192
Pitra, Frantisek, 145
Plamadeala, Leonid, 243
Planning, 43, 44, 45, 46, 48
PLO. See Palestine
Liberation Organization
Poja, Frigyer, 28(table)
Poland, 1, 120, 193-194,
299, 321
and CEMA, 2
church-state relations, 236,
237, 257, 260, 263-267

Poland (continued)
Council of State, 36,
 37, 48, 149, 212, 274,
 284
democratization, 48, 56
economy, 45
elections, 12, 14, 17, 18
Great Ribbon of the
 Order of the Polish
 People's Republic, 301
judiciary, 274, 277, 278,
 284-285
leadership, 209, 210.
 See also under Polish
 United Workers' Party
martial law (1981-1982),
 67, 122, 266, 284-285,
 289, 367
mass media, 45, 46, 48,
 127, 142, 173, 214, 215,
 216
noncommunist parties, 11,
 37, 61, 311
Sejm (national assembly),
 12, 13(table), 14, 18,
 34, 42, 45-46, 48, 143,
 148, 149, 264
and Soviet Union, 365,
 367, 369, 370
Union of Socialist
 Polish Youth, 326, 329,
 331, 333, 336
and Warsaw Pact, 2
 See also Front of
 National Unity; Polish
 United Workers' Party;
 Solidarity trade union;
 under Hungarian
 Socialist Workers'
 Party
Polednik, Jindrich, 331
Poles (in CSSR),
 41(table)
"Policy of Peace, Under-
 standing, and Coopera-
 tion" (Mladenov), 186
Polish Press Agency (PAP),
 67, 142, 216

Polish United Workers' Party
 (PZPR), 13(table), 193-194
admission, 82
Central Auditing Commission,
 67, 82, 137, 195, 196, 198
Central Committee, 67, 76,
 102, 115, 121-122, 123,
 126-127, 149, 173, 183,
 195, 196, 197, 198, 216
Central Committee membership
 composition, 136-139, 140-141,
 142-143, 146, 147-149
Central Committee Personnel
 Department, 154
Central Committee Press,
 Radio, and TV department,
 154
Central Control Commission,
 139, 163, 195, 196
and CPCZ, 155
democratization, 102, 121,
 126, 197, 210
8th Congress (1980), 136,
 137, 173, 189
leadership, 101-102, 127,
 155, 184, 185, 195-196,
 210, 211(table), 212, 214,
 215-216, 218
membership composition,
 66-67, 68(table), 84
9th Extraordinary Congress
 (1981), 67, 82, 121, 123,
 126, 136, 137, 139, 171,
 173, 183, 184, 186, 190,
 195-197, 198, 210, 213
organization levels, 95,
 96-97, 139, 183-184, 215
Politburo, 121, 127, 147,
 150, 154, 155, 173, 186,
 196, 214
press, 102, 260
primary party organization,
 95
purges, 66, 67, 94, 122, 195
resignations, 66, 67, 84
Secretariat, 127, 147, 161,
 162, 196
and SED, 155

(PZPR) continued
  and Soviet Union, 147,
    185, 189, 216
  and state system, 149
  3rd Congress (1959), 96
  wages and salaries, 82
  women in, 137, 139
  See also National Front
    (Poland)
Political clericalism,
  243, 267
Polityka (Polish weekly),
  142
Pop, Valeriu, 341
Popa, Dumitru, 162
Popescu, Dimitru Radu,
  129, 145
Popov, Atanas, 116
Popov, Zhivko, 283
Pozderac, Hamdija, 151, 152
PPF. See Patriotic
  People's Front
Prague spring (1968), 367
Pravda (CSSR daily), 90,
  266, 267
Pravda (Soviet Union), 93
Pravets (Bulgaria), 230
Premier, 209
President, 209, 213
Prespa's Bells (Talev),
  348
Presse, Die (Vienna), 352
"Pressing Issues in the
  Evaluation of the
  Control Activities of
  the Party" (Capka), 163
Private economy, 2
Procurator general. See
  Prosecutor general
Production and trade
  management, 79
Professional associations,
  356
Prihle, Karoly, 254
Prokopiak, Janusz, 121
Proletarian international-
  ism, 297, 300

Propaganda campaigns, 10,
  25, 53-55, 77, 78, 116,
  310, 315, 329-330, 333, 351
Prosecutor general, 277-279,
  282
Protestant church, 26, 245,
  263
Prumov, Ivan, 146, 161
Puder, Heinz, 79
Pullai, Arpad, 94, 162
Putrament, Jerzy, 121
Pyka, Tadeusz, 148
PZPR. See Polish United
  Workers' Party

Qaddumi, Faruq, 316

Rabotnichesko Delo (BCP
  daily), 92, 116, 119, 146,
  157, 226, 341, 348
Radio Hvezda, 249
Radio Tirana, 188
Radio Warsaw, 45, 48, 173
Radovic, Miljan, 151
Radulescu, Ilie, 145
Rajk, Laslo, 280
Rajnai, Sandor, 144
Rakosi, Matyas, 143, 209,
  210, 211(table), 218, 228
Rakowski, Mieczyslaw, 127
Ralin, Radoy, 340, 341
Rautu, Leonte, 145
Raychev, Aleksandar, 11
Rayon. See Districts
RCP. See Romanian Communist
  Party
Reagan, Ronald, 251
"Real Democracy--the Foundation
  of Socialism's Political
  System" (Todorov), 186
Regional party organizations.
  See Okrug
Religion. See Church-state
  relations
Reserve cadres, 82
"Resetting of Prices and
  Augmentation of Remuneration

of Working Personnel"
(RCP), 119
Revai, Jozsef, 210
"Review of Combat Ranks"
(Balev), 93
Revisionists, 2, 188, 322
Ribicic, Mitja, 151
Rokoszewski, Kazimiercz,
154
Roland, Ferenc, 320
Rolnicke Noviny
(Bratislava), 239
Romania, 1
arts and culture, 347,
348, 350
and CEMA, 2
church-state relations,
236, 243-244, 245,
253-254, 255, 257-258,
259, 261
Constitution, 35, 257
Council of Socialist
Culture and Education,
340
Council of State, 36, 245
elections, 17
Five-Year Legislative
Plan (1976-1980), 55,
284
food prices, 119
Grand National
Assembly, 34, 35, 44, 277
and Israel, 2, 289
judiciary, 277, 279,
283-284
leadership, 209, 210. See
also under Romanian
Communist Party
mass media, 145, 230, 259,
261, 340. See also
AGREPRES
and Mozambique, 295
political crime, 281
and Soviet Union, 289,
365, 368
Star Order of the
Socialist Republic of
Romania, 301

trade unions, 319, 323
Union of Communist Youth
(UCY), 85, 225, 326, 328,
330, 333
and Warsaw Pact, 2, 289
and Zambia, 295
See also Romanian Communist
Party; Socialist Democracy
and Unity Front; Union of
the Socialist Youth; under
Czechoslovakia
Romania Libera, 230
Romanian Communist Party (RCP)
admission, 85-86, 90
age distribution, 71
cadres policy, 85, 99, 212
card exchanges, 90-91, 92
Central Auditing
Commission, 126
Central Collegium, 163
Central Committee, 45, 69,
75, 76, 85, 86, 90, 91, 92,
99-100, 115, 117, 119, 120,
126, 145, 154, 220, 299,
341
Central Committee membership
composition, 129-130, 145
decision making, 158
elections, 159
11th Congress (1974), 126,
129(table), 189, 347
and Iraq, 158
and Jordan, 158
leadership, 162, 191,
211(table), 212, 218-220,
223-224, 227, 228-230, 231,
293, 313, 318
membership composition,
69-71, 85-86, 91-92
organization levels, 95,
126, 259
and Poland, 120, 158
Political Executive Committee
(Politburo), 76, 145, 149,
150, 154, 158-159, 355
press. See Scinteia
primary party organization,
95

(RCP) continued
  purges, 191
  Secretariat, 161, 162
  and Soviet Union, 304
  sports, 355
  and state system, 36, 45,
    55, 158, 159
  structure, 76
  10th Congress (1969), 55
  13th Congress (1984), 71,
    130
  12th Congress (1979), 126,
    129, 174, 189, 191, 279,
    347, 350
  women in, 69, 71, 75,
    85-86, 130
Romanian Orthodox Church,
  244, 245
Romanian Radio and
  Television, 145, 341
Roman Orthodox Church, 244
Rude Pravo (CPCZ daily),
  87, 90, 343, 345, 353
Rychlewski, Jan, 216

Sadecki, Jerzy, 127
Sakarev, Ivan, 146
SALT II. See Strategic
  Arms Limitation Talks, II
Sarlos, Istvan, 14, 28(table),
  248, 315
Schmidt, Helmut, 156
Schneeberger, Vilen, 245
Schuerer, Gerhard, 117
Scientific socialism, 345
Scinteia (RCP daily), 91,
  100, 218, 245, 257
Scornicesti (Romania), 229
Secrecy, 152, 213
Secret ballot, 17, 102,
  121, 139, 180, 184, 196,
  216
SED. See Socialist Unity
  Party
Sedition, 280
Sendov, Blagovest, 49
Serbia (Yugoslavia), 183,
  257

SFRY. See Yugoslavia,
  Socialist Federative
  Republic of
Shah of Iran, 303
Shehu, Fiqrete, 222
Shehu, Mehmet, 6, 174, 193,
  216-217, 222
Shopova, Stanka, 331
Sindermann, Horst, 190
Skrzypczak, first secretary,
  127
Skwirzynski, Tadeusz, 48
Slanski, Rudolf, 210, 280
Slavkov, Ivan, 225, 226
Slovak Communist Party,
  213, 303
Slovak Freedom Party, 310
Slovak National Council, 26
Slovak Renaissance Party,
  310-311
Slovaks, 34, 36, 41(table),
  177
Slovenia (Yugoslavia), 46,
  183(table)
Social courts, 276
Socialist Alliance of the
  Working People of
  Yugoslavia, 18, 309
Socialist democracy, 19, 21,
  22
Socialist Democracy and Unity
  Front (Romania), 18, 225,
  253, 309, 313
Socialist internationalism,
  297, 299, 303, 337, 367
Socialist society, 1, 292
Socialist Unity Party (SED)
  (GDR), 1
  age distribution, 65
  and Army, 200-201
  arts and culture, 343-344
  card exchanges, 88-89
  Central Committee, 21, 88,
    89, 115, 116, 117-118, 143,
    156, 178, 179, 299, 331, 343
  Central Control Commission,
    163
  decision making, 157, 179

(SED) (GDR) continued
  education in, 63, 65
  8th Congress, 179
  leadership, 211(table),
    218, 222, 318, 369
  membership composition,
    63, 65, 66(table), 74
  9th Congress, 179
  Politburo, 117, 150, 157
  press. See Einheit
  Secretariat, 161
  and Soviet Union, 179
  and state system, 36
  10th Congress (1981), 21,
    29, 63, 88, 157, 178-179,
    188, 190, 200-201, 246,
    319, 332
  Western Affairs Depart-
    ment, 116
  women in, 63
  See also under Polish
  United Workers' Party
Social mobilization, 5-6,
  10, 78
Soka, S., 249
Solidarity trade union
  (Poland), 45, 84, 121-
  122, 184, 215, 216, 237,
  257, 264, 265, 266, 267,
  315, 321, 322-323, 325,
  336, 367
Son of His People, a Son
  of His Time, A., 230
South Africa, 295
Soviet Union, 365
  army, 1
  creative unions, 352
  and international
  propaganda campaigns,
    54, 253
  and Iran, 303
  judiciary, 274, 277
  Komsomol, 326, 329, 333
  Supreme Soviet, 54
  See also Communist Party
  of the Soviet Union;
  Warsaw Pact; under

Communist parties;
  individual parties and
  countries
Spanish Communist Party,
  299-300
Speech, freedom of, 280, 281
Spornic, Aneta, 220
Sports unions, 355-356
Stalin, Joseph, 1, 264
State council chairman. See
  President
Statescu, Constantin, 283
Stefan Gheorghiu Academy
  (Hungary), 145, 229
Stefanski, Piotr, 45
Stepinac, Alojzije
  Cardinal, 256
Stojanovic, Nikola, 151
Stoychev, Vladimir, 11
Strategic Arms Limitation
  Talks (SALT), II, 253
Streit, Josef, 278
Strougal, Lubomir, 43, 194,
  213, 296, 297
Suhe Bator Order, 301
Sukrija, Ali, 151
Supreme Courts, 274-275
Suslov, Mikhail, 189
Svoboda, Ludvik, 221
Syrian Union of Youth of the
  Revolution, 333
Szabo, Istvan, 143
Szeged oil and natural
  gas plant (Hungary), 329
Szelenyi, Ivan, 352
Szentjoby, Tamas, 352
Szuros, Matyas, 144
Szydlak, Jan, 148

Takov, Peko, 186
Talev, Dimitur, 348
Tambo, Oliver, 302
Tanchev, Petur, 37
Tanev, Georgi, 103
Tanev, Mincho, 187
TANJUG (Yugoslav news
  agency), 256, 339

Tarsadalmi Szemle (MSZMP
   publication), 132
"Tasks of the Universities
   and Colleges in the
   Developed Socialist
   Society" (SED), 157
"Theses on Youth" (BCP),
   331
33-Year Old Woman, A
   (film), 348
Tisch, Harry, 317, 319
Tisza River chemical
   combine (Hungary), 329
Tisza River Locks II
   (Hungary), 329
Tito, Josip Broz, 2, 46,
   51, 121, 190-191, 209,
   210, 211(table), 228,
   369
   death (1980), 122, 365
Tobacco (Dimov), 348
Todorov, Stanko, 6, 35,
   40, 42, 47, 186, 220, 221,
   299
Tomal, Zdizislaw, 37
Trade unions, 309,
   316-326
Trofin, Virgil, 145
Trybuna Ludu (PZPR), 260
Tsanov, Vasil, 161
Tsolov, Tano, 152, 153
Tunisia, Communist Party
   of, 302
Typhoon on the Sea Coast
   (Albanian novel), 348

UCY. See Romania, Union
   of Communist Youth
Ukrainians (in CSSR),
   41(table)
Ulbricht, Walter, 209,
   210, 211(table), 218,
   221, 369
Under the Burning Arches
   (Albanian novel), 348
Uniform National Plan of
   the Socioeconomic

Development (Romania)
   (1982), 44
Union Of Bulgarian Journalists,
   342, 343
Union of Bulgarian Writers,
   349
Union of CSSR Journalists,
   342, 343
Union of CSSR Writers, 351
Union of Czech Brethren, 245
Union of Journalists,
   339-340, 342
Union of the Socialist
   Youth (Romania), 71
United fronts. See National
   front organizations
United Nations General
   Assembly, 263
United Peasants' Party
   (Poland), 13(table), 37,
   61, 311
United States, 251, 252, 284,
   292, 321, 332. See also
   under Communist Party of
   Czechoslovakia
"Unity and cohesion," 294
University admission, 327
Urban, Jan, 26
Uruguay, Communist Party of,
   302
Ust-Ulims celluloid combine
   (Hungary), 329

Vacations, 301-302
Varkonyi, Peter, 144
Varna Black Sea resort, 302
Vatican Radio, 255
Velechev, Boris, 100, 101,
   133, 161, 162, 210, 334
Verdet, Ilie, 219, 223, 227
Verner, Paul, 21, 161, 189
Vezhinov, Pavel, 11
Vidic, Dobrivoje, 151
Vietnam, 301
Vigilance, 79, 344
Vjesnik (Zagreb), 243

Vlad the Impaler
(prince of Romania),
230
Vlasic, Ferdo, 256
Voitec, Stefan, 245
Voivodeship, 76, 101, 139,
184, 185
Vojvodina (Yugoslavia),
183(table)
"Voluntary international
cooperation," 298
Voter registration, 18-19
Vulchev, Svetlin, 11

Walesa, Lech, 266, 315
Warsaw Pact, 2, 155, 185,
289, 312, 365, 367, 368
Warsaw Radio, 121
Weltanschauung, 261
West European Bureau of
the Comintern, 310
Wojtyla, Karol Cardinal,
264
Women
and communist party
membership, 62, 63, 69,
71, 72, 73(table), 75,
85-86, 87, 128, 130,
131, 133, 137, 139, 142
organizations, 309,
354-355
and trade unions, 323
Workers' parties, 1,
13(table)
Workers' productivity, 25,
92, 317, 318
World Council of Churches,
251-252
World Federation of
Democratic Women, 354
World War II, 1, 209, 256
Wraszyczyk, Tadeusz, 148
Writers' Union, 351-352
Wyszynski, Stefan Cardinal,
236, 263, 264, 265

Yambol Okrug (BPC), 100-101

Yosifov, Veselin, 343
Yotov, Yordan, 146, 341
Youth organizations, 309,
326, 336
Yugoslavia, Socialist
Federative Republic of
(SFRY), 1, 297-298
Army, 84
arts and culture, 352
assemblies, 15
Assembly of Intermunicipal
Communities, 15
Basic Organizations of
Associated Labor (BOAL), 15
and Bulgaria, 182
and CEMA, 2
Chamber of Associated
Labor, 15, 16(fig.)
Chamber of Communes, 15,
16(fig.)
Chamber of Republics and
Autonomous Provinces, 14,
16(fig.), 35, 46, 47
church-state relations, 238,
239-240, 243, 254, 256-257,
259, 262
Constitution (1974), 14-15,
17, 39, 51, 238, 274, 275,
276, 281
elections, 11, 14-15, 27
ethnic minorities, 181-182,
281
Federal (National) Assembly,
14, 15-17, 20, 27, 34-35,
39, 46-47, 51, 275
Federal Chamber, 14, 34, 39
judiciary, 274, 275-276
leadership, 209, 210, 313.
See also under League of
Yugoslav Communists
liberal attitude in, 46-47,
56
mass media, 122, 154, 243,
256, 259, 262, 321, 334
Muslims, 152, 240
and nonaligned movement, 2
political crime, 281

(SFRY) continued
 self-management system, 2
 Socialist Youth Federation,
  326, 330, 334
 Sociopolitical Chamber, 15,
  16(fig.)
 and Soviet Union, 2,
  365, 370
 State Presidency, 36-37,
  39, 51
 trade unions, 321
 Western press in, 7
 and Zambia, 295
 See also League of
  Yugoslav Communists;
  under Albania
Yugov, Anton, 218

Zabinski, Andrzej, 127
Zambia, 294-295
Zandarowski, Zdzislaw,
 147, 148
Zapotocky, Antonin, 210

Zawadzki, Sylwester, 53
Zeri I Popullit (AWP), 75,
 334, 348
Zhivkov, Todor
 and BCP, 24, 49, 50-51, 52,
  56, 62, 92, 93, 100, 101,
  103, 120, 133, 160, 174,
  176, 181, 183, 202, 203,
  211(table), 217, 218,
  220, 299
 family, 221, 226, 228
 and foreign leaders, 155,
  189, 190, 291, 293, 300,
  302, 303
 and national front, 314
 personality cult, 228, 230-231
 and writers, 349
 and youth organization,
  330, 332, 334, 335
Zhivkov, Vladimir, 226, 227
Zhivkova, Lyudmila, 133, 212,
 221, 223, 225-227, 228, 350
Zionism, 263, 300
Zycie Warszawy (daily), 142